ANTON ČECHOV 1860-1960

ANTON ČECHOV

1860-1960

SOME ESSAYS

EDITED BY

T. EEKMAN

LEIDEN
E. J. BRILL
1960

PRINTED IN THE NETHERLANDS

CONTENTS

FOREWORD

This jubilee year of 1960 has witnessed a stream of Čechov publications, productions, articles and studies in Soviet Russia as well as in other countries. Countless figures in the world of literature and the stage have chosen this occasion to give expression to the boundless admiration they feel for their honoured master. He is described as one of the greatest renovators of modern prose, one of the finest teachers of modern drama and literature and his popularity surpasses that of Dostoevskij, Tolstoj and other giants of Russian literature.

Čechov himself would undoubtedly have been shocked and terrified by such panegyrics and would certainly have given a great deal to stop them. We are therefore not acting in Čechov's spirit when we contribute still more to the stream of articles about him. Konstantin Paustovskij's sentiments on what has been written about Čechov do not apply to Russia alone: "It seems that all the words in the Russian language which can be applied to Čechov have already been spoken and used. Our love for him has outgrown our vocabulary. It has, like every great love, soon exhausted the stock of our best phrases and expressions. The danger of repetitions and commonplaces threatens. It is as if everything that can be said about Čechov has been said" (*Literaturnaja Gazeta,* 28 January 1960).

Yet it was just this love and admiration which prompted us to publish this volume. Love is determined to express itself, even if the object of that love dreads it and covers itself with a veil of shyness, even though there are no novel and unused words at love's disposal. The amazing thing about Čechov is not only his literary significance, but also the fact that his character as a person, which reveals itself in all his works and in all that is known about him, arouses in each new generation deep feelings of sympathy and affection. After all, the importance of a great writer, of an outstanding artist lies not only in the work he produces, but also in the fact that he is ever a model and an inspiration, a touchstone and a whetstone for new generations, that their ideas, opinions and ideals become impregnated through contact with him and consequently take on shape and form.

This volume contains some twenty essays which vary in length, theme and approach. They are written by students of Čechov from nine countries and in four languages. There are perhaps those who would have preferred a volume with a more uniform theme, a more dominant conception. But we feel that a volume such as this, which, for example, contains distinctly varying interpretations of stories such as "The

Duel", "The Black Monk", "The Student" or "A Boring Story", can
be useful too and may have its raison d'être. Certain writers seem to
regard Čechov as a saint, their attitude to him is unvariably one of awe
and reverence; another attitude would be simply inconceivable and unacceptable to them. One of his best biographers, A. I. Roskin, warns
against "making up Čechov according to a sort of standard of the 'ideo-
logically tried classical writer'. Such make-up is not necessary. The
great writers of the past are dear to us despite their doubts, errors
and transgressions. We may dispute with the great writers, but we
may not correct them" (*A. P. Čechov*, Moscow 1949, page 172).
In the compilation of this volume, therefore, we have not adopted a
one-sided, partial or biased attitude, — an attitude with which we
should have served Čechov least of all.

It may be called a favourable sign that authors from countries of
different political systems have come together to contribute to this
volume. That intellectuals, preoccupied with things of the mind, are
champions of peace and international concord is not surprising — it is,
after all, in their own interest, for no one is more hampered in his daily
work by international discord than the scholar. On the other hand, as
students of the human spirit and its developments, who themselves
set to work from certain accepted opinions and ideas, their starting
point fixed as it were against a certain spiritual background, as dis-
seminators of ideas, they become deeply involved in international ideological clashes. Yet this again is not altogether to be deplored. To say
that truth emerges out of the *choc des opinions* may not always
be correct, but the fact stands that it leads to the development, ripening
and enrichment of our ideas.

Thus we present a book which approaches the author from various
angles, in the hope that it will help the reader to approach Čechov.

THE EDITOR.

Russian words and names are given in the non-Russian contributions
in the most usual international transliteration. References to Čechov's
works are given (unless otherwise stated) according to the Complete
Edition of his Works and Letters, *Polnoe Sobranie Sočinenij i Pisem*,
20 vls. (Moscow 1944-1951) (abbreviated to PSSP, with the volumes
in Roman and the pages in Arabic numerals).

Евг. КАННАК

РАННИЕ ПОВЕСТИ ЧЕХОВА

Известен отзыв самого Чехова о своем раннем творчестве: „доселе я относился к своей литературной работе легкомысленно, небрежно, зря... Как репортеры пишут свои заметки о пожарах, так я писал свои рассказы: машинально, полубессознательно, нимало не заботясь ни о читателе, ни о себе самом" (письмо Григоровичу от 28-го марта 1886 г.).

Впоследствии, в 1899 г., просматривая свои произведения для издания Маркса, Чехов исключил из них большую часть своих ранних рассказов, как-бы подтверждая этим лишний раз свой строгий приговор. Разбросанные по многочисленным юмористическим журналам (*Осколки, Будильник, Спутник, Зритель* и др.) юношеские произведения 1880-83 гг. стали полностью доступны широкой публике лишь после издания полного собрания сочинений в 1944 г. Одновременно стали выходить в свет и другие материалы, касающиеся Чехова: неизданные письма, заметки и т.д.

В 1947 г. в книге *А. П. Чехов, Сборник документов и материалов* [1] были воспроизведены случайно сохранившиеся рукописи двух маленьких рассказов: *Двое в одном* и *Два романа* (1883 года). Обилие поправок, которые встречаются в этих рукописях буквально на каждой строке, заставляет нас относиться осторожнее и к приведенному выше отзыву Чехова и к распространенному мнению о чрезвычайной легкости чеховского творчества в юности. Правка рукописей сводится — что особенно характерно для Чехова — главным образом к сокращению фразы и уточнению стиля. Нельзя не предположить, что молодой автор вовсе не так уже „легкомысленно и небрежно" относился к своей работе; и это заключение повышает интерес читателя к раннему творчеству Чехова.

Советские исследователи посвятили за последние годы ряд работ юношеским произведениям Чехова. Но их внимание привлекали главным образом короткие рассказы и сценки, напечатанные в *Осколках*. Одни из них видят в молодом Чехове ученика и последователя Салтыкова-Щедрина, как он

---

[1] *Литературный Архив,* М. 1947, т. I, Огиз.

„умевшего открыть политику в быту." [2] Другие указывают
на влияние либерально-сатирического направления *Осколков*
на Чехова [3]. Как бы то ни было, Чехов-дебютант является
для большинства исследователей либо юмористом, яркими
вспышками освещавшим обывательское житье, либо сатири-
ком, высмеивавшим уродливые явления политического
режима.

Но молодой Чехов был не только автором коротких
рассказов. В начале своей литературной деятельности он
несколько раз пробовал раздвинуть узкие рамки, предписан-
ные ему юмористическими журналами и попытать свои силы
в области социально-психологического большого рассказа
или повести. Этим попыткам было до сих пор уделено мало
внимания; между тем, они далеко не лишены интереса.
Анализу этих ранних произведений мы и намерены посвятить
данную статью, ограничив поле исследования 1882 годом,
наиболее плодотворным в этом отношении.

В 1882 г. — Чехову было тогда 22 года и он совмещал
занятия медициной в университете с литературным „промы-
слом" — он написал ряд повестей, из которых *Ненужную
победу* и *Цветы запоздалые* можно без натяжки назвать даже
маленькими романами. Подпись под всеми этими произведениями: А. Чехонте. Заметим, что к этой литературной форме
Чехов вернется — если не считать *Драмы на охоте* (1884 г.) —
лишь в 1888 г. в рассказе *Степь*. Как *Пьеса без названия*
хранит в зародыше замыслы чеховских пьес, так в этих ранних произведениях — зачатки позднейшего творчества Чехова, с которым они связаны теснее, чем краткие юмористи-
ческие рассказы той-же эпохи. Здесь намечаются образы
будущих чеховских героев; его темы, настроения, литературные приемы зарождаются здесь на наших глазах.

Среди этих произведений особое место занимает маленький роман *Ненужная победа*. Любопытна история его воз-
никновения: среди русской читающей публики особым успехом пользовались в те годы социальные романы Ф. Шпиль-
гагена и венгерского писателя Мориса Йокая; Чехов, по
свидетельству его брата Михаила, поспорил однажды с редактором *Будильника,* утверждая, что и он способен написать
роман „не хуже заграничных". Он принялся, не откладывая,
за работу. Роман *Ненужная Победа* печатался в *Будильнике*
с июня до августа 1882 г. и вызвал большой интерес в чита-

---

[2] Б. Александров, *Семинарий по Чехову,* М. 1957, стр. 110.
[3] М. Гущин, *Творчество Чехова,* Харьков 1954, стр. 6-13.

тельской среде. Но уже в июле редактор остановил увлекше-
гося автора, попросив его поскорее закончить роман: „будем
лучше печатать мелкие рассказики..." [4] Чехову пришлось
покориться. Конец романа явно скомкан, не в мере запутанной
интриге недостает развязки, многие действующие лица
неожиданно исчезают из поля зрения читателя.

Ненужную победу принято считать лишь талантливой пародией на романы Йокая. Так-ли это? Центральный образ
барона фон Зайница привлекает особое внимание читателя.
Этот „знатный венгерец" — явно русского происхождения;
он — родной брат Платонова, первого драматического героя
Чехова (*Пьеса без названия*). Как и Платонов, барон ф.
Зайниц блестяще одарен, образован и остроумен; в молодости он привлекал всех к себе, пользовался неизменным
успехом у женщин; он много обещал; но при первом
препятствии, встреченном на жизненном пути, барон падает
духом, отрекается от прошлого, превращается в бродягу,
никчемного болтуна: он болен безволием, болезнью русских
интеллигентов. „Русская возбудимость", писал Чехов Суворину (30 дек. 88 г.), „имеет одно специфическое свойство: ее
быстро сменяет утомляемость". Это вполне приложимо и к
барону: циничные насмешки надо всем, да бутылка водки —
его единственное утешение. Возможно, что прототипом ф.
Зайница явились старшие братья Чехова, Александр и Николай, талантливые, но рано погрязшие в беспутной жизни и
пьянстве.

Центральное место в *Ненужной победе* занимает поэти-
ческая сказка-аллегория, которую барон рассказывает Ильке,
молодой девушке, ожидающей от него помощи и совета.

В некотором царстве жила-была девочка-фея; ее домом
был большой тюльпан, питалась она росой и медом и все
свое время отдавала заботам о насекомых: одевала их, лечила
и наставляла. Однажды пришел к ней страшный паук и по-
требовал, под угрозой смерти, чтобы она вышла за него
замуж. Насекомые, питомцы девочки, поклялись ее защитить:
„умрем, но не выдадим", закричали они хором. Но когда
паук явился к девочке за ответом, он увидел „не защитников,
а трусов, которые были бледны и дрожали всем телом. Он
громко засмеялся и на глазах всего насекомого мира...
зарезал бедную девочку"... „Нянька моя была отличный
педагог, прибавляет барон, она мне не лгала даже в сказках.

---

[4] *Собр. соч.,* том I, М. 1954, комментарии, стр. 104-5.

У нее не торжествовала добродетель. Паук и до сих пор сидит у себя в норе и кушает соус из мух, а подлые насекомые, больные и изорванные, небось чаще вспоминают о вкусных поминках, чем о девочке."

Беспросветным пессимизмом проникнута не только эта сказка, но и весь роман. Дурно устроено не только общество, в котором господствуют произвол, грубое насилие богатых и властных над бедными, неправедный суд — дурна и человеческая природа. Сильные жестоки, но слабые принижены и трусливы. Подл паук, но подлы и насекомые, „больные и изорванные". Пессимизм героя повидимому всецело разделяется и молодым автором.

Отметим еще два характерных чеховских мотива, которые встречаются в этом романе. Мотив „покинутого дома": барон ф. Зайниц сбивается с пути, становится пьяницей и бродягой, с того момента, когда ему заказано возвращение в родной дом. Разрыв с прошлым в связи с разорением старого гнезда — тема многих пьес и рассказов Чехова (*Пьеса без названия, Три сестры, Вишневый сад — У знакомых, Чужая беда* и др.). Тема эта носит несомненно биографический характер: вспомним, что когда Чехову было 16 лет, его отец, разорившийся лавочник, вынужден был продать свой таганрогский дом с торгов. Дом был куплен за бесценок другом П. Чехова, — и семья бывшего владельца осталась без крова.

Другой чеховский мотив, встречающийся в этом романе и повторяющийся впоследствии в *Чайке* — мотив убитой птицы. Подстреленная орлица падает на колени Ильки при первой ее встрече с бароном: это — символ трагической судьбы девушки, доверившейся слабому, безвольному человеку.

Реалистичнее *Ненужной победы,* искреннее и в художественном отношении зрелее — маленький роман *Цветы запоздалые.* [5] Фоном его является уже не фантастическая „заграница", о которой Чехов имел тогда представление лишь из книг, а хорошо ему знакомая Москва. Герои ее — московские типы: обедневшая дворянская семья, преданный слуга из крепостных, московская сваха, врач, вышедший из низов народа, путем долгих лишений добившийся образования. Здесь, как и в *Пьесе без названия,* намечается тема дворянского оскудения, к которой Чехов будет возвращаться неоднократно и которая полностью будет развернута в его последней пьесе: *Вишневый сад.*

---

[5] Впервые напечатан в журнале *Мирской толк* 1882 г.

Героиня романа, княжна Маруся, подобно *Трем сестрам,* живет надеждой на лучшую, осмысленную и полную жизнь. Закрывая глаза на действительность, она преображает в мечтах единственного человека, способного, как ей кажется, вывести ее из заколдованного круга пошлости, — доктора Топоркова, черствого корыстолюбивого эгоиста, который представляется ей подвижником науки, образцом действенного человеколюбия.

В конце романа, когда Маруся первая признается Топоркову в любви (как героини рассказов *Верочка* или *Страх*) чудо как будто совершается: Топорков готов отказаться от своей богатой практики, от нажитого капитала, готов всем пожертвовать для Маруси; ему стыдно вспомнить о преданных им „студенческих идеалах". Но Маруся умирает от чахотки — и все возвращается на прежнее место; как и раньше, Топорков лечит бездельных барынь и копит пятирублевки. В лице князя Егорушки, брата Маруси, пьяницы и мота, пошлость одерживает победу. Егорушка на правах брата вселился к Топоркову и тратит его деньги на кутежи: „Егорушка очень доволен".

Несмотря на тяжелый и неловкий слог, изобилующий еще провинциализмами, на недостаток об'ективности, в этом произведении есть уже существенный чеховский элемент: смешение трагического со случайным, нелепым и потому смешным, с которым мы встретимся в пьесах Чехова.

Намеченные здесь еще схематически персонажи принадлежат к подлинному чеховскому миру: верный Никифор, опекающий своих господ — как-бы набросок Фирса из *Вишневого сада*; доктор Топорков — чуть-ли не первый из многочисленных чеховских докторов — напоминает земского врача Ионыча, который так-же, забыв о „студенческих идеалах", копит деньги, толстеет и незаметно опускается.

Любопытно отметить, что пошлость топорковского быта, с которым он хочет порвать, символически представлена здесь конкретными деталями его обстановки: дорогим ковром „во всю комнату" и трехсотрублевыми часами. Все это в минуту духовного пробуждения кажется Топоркову „грязью", из которой надо вырваться. Так Надя, героиня последнего рассказа Чехова *Невеста,* бежит от картины изображающей „нагую даму и рядом с ней лиловую вазу с отбитой ручкой": бездарная картина — символ ожидающей девушку вульгарной и пустой провинциальной жизни.

Пошлость, грубая косная сила одерживает верх и в рассказе

Корреспондент, датированном тем-же 1882 г. [6] Весь рассказ построен на анекдоте: купец Тромбонов обещал пожертвовать деньги на школу, если старик Иван Никитич, корреспондент „московской и санкт-петербургской" прессы напишет о нем в газете. Иван Никитич действительно упоминает имя купца в своей статье, но на беду свою прибавляет: „последний обещал..." „Кто это последний? кричит возмущенный купец, это я последний?... Вон отсюда, чтобы и ноги твоей здесь не было!" Ивана Никитича изгоняют из дома и вслед за ним выбрасывают забытую им фуражку в „самую жидкую грязь." Но Иван Никитич не думает ни оправдываться, ни об'ясняться. Куда ему! Он забит, принижен, он боится всего и всех на свете: и купцов, и лакеев, и дворника, и собаки; и он смиренно семенит „по грязи на свою квартиру". Хоть он и пишет иногда в газетах и вспоминает с умилением о 60-х годах, „когда огня и правды в людях больше было", — в его жилах течет рабская кровь; он сам себя считает и называет „ноликом". И молодой автор, если и сочувсвует своему корреспонденту, презирает его в сущности не меньше чем полуграмотных купцов.

Упомянем, наконец, и о рассказе *Барыня,* первом крупном чеховском рассказе из крестьянской жизни. [7] С самого начала своей литературной деятельности Чехов шел своей дорогой: он не идеализировал крестьян, как требовало того народническое направление в литературе. В его рассказе крестьяне грубы, жадны, жестоки: сцены избиения Степана и особенно пьяной драки в трактире набросаны с беспощадным натурализмом, которого Чехов впоследствии будет избегать. На первый взгляд кажется, что крестьяне лишены всяких нравственных устоев: в гибели Степана повинна, конечно, молодая, красивая барыня, выбирающая любовников из подвластных ей крестьян; но не менее ее виновны и отец и брат Степана, толкнувшие его из корысти на „дурное дело", и даже сам Степан, по безволию и малодушию не сумевший себя отстоять.

Однако в отношении автора к своим героям есть существенная разница: барыня — подчеркивает Чехов — ни на минуту не задумывается о своей моральной ответственности. Узнав, что Степан убил свою жену, она восклицает: „Ужасный народ! Ах, какой народ! Негодяи! Хорошо-же, я им пока-

---

[6] Впервые напечатано в *Будильнике,* № 20 и 21, 1882 г.
[7] Впервые напечатано в журнале *Москва,* 1882 г.

жу...", и вскоре после драмы ищет утешения у прежнего любовника. Для Степана-же высшие этические нормы несомненно существуют. „А ежели душе грех?" спрашивает он брата (который уговаривает его пойти к барыне) — а отцу бросает с горечью: „В церковь ходите, а греха не боитесь!" Ему нечего ответить на упреки жены; он знает, что нарушил нравственный закон, что за это ему придется ответить; и он убивает Марью, чтобы не слышать голоса собственной совести.

Для молодого Чехова мужики в нравственном отношении стоят выше господ; этому взгляду он не изменит до конца, выразит его и в позднейших произведениях из крестьянской жизни (*Мужики, В овраге*), с особенной ясностью — в рассказе *Моя жизнь*. „Приглядываясь к нему (мужику) поближе, чувствуешь, что в нем есть что-то нужное и очень важное (...), а именно, он верит, что главное на земле — правда, и что спасение его и всего народа в одной лишь правде, и поэтому больше всего на свете он любит справедливость."

Интерес рассказов этой эпохи, главным образом, конечно, в том, что они своими темами, образами, мыслями предвещают будущего Чехова. Очень скоро — за три-четыре года — Чехов освободится от несовершенства стиля, от шаблонов, схематических образов, громоздкой композиции; на смену мелодраматическим сценам придут обыденные житейские события: „люди обедают, только обедают, а в это время слагается их счастье и разбиваются их жизни."

Изменится и его отношение к человеку: мрачный пессимизм юности смягчится и уступит место сдержанной жалости, а в конце его жизни — вере в людей. Голос Чехова будет звучать все глуше — и все слышнее будет его отклик в мире.

GERHARD DICK

ANTON ČECHOV UND GERHART HAUPTMANN

In der literarisch bedeutsamen Zeit um die Wende vom 19. zum
20. Jahrhundert war Gerhart Hauptmann neben Ibsen der ausländische
Dramatiker, der in Rußland den nachhaltigsten Erfolg hatte. Schon
im ersten Jahrzehnt seines Wirkens vermochte der deutsche Dichter das
russische Publikum zu begeistern, vor allem, als das im Jahre 1898
gegründete Moskauer Künstlertheater sich der Hauptmann-Stücke an-
genommen hatte. Hier kam der vertiefte Naturalismus Hauptmanns mit
seiner feinen psychologischen Analyse und dem Reichtum an inneren
Erlebnissen den künstlerischen Intentionen der Moskauer Truppe und
seiner verantwortlichen Leiter Stanislavskij und Nemirovič-Dančenko
sehr entgegen.

Unter diesen Umständen ist es nicht verwunderlich, daß auch Anton
Čechov sehr bald den deutschen Dichter kennen und schätzen lernte,
in dem er verwandte Saiten klingen hörte. In der Tat war den russischen Zeitgenossen die Verwandtschaft im Schaffen der beiden
Schriftsteller so offensichtlich, daß das Künstlertheater die Dramen
Hauptmanns (so *Einsame Menschen, Fuhrmann Henschel, Michael
Kramer, Die Weber, Die versunkene Glocke* und andere) mit dem
gleichen Erfolg wie Čechovs Stücke spielen konnte; ja, man sprach
sogar von einem „Čechov-Hauptmann-Künstlertheater". In einem
sinngemäß zitierten Gespräch mit Maksim Gor'kij heißt es, Hauptmann und Čechov repräsentierten „zwei parallele Richtungen des russischen Theaters von dazumal, beide gleich verwandt der russischen
Intelligenz in jener pessimistisch enttäuschten und zugleich nach
idealen Werten lechzenden, von Schönheit träumenden Zeit".[1] So
kommt es auch, daß Hauptmann, worauf noch eingegangen werden soll,
in einer Čechov-Aufführung des Künstlertheaters seine eigenen künstlerischen Absichten verwirklicht sehen konnte.

Auf diese Weise wirkte Hauptmann, der schon in jungen Jahren
durch die Lektüre von Turgenev, Doestoevskij und Lev Tolstoj beein-
flußt wurde und insbesondere dessen Drama *Vlast' t'my* verpflich-
tet war, wieder auf das russische Theater zurück.

Wann Čechov die erste Berührung mit der Dramatik Hauptmanns
hatte, läßt sich nicht genau ermitteln. Bekannt ist aus einem Briefe
Čechovs vom 15.4.1897 an Suvorin, daß er beabsichtigte, im Juni des

---

[1] *Gerhart Hauptmann und sein Werk.* Herausgegeben von Ludwig Marcuse,
Berlin/Leipzig 1922, S. 107.

gleichen Jahres in der Ortschaft Pokrovsk-Meščersk aus Anlaß eines Ärztetreffens Hauptmanns *Hannele* aufführen zu lassen; das seinerzeit in Moskau verbotene Stück schien ihm wegen des zu erwartenden Publikums wie aus den Gegebenheiten der dortigen Bühne („teatr osveščaemyj električestvom") gleichermaßen geeignet zu sein. So muß Čechov dieses Werk wie wahrscheinlich auch andere Dramen Hauptmanns bereits früher kennengelernt haben.

In Čechovs Bibliothek in Jalta befand sich Hauptmanns *Michael Kramer* in russischer Übersetzung, desgleichen der erste Band der 1902 begonnenen russischen Gesamtausgabe Hauptmans, die übrigens vier Jahre vor der ersten deutschen Ausgabe Gesammelter Werke Hauptmanns erschienen war.

Während Čechov, wie aus mehreren seiner Briefe hervorgeht, bereits Ende 1898 eine Übersetzung des *Fuhrmann Henschel* erhalten, das Stück dann aber doch nicht gelesen hatte, vertiefte er sich ein Jahr später gern in die Lektüre der *Einsamen Menschen*. Wie er am 19.8.1899 an Suvorin schreibt, sei es zwar ein altes Stück — es stammte ja bereits aus dem Jahre 1891 —, doch habe es ihn durch seine Aktualität („noviznoj") überrascht. Das Stück sei „očen' umna i sceníčna".

Im Frühling des Jahres 1900 sah Čechov dieses Stück erstmals auf der Bühne. Das Moskauer Künstlertheater war damals zu dem kranken Čechov auf die Krim gefahren und zeigte neben Čechovs *Djadja Vanja* auch Hauptmanns *Einsame Menschen*. Wie Stanislavskij berichtet, gefiel Čechov das Stück besser als seine eigenen Werke. „Das ist ein echter Dramatiker!" rief er aus. „Ich bin keiner, hören Sie, ich bin Arzt!" [2] Als das Künstlertheater die Krim wieder verließ, konnte es das Versprechen Čechovs mitnehmen, für diese Bühne ein weiteres Stück zu schreiben — *Tri sestry,* das Werk, das der Dichter noch im gleichen Jahre beendete.

Die hohe Wertschätzung, die Čechov dem dramatischen Schaffen Gerhart Hauptmanns entgegenbrachte, kommt auch in einem Brief zum Ausdruck, den er unter dem 2.3.1901 an Kondakov richtete. „...Hauptmann mne nravitsja, i ja sčitaju ego bol'šim dramaturgom."

Welche künstlerischen Merkmale sind es nun, die Čechov an Hauptmanns Dramen erkannte und schätzte?

Besonders auffällig erscheint die Verwandtschaft beider Dichter in der Tat in den *Einsamen Menschen.* Die an die „čechovskie nastroenija" erinnernde Stimmungslage der Hauptpersonen wird schon durch den Titel angedeutet — in Johannes Vockerat finden wir den Typ des haltlosen Intellektuellen, der zwischen Traditionsgebundenheit und fortschrittlichen Erkenntnissen hin und her schwankt, wie er in ähn-

---

[2] K. S. Stanislavskij, *Mein Leben in der Kunst,* Berlin 1951, S. 395.

licher Weise, nur in russisches Milieu übertragen, auch bei Čechov immer wieder auftritt. Die feine psychologische Charakterisierungskunst, die Sichtbarmachung innerer Vorgänge durch optische und akustische Mittel, die unmerkliche Verknüpfung der Handlungsfäden durch scheinbar unwichtige Details oder Gespräche — das alles sind Stilmittel, wie sie auch Čechov in seinen großen Dramen verwendete. Dazu kommt noch der dramaturgisch folgerichtige Aufbau des fünfaktigen Dramas, wie ihn Čechov in dieser Geschlossenheit zwar nicht nachahmte, der ihn aber zweifellos beeindruckte.

Auf der anderen Seite darf man aber den direkten Einfluß Hauptmanns auf Čechov nicht überschätzen. Abgesehen von allgemeinen Prinzipien, die beide Dichter unabhängig voneinander befolgten, die aber letztlich auf einer verwandten gesellschaftlichen Grundhaltung beruhen, finden sich in den letzten Dramen Čechovs kaum Ähnlichkeiten zu den *Einsamen Menschen*. Eher könnte man in *Višnevyj sad* einzelne Züge von Hauptmans Erstling *Vor Sonnenaufgang* wiederfinden; so etwa entspricht Hauptmanns Alfred Loth, der dem Mädchen Helene die Augen über die sozialen Nöte und Ungerechtigkeiten öffnet, weitgehend dem Studenten Tromifov bei Čechov, der Anja gegenüber genau so handelt. Die eingebildete Erhabenheit des abstrakt urteilenden Geistesmenschen gegenüber dem Gefühl des Herzens, die beiden Männergestalten eignet, führt aber bei Čechov nicht zu solch tragischer Konsequenz wie in Hauptmanns Drama, hatte doch Čechov auch den Selbstmord als dramaturgische Lösung, wie sie bei Hauptmann des öfteren angewandt wird, seit der *Čajka* verworfen.

Überhaupt läßt Čechov in seinen letzten Werken, so unaufdringlich beide Dichter in ihrer sozialen Tendenz auch sind, mehr optimistischen Zukunftsglauben durchschimmern als Hauptmann, der des öfteren das Gebiet des Realen verläßt und die Grenze zum Irrationalen überschreitet. Čechovs früher Tod setzte seinem Wirken ein jähes Ende, doch wäre er dem Deutschen auf dessen weiteren Wege wohl kaum gefolgt.

Gerhart Hauptmann seinerseits sollte Čechovs Dramatik erst postum kennenlernen. Bei dem ersten Gastspiel des Moskauer Künstlertheaters, das im Februar 1906 in Berlin stattfand, spielte die Truppe unter anderem zwei Čechov-Stücke, nämlich *Dadja Vanja* und *Tri sestry*. Stanislavskij berichtet nun in seinen Memoiren, daß Hauptmann die Vorstellungen mehrmals besuchte. „In den Pausen", so schreibt Stanislavskij, „sprach Hauptmann, der mit seiner Frau und seiner nächsten Umgebung in der Loge saß, ganz ungeniert und ziemlich laut seine schmeichelhafte Meinung über Čechov und unser Theater aus." Bei einem Besuch, den die beiden Theaterleiter Hauptmann abstatteten, habe der Dichter gesagt, er habe für seine Stücke immer von einer solchen Darstellung geträumt, wie er sie bei den Moskauer Künstlern gesehen — „ein einfaches, tiefes und inhaltreiches Spiel ohne sich aufdrängende Theatralik". [3]

Diese Darstellung wird in glänzender Weise durch Hauptmanns Biographen C. F. W. Behl bestätigt, der von einem Gespräch mit Hauptmann aus dem Jahre 1932 berichtet: „Höchstes Theatererlebnis war ihm das erste Gastspiel Stanislavskijs mit seinem Moskauer Künstlertheater, das 1906 ... stattfand. Die Nuancen einer Čechovaufführung sind für Hauptmann in allen Einzelheiten noch heute gegenwärtig. So stark war das damalige Kunsterlebnis." [4] Man beachte, daß dieses Gespräch mehr als ein Vierteljahrhundert nach der seinerzeitigen Aufführung stattfand!

In diesem Zusammenhang ist es interessant, daß Hauptmann in dem gleichen Winter, in dem er Čechovs Stücke in der Moskauer Inszenierung kennenlernte, sein Lustspiel *Die Jungfern vom Bischofsberg* beendete, das dann im Februar 1907 seine Uraufführung erlebte. Zwar hatte sich Hauptmann mit diesem Stoff, der auf persönliche Erlebnisse des Dichters zurückgeht, bereits seit dem Jahre 1892 beschäftigt und 1904 mit der endgültigen Abfassung des Werkes begonnen, doch können einige Züge des Stückes, die an Čechovs „Schwestern" erinnern, nicht übersehen werden.

Bei Hauptmann sind es nicht drei, sondern vier Schwestern, die nach dem Tode des Vaters auf sich allein gestellt sind. Wie bei Čechov ist auch hier die jüngste der Schwestern die lieblichste Gestalt. Der humanistisch gebildete Gymnasiallehrer Kulygin findet sein deutsches Gegenstück in dem pedantischen Oberlehrer Nast, wobei dieser eine weit schlechtere Figur macht und mehr an Čechovs Belikov, den „Mann im Futteral", erinnert. Im ganzen gesehen, hält aber Hauptmanns Lustspiel, das nicht zu seinen gelungensten Werken gehört, einen Vergleich mit Čechovs Schwesterndrama nicht aus.

So hat Hauptmann von Čechov als Dramatiker gewisse Anregungen empfangen, die er dann in eigener Weise verwertete. Zum mindesten wird man sagen dürfen, daß Čechovs Stück den deutschen Dichter veranlaßte, sein schon lange konzipiertes Werk nunmehr endgültig fertigzustellen.

Von einem Einfluß des N o v e l l i s t e n Čechov auf Gerhart Hauptmann ist allerdings nichts bekannt. In den *Einsamen Menschen* wird aus einer russischen Novelle zitiert, sie stammt aber nicht von Čechov, sondern von dem ihm geistesverwandten Garšin — es sind die *Chudožniki*. Nun ist allerdings 1890, als die *Einsamen Menschen* geschrieben wurden, Čechov in Deutschland noch fast unbekannt ge-

---

[3] K. S. Stanislavskij, a.a.O., S. 495/6.

[4] C. F. W. Behl, *Zwiesprache mit Gerhart Hauptmann*, München 1949, S. 17.

wesen — im gleichen Jahre war das erste Bändchen mit Erzählingen Čechovs unter dem Titel „Russische Leute" in Leipzig erschienen —, doch wird von Hauptmanns Biographen, im Gegensatz zu der bereits erwähnten Bühnenaufführung, der Name Čechovs im Zusammenhang mit seiner erzählenden Dichtung niemals erwähnt. [5] Wohl aber ließ sich der alternde Hauptmann aus Leskov vorlesen, und Maksim Gor'kij feierte er aus Anlaß von dessen Tode als Weltgenie. So dürfte Hauptmann den Novellisten Čechov kaum gekannt haben.

Diese Unterschätzung des erzählenden Werkes Anton Čechovs ist nun in Deutschland keine ungewöhnliche Erscheinung gewesen. Trotz zahlreicher Auflagen auf dem deutschen Büchermarkt, deren Höhepunkte in den Jahren nach der Jahrhundertwende sowie dem Jahrzehnt nach der Beendigung des ersten Weltkrieges liegen, ist Čechov in weiten Kreisen des gebildeten deutschen Bürgertums mehr als Dramatiker denn als Novellist geschätzt worden. Trautmann beklagte noch 1947, daß das literarische Porträt, daß man sich in Deutschland von Čechov gemacht habe, einseitig sei und der tiefen und bleibenden Bedeutung des großen Dichters nicht gerecht werde. [6] Erst in der dritten Kulminationsperiode Čechovs, die mit dem Jahre 1945 einsetzte, wird der Dichter nunmehr weiteren Kreisen der deutschen Öffentlichkeit eingehender und umfassender bekannt.

Bedeutende Schriftsteller deutscher Zunge, wie etwa Thomas Mann und Hermann Hesse, betonten in jüngster Zeit, daß sie Čechov erst sehr spät kennen, dann aber um so mehr schätzen gelernt hätten. Die Ursachen einer solchen mangelnden Würdigung Čechovs zu untersuchen, ist hier nicht der Ort. Es bleibt nur zu bemerken und zu bedauern, daß es Gerhart Hauptmann, der 1946 als Vierundachtzigjähriger starb, nicht mehr vergönnt war, seiner Erinnerung an den großen Dramatiker Anton Čechov noch die des bedeutenden Novellisten hinzuzufügen. Wenn sich auch beide Dichter in manchem unterscheiden, so gingen sie doch eine Zeitlang den gleichen Weg, einig in sozialem Verantwortungsbewußtsein, menschlichem Mitgefühl und künstlerischer Ausdruckskraft. Ihre literarischen Beziehungen sind ein interessantes Kapitel deutsch-russischer Wechselseitigkeit.

---

[5] C. F. W. Behl erklärt in einem Brief vom 18.2.1960 ausdrücklich, daß ihm von einer Beschäftigung Hauptmanns mit Čechovs Prosa nichts bekannt sei.

[6] R. Trautmann, *A. P. Tschechow,* Vorwort zu *Meistererzählungen,* Leipzig 1947, S. VII.

TOM EEKMAN

ČECHOV AND THE EUROPE OF HIS DAY

That Čechov is a European, a great, congenial, widely loved European, calls for no further explanation here. Much has been written
about the appreciation of his work and his personality in various
European countries. Many explanations have been produced to answer
the question why, of all Russian writers, he is the best loved by the
reading and theatre-going public of Europe. His popularity may be a
phenomenon belonging to a particular period of time; it is possible
that another period in our cultural evolution will champion other
literary figures and literary forms. But it is difficult to imagine that
Čechov will ever be forgotten or pushed completely into the background.

No answer has ever been given to the question as to what Čechov
thought of the Europe of his time (by Europe we mean central and
western Europe and especially the intellectually and artistically
developed lands: France, Germany, England and Italy — though this
conception is not altogether correct, as Russia belongs to Europe too
and is an inseparable part of it; but here we conform to usage in
Russia as it was in Čechov's time) and to the question as to what
Europe really meant to Čechov. Still, as far as I can see, it is important
to know Čechov's attitude to Europe and the chief European countries,
his conception of the latter and to what aspects of European life
and culture and to which expounders of these he felt most drawn.

To pose the problem 'Čechov and Europe' means broaching another,
far more extensive subject: the attitude of the Russian towards
European life and culture in general along the ages, the much-discussed
matter of 'Russia and Europe'. For hundreds of years, and especially
in the last 150 years, Russians have reflected deeply on their relationship to western Europe, felt the cultural bond between their own
country and the rest of Europe while realizing at the same time Russia's separate and single character. These men were aware of the
necessity to determine Russia's place in respect of Europe, to define
their point of view towards European mode of life, society and culture.
To name in the first place Fonvizin and Karamzin, a whole list of
Russian writers and thinkers have recorded their ideas on this subject.
They expressed in turn their admiration and their criticism; it is well
known that some expressed extremely contrary and even hostile sentiments against western culture as a whole, proclaiming to the world that
„Europe is in a state of putrifaction", to use the words of Pro-

fessor S. P. Ševyrev. It was, of course, in the first place they who
wished to save Russia by holding on to old traditions, to the orthodox
church, by clinging to the ancient social order of the peasants, they
who admired all that was authentically old-Russian, who ran down
western Europe: Gogol', Tjutčev, Dostoevskij and, of Čechov's contemporaries, Leont'ev with his aversion to the tendency to *pošlost'* and
levelling in the West, Rozanov with his contempt for 'the foul-blooded
continent', and Pobedonoscev, Attorney General of the Holy Synode,
with his sharp anti-western ideas.

Nevertheless it was not only conservative figures who thus rejected
things western. Did not Saltykov-Ščedrin in his sketches *Za rubežom*
attack the bourgeois order and the uncongenial imperialistic spirit of
Germany and ridicule 'the Republic without republicans' which he
found in France? Did not G. Uspenskij, staunch enemy of capitalism
after his travels through Europe, describe with feeling the poverty
and inequality he witnessed in Paris, London and Belgium? Did not
Korolenko express in bitter terms his disapproval of conditions he had
seen in the West, especially in America? And we have only to call to
mind "The City of the Yellow Devil" by Gor'kij and to realize his ideas
concerning the bourgeois and capitalistic West. And finally we can
point to Tolstoj's passionate condemnation of middle-class mentality,
society, culture and art found in western Europe. I would point out
that these — Tolstoj, Uspenskij, Korolenko, Gor'kij — were not only
contemporaries of Čechov, but personal acquaintances of his and,
generally speaking, appreciated or admired by him.

All this suggests that the predominant tone of Russian publicists,
writers and philosophers in regard to western Europe was exclusively
negative, that Russian intellectuals were critical and suspicious in their
attitude to European culture. This is however not so. We need only
mention Turgenev and his sympathy for the West; how in *Dym* he
poked fun at the nonsense some Russians spouted about the rottenness
of the West and Russia's divine calling. Yet it must be admitted that
few writers had a complete and unconditional admiration for the West.

Would it be correct to talk of two equal camps, one for, and one
against western civilization, to which nineteenth century Russian
educated people belonged? Such a classification would not tally entirely
with the facts. A striking fact is that the attitude of many who
criticized the West was due to the disappointment they experienced
during their first visit to Europe, when they really saw at last countries
they had heard and talked and dreamed so much about; which means
that they, too, had had great expectations. Was not Europe "the land of
holy wonders" (A. Chomjakov), in which "we believe as the Christians
believe in Paradise" (A. Herzen)? Reality however did not come up to

such expectations, and the Russian traveller felt deceived and disillusioned. The process of disenchantment can be easily discerned in the works of several Russians such as Karamzin, Herzen, Korolenko and others: they too had had at first a favourable and idealized idea of Europe.

It is a generally known fact that from the eighteenth century onwards the educated classes in Russia were turned to western Europe, had been brought up in the European way, spoke European languages and were imbued with western culture, literature and the western mode of life. It has been said that this preoccupation with Europe diminished in the third quarter of the nineteenth century, when *raznočincy* appeared, that is when, in all fields of Russian culture, members of the lower layers of society made their presence felt, personalities less European in their education, more united with the people, farther removed from the European spirit and inclined to be hostile to the West. [1] It is doubtful whether this is altogether correct, for it is a known fact that lower social groups always try to imitate and to acquire the manners and customs of the higher classes; and so we see how in Russia too the lower classes, the half educated layers of society, the new intelligentsia, the increasing class of civil servants, the bourgeoisie which came into being in the 'seventies, 'eighties and 'nineties strove to adopt the common European way of life. We must not forget that most of the stories written by the young Čechov are enacted in these classes of society and that he himself belonged to them.

We cannot therefore speak of two camps, one for and the other against Europe, but the large majority of the educated and half-educated classes were in many ways strongly influenced by western Europe and the greater part submitted to this influence unconditionally. The critics mentioned above (as far as they uttered ideas that were their own) might be considered as universal 'culture critics'. What they judged and critized was not so much a foreign culture as a culture to which they belonged and were bound by ropes of steel. In the West itself there were critical thinkers who attacked the social and cultural (pseudo-cultural) order in which they found themselves. It often happened that Russian critics, wittingly or unwittingly, imitated West-European thinkers (like Rousseau, de Maistre, Saint Simon and so on). Besides, the activities of many of these Russian critics were not limited to negative judgement of the West; they were the most conscious thinkers of their time who took a grave view of the mistakes and injustices of the surrounding society and took up the cudgels against them. The above mentioned contemporaries of Čechov: Salty-

[1] A. von Schelting, *Russland und Europa im russischen Geschichtsdenken*, Bern 1948, p. 269.

kov-Ščedrin, Uspenskij, Tolstoj, Korolenko were all fanatically opposed to the existing political and social structure in Russia.

And finally this aversion from western Europe often went hand in hand with a strong dislike of all kinds of imitation of the western way of life, manners and culture in Russia. Let us remember how Fonvizin ridiculed francophiles in his "Brigadier", how Griboedov, too, ridiculed Russian xenomania and how Tolstoj attacked imitation of things foreign by the upper classes of Russian society. Undoubtedly the Russian aversion to Europe can be explained by deep feelings of patriotism, by national pride which was felt to be offended. This again does not mean that westernizers like Turgenev or T. N. Granovskij were not patriotic; they simply had a different way of thinking; they believed that the western way of life and culture held many valuable elements — valuable to Russia too.

Čechov belonged undoubtedly to these westernizers. Many research scholars have drawn attention to Čechov's realism, to his true-to-life pictures of the Russia of his day. W. H. Bruford even wrote a socio-logical treatise on Russia under the Tsars based on Čechov's stories and plays, entitled *Chekhov and his Russia*, wherein he observes: "With hardly any exceptions he took his subjects from contemporary Russia, and aimed at making his pictures completely convincing in their representative quality". [2] And Čechov does indeed produce scenes which are typical of the classes and circles he describes. We can be sure that on the subject of the relationship to the West which interests us here he also gave (in his own particular airy, humorous, smiling, yet some-times caustic way) an authentic picture of the truth. We have already pointed out that it was usual for the groups he described, particularly in his youth (the petite bourgeoisie of the towns, *meščanstvo*, the in-telligentsia and official circles), to imitate the West and borrow all sorts of ideas and manners from western countries. And actually, when we turn up any of Čechov's stories, articles, plays or light-hearted sketches from his early years — they all bear the mark of West-European influence.

The first thing to strike us is his predilection for foreign words, especially French ones, and also Latin, German, English and Italian. I do not mean the ordinary borrowings, rooted in the language, but all sorts of fashionable words, expressions, sayings and clichés bor-rowed straight away from other languages and written in Latin letters (but also in cyrillic script, especially when Čechov puts them into the mouths of uneducated persons).

His stories teem with *monsieur, madame, mademoiselle, pardon,*

---

[2] London 1947; p. 20.

au revoir, ma ch'ère and *adieu,* with *salon* and *jeune premier, tête-à-tête*
and *nouveauté,* etc. etc. The mere use of such words proves what an
enormous significance notably French culture and the French way of
life had in the educated and semi-educated layers of Russian society.
French was spoken to make class distinction felt or in order not to be
understood by inferiors. In addition Čechov is full of Latin expressions. It is a known fact that Russian gymnasia attached great importance to classical training, to Latin and Greek. Čechov showed in all
his literary works a great interest in ancient Roman writers, a
considerable knowledge of Latin and an exceptional memory in this
respect. He had a great liking for Latin expressions, and particularly
his doctors and apothecaries often speak Latin (dog-Latin). Sayings
like *mens sana in corpore sano* and *sapienti sat* and so on are to be
found again and again in his work. A separate article could be written
on the influence of Latin and the ancient classics in his work. But let
us turn to modern languages.

From English he borrowed a few words, but less than from French:
words like *gentleman, milord, setter, lord-mayor, bye-bye.* He knew
no English, as this language was far less popular than French and
German among educated Russians. From Italian, too, he borrowed
only a few words: *salto mortale, in tutti quanti, signore, buona sera,
finita la comedia.* Much larger is the number of words taken from
German. The middle-class characters whom he described loved to
sprinkle their conversation with words like *Mutter(chen), Vater,
Spitzbube, Rheinwein, Ich liebe dich, Schnaps trinken, Sprechen
Sie deutsch?* [3] *Da ist der Hund begraben, Herr Professor* (as
Serebrjakov is called in "The Wood Demon" and later in "Uncle
Vanya"). There are hardly any words from other European languages,
not even from the Slavic (except the South-Slavic *živio,* and a most
difficult to pronounce Polish sentence in the story "Slime", V 209).

Speaking generally we can say that a study of Čechov's works
proves that he was interested in foreign languages, loved to use them
and, when he could, play on them: here too his sense of humour is
apparent. He uses or makes his characters use the Latin saying *de
mortuis nihil nisi bene;* but in one of his journalistic "Fragments on
Moscow Life" he exclaims: *aut redactor, aut nihil* (II 353), and
elsewhere he says of older people *aut bene, aut nihil* (III 213), in
the story "The Orator": *aut mortuis nihil bene* (V 251), and Šamraev
says in "The Seagull": *De gustibus aut bene, aut nihil.* [4] Already in his
first "Play without a Title" someone remarks: *De mortuis aut bene aut*

---

[3] Of the Muscovites he says: "Nine-tenths of them know no more German
than: "Sprechen Sie deutsch?" and "Schnaps trinken." (II 442).
[4] XI 150; also in his Notebook, XII 285.

nihil, but Platonov corrects him: "No, that is a Latin heresy. In my opinion it is: *de omnibus aut nihil aut veritas.* But *veritas* is better than *nihil*." (XII 21). Čechov loves to put bungled or invented French and German words into the mouths of his heroes, especially the half-educated ones: *moja šarmanočka!, bonžurte!, amurčik!, movetonstvo, komil'fotnost', kel'-vyražansy, že vu pri alja trimontran, ona robko zamersikala*; and *gešeftmacherstvujuščie moskviči, nemecko-libergott-skaja erunda.* There are many such examples.

Čechov keenly realized the importance of knowing foreign languages. "Without languages I am like a bird without wings", says one of his heroes (VI 319). Whenever he refers to one of his characters as an educated person he adds that he (or she) knows (or speaks, or has learnt) German and French, and sometimes even English and Italian, or he simply adds: "...he knows foreign languages". In the story "The Steppe", Father Christofer says to Egoruška: "Learn Latin, French, German (...). If you know this all, every job will be easy to you (...). Think ... the Holy Apostles spoke all the languages — you too: learn languages". (VII 104-105). We might add that Čechov himself had a modest school knowledge of French and German; during his longest stay in France, in 1897, he studied French seriously, he wrote French letters, and he even contemplated making a translation into Russian of one of Maupassant's works. [5]

One might think that Čechov would describe the characters from the above mentioned milieux with irony, that he would treat them with sarcasm and ridicule their uncritical and stupid use of foreign words. This he does too sometimes, but not always. He was not a purist, and no Fonvizin. Čechov was, as has often been emphasized, a *Kulturträger*. He ardently wished that a general human culture would take root and flower over the entire world, and especially in Russia. He was keenly aware that the cultural level of the Russian people should be raised. The lack of education and culture which he saw around him grieved him, especially in his later years. But he was not one to become embittered and express himself in fiery reproaches. For this reason he could not possibly be opposed to or reject the influence on Russia — and on the Russian language too — of the countries with a traditional high cultural level. He sometimes makes fun of the incorrect use (pointing to ignorance) of foreign words, or, e.g., of people who study with gusto a dictionary entitled "30,000 Foreign Words". But the use of foreign words, as such, he does not condemn. The foreign words and phrases he uses do not always fall from the lips of his characters; he introduces them too when he himsef is talking. His letters prove even

---

[5] Cf. R. Hingley, *Chekhov*, London 1950, p. 146-7.

more clearly how eagerly and frequently he makes use of such words, and this often in his well-known playful way. We recall the fact that his first letter but one, from his boyhood, was written in German! Čechov, and especially the young Čechov, Antoša Čechonte, journalist, dramatic critic and humoristic contributor to second rate papers had great fun — obviously — showing off his knowledge of languages, especially of French and Latin (although he used to say jokingly that he "knew all the languages except the foreign ones"). On the other hand, he could not say like Professor Nikolaj Stepanyč in "A Boring Story": "It is easier for me to write German or French that Russian" (VII 226). [6]

To return to the French element in the language of Čechov's work. Without making a profound analysis of it, which would hardly be in place here, we may pause a moment to ascertain in what branches of life, according to the words used, the influene of the French was most noticeable. We find that these branches were in the first place clothes and dress, and food and drink. To quote Puškin:

Ja mog by pred učenym svetom
zdes' opisat' ego narjad;
... no pantalony, frak, žilet,
vsech ětich slov na russkom net.

And indeed, these words did not exist in the Russian language, and thus we find Russian townfolk visiting *galanterejnye magaziny, Parižskie novosti* or *Maison de Paris,* and buying there all kinds of *plumages, agréments, corsets, tournures* and so on. The shop-assistant in the story "Polin'ka" says: "There are two sorts of lace, madam! Cotton and silk. *Oriental, British, Valenciennes,* crochet, *torchon* are of cotton and *rococo, soutache, Cambrai* are of silk" (VI 49).

As for food and drink, all Muscovites and Petersburgers ate only 'French rolls', bought or made *compôte, mayonnaise, consommé, blanc-manger, sauce provençale* and so on (cf., e.g., I 181) and ordered in their restaurants with foreign names all kinds of French dishes. And when they drank — and Čechov's characters were heavy drinkers —, then it was certainly French wine — *vinum rubrum gallicum,* as Čechov loved to say — and preferably *šampanskoe* (or even better: *fin' šampan'*). Champagne plays a very important rôle in Čechov's

---

[6] Čechov's appreciation of language-knowledge is, as so often is the case with him, ridiculed by himself: in his Notebook we find the following comment, intended for the story "Ariadna": "Ariadna speaks three languages fluently. Women learn languages quickly because they have lots of empty space in their head" (XII 221).

stories. And of course there are all kinds of *likery, rom, kon'ak, lafit* etc.

The influence of France is naturally not restricted to these two fields. Town life is full of it. The furniture in the houses was *Empire* or *Louis XVI*. Names given to members of the family reflect the French influence too: *maman, cousine, belle soeur*. Peter is no longer Petr but Pierre, Michail becomes Michel, Ivan becomes Jean, Sof'ja Sophie and Marja, Marie, not to mention the many Mimis and Fifis and Doudous. There was a very strong French, or rather Parisian, mark to be found in the world of amusement and in the theatres of a lighter kind: *cancan, Moulin Rouge, vaudevilles* etc. The spirit of Paris under the second Empire and the years that followed, its amusement, its gaiety and brilliance was a great attraction in Moscow as in nearly all the cities of Europe. "Off to Paris!" [7] was the cry of the average citizen of that time (cf. Glagol'ev jr. in "Play without a Title", or the story "Off to Paris", IV 546, or Jaša in "The Cherry Orchard").

The German element in Russian town-life finds expression in a very different way. It was, of course, also felt in everyday-life in Russia, but Čechov expresses it less in the use of borrowed words and phrases. It is to be seen in the first place in the frequent occurrence of German surnames in Čechov's work. This proves the fact that in Russia, and especially in the towns, the German inhabitants formed a not unimportant colony. There were also some Swiss, Czechs, Scandinavians, Dutch etc., but these were few as compared with the number of Germans. They are chiefly to be found in trade and business and in some of the intellectual professions such as doctors, apothecaries and teachers. There was in Moscow a complete German theatre, which Čechov, with his predilection for anything to do with the stage, found most interesting. In "Fragments from Moscow Life" he wrote that it would soon be the best theatre in Moscow (II 387). There were also German land-owners and important civil-servants, high officers and the so-called Baltic barons. Many of these were Russianized in different degrees. Čechov has depicted Germans of all these sorts and types: let us recall only von Koren in "The Duel", Tuzenbach (baron Tusenbach-Krone-Altschauer) in "The Three Sisters" and the uncongenial son-in-law of the hero in "A Boring Story", Aleksandr Adol'fovič Gnecker. Nearly every page of Čechov's early work contains Germans or at least German surnames, to begin with "Letter to my Learned Neighbour, Dr. Friedrich", dated 1880, the first of his writings to go into print. To take one category: all dentists in his work, without exception, have German names: Gwalter, Krachter, Karkman, Grum-

---

[7] "Valjaj v Pariž!" (*Ivanov,* old wording, XI 478.)

mer etc.; the same is true of most of the doctors (Gefter, Stroh-binder, Franstein, von Sterck, Adolf Magnus, von Brun, Prechtel, Moselweiser etc.) and pharmaceutical chemists. Nevertheless, we must be careful not to forget the numerous Jews who lived in Russian towns. These had mostly German names and it is often difficult to make out whether a certain character of Čechov's is German or Jewish. The subject of Jews and their treatment in Čechov's works is a study on its own, which we will leave to one side now.

Besides the professions mentioned above we find in Čechov's stories and plays droves of German officers and teachers, French governesses and tutors (often with peculiar names like Monsieur Pasdequoi, Madame Tremblant, Tresbien, Entrenoussoitdit, Jevous-aime), Polish bailiffs (landagents are nearly always Polish in Čechov's work). It is obvious that Čechov liked to brighten his work, describing Russian life, with foreign persons.

And now we come to the question: How did Čechov depict all these foreign elements? What was his own attitude towards them? Did he attempt to point out that, despite the obvious excellence of foreign lands and foreigners, the Russian was nevertheless superior, as we find in the work of his older contemporary N. S. Leskov? (cf. his stories "The Left-Handed Smith" or "The Iron Will"). Was he sadly aware of the social injustice of the West, even as Tolstoj, Uspenskij and others? Or that western culture was doomed to perish, as so many nineteenth century Russian publicists were convinced? No, there is no question of such sentiments in Čechov. Nowhere has he expressed an opinion or written a treatise or essay on western culture in general or on the relationship of Russia to Europe. [8]. But from his earliest years he had had a hatred of coarseness, ignorance, dirt and narrow-mindedness. He complained over the *aziatčina* he saw around him. [9] When in the provincial town Taganrog he comes across a clean, tidy street, he cries out: "It breathes of Europe!" (XIII 307). But in general he must have

[8] An exception is his necrology of the explorer N. M. Prževal'skij (1888), who had uphold "the honour of the fatherland and knowledge" and who had distinguished himself by a "fanatic faith in Christian culture and in science". He continues thus: "In our sickly times, when European societies are overcome with inertia, weariness of life and scepticism, when there prevails everywhere a strange mixture of aversion to life and fear of death, when even the best type of individuals sit with their arms crossed, justifying their inaction and immorality by saying that life is aimless, — in these times, undaunted contenders [like Prževal'skij] are necessary as the sun" (VII 476-477). This unsigned article in *Novoe Vremja* seems to belong to Čechov; its tone fits well in with the paper, but it is rather an exception in Čechov's work.

[9] Cf. his Notebook: "We have a European self-love and conceit, but an Asiatic education and behaviour" (XII 268). By "European" he certainly meant here: "as if we were educated Europeans".

agreed with the Head of the Fire Brigade in his short comedy entitled "The little-bourgeois gentlemen" (1884) who says with a sigh: "We are still far from Europe...!" (III 82).

Čechov must have been impressed by and must have admired the culture and refinement which he attributed to West-European countries. With conviction he exclaims in a letter: "We should send our young writers on assignments abroad, honestly we should!" [10] As W. H. Bruford states:"... He early became an admirer of the literary, artistic and scientific culture introduced by the aristocracy from the West. He knew the peasant too wel to idealize him in the manner of the *narodniki* and Tolstoj, and he believed too firmly in the spiritual achievements of western culture and their enrichment of life to practise the cultural ascetism of the *narodniki* and those who sympathized with them." [11] And the Soviet-Russian biographer A. Derman confirms: "... In general, he continued to be all his life a Westernizer and a *kul'turnik*". [12]

He was deeply interested in what happened in foreign countries and all that emanated from them. Nearly every page of his work and every letter he wrote testify to this. We can therefore say that Čechov's attitude to other countries differed from that of the contemporary writers mentioned above and was in agreement with that of the majority of the educated and semi-educated classes we have discussed. As a student of twenty-one he reviewed the performances of Sarah Bernhardt in Moscow, calling her a "child of Paris" who had "come at the right moment to shake us out of our dreadful lethargy" (I 478). In this article he gives a detailed description of Paris, so that we have the impression that he himself had been there and knew the city very well (I 485). With Čechov certainly obtains Doestoevskij's well-known sentiment that the Russian has two fatherlands — Russia and Europe.

When he depicts foreigners he does so sometimes with irony; as examples may serve the character of the English governess Miss Willka Charlesovna Twice in the story "A Daughter of Albion" (1883) or the heroes of "The Grateful German" (1883) and "A Good German"

---

[10] To Suvorin, Dec. 14, 1897 (*Pis'ma A. P. Čechova*, vol. V, M. 1915, p. 129). The phrase was omitted from the PSSP (XVII 189), characteristically enough. We quote the translation of Professor Gleb Struve, who signalized these omissions in his article *Chekhov in Communist Censorship* (*American Slavic & East Eur. Review*, vol. 33 no. 81, June 1955, p. 333). — Čechov had a poor opinion of the cultural level of Russian writers; cf., e.g., his rather strongly worded condemnation in his letter to Suvorin of May 15, 1889 (XIV 369), where he compares them with French writers like P. Bourget.

[11] W. H. Bruford, op. cit., p. 198.

[12] A. Derman, *Anton Pavlovič Čechov, kritiko-biografičeskij očerk*, M. 1939, p. 116; cf. also p. 119: Čechov was a "convinced supporter of western culture".

(1887). But it often happens that we meet congenial foreigners in his work, and his irony is directed sometimes rather at Russians or at Russian circumstances in their relation to foreigners. [13] Bitter attacks on foreigners or on foreign lands are not present in Čechov. At the most it is with ironical humour that he depicts characters who are over-enthusiastic about outlandish, i.e. western customs and things and hold their country in contempt, as in the case of young Glagol'ev in the "Play without a Title" or Jaša in "The Cherry Orchard". When reviewing an industrial exhibition he is struck by "the French tendencies of the exponents", who label the half of their wares in French; "but", adds Čechov, "as even servant girls wear *tournures*, it would be unseemly for the exponents (. . . .) to lag behind civilization" (II 482). The young Čechov felt little admiration for Moscow's tasteless imitations of Parisian centres of amusement or for those who frequented such places, as can be seen from his review "Salon des Variétés" (1881), which he closes with the following words: "Let's go. How nice the exit is! If I were the proprietor of this place I should levy an exit fee and not an entrance" (I 477). He repudiated unconditional imitation, though we must take into account a certain amount of Čechovian irony in his comical lamentation: "The whole human race is going to rack and ruin from imitation of things foreign" (II 218).

Keen observer that he was, he studied closely the foreigners around and about him. Note for example his short sketch of a German girl in a Moscow place of entertainment, taken also from "Salon des Variétés" (1881):

„Fräulein Luise is sitting at a small table. She is big and fat, sweaty and cumbersome as a snail (...). The lines of her corset can be clearly seen along her massive back. What a good thing that she is hiding her hands and her feet! Her hands are large, red and horny. A year ago she still lived in Prussia, where she scrubbed floors, cooked for the reverend Biersuppe and looked after little Schmidts and Müllers and Schulzes... But fate willed that the even tenor of her life be disturbed. She fell in love with Fritz and he with her. But Fritz could not marry a poor girl; he would call himself a fool to marry a girl with nothing! Luise vowed eternal love and quit her dear Vaterland for the cold Russian steppes to earn a dowry... And now she visits the Salon every night. All day long she

---

[13] For example in *Patriot svoego otečestva* (II 162), *Russkij ugol'* (III 243), or *Na čužbine* (IV 59). In the same story *Doč Al'biona* Čechov's ridicule is directed as much against the unmannered Russian landlord as against the English girl! In *Ušla* (II 124) the swindler is a German, but a Russian turns out to be an even greater rogue. Direct mockerey at foreigners we find in *Obyvateli* (VI 438), where a Pole and a German revile the lazy Russians, but do not do a stroke of work themselves...

sticks little boxes and crochets a table cloth. Once she has saved
a certain sum she will return to Prussia and marry her Fritz..."
(I 475).

But it is only a short sketch (which, incidentally, calls to mind the
story "The Iron Will" written a few years earlier by Leskov). Čechov
never wrote lengthy descriptions of foreigners in Russia or stories
about them. His Germans appear more or less incidentally among the
Russians and in the scene of Russian life.

Not only the atmosphere and the way of life, the *byt*, fashions and
foreign influences are mirrored in Čechov's work, but also the course
things took in Europe as far as this was known in Russia, — for
example, the political events. In young Čechov's stories, jokes and
articles, we come across all important figures from the political stage
of those days: Bismarck and Gambetti, Gladstone and Beaconsfield,
Battenberg and Cankov, Kruger and Boulanger. There are echoes of
the so-called Eastern Question, the riots in the Balkans, the peace of
S. Stefano, the formation of East Rumelia, the situation in France,
the Panama scandal and so on. We read arguments over the chances
of a new Franco-German war and about Austrian politics. It is clear
that Čechov followed political events in Europe. But it is clear too, as
far as I can see, that he hardly attached great importance to them.
His characters often talk politics, but what they say is only senseless
twaddle, emphasizing, as it were, the stupidity and emptiness of these
small middle-class figures [14]). The young Čechov showed no political
passions or strong sympathies, there is no evidence of his taking sides
in the political struggles of Europe. He was careful, retiring and
neutral on this score. In later life he took a more serious view of
political and social affairs in the West — as his letters from France
testify, in which he shows his interest in the Dreyfus affair.

It is striking to note that all Čechov says in his early work about
the different European nations coincides more or less with general
and current views on them. To him the French are frivolous, and
especially French women (*francuzjanki*), who are at the same time
attractive in appearance, which makes them dangerous women indeed.
He seems to have been attracted to the type of the highspirited French-
woman. In his accounts the Frenh are lively, gay and carefree (cf. III
274), have good taste and refinement. France has a high standard of

---

[14] Cf. "Psychopaths", IV 408-409, or VI 249. His later life-experience seems
to confirm this opinion: in a letter to Suvorin he writes in 1894: "The Russian
has always been more interested in foreign politics than in his own, Russian, and
when you listen to the conversations, you see now how naive and superstitious
Russian educated people are and how little knowledge they have" (XVI 190).

culture, even though the standard of their morals is not quite so high; a talented, but a degenerated people. (As we know, in the eyes of Russian observers, France is already for two centuries constantly degenerating). [15] In his later life, Čechov had a high opinion of the French and their significance for European culture. [16]

The English are in turn phlegmatic, dispassionate and unperturbable, but correct, tenacious and obstinate. "The Englishman", says one of his characters, "is descended from a frozen fish" (II 218). He is always matter of fact ("time is money," see II 275).

As for the Germans, they are hard workers, patient, accurate, honest, respectable, inclined to the sentimental and patriotic; sometimes they are pedantic, ambitious and cold-blooded [17]; Russians are astonished and often laugh at their customs, at their pronounciation of Russian (the Germans were the only foreigners who settled in Russia in large numbers and retained their native customs, and who could be observed by the Russians). There are evidences that Čechov did not care very much for the Germans [18]; he liked to make fun of them. But in his works he refrained from making unfair generalizations, as so many Russians did. A characteristic anecdote is to be found in his "Boring Story", where he tells how a certain Krylov "when bathing (...) in Reval became furious because the water was so cold and cried: 'The Germans are rogues!'" (VII 268). He appreciated the high standard

---

[15] But not in the eyes of all Russian observers. See Il'ja Erenburg, *Francuzskie tetradi*, M. 1958, p. 3-4. This little book stands out for its warm support of French culture and mode of life.

[16] Cf. his letter to Suvorin of Nov. 24, 1897 from Nice; after giving his opinion on the memoirs of ex-minister Baihaut, he remarks: "How suffers this people, how dear it has to pay for the sins of all the others — this people, which walks at the head of all nations and calls the tune of European culture" (XVII 176).

[17] Cf. his characteristic of the Russians, the Germans and the French in his letter to Suvorin, Dec. 30, 1888 (XIV 274).

[18] It is true that we meet unfavourable remarks in his letters, where he expressed himself with less restraint than in his works — cf. the letter of Nov. 20-25, 1888 to Suvorin (XIV 240): "You ought to write [in *Novoe Vremja*] that the money spent on the Hun university of Derpt, where useless Germans are studying, should be spent by the ministry on schools for the Tatars, who are useful to Russia". Some of his persons with German surnames (Gnecker in "A Boring Story", Von Diederitz in "The Lady with the Dog" and others) are rendered rather unfavourably, but there is no evidence that this was done intentionally. And some remarks of his heroes (as when someone says: "I don't like those Germans; in every hundred, ninety-nine are idiots and one is a genius", I 366) do not necessarily express Čechov's own opinions. He was convinced of the significance of German education: "The mother of all evils in Russia", he wrote to Suvorin, "is gross ignorance, which is proper to all parties and directions in the same measure. You praise German culture, (...) therefore you will be in Paradise, and therefore I respect you very high" (Oct. 28, 1889, XIV 423).

of German civilization and science, the German civic spirit. In a
letter to Suvorin, attacking Tolstoj and the French writer Paul Bourget,
he remarks: "Germany doesn't know writers as Bourget or Tolstoj, and
that is its good fortune. It has science and patriotism and good diplo-
mats and everything you like. It will defeat France, and French writers
will be its allies..." (This is one of the passages which were omitted
for political reasons from the PSSP). [19] There is a second place in
his correspondence where he prefers the Germans to the French, who
are in general congenial people in his eyes: perhaps this utterance is
due to the influence of his friend Suvorin. "I share your feeling of
disgust at the French", he writes him in 1892. "The Germans stand
much higher, although for some reason they are called blunt. I like the
Franco-Russian sympathies just a s much as Tatiščev [a tedious 18th
century historian]. There is something dissolute in those sympathies..."
(XV 420).

Proof that he did no hate the Germans, Germany and the German
element in Russia can be found not only in his letters from Germany
written in the last months of his life, but, after all, also in the fact
that he married... Ol'ga Knipper, his *nemčuška* (dear little German
girl). [20]

Thus from Čechov's works a complete typology of West European
nations in Russian eyes could be made. To this can be added that there
is no sign whatever of Slavophilism, on the contrary. In "Three Years"
Fedor Laptev writes an article with more or less slavophile sentiments:
Europe, he writes, must be saved through idealism, whereupon his
brother asks in a matter-of-fact way: "From what must Europe be
saved?" (VIII 461-462). This laconic question seems to come from
Čechov himself. [21] With obvious repugnance he depicts russophile
prattles in his story "Good-for-Nothings" (1885). About other Slavic
peoples he talks seldom, and then without any feeling of affinity. Now
and then he introduces a Polish bailiff (usually a rather unpleasant
figure; in "The Princess" these bailiffs are called dangerous spies
(VII, 216)), a Czech teacher (there was one in the Taganrog school
in his time). On his journey to Sachalin, he met Poles in Siberia, whom

---

[19] This omission was not noticed by G. Struve. The passage appears in *Pis'ma
A. P. Čechova*, vol. II, M. 1912, in letter no. 246 of Dec. 27, 1889 (PSSP XIV
459).
[20] Although he makes one of the characters in his early story "Which of the
three" (1882) think: "She is a good and noble girl (...), daughter of a Privy Coun-
cillor, and add to this that she is beautiful! But one thing is annoying: she has a
German surname..." (I 359).
[21] The passage emerges still more clearly from the note in his Notebook
(XII 209).

he called "Good, hospitable and very refined people." [22] When travelling
in the West he visited Poland (L'vov) and Prague, but he hardly ever
talks about these places except to remark that in L'vov there are many
Jews and that Russian literature is highly appreciated in Prague and
has been translated for many years. Opatija (Abazzia), which he
visited in 1894, he found most unpleasant; in "Ariadna" he describes
the place as an "awful, dirty little Slavic town" (IX 72-73), and in a
letter he compares the luxurious French Mediterranian coast with
"Abazzia and the whole of this uncivilised brotherly Moldavia. For
here we have our brethren the Slavs!" [23]

It seems that Čechov knew the history of ancient and modern Europe
better than that of his own country, owing undoubtedly partly to the
way history was taught in the Russian schools in those days. All his
pictures and figures derived from history, with only a few exceptions
(Pečeneg, Rjurik, Potemkin), are taken from ancient and western
history: if he wants to mention some outstanding hero of the past, then
he takes Alexander the Great or Napoleon, but never Jaroslav, Ivan
the Terrible or Peter the Great.

Up to this point we have discussed the imitation and the echo
in Russia of European fashions and way of life, of European politics
and history. But what in reality did Europe mean to Čechov in his
own field, the field of literature, and of culture in general? He had
always read a lot, from his childhood onwards, foreign literature too,
mostly in translation, but, at least in his later life, also in the original
French and German [24]. As a boy he was at first deeply moved by
Uncle Toms Cabin, though later he took a critical view of it. He was
impressed by *The Children of Captain Grant* and "Don Quichotte",
by Cooper and Myne Reed. As early on as the years in Taganrog he
had read plays of Shakespeare, works of Humboldt, of Schopen-

---

[22] To his sister, May 14-17, 1890 (XV 77).

[23] We quote again the translation of G. Struve, op. cit, p 332, because this
passage was equally suppressed from the PSSP (letter of Sept. 22, 1894, XVI
168). Čechov somewhat disdainfully uses the term "brotherly Moldavia" (*bratuš-
kinskaja M.*), alluding to the word *bratuški,* applied by slavophile-minded Russians
to the Balkan Slavs.

[24] Čechov had read deeply in classical and contemporary literature of the
western countries, but he also knew Russian literature, ancient and modern,
and appreciated much in it, as he has clearly shown on many occasions. In the
following comment, which appears in a rough sketch for one of his stories, rings
a note of disapproval: "He liked most literary works which did not disturb or
upset his feelings: Shakespeare, Homer (...); he discovered that Homer, Hugo
and Dickens had certain traits in common (...). He never read one of the
Russian writers, whom he hated" (XII 327). — That Čechov as a boy read
German books appears, a.o., from a letter of Feb. 8, 1877 ("načitalsja nemeckich
romanov").

hauer. His first experience of the stage, in Taganrog too, was a performance of Jacques Offenbach's operetta *La Belle Hélène,* then he saw the French cabaret "Delo v trech šljapach", the melodrama "The Beggars of Paris", the operetta "The Tea Flower" etc. In Moscow, as student, journalist and beginning belletrist, he continued to interest himself in foreign literature and the foreign stage: we know that he was absolutely at home in the theatres of Moscow, the popular as well as the classical. He knew all the popular operas and operettas, vaudevilles and farces of those days.

It is not difficult to determine which foreign writer or dramatist made the deepest impression on him; for Čechov Shakespeare stood out above all others as a giant. The biographer A. N. Roskin writes as follows in his recently re-published book on Čechov in reference to a quotation from Hamlet in "The Seagull":

"Through all Čechov's works, his letters, note-books, and conversations, fixed in memoirs, his deep, never-waning interest for Shakespeare's *Hamlet* runs like a red thread. Even during the period when he contributed to humorous periodicals, Čechov wrote a remarkable article on 'Hamlet on the stage of the Puškin Theatre' (...). Single lines from Hamlet or reflections on Shakespeare's tragedy appear in all Čechov's work: in his plays, in a large number of his stories, in his letters and notes. — The lines from Hamlet in 'The Seagull' do not sound like a quotation, but rather as a *Leitmotiv,* one of the *Leitmotivs* of the piece. — Up to a point the critic was indeed right who called 'The Seagull' Čechov's Shakespearian piece." [25]

But besides Hamlet, Čechov knew other plays of Shakespeare's well and repeatedly wrote about them. Without paying too much attention to statistics, we may call it still significant that Shakespeare's name or that of one of his plays appear 73 times in his letters, that is oftener than the names of all the other classical writers put together. Whenever he lists the names of a number of outstanding figures, which he does repeatedly, e.g., as a contrast to the commonplace middle-class circles he is describing, Shakespeare's name appears in every case without exception.

A second great literary figure to whom Čechov gave special attention was Goethe, and especialy his *Faust,* which he seems to have known very well. He makes small mention of other English and German classical writers. Only occasionally he refers to Scott, Byron, Dickens, to Heine and Schiller, and to Lope de Vega and Calderon. More frequently appear the names of the great French classics: Voltaire,

---

[25] A. Roskin, *A. P. Čechov,* M. 1959, p. 131. Cf. *id.,* Antoša Čechonte, M. 1959, p. 343.

Molière, Balzac, and Victor Hugo, whom he described as "the general of French literature" (I 480).

Speaking generally we can say that French cuture, in its universality and great radiating power, made the strongest impact on Čechov, as in the case of many Russians.[26] His interest in contemporary writers naturally varied and sometimes changed completely. In his early years in Moscow he knew and mentioned Jean Ripchen, François Koppe, Ponson du Terrail and other second-rate French belletrists, Jules Verne, the Germans Berthold Auerbach and Friedrich Spielhagen, the detective-story writer Gaborio and the popular German novelist Eugenie Marlitt. How well he knew some of them can be seen from the parodies he loved to write (e.g., of A. Daudet, Jules Verne and Mór Jokai). In later years he developed a lively interest in modern play-wrights, Ibsen especially, and Hauptmann, Strindberg and Maeter-linck, and in belletrists, especially French ones, like Paul Bourget, Flaubert, Daudet, Dumas, Flammarion, Zola, Maupassant. Some of these, chiefly Maupassant, left a certain mark on his work.[27]

Less often appear references to composers and musicians, although Čechov loved music very much. Most frequently he mentions Beet-hoven; also Bach, Mozart, Chopin, Mendelssohn, Brahms, Wagner and the in his time so popular Gounod, — Franz von Suppé's operetta *Boccaccio*, Saint Saens' *Chant du Cygne*, Meyerbeer's opera *Les Huguénots* and Offenbach's operettas were well-known to him, even as the fashionable French, German and Italian romances. In 1884 he wrote on the occasion of Lentovskij's production in Moscow of Strauss's "Carnival in Rome" a parody entitled *Kavardak v Rime* (III 491). Quite often in his stories and articles Italian singers appear, great ones and famous, who appeared in Moscow and St. Petersburg, and less well-known ones, who toured the provinces. He wrote about the Russian tour of the ballerina Cucchi and later expressed his enthusiasm for the great actress Eleanora Duse.[28]

Of the European philosophers and scholars Čechov mentions

---

[26] See I. Erenburg, op. cit.: "Along the ages, France has had the gift to focus, as it were, the ideas and moral aims of Europe" (p. 11).

[27] Cf. H. Halm, *A. Tschechows Kurzgeschichten und deren Vorläufer*, Weimar 1933. — On his interest in foreign writers cf. M. P. Čechov, *Vokrug Čechova*, M. 1959, p. 68. In 1892, he intended to adapt a play of Hermann Sudermann (XV 336).

[28] He saw her the day before his departure to western Europe in 1891 and wrote the same night to his sister: "A remarkable actress. I have never seen anything like it before. I kept looking at this Duse and was harassed to the point of anguish by the thought that we have to exercise our temperaments and tastes on such wooden actresses as N. and her like (...). Looking at Duse, I realised why one feels so bored in the Russian theatre" (March 16-17). I quote the transla-tion of G. Struve (op. cit., p. 331): part of the passage is omitted from the PSSP.

repeatedly Spinoza, Kant, Proudhon, Lessing, and in later years Max
Nordau and Nietzsche. He seems to have been acquainted with the
scientific works, popular at the time, of John Stuart Mill, Spencer,
Buckle, Vogt, Moleschott, and he frequently refers to Darwin, Pasteur,
Koch and Edison (whom he described as "the professor in black magic,
the magician"), as well as to the famous explorers Stanley and Living-
stone. Frequently Čechov puts the names of such famous scholars,
artists or other great figures or reflections on them into the mouths
of his middle-class characters, thus achieving again the effect of
emphasizing the spiritual poverty, stupidity and narrow-mindedness of
the latter. Or he points out how in their youth they were moved by
these great figures, were at least acquainted with their works, and how
later they lost their ideals and the fire of their enthusiasm died out.
There are many examples of this. [29]

Up to now we have paid attention chiefly to the early period of
Čechov's work. Are there evidences of change and evolution in his
ideas? To answer this question we must first devote our attention to
his travels in the West in the 'nineties. He had long wanted to travel
abroad [30] and in 1889 there was talk about a trip to Suvorin and
Grigorovič in Tirol, but this fell through. [31] In March 1891, however,
soon after his return from Sachalin, he set off with his friend Suvorin
for Vienna and then on to Italy and Paris. September 1894 found him
again in Vienna and Italy and in Opatija and Nice. His longest stay
abroad was between September 1897 and May 1898; during these
eight months he was mostly in Nice, but he went to Biarritz and Paris
too. Nice lured him again in December 1900 and in February 1901 he
returned from there via Italy. The trip he made with his wife via
Berlin to Badenweiler in 1904 was the last he made in his life.

If we study his reactions on these trips as expressed in his letters
and elsewhere, we find that personal acquaintance with foreign parts
did not lead to the disillusionment experienced by some other Russian
writers discussed earlier in this article. Čechov seems rather to have
confirmed alll he already thought and knew about Europe. His first
impressions of western peoples from his travels go as far back as

---

[29] "In the beginning", says one of the chief characters in "The Duel", "we had
kisses (...), pledges, Spencer, ideals..." (VII 329) (and he suggests that later all
these things disappeared). The following comment in his Notebook is also
characteristic: "I have not read Spencer. Tell me about his work. What does he
write about?" And Čechov adds in brackets that this is said by a "tiresome lady"
(XII 252).
[30] "How I would love to go to Biarritz or some such place, where there is
music and women galore... Later (...) I shall certainly go to Europe now and
then" (May 1889 to Suvorin, XIV 354). Čechov kept to this decision.
[31] See G. Struve's article in this volume.

October 1890, when he visited Hongkong on his return-journey from
Sachalin. After his arrival in Moscow, he wrote to Suvorin about this
town:

"...excellent roads, tramcars, a railway going up the hill, museums,
botanical gardens; wherever you turn you can see the tenderest
solicitude of the British for their employees; there is even a club
for sailors. I was driven in a jinricksha, that is, by men. I bought
all kinds of junk from the Chinese, and I waxed indignant when I
heard my Russian fellow-travellers criticise the British for their
exploitation of the natives. Yes, I thought to myself, the Englishman
does exploit the Chinese, the Sepoys, the Hindoos, but in return he
gives them roads, drains, museums, and Christianity, and what about
you — you also exploit, but what do you give?" [32]

His first letters from his journey to the West, from Vienna and
Venice, are full of sincere, childish enthusiasm:

"...From Warsaw to Vienna I travelled like a railway *Nana*, in a
luxurious compartment of the 'International Sleeper Company': beds,
mirrors, huge windows, carpets etc. — Ah, my friends the Tun-
guzes, if only you knew how wonderful Vienna is! It is incomparable to any other city I have ever seen in my life. Wide streets
(...), and the shops are not shops but dreamland itself. Of ties alone
there are milliards in the windows! (...). Everything is simply
splendid, and only yesterday I realized that architecture is an art
(...). In every street there is surely a bookshop. There are Russian
books too in the bookseller's windows, but, oh Lord, these are not
the works of Al'bov, of Barancevič or of Čechov, but of all kinds
of anonymous writers, who write and publish their works abroad...
Strange that you can read and say just what you like here..."
(XV 175).

Farther on in this letter he writes with enthusiasm about the splendid
cabs, the wonderful food, the beautiful and elegant women, etc. With
rupture he writes about Venice too:

"Never in my life have I seen such an extraordinary city as
Venice. It is full enchantment, glitter and joy of life. Instead of
streets and roads there are canals, instead of cabs — gondolas; the
architecture is fantastic, and there isn't a place which is not of

[32] Dec. 9, 1890; *Pis'ma A. P. Čechova*, vol. III (1890-91), M. 1913, p. 145. The
passage is quoted by A. Derman, op. cit., p. 116; but it was suppressed in the
PSSP! (XV 130). This was signalized by G. Struve (op. cit., p. 330); we quoted
the translation in his article. We think Derman was right when he commented
(ibid.): "Here we have the admission, formulated on the base of concrete mate-
rials, of the superiority of the developed bourgeois system to a backward system.
In Čechov's outlook on life this is a very essential feature, which comes now
clearly to the fore".

historic or artistic interest (...). The sculptures and paintings are of
a beauty undreamed of by us. In a word, I am bewitched by all I see
(...). I feel I am in the presence of an astonishing beauty which
I enjoy deeply. And the evening! Sweet God! The evenings are so
beautiful you nearly die, everything is so extraordinary! It is not
difficult for a poor and humble Russian to go off his head in this
world of beauty, wealth and freedom. I would willingy stay here
forever..." (XV 177).

Later he sums up his impressions of Italy:

"It is a fairyland. If I were an independent artist with money
I would spend the winters here. Apart from the beauties of nature
and the warm climate, Italy is indeed the only country where you
feel convinced that art is truly the be all and end all, and this conviction gives a man courage" (XXV 185).

He is equally enthusiastic about Nice, and about Paris. "An excellent people" he exclaims about the French (XV 194). Nevertheless his
criticism is aroused. He complains about the "railway conditions"
abroad, which are "worse than in Russia" (XV 189). "Rome", he
finds, "on the whole resembles Char'kov and Naples is dirty. The sea
does not rouse my enthusiasm — in November and December [when he
returned from Sachalin] I was fed up with it" (XV 191). The French
paintings he saw at an exhibition in Paris did not arouse his admiration,
he preferred the contemporary, Russian painters (XV 194). And when
he is satiated by the spectacle of the tourism of the rich in Nice and
Monte Carlo and of the roulette, he writes:

"How despicable and dirty is this life with its artichokes, palms
and the scent of orange blossoms! I like luxury and wealth, but the
roulette luxury here reminds me of a luxurious lavatory. There is
something in the air which offends one's feeling of decency and
reduces nature, the murmur of the sea, the moon to something trite
and commonplace" (XV 191).

In his notebook he wrote the following comment on Monte Carlo:

"Cocottes in Monte Carlo, a cocotte atmosphere; it seems as if
the palm is also a cocotte and the chicken too..." (XII 240).

Nevertheless his indignation was aroused when Grigorovič wrote
to Suvorin that Italian cities, whose art was unknown to Čechov,
"were nothing for Čechov" and that he "belonged to a generation which
was obviously turning away from the West". He reacted furiously to
this in a letter to Suvorin dated May 27th, 1891:

"You must be an ox indeed if, when you see Venice and Florence
for the first time, you "turn away from the West". "Who has been

trumpetting forth to the whole world that I did not like it abroad?", he then exclaims: "What did he expect me to do? Roar with rapture? Break windows? Kiss the French? Didn't I come away with ideas? I think I did" (XV 209).

Suvorin's remark, which aroused Čechov's indignation, is confirmed by Suvorin himself:

"He loved all that was living, all that was moving or moved itself, all that was colourful, gay and poetical in nature and life. (...) We went abroad together twice and both times visited Italy. Art — sculpture, paintings and churches — interested him very little. We had only just arrived in Rome when he wanted to lie in the grass. The originality of Venice fascinated him, but the serenads and the way the people lived far more than the Doge's palace". [33]

The writer D. Merežkovskij, who met Čechov in Venice, wrote in the same trend:

"I talked enthusiastically with Čechov about Italy. He was walking alongside me, tall, stooping slightly as usual, and he smiled quietly. It was his first visit to Italy too. For him too Venice was the first Italian city to see, but I saw no sign of enthusiasm in him. I felt even somewhat hurted by it. He noticed small unexpected details which seemed most unimportant to me: the guide and his completely bald head, the voice of the woman selling violets on the San Marco Square, the uninterrupted ringing on Italian stations..." [34]

His interest in unexpected details, in "all things colourful, gay and poetical" was well noticed by both. Yet they seem to have underestimated Čechov's admiration and enthusiasm for the wonders of Italian art, as it appears from his letters. Čechov was not the man to "roar with rapture and break windows".

After his journey, he was for some time not eager to go abroad. To Suvorin, who was in 1892 in Biarritz, he wrote:

"I don't envy you your sea, your freedom, the good disposition one has abroad. The Russian summer is better than anything else. To tell you the truth, I don't feel very much like going abroad. After Singapore, Ceylon and, perhaps, our Amur, Italy and even the Vesuvius crater don't seem tempting to me. When I sojourned in India and China, I did not see a great difference between foreign countries and Russia" (XV 421).

But afterwards his longing for travelling and foreign countries increased again, as is shown by many letters:

---

[33] Sophie Laffitte, *Tchekhov par lui-même*, (Paris) 1957, p. 110.
[34] Iibd., p. 109-110.

"Money! Money! If I had money, I'd travel to South Africa, about which I am reading most interesting letters now. One must have a purpose in life, and when you travel, you have a purpose" (to Lidija Mizinova, XVI 80).

His impressions during his second visit are of the same nature as during his first. "The scenery in Lombardy is wonderful", he writes, "more beautiful perhaps than anywhere else in the world" (XVI 171). "I am coughing and coughing all the time. But I feel fine. It is amazing what good it does me to be abroad!" (XVI 173). Only Opatija he did not like: at first he found "Abazzia and the Adriatic Sea beautiful, but the Luka and the Psel [small rivers in South Russia where in earlier times he had spent the summers] are more beautiful" (XVI 167). The very next day he writes: "It is raining. It is boring here in Abazzia. The sea is not so beautiful as in Jalta" (XVI 168).

When he heard six months later that Suvorin was going to Italy he wrote (March 23rd, 1895):   .

„Give my love to Italy. I adore Italy, although you told Grigorovič that I lay down in the San Marco Square and said: "How nice it would be to lie in the grass somewhere in our Moscow province now" (...). Lombardy touched me so that, I think, I remember every tree, and if I close my eyes I see Venice clearly" (XVI 229).

It was not until three and a half years had passed that he went abroad again. He spent some months in Nice, and wrote:

"I have made an ass of myself up to now not to spend long times abroad. It seems to me now that, when I shall live, I shall winter no more in Moscow, not for all the world. As soon as it is October — away from Russia! Nature here does not move me, it is strange to me; but I have a passion for warmth, for culture... And culture oozes from every shop window and every wicker basket; every dog smells of civilization". [35]
But in the long run his idle life far from home palled upon him: "I am healthy to the core, but my privileged position of an idle and well-contented person begins to bore me, and sometimes — I am longing for snow. It is possible to work here, but something is missing, and when I am working I feel an inconvenience, as if I were hanged on one leg" (XVII 176).

However, he soon overcame this feeling, as it seems, and was drawn to Paris. From there he wrote: "Here I find life interesting and gay and I would not mind to stay a week longer" (XVII 259-260). After returning home he wrote repeatedly from Melichovo with admiration

---

[35] To Mrs. Suvorina, Nov. 10, 1897; XVII 171-2.

and longing about Paris: "I think with great pleasure of Paris. What a marvellous city it is!" (XVII 273). And two months later he declared to Suvorin: "I intend in future to go to Paris every spring" (XVII 361).

He realized however that his health could not cope with travelling about and certainly not with the winters abroad, which he described as "dreadful" and as "putting him out terribly" (XVII 300). He saw that he was obliged to lead a quiet life, take care of himself, and this he found annoying. He often dreamed of journeys to distant parts, of returning to spots abroad which he loved. The following quotation is taken from one of his letters from Jalta:

"In short, I have the life of a Prince. Yet I am not content. Again and again the longing seizes me to sell the house, rush to Monte Carlo and put at once 100 francs on *quatre-premier*. A quiet, orderly life, and that in the provinces, is a long life, each month being like a year..." (XVII 360).

When at last he was able to cross the border, at the end of 1900, he again enjoyed himself immensely:

"It is perfectly delightful here", he writes to his sister from Nice. "(...) It is Paradise to one who has lived so long in Jalta" (XVIII 424). From Florence he writes his wife: "It is wonderful here. He who has not been to Italy has not yet lived!" (XIX 32). And then from Rome: "Oh, what a delightful country is this Italy! A marvellous country! Every corner, every decimeter of ground has something to teach the observer..." (XIX 34).

Yet even in Italy and Nice he finds that he has seen everything there is to be seen, and there is nothing new to impress him. After his return to Jalta he writes: "I have been abroad, but there is nothing new, I have nothing to write about" (XIX 39). A few days later however his mood is different: "At the moment nothing interesting is happening here", he tells his wife, "and were it not that my mind is filled with thoughts of you I would go abroad again" (XIX 43). It is amazing that as late as the spring of 1904, a few months before his death, he writes of his plan to go to the Russian-Japanese warfront in his capacity as medical man (XX 248, 270).

His last trip gave him great pleasure again: "I had a good and pleasant journey", he writes from Berlin to his sister in June 1904. "We have a comfortable room here (...) in the best hotel. Everything is first-rate"; "I like Berlin" (XX 293). Yet, notwithstanding his general contentment, his criticism is aroused:

"The worst thing of all here and something that knocks you in the eye is the way the women dress. What a dreadful lack of taste! Nowhere are people so badly dressed, without an atom of taste.

I haven't seen one pretty woman and not one who doesn't wear some ridiculous bow or other. At last I can understand why it is so difficult to develop some sense of taste in the Germans in Moscow" (XX 294-295).

And in another letter:

   "The Germans have either lost their sense of taste or they never had one. The way German women dress is worse than in bad taste — it is simply messy; the men too. In all Berlin there is not one pretty woman to be seen, not one who is not disfigured by her clothes. On the other hand they are marvellous housewives; in this field they have attained what are for us unattainable heights" (XX 297). And elsewhere: "I live amongst Germans. I am used to my room and my daily routine, but I cannot get used to German quiet and calm. In the house and outside there is not a single sound to be heard — only at seven o'clock and at midday there is the music in the garden, expensive music, but very unmusical. There isn't a grain of talent to be felt in anything, not a grain of taste, but on the other hand, everything is well ordered and as honest as you like. Our Russian life is much more talented, not to mention the Italian and the French" (XX 299).

And again in his last letter, one of the last lines he wrote:

   "Not one well-dressed German woman — bad taste which is most disheartening..." (XX 306).

Thus at the end he strikes yet a critical note, adding to his interpretation of the German type.

One may wonder what significance Čechov's journeys in foreign parts had on his work, what nature of response they found in it. It seems that these were limited indeed. His first journey is reflected in "An Anonymous Story" (1893), wherein towards the end the story-teller and the heroine travel to Italy and stay there for a time. His second trip is summed up in "Ariadna", which also describes a journey abroad with a woman. But that is all.

What conclusions can we draw? That travelling and visits to foreign countries did not affect him as deeply as we might expect? It is possible that as Čechov grew older and his health deteriorated, not only his ability to work diminished, but also his ability to give artistic form to new impressions, his ability to create something out of new, fresh experiences. It often happens that a writer as he gets older feeds more and more on his memories and less on recent events in his life. However that may be, the fact remains that Čechov introduced many more foreign and international motives into his early work than into his later, more mature work, despite his personal experiences abroad. We can enlarge on this: the work Čechov produced in the last ten years of his life has far less references to conditions and occurrences abroad, far less foreign characters, far less French and Latin and other foreign words and phrases, sayings and names, far less discussions on European politics etc. than in the first ten years of his career. This does not mean to say that they have disappeared; but they have a less important place, although (as we have seen) his interest in Europe and all kinds of events in European life and developments in European culture was as strong as ever. But we can say that, generally speaking, the work produced by Čechov in these last ten years of his life differs from the rest by its more intimate character, by a certain mood which runs through it and is transferred to the reader, by its subtle human feelings and reflections, by its greater richness of ideas, so that there is less room for things exotic and for current events. Besides, Čechov probably no longer felt the urge to show off his knowledge of foreign languages and foreign affairs, as Antoša Čechonte had done. In this connection it is significant that when revising his stories, or preparing them for publication in his Complete Works, he replaced many a foreign phrase with the Russian counterpart. In the title of his first short story, "Letter to a Learned Neighbour", the name 'Dr. Friedrich' was afterwards crossed out. In "Misery" (1886) he had originally written: "... *i gul uličnoj sumatochi dostigaet svoego forte*" — but he changed this subsequently to: "... *i uličnaja sumatocha stanovitsja šumnee*" (IV 608). Elsewhere he replaced the word *lingvistika* by *znanie jazykov*; the word *kanal'i* is scratched out in "Ariadna", *alia jacta est* in "Three Years"; Uncle George in "The Wood Demon" becomes Uncle Vanja in the piece of the same name, and so on. In a letter to Gor'kij, he points to "the unsuitability of foreign, not genuine Russian or seldom used words". [36]

In the above we have convinced ourselves that Čechov was a Westernizer, that is to say he was a European, and a man who contemplated with eagerness distant horizons and willingly left all kinds of limits and boundary lines — land-frontiers as well — behind him. But no one can doubt for one moment that he was a real Russian. [37] Would it be

---

[36] Jan. 3, 1899 (XVIII 11). "I can reconcile myself to *kolležskij assessor* and *kapitan vtorogo ranga* in descriptions", Čechov continued, "but *flirt* and *champion* (when they occur in descriptions) arouse my aversion".

[37] Strong national feelings appear seldom in Čechov, as may be clear from the above. (Characteristic of him is this comment in his Notebook: "National science does not exist, even as a national multiplication table does not exist. That which is national about it is no science", XII 225). That he loved Russia is a fact beyond doubt, even though he seldom said so (He speaks, e.g., with warmth of Jarcev's and Kostja's love for their country in "Three Years", VIII 425). And

correct to say that his fame and popularity in the West are due to the fact that more than most Russian writers he turned to the West and had what can be called a European character? I do not think we can put it quite that way. His popularity abroad as well as at home is due, I think, not only to his gifts as an artist, but to the congenial traits in his character, which reveal his deep humanity. By dint of these qualities Čechov belongs not only to his fatherland, not only to Europe, but to the whole world.

---

we feel sure in the following comment that he does not particularly admire the women in question: „Russians abroad: the men love Russia passionately, but the women forget her very soon and do not love her" (XII 238). When he was compelled to live in Jalta, he repeatedly expressed his longing for Moscow and the "real" Russia. Cf. V. Ermilov, *A. P. Čechov,* M. 1959, p. 413-414.

NINA GOURFINKEL

ČECHOV CHRONIQUEUR DE LA VIE THÉÂTRALE

Le 2 novembre 1896, Čechov écrivait à Suvorin: „En votre qualité
d'amateur de choses de théâtre, je tiens à vous faire savoir ceci: vous
connaissez Garin, l'acteur moscovite, grand excentrique qui se déplace
à la Hamlet, porte la cape et s'exprime avec majesté. Il a écrit un livre:
„Les erreurs théâtrales", et la revue „l'Amateur de théâtre" en a déjà
publié cinq feuilles sous forme de supplément. Imaginez-vous que cet
excentrique a réussi à produire un ouvrage original. Ces „Erreurs
théâtrales" sont une étude sérieuse, riche de pensées utiles et de faits
intéressants. Les acteurs, qui se jugent infaillibles comme le pape et
n'admettent jamais qu'ils puissent se tromper, accueilleront sans doute
ce livre avec mépris. J'ai écrit à l'auteur pour qu'il m'envoie tout ce qui
a déjà paru. Lisez-le. Il arrive donc que les excentriques sont bons
à quelque chose! Si c'est aussi votre avis, je lui écrirai de ne pas laisser
refroidir son zèle et de poursuivre sur le même ton." [1]

En ces jours — deux semaines à peine après l'échec cuisant de
„la Mouette" au Théâtre Alexandrine, échec dû pour une bonne part à
l'incompréhension et à la fausse interprétation de la pièce par une
troupe entraînée à un répertoire conventionnel, — Čechov devait être
particulièrement sensible aux critiques que Garin, acteur lui-même,
adressait à ses confrères. Il s'en prenait à leur paresse d'esprit,
à leur ignorance, à leur manque de conscience professionnelle et de
préparation, surtout parmi les seconds rôles et les doublures. Il criti-
quait de même l'incompétence des régisseurs qui, trop souvent, se can-
tonnaient dans leurs fonctions administratives. Sans se soucier de la
présentation d'ensemble du spectacle, ils s'en remettaient, pour ce qui
leur semblait n'être que des „détails matériels", aux „spécialistes":
machinistes et décorateurs.

Pourtant, n'eût été leur ignorance, leur indifférence ou leur scepticisme, ils auraient pu, en cette année 1896, assister à autre chose
qu'à des discussions théoriques, ils auraient pu découvrir des signes
précurseurs de l'avènement du nouveau maître du spectacle: le metteur
en scène. En effet, depuis des années, sur les minuscules plateaux de

---

[1] PSSP XVI 380. *Teatral'nye Ošibki*, Moscou 1896, 128 p. (Supplément à la
revue „l'Amateur de théâtre" — *Teatral. „Experto credite"*). Dans la 2e édition,
sensiblement complétée, de son livre (Moscou 1901, 332 p., Première Imprimerie
Féminine E. K. Gerbeck), Garin cite Čechov parmi les personnalités, pour la
plupart universitaires, qui ont apporté leur adhésion à ses idées.

clubs moscovites où se produisait la Société d'Art et de Littérature,
Stanislavskij donnait des exemples éclatants du nouvel art scénique.
Mais les „connaisseurs" et les professionnels, à quelques exceptions
près, qualifiaient son effort d'„amateurisme". Deux ans après, „l'amateur" était porté en triomphe et imposait ses „fantaisies excentriques",
grâce surtout à cette même „Mouette", si scandaleusement sifflée lors
de sa création. Le miracle était dû à la rencontre providentielle du nouveau metteur en scène avec un dramaturge novateur. La fameuse
boutade moscovite: „Le Tréâtre d'Art a rendu Čechov čechovien, et
Čechov a rendu artistique le Théâtre d'Art", allait rapidement devenir
une vérité première.

C'est en connaissance de cause que Čechov faisait siennes les critiques
de Garin. Car il connaissait l'envers du décor. Il savait de quoi il parlait,
lorsque, quelques années après, il insistait pour que Gor'kij vînt en
Crimée suivre la tournée de ce même Théâtre d'Art: „Pour écrire une
pièce, il faut que vous vous approchiez de ce théâtre, que vous le voyiez
de près. En assistant fréquemment aux répétitions, vous vous ferez
plus aisément la main. Rien ne permet mieux de comprendre les conditions de la scène que le désordre qui règne aux répétitions." [2]

Les répétitions, Čechov les avait fréquentées dès l'âge de dix-sept
ans. Encore adolescent, non content d'être spectateur assidû et acteur-
auteur du cercle de lycéens amateurs, il avait eu accès aux coulisses
grâce à un condisciple, fils d'un acteur de la troupe de Taganrog. C'est
ainsi qu'il fit connaissance de Solovcov, artiste connu, qu'il devait
retrouver plus tard chez Korš et auquel il allait dédier „l'Ours".

A Moscou, pendant ses années estudiantines, Čechov devint un colla-
borateur plus que constant: forcené, des revues humoristiques; les
minces honoraires qu'il en recevait constituaient une source de revenus
appréciable pour sa maigre bourse. Or, dans les rubriques de ces revues
et surtout pendant la saison, [3] le théâtre figurait en bonne place, sous
forme d'échos et de potins sur les acteurs. Ces revues, destinées à un
public moyen, de médiocre culture, demandaient au chroniqueur moins
un jugement qu'une information facile ou un rapide délassement et
imposaient un certain style, assez banal et un brin vulgaire. Avant
de devenir Anton Čechov, Antoša Čechonte pécha fréquemment contre
le bon goût. Ausi, l'écrivain condamnait-il sans pitié ce qu'il appelait
ses „excréments littéraires", se refusant à les inclure dans ses éditions
ultérieures. Pourtant, dans les pages qui suivent, nous y ferons constamment appel, car, malgré leur absence de valeur littéraire, ces

---

[2] Lettre du 6 mars 1900. M. Gor'kij et A. Čechov, „Correspondance, articles,
témoignages", Moscou 1951.
[3] Voir A. Myškovskaja, „Čechov dans les revues humoristiques des années
1880", Moscou 1929.

récits et articulets offrent une précieuse documentation. D'abord, ils montrent dans quelle mesure le futur créateur de chefs d'oeuvre partout acclamés aujourd'hui, était familier des choses de théâtre et dans quel esprit il aborda sa réforme dramaturgique; ensuite, ils présentent, des moeurs théâtrales de son temps, un tableau véridique, comparable par sa richesse et son authenticité à celui qu'en a donné Ostrovskij. Jeune contemporain de l'auteur des „Talents et admirateurs" et de „Ce n'est pas de leur faute", Čechov le prolonge dans ce domaine, et bien souvent les images et les personnages suscités par l'un et par l'autre se recoupent et se complètent.

Une observation préalable: Čechov prend soin de situer ses récits théâtraux en province. N'empêche que les déductions qui en découlent sont valables pour Pétersbourg et Moscou et concordent avec ses jugements sur les milieux et l'art des scènes des deux capitales. Il en est ainsi de Garin qui feint de ne parler que des troupes de province ou des entreprises privées. Pour tous deux, jouent, d'abord, des considérations de prudence: à l'époque, on ne s'attaquait pas impunément aux scènes impériales ni même aux scènes privées moscovites et pétersbourgeoises. D'ailleurs, le lieu d'action de toute l'oeuvre de Čechov est la province. Mais plutôt que de limiter le champ d'observation, l'immense espace russe qui sert de toile de fond à ses petits récits, leur confère, au contraire, une résonance à l'échelle nationale. Ainsi en fut-il des „Ames mortes" et, particulièrement, du *Revizor*: Gogol', après s'être brûlé les doigts avec „l'Ordre de Vladimir" qui devait se dérouler à Pétersbourg, transporta sa satire dans une ville „d'où l'on pouvait galoper trois ans sans arriver à un état quelconque", et cela sans que sa pointe s'en trouvât moindrement émoussée.

Enfin, les caractéristiques brossées par Čechov à propos du théâtre, comportent, à côté de particularités nationales, nombre de traits généraux, inhérents au métier même d'acteur et communs à la corporation dans le monde entier. La déformation professionnelle de gens qui, ainsi que tous les personnages čechoviens, ne sont ni très bons ni très méchants, mais sont comme tout le monde, ne les rend que plus universellement humains.

2.

Essayons de systématiser tant soit peu les images évoquées par Čechov dans ses „contes de Melpomène", pour employer ce titre caractéristique qu'il donna à son premier recueil, [4] mais en l'étendant à

---

[4] Publié à Moscou en 1884 à frais d'auteur, ce recueil de 96 pages réunissait six récits, précédemment parus dans les revues „Baragoin" (*Mirskoj Tolk*): „Lui et elle", „Deux scandales", „Le Baron" et „La Vengeance"; dans „Le Réveil-matin" (*Budil'nik*): „Femmes d'artistes"; et dans „Les Éclats" (*Oskolki*): „Le Tragé-

tous ses écrits sur le monde du théâtre. Dans toute son oeuvre, d'ailleurs, il évoque fréquemment le théâtre. Mme L. Frejdkina [5] a montré
avec justesse que ses personnages sympathiques s'ennuient loin du
théâtre qui est, pour eux, synonyme de culture (Laevskij dans „Le
Duel", Andrej Efimovič dans „La Salle N° 6", le narrateur de „Ma
vie"), alors que les coeurs secs, les méchants détestent le théâtre (tels
l'architecte de „Ma vie", le père de l'actrice dans „l'Office des morts",
ou le héros de „l'Homme à l'étui" et ses pareils).

Čechov débutant consigne ses impressions théâtrales en décembre
1881, à l'occasion de la tournée de Sarah Bernhardt en Russie. Voici
pour le ton „humoristique":

> „Celle qui a visité les deux pôles, qui de sa traîne a balayé en long
> et en large les cinq continents (…), Sarah Bernhardt, mille fois
> renommée, a daigné honorer de sa présence notre Ville aux blanches
> murailles". [6] Ou encore: „Il y a deux jours, Moscou ne connaissait
> que quatre éléments, aujourd'hui elle ne fait que deviser sur le
> cinquième. Elle connaissait sept merveilles; maintenant, toutes les
> trente secondes, elle proclame l'existence d'une huitième…" „L'artiste
> est devenue notre *idée fixe*. Dans nos têtes règne une espèce de
> folie primaire…."

Le portrait de la vedette, supposé extrait d'une lettre du docteur
en médecine Ferfluchtenschwein à un collègue, constate sa „poitrine
plate de paralytique et ses systèmes osseux et musculaire déficients";
„le cou est si long et si maigre qu'on distingue non seulement la carotide
mais aussi les veines jugulaires", etc. etc.

Tout, cependant, n'est pas du même acabit. Dans une autre critique,
après les „mots d'esprit" d'usage, Antoša Čechonte glisse quelques
observations autrement sérieuses:

> „Nous sommes loin d'admirer le talent de Sarah Bernhardt. Il lui
> manque (…) le feu, qui seul est capable de nous toucher jusqu'à
> faire couler nos larmes, jusqu'à nous faire perdre conscience (…).
> Fort intelligente, cette dame possède des procédés à effet, elle connaît
> le coeur humain, elle a accumulé tout le savoir possible et imaginable,
> et c'est avec justesse qu'elle exécute les tours de prestidigitation
> qui se produisent dans notre âme. Elle fait de ses héroïnes des fem-
> mes aussi extraordinaires qu'elle-même. Son but est de frapper,
> d'étonner, d'éblouir…" Son jeu „est une leçon bien apprise", „il
> reflète moins le génie qu'un labeur puissant, gigantesque".

---

dien". Un seul de ses récits trouva grâce aux yeux de son auteur et fut inclus
par lui dans ses éditions ultérieures.

[5] L. Frejkina, „Le thème du théâtre dans les récits de Čechov", dans la revue
Teatr, Moscou 1960, 1.

[6] Surnom de Moscou.

Et l'auteur de parler de „dressage", d'„artifice", — non pour s'en indigner, cependant. Sans les aimer, il les constate et leur rend même hommage. Le jeu des artistes russes „plein d'âme" lui est plus proche, et pourtant il voudrait que ces artistes prennent exemple sur la Française, car „ils sont paresseux, ne travaillent guère et manquent de culture." [7]

C'est aussi „le manque de culture" qu'Antoša Čechonte reproche à Ivanov-Kozel'skij, acteur provincial qu'il voit dans Hamlet. „Son jeu, dit-il, a beaucoup de charme, mais ce charme est dû exclusivement à son aptitude à éprouver des sentiments!" [8]

Ce critique de vingt et un ans a fait son choix entre les deux grandes traditions scéniques russes: il rejette celle du *nutro* („le dedans") au jeu passionné, déchaîné, avec des éclairs de génie mais dans l'ensemble désordonné, inégal et s'en remettant entièrement à l'inspiration; c'est la tradition de Močalov, „le Kean russe", à laquelle s'attache justement Ivanov-Kozel'skij. Čechov lui préfère la tradition de Ščepkin qui modère et éclaire par l'intelligence l'âme russe débordante. C'est là une des causes profondes qui le rapprocheront du Théâtre d'Art de Moscou, continuateur direct de Ščepkin. [9] C'est aussi pourquoi sa plus forte émotion théâtrale lui viendra d'Eléonora Duse qui réunit miraculeusement l'âme et l'intelligence, la technique et la sensibilité. Rentré tard dans la nuit du spectacle, il éprouve le besoin irrésistible de s'épancher et il écrit à sa soeur. Son admiration pour l'artiste l'incite à un retour sur les acteurs nationaux: „Je regardais cette Duse et je ressentais de la tristesse en pensant que nous en sommes réduits à faire l'éducation de notre goût et de notre tempérament sur l'exemple d'actrices inexpressives telles que X et autres, que nous tenons en estime, parce que nous n'en avons pas de meilleures. En regardant la Duse, j'ai compris pour quoi on s'ennuie au théâtre russe..." [10]

En 1891, à propos de l'Italienne, il exprime les mêmes vues que, dix ans auparavant, il exprimait à propos de la Française; dix ans après, le fond de sa pensée n'aura pas changé. Très tôt aussi il comprend combien et en quoi est insatisfaisante la dramaturgie de son temps. Le monstre informe qu'est sa „Pièce sans titre", écrite à l'âge de vingt ans et dans laquelle ont été taillées les malheureuses adaptations connues sous le nom du héros principal — Platonov (adaptations

---

[7] „Sarah Bernhardt", „Encore sur Sarah Bernhardt", „Lettres et télégrammes d'Antoša Čechonte", 1881, PSSP I.

[8] „Hamlet au Théâtre Puškin", 1882, PSSP I.

[9] Čechov oppose les deux traditions sur un mode plaisant dans „Le Critique", 1887, PSSP VI.

[10] Cité d'après les „Lettres de Čechov" éditées par sa soeur, Moscou 1913, vol. III.

anglaise, française et récemment russe), contient en germe presque
tous les thèmes et personnages qu'il développera dans ses oeuvres
scéniques ultérieures. Seule se perfectionnera sa technique. On dirait
que le destin qui devait faire mourir cet homme si jeune, compensait
la brièveté de son essor créateur par une maturité de pensée étonnem-
ment précoce.

3.

Pendant les années de sa collaboration aux revues humoristiques,
Čechov explore les coins et recoins du monde théâtral. Ses pages four-
millent de charges d'acteurs, de directeurs, d'amateurs, et il s'en prend
aux entreprises théâtrales, à la critique, au public et aux dramaturges,
déblayant ainsi le terrain pour son oeuvre future.

Commençons par les acteurs.

Selon le jeune Čechov, l'impression la plus fréquente qu'on éprouve
au théâtre, est l'ennui. Il attribue la monotonie et la grisaille des spectacles d'abord au manque d'intelligence (*razumenie*) des acteurs, même
de premier plan. Il remarque que si le nouveau „Théâtre près du
monument Puškin" se qualifie d'„accessible", il l'est moins au public
qu'aux mauvais comédiens. Il déplore que les cercles d'amateurs qui
prolifèrent à Moscou, soient, à des rares exceptions près, d'un niveau
aussi déplorable. [11] Mais les portraits des professionnels qu'il croque
ne sont pas beaucoup plus brillants.

Voici — à tout seigneur tout honneur — le tragédien Vasilisk
(Basilic) Afrikanovič Tigrov, dont le prénom, le patronyme et le nom
de guerre trahissent la propension aux rugissements qu'il doit pousser
sur le plateau. [12] Ses collègues lui offrent un banquet pour célébrer
les vingt cinq ans de son activité au service de l'Art. A la place d'honneur, dans un fauteuil emprunté au magasin des accessoires (et qu'il
faudra restituer pour *Hamlet,* sous peine de priver Claudius de son
trône), il se pavane entre „la grande dame" Svirepeeva (nom parlant :
Féroçova) et l'ingénue Unylova (nom parlant dérivé de „dolente"),
et flanqué de deux rangs d'hommes aux visages rasés (trait profession-
nel : on est en 1886 !). Discours du raisonneur Babelmandebskij [13] et
surtout du jeune premier, „sans talent mais jouissant d'une réputation
d'acteur instruit, parce qu'il nasille, possède dans sa chambre d'hôtel
le dictionnaire : „30.000 mots étrangers" et est passé maître dans l'art
des longues palabres." Que de phrases ronflantes sur „l'art sacré", „les
étoiles" et, „guettant l'acteur, les précipices, pleins de reptiles sifflants

---

[11] PSSP II, pp. 358, 375, 483s., 487 et *passim.*
[12] „Le Jubilé" (*Jubilej*), 1886, PSSP V.
[13] Čechov aime beaucoup les noms parlants ou amusants et les note souvent
dans ses Carnets.

et de monstres amphibies." Mais c'est la vodka qui domine tout, et lorsque les fonds s'épuisent, les convives décident de s'en procurer encore en mettant en gage l'album de photos offert au jubilaire par ses collègues et où „il n'y a pas une seule figure humaine tant soit peu convenable."

L'acteur a toujours l'escarcelle vide. Après avoir empoché, grâce à sa représentation à bénéfice, la somme, pour lui pharamineuse, de 123 roubles 30 kopcks, le tragédien Unylov (nom parlant dérivé de „dolent"), en compagnie de Tigrov, le père noble, fait de beaux projets: il rêve d'organiser une compagnie théâtrale inspirée du „principe collectif, avec parts coopératives, solidarité et autres idéaux d'acteurs". Mais encore une fois, les compères boiront la forte somme jusqu'au dernier kopek „à la santé de l'amour de l'art". [14]

Vu de la salle, le tragédien était superbe: „Il tonitruait, sifflait, frappait du pied, déchirait sa veste (...), trépignait (...), étouffait bruyamment..." La fille du chef de police s'y laissa prendre; elle s'enfuit avec lui, et l'acteur l'épousa dans l'espoir de toucher la dot. Mais le père outragé ne l'entend pas de cette oreille, et le tragédien se jugeant trompé, se venge de son dépit sur la jeune femme. Desespérée, elle écrit: „Papa, il me bat! Pardonne-nous! Envoie-nous de l'argent!" [15]

Le jeune premier choisit d'habitude un nom de guerre double, aux syllabes sonores. Tel Brama Glinskij, chaussé de souliers prunelle, la main gauche gantée, un cigare aux lèvres et répandant un parfum d'héliotrope. Cela ne l'empêche pas de „ressembler à un voyageur, perdu dans un pays où il n'y a ni tailleurs, ni blanchisseuses, ni établissements de bains..." [16]

Il arrive que le jeune premier présente bien: „Svelte, élégant, le visage ovale et des pochcs ovales sous les yeux", il porte des chaussettes rouges et éblouit la société provinciale par ses propos sur l'ascendant moral que l'artiste exerce sur le public grossier. Quant à ses succès personnels, il raconte modestement qu'ils sont tels qu'à un moment de gêne il a pu vendre à un épicier 32 kilogs de feuilles de lauriers provenant de ses couronnes. Et ses exploits amoureux!... Mais là, ce Chlestakov théâtral fait fiasco: il cite mal à propos le nom d'une de ses prétendues admiratrices et, mis en demeure de se battre en duel ou de faire des excuses, se rétracte lamentablement. [17]

Les acteurs sont méchants entre eux, ils se jalousent, se volent, se jouent des tours pendables, et quand il s'agit d'argent, sont capables de

---

[14] „Après la représentation à bénéfice" (*Posle benefisa*), 1885, PSSP IV.
[15] „Le tragédien" (*Tragik*), 1883, PSSP II. C'est le seul des six „Contes de Melpomène" que Čechov ait inclus dans ses éditions ultérieures.
[16] „La fin de l'acteur" (*Akterskaja gibel'*), 1886, PSSP V.
[17] „Le jeune premier" (*Pervyj ljubovnik*), 1886, PSSP V.

s'entretuer. Ce dernier récit, d'un humour macabre, comporte une
„Moralité: Lorsque, les larmes aux yeux, un acteur vous parle de ses
chers camarades, d'amitié et de „solidarité", lorsqu'il vous prend dans
ses bras et vous embrasse, ma foi, ne vous y fiez pas trop." [18]

Dans sa famille, l'acteur est insupportable. Sa femme, victime de
sa vanité, comme, d'ailleurs, la femme d'un peintre, d'un musicien,
d'un chanteur, d'un sculpteur ou d'un romancier, doit lui servir de
muse, de confidente, de public — parfois son seul public, à l'enthousiasme obligatoire, et c'est elle qu'il rend responsable s'il n'y a rien
à manger. Moralité: n'épousez pas un artiste. [19]

Čechov n'est pas tendre pour les actrices. On trouve dans ses Carnets ce canevas de récit:

> „Une actrice. Jusqu'à sa dernière heure, elle a été une bien mau-
> vaise interprète. On ne l'aimait pas, on évitait d'aller la voir jouer,
> elle gâchait les meilleurs rôles, ce qui ne l'empêcha pas de se pro-
> duire sur la scène jusqu'à l'âge de 70 ans." [20]

Voici un autre canevas comportant une conclusion d'ordre général:

> „Destin d'une actrice: ses origines — une excellente famille aisée
> à Kerč. La vie lui paraît ennuyeuse, les impressions qu'elle reçoit
> sont pauvres. Scène, vertu, passion, enfin, amants. Aboutissement:
> elle s'installe chez un oncle, bien dodu, et jouit de la solitude. L'ex-
> périence a prouvé que l'artiste doit savoir se passer de vin, de
> mariage et de ventre. La scène deviendra art seulement dans l'avenir;
> en attendant, elle n'est qu'une lutte pour cet avenir." [21]

Aussi artificielle que soit parfois l'affabulation (du „Portefeuille"
ou des „Deux scandales", par exemple), aussi mince l'anecdote et grosses les ficelles, les caractères et la peinture du milieu sont à peine
outrés. Ces récits burlesques correspondent au tableau de l'affligeante
existence des acteurs dans les années 1870 et 1880, telle que la font
revivre les mémoires tristement véridiques d'un Medvedev ou d'un
Davydov, bien que ce dernier soit, par tempérament, plus optimiste. [22]
Un lourd et récent passé pesait sur les acteurs. L'abolition du servage
ne remontait qu'à 1861, et depuis la formation du théâtre russe, la
plupart des troupes étaient constituées de serfs. Certes, de très grands

---

[18] „Le portefeuille" (*Bumažnik*), 1885, PSSP IV. Voir aussi „La vengeance"
(*Mest'*) ou „Deux scandales" (*Dva skandala*), 1882, PSSP II, ou encore „Les
bottes" (*Sapogi*) ou „L'Acteur comique" (*Komik*), 1883, PSSP III ou „Le
Critique" (*Kritik*), 1887, PSSP VI.

[19] „Femmes d'artistes" (*Žony artistov*), 1882, PSSP I.

[20] Carnets, notations des années 1897 à 1904, PSSP XII.

[21] *Ibid.*

[22] P. P. Medvedev, „Souvenirs", „Acad.", Len. 1929. — V. N. Davydov,
„Récit sur le passé", „Acad.", Len. 1931.

artistes en sont sortis — un Ščepkin, un Močalov, pour ne citer qu'eux mais la masse demeurait inculte et timorée, telle que l'avaient façonnée les „fantaisies mi-seigneuriales" (*polubarskie zatei*) de maîtres trop souvent frustes et incultes eux-mêmes. Les temps nouveaux avaient bouleversé les assises sociales et économiques d'une société en fermentation, brusquement engagée dans une industrialisation vertigineuse. A la décadence d'une noblesse terrienne incapable de s'adapter à des méthodes d'exploitation rationnelles, correspondait la promotion du tiers état. Dès le premier quart du siècle avait commencé la liquidation des troupes et orchestres serfs, trop coûteux. „Les amours et les zéphyrs, vendus un à un", encombraient le marché du travail théâtral où venaient les rejoindre les nombreuses épaves, rejetées par la vie moderne: les nobles déchus, dont les pères avaient possédé leurs propres „amuseurs", les roturiers ratés qui avaient vainement espéré faire une rapide carrière, les petits fonctionnaires malchanceux, les étudiants stoppés dans leur études. Tous croyaient trouver un refuge facile dans la carrière d'acteur qui ne semblait requérir aucun savoir spécial. Mais ils ne faisaient qu'échanger une misère contre une autre. Aussi, la vodka était reine. Il faut connaître ce fond de toile décevant pour discerner les résonances profondément véridiques d'une charge aussi grosse que le récit de Čechov: „Un remède contre la dipsomanie". [23]

Un acteur renommé, Feniksov-Porc-Epic II (Feniksov-Dikobrazov), arrive dans une ville de province où sont annoncés ses spectacles. Il sort superbement d'un compartiment de première classe, mais ceux qui l'attendent sur le quai, y compris le directeur du théâtre, savent qu'il a acheté son billet de première à l'avant-dernière station, pour jeter la poudre aux yeux, et que jusque là il avait voyagé en troisième. „Ils voient que, malgré le froid automnal, cette célébrité ne porte qu'un macfarlane d'été et une petite toque en loutre pelée (...). „N'empêche qu'à l'apparition de la physionomie bleuâtre et mal éveillée de Porc-Epic II à la portière, tout le monde est pris d'un certain frémissement et se sent le désir de lui être présenté."

Hélas! l'illustre acteur dont le nom a rempli la caisse du théâtre, sombre soudain dans une crise aigue de disposomanie. Heureusement, la chose, assez fréquente, est prévue: la petite ville possède un spécialiste de ces situations, un coiffeur qui inflige au comédien, plongé dans le néant, un traitement *sui generis*: il lui fait ingurgiter un mélange de vodka, de sel, de savon, d'ammoniaque, de soufre, de colophane, etc., et alterne l'absorption forcée de l'infâme breuvage avec des coups de poings vigoureux sur le crâne de la célébrité. Celle-ci reprend ses sens... On ne sera pas contraint de rembourser le public!

---

[23] *Sredstvo ot zapoja*, 1885, PSSP IV.

Dans sa misère, l'acteur est affreusement seul. En voici un, „un homme au pardessus râpé, à la physionomie glabre d'un rouge violâtre, portant sous le bras une bouteille de vodka; un saucisson enroulé dans du papier sort de sa poche." L'homme rôde dans un cimetière, il cherche une tombe, une pauvre tombe délaissée, avec une croix à bon marché plantée de travers. „Les confrères et les journaleux, explique-t-il, avaient bien réuni assez d'argent pour un monument décent, seulement, voilà (...) c'est parti en vodka...."

Après tout, personne ne songe plus au défunt, lui seul ne l'a pas oublié à cause du mal qu'il lui avait fait:

> „Il a agi à mon égard comme un brigand, comme un scélérat, que Dieu ait pitié de son âme. C'est à force de l'admirer et de l'écouter que je me suis fait acteur. Par son art, il m'a fait quitter la maison paternelle, il m'a tenté par la vanité. Que de choses il m'a promises, pour ne me donner que de la peine et des larmes... Le sort de l'acteur est dur! J'ai perdu ma jeunesse, ma sobriété, mon image de Dieu (...). Pas un sou en poche, des talons éculés, un pantalon rapiécé et effrangé. Quant à mon visage, ne dirait-on pas qu'il a été rongé par des chiens (...). En outre, il m'a fait perdre la foi, mon bourreau! Si au moins j'avais eu du talent, mais non, j'ai tout perdu pour rien, pour rien!... Buvons à son repos éternel! Bien que je ne l'aime pas, bien que ce soit un mort, c'est tout de même le seul être que j'aie au monde..." [24]

Cependant, dès ses premiers récits, Čechov a découvert l'autre aspect du théâtre, celui où l'illusion devient vérité et poésie.

Voici un couple disparate, comme il y en a tant dans ce milieu: elle est une cantatrice célèbre, et lui, il est le mari de sa femme, son caissier, son impresario, son valet. Ils sont toujours en voyage, à l'hôtel, en route d'une capitale à l'autre. Ils ne sortent que le soir, en voiture fermée, pour se rendre au théâtre, et se réveillent tard et de mauvaise humeur. Elle est laide. Il la déteste, la méprise, la vole. Mais la voilà sur le plateau, et tout change:

> „Regardez-la, cette mégère, lorsque, fardée, léchée, corsetée, elle s'approche de la rampe. C'est la rivale du rossignol et de l'alouette! Que de dignité, de charme dans cette prestance de cygne... Quand elle lève le bras et ouvre la bouche, ses yeux, étroits comme des fentes, s'agrandissent et s'emplissent de passion et de lumière..."

L'ayant ramenée à l'hôtel, il s'approche d'elle, ivre d'amour... Elle n'est pas dupe, mais elle tient à lui, parce que, dans sette atmosphère de mensonge où elle vit, c'est le seul être qui parfois a le courage de s'écrier: „Ce n'est pas vrai!" [25]

---

[24] „Au cimetière" (*Na kladbišče*), 1884, PSSP III.
[25] „Lui et elle" (*On i ona*), 1882, PSSP II. Cf. le récit: *Mari d'elle* (sic!),

Vrai, l'acteur ne le devient qu'à sa dernière heure, quand, dans un sordide garni, triste et solitaire, mal soutenu par la sympathie inefficace des ses camarades, il éprouve la poignante nostalgie de son pays natal. [26]

Il y a aussi cette minute de vérité lorsque, après force libations, ayant passé des grandes phrases sur „l'art sacré" aux injures, et des injures aux anecdotes croustillantes, celles-ci épuisées à leur tour, les acteurs se mettent à se souvenir. „L'acteur russe, dit Čechov, est infiniment sympathique quand il est sincère et que, au lieu de proférer des imbécillités sur les intrigues, la décadence de l'art ou l'iniquité de la presse, etc., il raconte simplement ce qu'il a vu et entendu. Il vous suffit parfois d'écouter un comédien, piteux et émacié, se remémorer son passé, pour que votre imagination recrée la figure poétique et attrayante d'un homme qui, jusqu'au tombeau, est resté étourdi, fantasque, vicieux peut-être, mais, vagabond infatigable, ardent, tenace et toujours malheureux, n'en garde pas moins la foi en son art. Par sa largesse, par son insouciance, son mode de vie excessif, il rappelle les anciens preux ... Il suffit alors de l'écouter, pour lui pardonner ses erreurs, volontaires ou non, se laisser séduire et, qui sait, se mettre à l'envier." [27]

Derrière les belles phrases qui sonnent faux, se cache parfois une passion authentique, indéracinable du théâtre. Parmi ces récits trop souvent bâclés, il y a au moins un chef d'oeuvre: *Kalchas*, qui prend tout son relief dans l'adaptation scénique qu'en fit Čechov, sous le titre: „Le chant du cygne". [28] Cette brève „étude dramatique en un acte" évoque de manière saisissante le drame de l'acteur vieillissant. L'acteur comique Svetlovidov (encore un nom à résonance, apparenté au mot „lumière"), âgé de 68 ans, après avoir joué Calchas lors de sa représentation à bénéfice et arrosé cet événement comme il se doit, s'est endormi dans sa loge „à la suite de cette rencontre de Bacchus et de Melpomène". La nuit, il se réveille, seul dans le théâtre vide. Encore affublé de son costume ridicule, il monte sur le plateau désert et en désordre, avec ses portes mal jointes qui mènent vers les minables loges d'artistes et le bric-à-brac scénique amoncelé dans un coin. Devant lui, le trou noir et béant de la salle, „qui a bouffé trente cinq ans de son existence". Il se souvient ... Il y a bien eu jadis dans sa vie une charmante jeune fille; pour l'épouser, elle exigeait qu'il cessât

---

1885, PSSP IV: Un petit comptable a ressenti comme un déshonneur la décision de sa femme de faire du théâtre et l'a chassée. Mais lorsqu'il apprend qu'elle est devenue une cantatrice renommée à gros cachets, il s'empresse de lui „pardonner". Depuis, il vit à ses crochets.

[26] „La fin de l'acteur" (*Akterskaja gibel'*), 1886, PSSP V.

[27] „Le Jubilé" (*Jubilej*), 1886, PSSP V.

[28] „Calchas" (*Kalchas*), 1886, PSSP V; „Le chant du cygne" (*Lebedinaja pesn'*), 1887, PSSP XI.

d'être „un bouffon". Mais il était chevillé au théâtre. Avec le temps
ses yeux se dessillèrent:

> „Je compris que je n'étais qu'un esclave, un amuseur d'oisifs, je
> compris que l'art sacré n'existe pas et que le théâtre est délire et
> supercherie! Je compris le public!... Ils m'applaudissent, ils dé-
> pensent un rouble pour ma photo, mais je reste pour eux un étranger,
> un être inférieur, une espèce de cocotte! Ils me recherchent par
> vanité, mais jamais ils ne s'abaisseront à me donner pour femme leur
> soeur ou leur fille..."

Et maintenant, il est vieux. „A 68 ans, les gens vont aux offices,
se préparent à la mort, et moi... Des propos impurs, la gueule de
bois, ce costume de paillasse..."
Réveillé par ses éclats de voix, apparaît le vieux souffleur Nikita:
„Vous ne me trahirez pas, supplie-t-il. Je couche ici dans les loges...
Je n'ai pas d'autre coin où aller, croyez-moi, pour l'amour de Dieu..."
Les souvenirs affluent, et le vieil acteur, dans son accoutrement de
Calchas, évoque ses anciens rôles, les *vrais*: Boris Godunov, le roi
Lear, Hamlet... Le souffleur lui donne la réplique. Tout est trans-
formé. L'acteur éclate d'un rire heureux, il applaudit: Bravo! bis!
La vieillesse? Quelle blague! Ça n'existe pas! Ah, cette fontaine de
Jouvence! „Là où il y a du talent, Nikita, il n'y a pas de vieillesse!..."

4.

Le vieux Nikita du „Chant du cygne" n'est pas chez Čechov un personnage épisodique. L'écrivain est bon pour les humbles de la scène: la
craintive petite choriste qui se laisse dépouiller, [29] l'accompagnateur, [30]
et surtout le souffleur, auxiliaire effacé dont il a deviné le drame. „Le
baron" [31] est le surnom d'un vieux souffleur, si misérable qu'il ne
réagit plus aux pires humiliations. Comme Nikita, il n'a pas de chez
soi et dort dans le réduit de la caisse du théâtre. Au fond de son
coeur, il chérit la haute tradition de Rossi et de Salvini et admire les
acteurs qui ont l'audace d'interpréter Shakespeare et Schiller. Toute
sa vie il a rêvé de se faire acteur, mais il n'a pas osé. Et maintenant,
il est trop tard. Au moins, de toutes les fibres de son âme, reste-t-il
attaché au théâtre. Plus pour longtemps, — et c'est l'anecdote autour
de laquelle s'enroule le récit, — car il a provoqué un scandale et va
être chassé de son paradis: devant un exécrable Hamlet, il n'a pu se
maîtriser et au lieu de lui souffler, l'a couvert d'injures...
On trouve dans les Carnets de Čechov une variante de ce sujet:

[29] „La choriste" (*Choristka*), 1886, PSSP V.
[30] „L'accompagnateur" (*Taper*), 1885, PSSP IV.
[31] „Le baron" (*Baron*), 1882, PSSP II.

„Il a été souffleur, puis il en a eu assez; après quinze ans pendant lesquels il n'a pas mis les pieds au théâtre, il finit par y retourner. Il assiste à une représentation et fond en larmes." [32]

Le trou du souffleur n'a rien de paradisiaque. „Seul l'extérieur du coffre est enduit d'un blanc étincelant, dit Čechov; à l'intérieur, ses parois sont écaillées, couvertes de toiles d'araignée et d'échardes, et ça sent là-dedans l'humidité, le poisson fumé et l'alcool." [33]

Le petit monde des coulisses, à la fois humble et arrogant, vaniteux et famélique, se pavane dans ses minables oripeaux d'emprunt. Irrésistiblement amoureux du rêve et prêt à tous les sacrifices, il a trouvé en Čechov un chroniqueur incomparable, lucide et fraternel.

5.

A l'exception de quelques villes qui possédaient des bâtiments de théâtre décents, [34] les troupes nomades étaient condamnées à se produire dans des conditions lamentables. Voici comment Čechov décrit un de ces temples de Melpomène:

„Le théâtre se trouve au bout de la rue, à trois cents pas de la prison. Peint en rouge brique, la couleur recouvre tout, sauf les lézardes révélant qu'il est en bois. Ce théâtre fut jadis une grange où l'on entassait des sacs de farine. Ce ne sont pas ses qualités qui lui ont valu d'être promue au rang de théâtre, mais c'était la construction la plus élevée de la ville." [35]

C'est entre des salles de ce genre — quelles devaient y être les loges d'artistes! — et les sordides garnis aux lits inconfortables: ressorts cassés, plumes sortant des oreillers, poussière, désordre, [36] que les acteurs partageaient leur existence. Il en allait différemment pour ceux des scènes impériales: leurs contrats étaient assurés et ils s'em-

---

[32] PSSP XII.

[33] „Le baron", note 31. — Cf. Garin, dans son livre précité (note 1): „Dans les théâtres de province où j'eus à travailler, aucune installation n'était prévue pour le souffleur (...). On lui ménageait sous la scène un siège qui n'était à l'abri ni des courants d'air, ni de la poussière, ni du froid" (p. 7). „En été même, son sort était lamentable: à défaut d'un petit banc de bois sous les pieds et d'un revêtement du coffre, il lui arrivait, pendant de grosses pluies, d'avoir de l'eau jusqu'aux genoux..." (p. 9). Ce passage dut certainement aller droit au coeur de l'auteur du „Baron".

[34] Ce qui n'était pas toujours le cas même pour les scènes privées des capitales. Qu'on songe au retentissement qu'a eu la conception du nouveau bâtiment du Théâtre d'Art de Moscou, en 1902, où, pour la première fois, on avait songé non seulement au confort du public mais aussi des artistes.

[35] „La vengeance", note 18. Cf. la triste indication scénique préliminaire du „Chant du cygne".

[36] Tels sont les garnis évoqués dans la plupart des récits précités.

bourgeoisaient souvent; cependant, eux non plus n'étaient pas garantis contre les excès d'un régime théâtral bureaucratique frisant les rigueurs policières. Quant aux acteurs des scènes privées, surtout en province, ils étaient exposés à l'arbitraire des gouverneurs qui se trouvaient être souvent des cousins germains de celui que nous montre „Le Révizor", ou en proie aux bontés suspectes de „mécènes". [37]

Et puis, il fallait compter aussi avec le directeur de la troupe. La prolifération des théâtres, surtout depuis l'abolition du monopole, en 1881, avait créé ce nouveau type d'homme d'affaires qu'on appelle en russe „entrepreneur" (*antreprener*). C'était généralement un petit profiteur sans scrupules qui, sous de belles phrases, dissimulait une totale indifférence pour l'art. Čechov esquisse le portrait de ce personnage, lâche, cupide, phraseur et menteur, dans „Un directeur de théâtre sous le divan" [38]; il fait apparaître sa silhouette dans la fameuse *Dušečka*, à travers les propos de sa femme-perroquet. [39] Dans „Le Jubilé", le directeur est le seul qui n'a pas versé sa cotisation pour le banquet et qui profite de l'euphorie générale pour s'empiffrer subrepticement. [40]

Dans le cortège de masques de carnaval, voici un *Renard*:

„Ses paroles sont sucre et miel; à l'entendre, il est victime des intrigues et de l'ingratitude. Il larmoie, il cherche à éveiller votre compassion. Écoutez-le, mais ne vous laissez pas prendre: il vous dépouillera, il vous laissera sans chemise, car c'est un directeur de théâtre." [41]

Parfois les dupes se vengent. Ainsi, cet acteur, connu pour sa force physique, qui se vante d'avoir battu comme plâtre au cours de sa carrière pas moins de trente trois directeurs de théâtre, „sans compter les collègues de moindre importance". [42]

On sait par la correspondance de Čechov qu'il se proposait d'écrire, en collaboration avec l'écrivain A. S. Lazarev-Gruzinskij, un vaudeville satirique dont le titre eût été... „Hamlet, prince du Danemark". Dans l'énumération des caractéristiques de ce projet qui ne fut pas réalisé et dont on peut seulement deviner qu'il s'agissait d'une satire sur les

---

[37] Dans un de ses tout premiers contes: „L'inutile victoire" (*Nenužnaja pobeda*), 1882, PSSP I, dont l'action se déroule soi disant en Hongrie, Čechov raconte sur un mode romantique les malheurs d'un violoniste et de sa fille harpiste qui boivent jusqu'à la lie la coupe des humiliations que leur infligent les puissants de ce monde.

[38] *Antreprener pod divanom* (*Zakulisnaja istorija*), 1885, PSSP IV.

[39] 1889, PSSP VII.

[40] V. note 12.

[41] „Les masques" (*Rjaženye*), 1886, PSSP IV.

[42] „La fin de l'acteur" v. note 16.

acteurs, Čechov insiste sur ce point: „Critique de l'organisation théâtrale; sans critique, notre vaudeville n'aurait aucune portée." [43]

Le premier souci du directeur de théâtre est de gagner de l'argent; pour y réussir, il lui faut donc plaire au public. Or, écrit Čechov,

„si nos théâtres sont mauvais, la faute en est au public. Partout et toujours, c'est le même public: il est bête ou intelligent, réceptif ou impitoyable, selon son humeur. Ce n'est qu'un troupeau qui a besoin de bons bergers et de chiens, et qui marche toujours dans la direction où le mènent ces chiens et ces bergers. Vous vous indignez d'entendre les spectateurs s'esclaffer pour de bons mots plats et applaudir des phrases ronflantes, et c'est ce même public stupide qui fait les salles combles à *Othello* et verse des larmes en écoutant l'opéra *Evgenij Onegin* (...). Aussi bête qu'il soit, le public est, en somme, plus intelligent, plus sincère et plus bienveillant que Korš [44], les acteurs et les dramaturges, bien que Korš et les acteurs soient d'avis contraire. C'est un malentendu mutuel." [45]

Le public, ce sont les hommes et les femmes qui vivent dans les pages de Čechov, eux aussi „intelligents ou bêtes, réceptifs ou impitoyables, selon leur humeur". Dans ses lettres, l'écrivain étudie avec une curiosité passionnée les réactions de la salle qui ont transformé en scandale la première d'„Ivanov" (1887) et celle de „La Mouette" (1896), un des fours les plus mémorables de l'histoire du théâtre.

Voyez ce canevas caractéristique:

„Au théâtre. Un monsieur demande à une dame d'enlever son chapeau qui le gêne. Mécontentement, agacement, prières. Enfin, l'aveu: „Madame, je suis l'auteur de cette pièce!" Réponse: „Que voulez-vous que ça me fasse?" [46]

Mais voici un amateur sérieux, passionné de Shakespeare. Il discute avec un ami, il émet des vues profondes sur l'art dramatique. Arrive le neveu du connaisseur, un lycéen d'une douzaine d'années qui interrompt la discussion. Tremblant et éploré, l'enfant remet à son oncle un billet de la part de sa mère. L'amateur éclairé s'excuse et passe dans la pièce à côté d'où retentissent bientôt des cris déchirants: sa soeur, veuve, lui a demandé de „corriger" l'enfant. L'amateur de théâtre s'acquitte au mieux de la besogne et, content de lui, revient à Shakespeare. Le récit est intitulé: „A propos du drame." [47]

Dans son immense majorité, le public ne demande qu'une chose: qu'on le divertisse. Personne ne veut voir des pièces sérieuses. Čechov

---

[43] Lettre du 15 novembre 1887, XIII 391.
[44] Directeur du théâtre moscovite du même nom où fut créé *Ivanov*.
[45] Lettre du 7 novembre 1888 à Suvorin, XIV 224.
[46] Carnets, PSSP XII.
[47] *O drame*, 1884, PSSP III.

avait fondé quelque espoir sur l'entreprise de Lentovskij, acteur, metteur en scène et impresario connu, qui jure de faire de son théâtre
moscovite une scène populaire et éducative. Hélas ! les impératifs de la
trésorerie l'emportent et, de guerre lasse, Lentovskij est obligé d'af-
ficher „Les Cloches de Corneville"... [48]

Dans une satire, Čechov présente le public sous les traits de la
fameuse dame gogolienne „aimable sous tous les rapports" et qui, ici,
„avale tout ce qu'on lui sert". Sa cible préférée est le répertoire de
Lentovskij. Ainsi, spécialiste de la mise en scène à grand spectacle,
celui-ci monte un mélo „Les lépreux et les purs", adapté de l'allemand
et farci d' „effets". Le IIe acte à lui seul montre une avalanche de
neige et un incendie et fait assister à la destruction d'un village.
Čechov en écrit une parodie dont la portée, comme le montre son titre,
va très loin : „Tragédiens impurs et dramaturges lépreux", „Tragédie
horrible, terrible et d'un désespoir révoltant en beaucoup d'actes et
encore plus de tableaux." [49] Parmi les personnages, figurent Lentovskij
en personne, „homme et directeur", et Tarnovskij, adaptateur du mélo,
„un individu impressionnant qui tutoie les diables, les baleines et les
crocodiles ; son pouls bat à 225 pulsations, et sa température est de
42,8°." La pièce commence par l'Épilogue, parce que, explique l'auteur,
„on m'a dit à la rédaction que moins c'est vraisemblable et mieux ça
vaut. A leurs souhaits !"

L'indication scénique préliminaire, sous sa forme de plaisanterie,
déclare la guerre au mélodrame et à son attirail fracassant. [50] Les six
actes de la parodie condensent en trois pages prisons, supplices, absorption de viande crue, etc., ce qui n'empêche pas Lentovskij de déclarer
à la fin : „Malgré tout ça, je ne suis pas satisfait !"

Une autre parodie ridiculise la mise en scène du „Carnaval à Rome",
opéra comique de Johann Strauss, monté par le même Lentovskij et que
le public avait commencé par bouder. Čechov écrit „Tohubohu à Rome",
„bizarrerie comique en 3 actes et 5 tableaux, avec prologue et deux
fiascos". [51] Parmi les personnages : la Lune, encore Lentovskij, déçu et
armé de ciseaux (allusion aux larges coupures qu'il a pratiquées dans
le texte), et la Caisse, vieille fille flanquée de ses deux enfants, Grande

---

[48] PSSP II, *passim*.

[49] 1884, PSSP III.

[50] La voici : „Cratère d'un volcan. Tarnovskij est assis devant une table à
écrire couverte de sang ; sur ses épaules, en fait de tête, un crâne ; dans sa bouche
brûle du soufre. Il trempe sa plume dans la lave que touillent des sorcières. On
frémit d'angoisse. Des courants de froid dans le dos flottent dans l'air. Au fond
de la scène, des genoux fléchissant de peur sont suspendus sur des crochets
chauffés à blanc. Foudres et tonnerre... Chaos, horreur, terreur... La fantaisie du
lecteur complètera le reste."

[51] 1884, PSSP III.

Recette et Petite Recette, la seconde affamée, sans parler de tambours, fakirs, nonnes, grenouilles, mille espérances, mauvais génies, etc. A travers une série de péripéties romanesques, Lentovskij s'acharne à tuer Petite Recette. La Lune, „planète aimable sous tous les rapports", „fait, d'ennui, une éclipse". Enfin, un bon génie prend la défense de la Caisse.

L'allusion répétée au personnage gogolien n'est certainement pas fortuite : le jeune Čechov continue la lutte commencée par Gogol' contre le mélodrame et le vaudeville imbéciles. L'arme a changé, mais le sens du combat est le même.

Le manque de discernement des directeurs de théâtre et leur soif d'inédit leur font accepter n'importe quelle ineptie. [52] Un journaliste plus perspicace voudrait-il donner son avis que mille considérations personnelles l'en empêchent. [53]

Čechov réserve ses flèches les plus acérées à ceux qu'il appelle „les fabricants de drames" (dramodely).

„Un personnage terne au regard éteint, à l'aspect catarrheux, entre dans le cabinet d'un médecin. A en juger d'après les dimensions de son nez et l'expression lugubre de son visage, le bonhomme ne doit pas être ennemi des boissons alcooliques ; il est enclin en outre à un rhume chronique et à la philosophie."

Plein de respect pour ce client, le médecin l'interroge sur son mode de vie. D'après les réponses, le patient passe son existence à boire et à jouer au billard. Le soir, il va au théâtre, puis se remet à boire parce qu'il en revient ému et excité.

„— Et quand écrivez-vous vos pièces ?
— ... C'est selon....
— Décrivez-moi votre processus de travail...
— D'abord, par hasard ou grâce à quelque ami, — car je n'ai pas le temps de m'en occuper moi-même ! — un truc français ou allemand me tombe sous la main. S'il me convient, je le porte à ma sœur ou j'engage un étudiant pour cinq roubles... Ils le traduisent, et moi, vous comprenez, je l'arrange en l'adaptant aux mœurs russes : je

---

[52] C'est du moins ainsi que semble devoir s'interpréter le canevas de récit, noté dans les Carnets, XII 262 : Un directeur de théâtre vient difficilement à bout d'un manuscrit : la pièce est nulle. Il est furieux mais la monte tout de même. Ce sera, évidemment, un échec.

[53] Ibid., p. 245 s. : „Le critique théâtral N. a pour maîtresse l'actrice X. Représentation à bénéfice de celle-ci. La pièce est mauvaise, l'interprétation détestable, mais N. est obligé de dispenser des éloges. Brièvement, il écrit : „La pièce et l'interprète ont remporté un grand succès. A demain, les détails". Il pousse un soupir de soulagement. Le lendemain il se rend chez X. Elle le reçoit, se laisse embrasser, puis, vipérine, lui dit : „A demain, les détails !"

remplace par des noms russes les noms de famille étrangers, etc. (...)
C'est tout (...). Mais quel travail! Quel travail!..." [54]
Parmi les masques de carnaval s'avance

„un dramaturge endimanché. Il cache quelque chose sous les basques
de son habit et jette des regards furtifs comme s'il venait de commettre un larcin... Habillé comme un gandin, il babille le français
et se vante d'entretenir une correspondance avec Sardou. C'est un
talent extraordinaire, il cuisine les drames comme des crêpes et il
est capable d'écrire des deux mains à la fois. Cependant, les contemporains ne l'apprécient guère (...). Ils savent que sous l'enveloppe du
dramaturge se dissimule *le coupeur d'un atelier de confection..."* [55]

Loin d'être hostile aux vrais hommes de lettres, Čechov, au contraire,
prend leur défense contre ces imposteurs. A l'occasion d'une pièce à
succès donnée au Théâtre Korš et qui, parmi de nombreux „effets":
bébés, noyés, guitares, etc., mettait en scène un écrivain, il exhala sa
colère dans l'article: „Un effet à la mode". [56] Les fabricants de drames,
disait-il, ne savent plus qu'inventer. „Ils ont utilisé sur la scène tout
ce que la nature offre de plus terrifiant", au point que, même pour les
décorateurs de province, ce ne sont plus que vétilles.

„Les héros et les héroïnes se pendent, se noient, se tirent des
balles, se jettent dans des précipices ou deviennent hydrophobes...
Ils meurent de maladies abominables qui ne figurent pas dans les
manuels de médecine les plus complets. Quant à la psychologie et la
psychopathie, nos dramaturges avancés en sont si friands que c'en
est une belle pagaïe! (...) Des abîmes, des effondrements, des sauts
du cinquième étage (...). Voici, par exemple, un tour de prestidigita-
tion: l'héroïne est capable simultanément de pleurer, de rire, d'aimer,
de haïr, d'avoir peur de grenouilles et de se servir d'un énorme
revolver à six coups (...). Il ne nous manquait qu'un seul effet,
le plus impressionnant, le plus ronflant, le plus époustouflant, un
effet qui donne la chair de poule et prétend en même temps susciter
des idées: *l'homme de lettres* porté à la scène."
Le drame s'en est emparé:
   „C'est généralement un personnage à figure bestiale, échevelé, avec,
dans sa crinière, du duvet et de la paille. Il n'use ni de cendriers
ni de crachoirs, il emprunte sans rendre, il ment, il boit et il vous fait
chanter. En parlant de lui, il dit: „nous" ou „la littérature contemporaine"". Et Čechov de s'indigner: „Mais a-t-on jamais vu de pareils

---

[54] „Le dramaturge" (*Dramaturg*), 1886, PSSP V.
[55] „Les masques", note 41. Cf. „La déclaration forcée" (*Vynuždennoe zajav-
lenie*), 1889, PSSP VII, parodie d'une pièce suivie de la déclaration comique d'un
membre de la Société des Auteurs dramatiques ridiculisant les adhérents à la
Société qui n'ont rien à y faire.
[56] *Modnyj effekt*, 1886, PSSP IV.

écrivains? Les auteurs se comptent en Russie non par centaines mais par unités ou par dizaines et ils sont plus ou moins connus sinon du public du moins de leurs confrères... Qui donc a pu servir de modèle à ce personnage? De quel point d'observation l'auteur du drame a-t-il étudié ce „type"?"

<h2 style="text-align:center">6.</h2>

Les jugements sur les acteurs, les entreprises théâtrales et les milieux du théâtre que Čechov exprime dans ses lettres, se multiplient à partir du moment où, auteur d'„Ivanov", il devient lui-même maître d'oeuvre. Ces jugements concordent point par point avec le tableau brossé dans ses chroniques et récits. Le cadre de la présente étude ne permettant pas de citer les résultats du dépouillement de sa correspondance auquel nous nous sommes livrée, nous devrons nous contenter de quelques exemples de ses opinions, formulées à diverses époques mais toujours dans le même esprit.

Le 26 mars 1883, Čechov écrivait à A. Kanaev, dramaturge et pédagogue: „Quelque chose cloche chez nos acteurs (...), quelque chose d'étrange (...), je ne m'aventure pas encore à en parler (...). Dommage pour le théâtre russe..." Et il rappelle à son correspondant la conversation qu'ils avaient eue à propos des scandales et des intrigues au Théâtre Korš, conversation, qui, dit-il,

„prit rapidement un tour mineur: nous étions d'accord sur ceci: nos acteurs possèdent tout, sauf l'éducation et la culture et, passez-moi l'expression, ils ne sont pas des gentlemen dans le vrai sens de ce mot (...). Je vous avais exprimé mes craintes pour l'avenir du nouveau théâtre. Le théâtre n'est ni un débit de boissons ni un restaurant tatare (...) et si l'on y introduit ces éléments, il finira mal, comme finira mal l'université qui fleure la caserne..." (XIII 54/55).

A propos de ce théâtre moscovite, Čechov parlait de „linge sale et de petits acteurs", [57] et dix ans après, il dira dans une note de journal au sujet de la scène dramatique impériale de Pétersbourg: „Il y a dans le régime de la scène alexandrine quelque chose de funeste pour la jeunesse, la beauté et le talent, quelque chose qui nous fait trembler pour ceux qui débutent." [58]

Ce n'est qu'en 1898 que Čechov, après avoir assisté à une répétition du Théâtre d'Art de Moscou, quelques jours avant son ouverture, constatera: „J'ai été agréablement touché par le niveau intellectuel de cette troupe." Ce théâtre lui apparaîtra comme „une île bienheureuse" qu'il a eu la chance d'aborder dans la mer théâtrale déserte et désolée. Cette

[57] Lettre du 25 ou 26 juin 1883, XIII 67.
[58] Note sur l'artiste Potockaja, 1893, PSSP VIII.

rencontre n'était pas fortuite. Les voies du Théâtre d'Art et de *son*
dramaturge convergeaient depuis longtemps, bien avant qu'ils ne se
fussent connus. Il suffit de comparer les notes du jeune Stanislavskij
et, par exemple, les réflexions que, dès 1889, Čechov mettait dans la
bouche du professeur dans „Une ennuyeuse histoire":

> „Il est possible, disait le vieux professeur, de persuader à la
> foule sentimentale et crédule, que le théâtre, sous son aspect présent,
> est une école (...). J'ignore ce qu'il en sera dans cinquante ou cent
> ans, mais dans les conditions actuelles, le théâtre ne peut servir que
> de divertissement. Seulement, ce divertissement nous coûte cher (en
> jeunesse et en forces gaspillées)."

Non content de s'attaquer à l'institution, le professeur s'en prenait
aussi à l'esthétique:

> „Lorsqu'un acteur, garrotté de la tête aux pieds par des préjugés
> et des traditions, s'efforce de débiter avec sifflements et convulsions
> un monologue aussi clair et aussi simple que „Être ou ne pas être",
> je sens venir de la scène le même souffle de routine qui m'ennuyait
> il y a quarante ans, au temps où l'on se frappait la poitrine en pous-
> sant des hurlements classiques."[59]

En 1889, Stanislavskij et Nemirovič-Dančenko pensaient déjà,
chacun de son côté, comme le personnage čechovien, mais ils n'allaient
le dire tout haut qu'en 1898, et justement grâce à cette „Mouette" dans
laquelle Čechov avait mis toute son expérience du théâtre et dont il fit
son manifeste dramaturgique.

---

[59] „Une ennuyeuse histoire", 1889, PSSP VII. Une autre coïncidence prémoni-
toire: le professeur se dit incommodé par „la musique qui, on ne sait pourquoi,
joue aux entr'actes en ajoutant aux impressions reçues de la pièce, des impressions
discordantes." Or, pour sauvegarder l'unité du spectacle, Stanislavskij supprima
la musique pendant les entr'actes, ce qui, à l'époque, fut considéré comme une
réforme révolutionnaire. D'autre part, le personnage de Katja, campé dans cette
nouvelle, préfigure celui de Nina Zarečnaja, de „La Mouette", laquelle porte à
sa pleine expression les traits fugitifs des héroïnes théâtrales précédemment
esquissées par Čechov.

HANS-BERND HARDER

ZUR ENTWICKLUNG DER POETIK ČECHOVS — 1886 BIS 1890

1

Die Bedeutung Čechovs für die russische Literatur am Ende des 19. Jahrhunderts dokumentiert sich in einer Fülle von Arbeiten. Sie alle bleiben aber — soweit sich übersehen läßt — hinsichtlich eines Punkts unbefriedigend: sie befassen sich nicht mit der Entwicklung der Poetik. [1]

Dabei läßt sich gerade für die Jahre von 1886 bis 1890 eine Entwicklung innerhalb des dichterischen Werks bei Čechov feststellen: die humoristische Kurzgeschichte wird nach und nach von der ‚ernsten‘, größeren Erzählung verdrängt, den Versuchen zur größeren Form der Erzählung schließt sich die Bemühung um die Form des Romans an, schließlich scheitern aber beide. Diese Entwicklung, die sich im dichterischen Werk selbst vollzog, fand ihren Niederschlag in einer Fülle von Aussagen zur Poetik im Briefwechsel dieser Jahre. Sie erlauben es, diese Entwicklung im theoretischen Bereich zu verfolgen.

Freilich liefert die Darstellung nach dem Briefwechsel nur ein unvollständiges Bild. Sie bedarf der Heranziehung des dichterischen Werks selbst. Von der Aufstellung der Poetik nach den Briefen in einer Entwicklung gehen aber erst die Fragen aus, die dann an das Werk selbst zu stellen sind.

2

Das Verhältnis Čechovs zur literarischen Arbeit ändert sich zu Anfang des Jahres 1886 grundlegend. Die Wende wird eingeleitet durch einen Besuch Čechovs in Petersburg am Ende des Jahres 1885. In der folgenden Zeit zeigt sich eine Beunruhigung, die aus den Gesprächen mit Suvorin und Grigorovič herrührt. So schreibt er am 4.1.1886 an seinen Bruder Aleksandr:

„Суворин, Григорович, Буренин... все это приглашало, воспевало... и мне жутко стало, что я писал небрежно, спустя рукава. Знай, мол, я, что меня так читают, я писал бы не так на заказ...‘‘ (XIII 157)

---

[1] Vergl. allgemein zur Aufstellung der Poetik den Aufsatz von I. S. Ežov *Literaturnye vzgljady Čechova* in *Čechova i ego sreda*, Leningrad 1930.

Schließlich erhält er von Grigorovič einen Brief, der ihn nach eigenen Worten wie ein Blitz traf, und er beeilt sich am 28.3. zu antworten:

> „Доселе относился я к своей литературной работе крайне легкомысленно, небрежно, зря ... Писал я и всячески старался не потратить на рассказ образов и картин, которые мне дороги и которые я, Бог знает почему, берег и тщательно прятал ... От срочной работы избавлюсь, но не скоро ... Выбиться из колеи, в которую я попал, нет возможности ... Летом, когда у меня досуга больше и проживать приходится меньше, я возьмусь за серьезное дело ... Вся надежда на будущее. Мне еще только 26 лет. Может быть, успею что-нибудь сделать, хотя время бежит быстро" (XIII 194).

Tatsächlich gibt Čechov die kleinen Arbeiten nur zögernd auf. Er beginnt aber an der ‚seriösen' Zeitung *Novoe vremja* mitzuarbeiten, deren Herausgeber Suvorin ist. Es kristallisiert sich jetzt eine Poetik der Erzählung heraus, deren Spuren sich in den Briefen finden.

Eine Fixierung der Poetik einer Erzählung liegt in einem Brief an seinen Bruder Aleksandr vom 10.5.1886 vor. Čechov gibt ein ganzes Program. Er schreibt:

> „Город будущего" ... выйдет художественным произведением только при след[ующих] условиях:
>
> 1) отсутствие продлинновенных словоизвержений политикосоциально-экономического свойства; 2) объективность сплошная; 3) правдивость в описании действующих лиц и предметов; 4) сугубая краткость; 5) смелость и оригинальность; беги от шаблона; 6) сердечность.
>
> По моему мнению, описания природы должны быть весьма кратки и иметь характер à propos. Общие места ... надо бросить. В описаниях природы надо хвататься за мелкие частности, группируя их таким образом, чтобы по прочтении, когда закроешь глаза, давалась картина ...
>
> В сфере психики тоже частности. Храни бог от общих мест. ...нужно стараться, чтобы оно [душевное состояние] было понятно из действий героев ... Не нужно гоняться за изобилием действ[ующих] лиц. Центром тяжести должны быть двое: он и она. ..." (XIII 214/15).

Das ‚Programm' überrascht durch seine Reife. Die Grundzüge der Poetik sind in ihm ausgesprochen. Besonders überrascht die Mitteilung zur Beschreibung und Darstellung der Natur und der Personen und die Angabe des Kompositionszentrums in Form eines Paares.

Mit dieser Vollständigkeit setzt sich das Programm scharf von den poetischen Aspekten, wenn man überhaupt davon sprechen kann, der vor 1886 liegenden Zeit ab. Sie sind nicht umfangreich und lassen sich dem Zweck seiner damaligen Arbeiten entsprechend in zwei Punkten skizzieren: Gegenwartsnähe mit Genauigkeit und Kürze. Beide haben aber noch nicht das scharfe poetische Profil der Jahre von 1886 an. Ihre Fixierung liegt in einem Brief an seinen Bruder Aleksandr vom 17./18.4.1883 vor. Čechov schreibt:

> „Главное: 1) чем короче, тем лучше, 2) идейка, современность, à propos, 3) шарж любезен, но незнание чинов и времен года не допускается" (XIII 56).

Diese Punkte machen nach Čechovs Ansicht eine gute humoristische Erzählung aus. Hinsichtlich des Themas schreibt er:

> „Темы едва ли теснят тебя... Не будь узок, будь пошире..."

Dabei verdient hervorgehoben zu werden, daß die Kürze sich in dieser Zeit nur auf den Umfang der Erzählung bezieht. Sie scheint ein gängiger Begriff für Lejkin im Umgang mit seinen Mitarbeitern gewesen zu sein. [2]
Ein Zusammenhang zwischen dem Thema und der Form der Erzählung scheint ebenfalls nicht zu bestehen. Allerdings zeigen sich in den frühen Erzählungen schon Anklänge an den ‚byt', in dessen Benutzung sich eine Aufname der ‚intrigenlosen' Erzählung zeigt. Bezeichnend ist es, daß sich in dieser Zeit auch schon ernste Themen unter den Erzählungen finden. [3]
Es bleibt also bemerkenswert, daß mit dem Programm zwar inhaltlich kein Bruch vorliegt, wohl aber ein Sprung, dessen Anlaß in der Wende zur ‚seriösen' Arbeit liegt.

3

Man wird das Programm nicht überinterpretieren dürfen. Es ist aber für diese Zeit — das Jahr 1886 und weitgehend auch noch 1887 — eine ziemlich vollständige, lose Fixierung von Čechovs Ansichten. Den Nachweis dieser Annahme können entsprechende Bemerkungen in den Briefen dieser Zeit erbringen. Es ist aber nicht zu vergessen, daß viele Stellen Adhoc-charakter haben, d.h. in einer bestimmten Situation einer bestimmten Person zugerechnet sind. Das Programm exakt aus dem speziellen Bezug zu lösen, ist aber mit diesen Bemerkungen nur in der Andeutung möglich.

---

[2] z.B. schreibt er am 12. od. 13.2.84 an Lejkin: „Ne posylaju Vam (die Erzählung), bojus' ogorčit' Vas dlinoju" (XIII 93).
[3] Seine ‚Entdeckung' durch Grigorovič und Suvorin geht von der Erzählung *Eger'* (1885) aus.

Die Bemerkungen über die Darstellung bleiben im wesentlichen unverändert auch für den späteren Čechov. Ebenso bleibt das Paar als Zentrum der Erzählung sogar der Ausgang bei der Komposition für den Roman und die größere Erzählung. Im ersten Teil — in den 6 Punkten — zeigen sich späterhin Änderungen, in der ersten Zeit bleiben sie aber unverändert oder unproblematisch, d.h. sie werden nicht herangezogen.

Das Fehlen politisch-sozialer Erörterungen richtet sich gegen den dilettantischen Gebrauch der Literatur als Sprachrohr für politisch-soziale Ideen. Mit der begrifflichen Fassung als Prätention, als Tendenz, durchzieht ihre Ablehnung seine Poetik. Bis 1888 kommt sie aber nur selten und mehr nebensächlich vor. [4] Ebenso wird der Begriff der Objektivität nur einmal herangezogen, wo er auch gleich eine Erweiterung erfährt. Mit seiner Erörterung in einem Brief an M. V. Kiseleva vom 14.1.1887 wird die spätere Entwicklung der Poetik bereits anvisiert. Čechov antwortet aus Anlaß einer Kritik an der Wahl des Themas der Erzählung *Tina*. Er verteidigt die literarische Gleichwertigkeit aller Themen:

> „Думать же, что на обязанности литературы лежит выкапывать из кучи негодяев „зерно", значит отрицать самое литературу. Художественная литература потому и называется художественной, что рисует жизнь такою, какова она есть на самом деле. Ее назначение — правда безусловная и честная." ... „Я согласен, „зерно" — хорошая штука, но ведь литератор не кондитер, не косметик, не увеселитель; для химиков на земле нет ничего нечистого. Литератор должен быть так же объективен, как химик; он должен отрешиться от житейской субъективности и знать, что ... злые страсти так же присущи жизни, как и добрые" (XIII 262-263).

Auffällig sind in dieser Stellungnahme die Anklänge an Gedanken Zolas. [5] Über die Forderung im ‚Programm' geht dieser Begriff aber schon hinaus. Dort bezog er sich nur auf unvoreingenommene Darstellung, da die Objektivität einem schon gegebenen Thema gefordert wird — in diesem Brief richtet sie sich auf die Unvoreingenommenheit dem Thema gegenüber. Die ‚Wahrhaftigkeit in der Beschreibung der handelnden Personen und Gegenstände' durchzieht ebenfalls seine Poetik als Forderung. Am 6.4.1886 schreibt er seinem Bruder Aleksandr:

> „Не выдумывай страданий, к[ото]рых не испытал, и не рисуй картин, к[ото]рых не видел, — ибо ложь в рассказе

---

[4] Vergl. Brief an A. S. Suvorin vom 18.3.1887.

[5] Vergl. *Les romanciers naturalistes,* 3. Aufl., Paris 1881, den Abschnitt über Flaubert.

гораздо скучнее, чем в разговоре..." (XIII 203); oder
Čechov kritisiert Lejkin am 7.10.1887:

„...у Вас на охоте охотники стреляют куропаток в лесу.
Куропатки бывают на опушке леса, а в лесу на деревьях
никогда" (XIII 370). Die Beispiele ließen sich fortsetzen.

Die ‚Kürze' ist neben der Objektivität der zweite Zentralbegriff
seiner Poetik. Ursprünglich nur auf den Umfang der Erzählung bezogen (Vergl. Brief No. XIII 62, 118, 180), wird sie im Lauf der Zeit
zu einer Forderung, die Mittel der Darstellung und Teile der Erzählung
betrifft. Sehr häufig ist sie auch nur der Ausdruck einer gelungenen
Stelle, wobei nicht weiter differenziert wird. Z.B. schreibt er zwischen dem 6. und 8.10.1887 an den Bruder Aleksandr:

„Пьеса у меня вышла легкая, как перышко, без одной
длинноты" (XIII 371);

oder am 14.1.1887 kritisiert er die Erzählung *Lar'ka* der Kiseleva:

„...есть шероховатости, но краткость и мужская манера рассказа все окупает" (XIII 261), wobei der Begriff nur einen allgemeinen Eindruck wiedergibt. Welche Nuance der Begriff im ‚Programm'
hat läßt sich ebenfalls nur vermuten. Die Bedeutung der „Kompaktheit"
wie sie späterhin meist gebraucht wird schimmert in diesen Stellen
schon durch. Die Forderung nach Originalität korrespondiert der
Ablehnung der Schablone. Gerade bei den Themen der Erzählungen
warnte Čechov vor der Schablone: z.B. am 4.1.1886 an den Bruder
Aleksandr:

„Брось ты, сделай милость, своих угнетенных коллежских
регистраторов! Неужели ты нюхом не чуешь, что эта тема
уже отжила и нагоняет зевоту?" (XIII 156).

Die Schablone im Stil ist der Gemeinplatz, den er am 10.5.86 in dem
‚Programmbrief' rügt. Die Schablone kann sich aber auch nach Ansicht
Čechovs in den Gedanken zeigen. So schreibt er wieder an seinen Bru-
der am 23.2.1887:

„Не понимает [Билибин], что оригинальность автора
сидит не только в стиле, но и в способе мышления, в
убеждениях и проч., во всем том именно, в чем он шабло-
нен, как баба" (XIII 286-7).

Einen Reflex der ‚Herzlichkeit' kann man vielleicht in dem Begriff
der Wärme sehen, der allgemein eine Erzählung in ihrer Stimmung
und Darstellung meint. So etwa die Bemerkung über Leont'ev
(Ščeglov) am 5.2.1888 an Pleščeev:

„Этот не так смел и красив, но теплее Короленко. . .”
(XIV 32).

Somit lassen sich die Forderungen des Programms mehr oder
weniger in den Bemerkungen des Jahres 1886 und weitgehend auch
noch für 1887 aufzeigen. Dabei erfahren die Begriffe der Kürze und
Objektivität eine Erweiterung ihrer Anwendung oder Präzisierung.
Die strengere Fassung der Objektivität ließ im übrigen erkennen,
daß die ‚intrigenlose Erzählung’ der Typus der Erzählung in den
folgenden Jahren in der Theorie sein würde. Čechov knüpfte damit
an Aspekte seiner früheren Arbeit an. Grigorovič und Turgenev hatten
dazu Vorstufen im sogenannten ‚byt’ geliefert, einer kurzen Skizze,
die ein Milieu schildert, die Handlung stark reduziert. [6] Seine frühen
Arbeiten knüpfen, soweit sie nicht etwa auf einer Anekdote beruhen,
an diesen Typ der Darstellung an.

Mit diesem Ansatz war freilich eine Theorie der größeren Erzählung oder gar des Romans kaum im Blickfeld. Hier hatte die
Poetik eine Lücke, die nicht einfach durch Erweiterung zu schließen
war. Mit der Aufgabe der größeren Form, die sich Čechov stellte, war
die Frage, ob er das Modell der intrigenlosen Erzählung verwerfen
konnte. Konnte er es nicht, so mußte er innerhalb dieses Rahmens eine
Theorie der größeren Erzählung und des Romans liefern. Dabei mußte
der Roman zum Gesellschaftsroman werden.

Erst mit der Aufnahme der größeren Form, gerieten die poetischen
Zentralbegriffe der Kürze und der Objektivität in eine Krise.

4

Der Anstoß zur Zuwendung zur größeren Form geht auf die
Wende in Čechovs Werk zu Anfang des Jahres 1886 zurück. Auf den
erwähnten Brief von Grigorovič antwortet er, daß er im Sommer etwas
Ernsthaftes (‚ser’eznoe delo’) beginnen wolle. Und zunächst zeigt sich
der Vollzug in seinen Arbeiten nur in der Mitarbeit an der von
Suvorin herausgegebenen Zeitung *Novoe vremja*. [7] Gleichzeitig aber
arbeitet er weiter in den *Oskolki* von Lejkin und in der *Peterburgskaja
gazeta*. Seine Beiträge in dem *Novoe vremja* zeichnen sich durch
‚ernste’ Themen aus. Damit ist unabhängig von der wohl immer wieder
von Grigorovič und anderen geforderten Zuwendung zur größeren

---

[6] Unter diesem Gesichtspunkt wäre das Verhältnis Čechovs zu Turgenev neu zu
untersuchen unter Berücksichtigung der Probleme, die aus diesem Ansatz für
die Poetik folgten.

[7] Im Jahre 1886 erscheinen in *Novoe vremja* 17 Arbeiten. Ihr Umfang
schwankt zwischen 7 und 18 Seiten. Im Jahre 1887 geht ihre Zahl auf 11 ver-
öffentlichte zurück. Ihr Umfang steigt leicht an. Die Mitarbeit in *Oskolki* geht
1887 sehr zurück.

Form, der Anstoß zu einer Beschäftigung gegeben. Mit dem ‚ernsten' Inhalt vollzog sich nicht nur ein Übergang, der einen Wechsel im künstlerischen Anspruch belegte, sondern dieses ernste Thema verlangte auch einen größeren Entfaltungsraum, wie es auch seiner Art nach vielschichtiger sein mußte und sich der einfachen Darstellung entzog. So wurde auch von hierher die Entwicklung in Gang gesetzt, die schließlich etwa in der zweiten Hälfte des Jahres 1887 in den Versuch, größere Formen zu schreiben, einmündet. Für die Zeit bis zu diesem Punkte ist eine wachsende Unzufriedenheit mit seiner früheren Arbeit, seiner Arbeit nach 1886 und insbesondere eine Unsicherheit während des Schreibens selbst charakteristisch.

Erste, wenn auch nicht eindeutige Nachrichten ergeben sich für den Juli 1887, wo von einem Roman die Rede ist. [8] Auch nicht ganz zuverlässig ist Čechovs eigene Mitteilung an seinen Bruder Aleksandr um die Mitte des Oktober:

„У меня есть роман в 1500 строк ..." [9]

Im Oktober liest er auch Korolenkos *Les šumit* und urteilt über die Architektur eines Romans des amerikanischen Schriftstellers Henry Thoreau. [10] Er muß aber noch gegen Ende des Jahres 1887 an einem Roman gearbeitet haben, wie aus einem Brief vom 12.1.1888 an Grigorovič zu ersehen ist, wo von einem angefangenen Roman die Rede ist. Dieser Brief enthält auch die Antwort auf eine erneute Aufforderung sich größere Arbeiten vorzunehmen. Diesmal kann Čechov schreiben:

„Вот Вам ответ на существенную часть Вашего письма: я принялся за большую вещь" (XIV 14).

Gemeint ist hier die spätere Novelle *Step'*, die er auf einen Rat Korolenkos hin begann. Sie liegt im Anfang des Februar vor. Den März über arbeitet Čechov an der größeren Erzählung *Ogni*, die er schon im Februar begonnen hatte. Sie wird erst Ende April abgeschlossen. Im Mai entstand die größere Erzählung *Žitejskaja meloč'* und erst im August schreibt Čechov wieder am Roman. Er unterbricht aber wieder, schon unsicher geworden, um in der zweiten Hälfte des September die Erzählung *Imeniny* zu schreiben. Im Oktober beschäftigt ihn der Roman, der aber nicht vorwärtskommt. Schließlich entsteht

---

[8] Vergl. Lazarev-Gruzinskij in *Čechov v vospominanijach sovremennikov*, o.O., 1952, S. 102.

[9] Der Roman ist nicht erhalten. Man bezweifelt, ob es ihn gegeben hat. Jedenfalls kann er nicht umfangreich gewesen sein, denn *Pripadok* mit fast 2000 Zeilen (Brief No. XIV 511) hat gedruckt 23 Seiten.

[10] Čechov las den Roman *Walden; or life in the woods* (1854).

die Erzählung *Pripadok,* deren Thema er schon im September mitteilt. Über das Jahr verstreut entstanden die kleinen Erzählungen: *Spat' chočetsja, Krasavicy, Skazka,* später *Pari* genannt, und *Sapožnik i nečistaja sila.*

So nimmt Čechov die Arbeit am Roman — unbewältigt im Jahre 1888 — im folgenden Jahr wieder auf. Im März schreibt er intensiv und zuversichtlich. Er verändert das Vorliegende und schwärmt von seiner Arbeit. Zuversichtliche Nachrichten liegen auch noch im April bis in den Mai hinein vor. Ende Mai aber schreibt er bereits von einem Abschluß in zwei bis drei Jahren, aber er arbeitet noch im Juni.

Zwischen Juli und August beginnt er die Erzählung *Moe imja i ja,* die spätere *Skučnaja istorija,* und beendet sie Ende August. Danach fehlen die Spuren größerer Arbeiten. Im Jahre 1890 verfaßte er bis zur Abreise nach Sachalin nur die Erzählung *Čerti,* später unter dem Titel *Vory.* An kleineren Arbeiten fällt in das Jahr 1889 nur die Erzählung *Knjaginja.* [11]

Die Aufstellung der Arbeiten dieser Jahre belegt die Bemühung um die größere Form. Der Roman, zu dem es verschiedene Ansätze gab, ist nicht geschrieben worden. Auf dem Hintergrund der Werkgeschichte, sich in ihr spiegelnd, sie wiederum bestimmend, vollzog sich die Bewegung und Entwicklung der poetischen Zentralbegriffe.

5

Mit der Bemühung um die größere Form der Erzählung mußte der Stoff der Erzählungen sich zwangsläufig ändern. In dieser Änderung spiegelt sich die Bewegung, die Čechovs Arbeit 1887/88 erfaßt, deutlich wider.

Theoretisch stellte sich Čechov folgende Aufgabe: die Szene, die Situation, die seinen bisherigen Erzählungen zugrunde lag, ließ sich nicht ohne weiteres zu einer größeren Form dehnen. Für die intrigenlose Erzählung — und es gibt keine Anzeichen dafür, daß er diesen Typ aufgeben wollte — mußte die Situation, die Szene der Mittelpunkt bleiben. So blieb nur die Möglichkeit Situationen aneinander zu reihen, eine Form der Verknüpfung zu finden. Tatsächlich ist es auch für die Darstellung eines Stoffs durch Čechov charakteristisch, daß eine Reihe von Situationen und die Typen von Personen angegeben werden. Die Zusammenstellung der Wiedergaben von Stoffen in seinen Briefen soll also einmal diese Eigentümlichkeit belegen, die die praktische Existenz des erwähnten theoretischen Problems nachweist, zum

---

[11] Die dramatischen Arbeiten sind nicht berücksichtigt. Sie haben eine spezielle Poetik und tragen zur Entwicklung der Poetik der Erzählung und des Romans nichts bei.

anderen erschließt die Erwähnung nicht bearbeiteter oder vollendeter
Stoffe damit neues Material zur Poetik Čechovs.

In den Briefen nimmt die Erwähnung der Stoffe von 1887/88 an
einen großen Raum ein.

Die erwähnte Aufzählung von Situationen, Bildern und Typen [12]
findet sich schon in der Mitteilung des Stoffs der *Step'* an Grigorovič
am 12.1.1888:

> „Я изображаю равнину, лиловую даль, овцеводов, [...],
> попов, ночные грозы, постоялые дворы, обозы, степных
> птиц и проч." (XIV 14).

Ebenso schreibt Čechov an Ja. P. Polonskij am 18.1.1888 über den
Stoff von *Step'*:

> „В небольшой повести я изображаю степь, степных
> людей, птиц, ночи, грозы и проч."

Er schränkt aber den Wert des Stoffs gleich darauf ein, wenn er
fortfährt:

> „Для современной читающей публики такой сюжет, как
> степь с ее природой и людьми, представляется специальным
> и малозначащим" (XIV 19).

Das Übergewicht der Naturbeschreibung formuliert er selbst am
19.1.1888 an Pleščeev:

> „... Выйдет у меня 4-5 печатных листов; из них два листа
> заняты описанием природы и местностей — скучно!" (XIV
> 21).

Ebenfalls empfindet er diesen Mangel, wenn er am 3.2.1888 wiederum an Pleščeev schreibt:

> „Вы увидите в ней не одну фигуру, заслуживающую вни-
> мания и более широкого изображения" (XIV 26).

Als Grigorovič ihm noch während der Arbeit an *Step'* das Thema
eines Jungen, der in der Großstadt durch Selbstmord endet, vorschlägt,
weist er es als zu schwierig für die Schriftsteller seiner Generation
zurück. Nach Beendigung der *Step'* denkt er an eine Fortsetzung mit
diesem Thema. Am 5.2.1888 entwirft Čechov das Thema allgemein
und stellt eine besondere Forderung:

> „Вся энергия художника должна быть обращена на две
> силы: человек и природа. С одной стороны, физическая

---

[12] Vergl. Lazarev-Gruzinskij in *Čechov v vospominanijach sovremennikov*,
S. 115. Dort gibt er die Beschreibung einer Beerdigung wieder, die aus einem
Romananfang von 1887 stammen soll.

слабость, нервность, ранняя половая зрелость, страстная
жажда жизни и правды, мечты о широкой, как степь, деятельности...; с другой — необъятная равнина, суровый
климат, серый, суровый народ..." (XIV 33).

Damit hatte er sich vom Stoff her eine neue Aufgabe gestellt, denn
wenn er wirklich den Untergang des Jungen mit Einbeziehung der Natur beschreiben, ja sogar erklären wollte, so hatte er sich mit der
Darstellung des Selbstmords ein Ziel gesetzt, dem schließlich sein
bisheriges Verfahren der losen Verbindung von Bildern der Natur
und Typen nicht genügen konnte. Freilich ist diese Fortsetzung von
Step' nicht geschrieben worden.

Seine Vorstellungen von einem Stoff müssen sich aber in diesem
Zusammenhang doch geändert haben, wie eine Erwähnung seiner
Erzählung *Sčast'e* (1887) erkennen läßt. Er erklärt sie am 25.3.1888
für die beste aller seiner Erzählungen und gibt ihren Stoff in folgender Form an:

„В рассказе изображается степь: равнина, ночь, бледная
заря на востоке, стадо овец и три человеческие фигуры,
рассуждающие о счастьи" (XIV 58/59).

Die Angabe, daß die Personen über das Glück urteilen, ist nicht
zu übersehen. Dieses Thema der Personen der Erzählung bestimmt
ihren Ablauf. Nach diesem Modell hat Čechov dann die Erzählung
Ogni geschrieben. Dort urteilen oder diskutieren die Personen über
den Pessimismus. Angaben über den Stoff von *Ogni* sind aus dieser
Zeit nicht erhalten. Nur eine Bemerkung Leont'ev (Ščeglov) gegenüber läßt seine Unzufriedenheit mit dem Stoff erkennen. [13] Ebenso
enthält der Briefwechsel keine Bemerkung über den Stoff von
Žitejskaja meloč'. Auch *Imeniny* wird nicht erwähnt, abgesehen von
der allgemeinen Bemerkung, die Erzählung sei ‚s napravleniem' geschrieben. [14]

Selbst diese Stoffe verläßt Čechov aber aus Anlaß der Mitarbeit an
einem Sammelband für den Dichter V. M. Garšin, der in diesem Jahre
seinem Leben durch Selbstmord ein Ende gemacht hatte. Am 15.9.1888
teilt er Pleščeev den Plan mit:

„... Впрочем, есть у меня еще одна тема: молодой человек гаршинской закваски, недюжинный, честный и глубоко
чуткий, попадает первый раз в жизни в дом терпимости"
(XIV 168).

Čechov fährt fort und deutet die Richtung an:

---

[13] Vergl. Brief vom 18.4.1888. Desgleichen den Brief vom 17.4.1888 an Pleščeev über die Schwierigkeiten der Ausführung.
[14] Vergl. Brief XIV 172 an Pleščeev.

„Так как о серьезном нужно говорить серьезно, то в
рассказе этом все вещи будут названы настоящими их
именами.”

Unschwer erkennt man hier ein verwandtes Thema zu dem der
Fortsetzung von *Step'*. Es ist ein aktuelles Thema, das freilich auch als
eine Reverenz vor Garšin zu verstehen ist, aber daß Čechov sich in
dieser Zeit solchen Themen gegenüber nicht ablehnend verhält, belegt
eine Besprechung eines Romans von Lejkin am 5.10.1888 :

Стукин имеет значение серьезное и стоит многого [по
моему мнению] и будет служить чуть ли не единственным
памятником банковских безобразий нашего времени; к
тому же фигурируют в нем не Акулина и не Катерина, а
птицы более высшего порядка” (XIV 178).

Im Oktober des Jahres 1888 wendet Čechov sich dem Roman zu. Die
Mitteilungen vor diesem Zeitpunkt sind sehr allgemein und lassen kaum
Näheres erkennen. [15] Jetzt schreibt Čechov am 9. 10.1888 an Grigoro-
vič :

„Хочется писать роман, есть чудесный сюжет... Те
мысли, женщины, мужчины, картины природы, которые
скопились у меня для романа, останутся целы и невре-
димы... Роман захватывает у меня несколько семейств
и весь уезд с лесами, реками, паромами, железной дорогой”
(XIV 182/183).

Diese Aufzählung geht kaum über die Angaben hinaus, die er schon
am 12.1.1888 gemacht hatte. Es zeichnet sich jetzt aber die Form eines
Gesellschaftsromans ab. In ihr lag eine Konsequenz der intrigenlosen
Erzählung. Damit stellten sich aber neue Probleme. In *Ščast'e* hatte
das Thema des Glücks, in *Ogni* das Thema des Pessimismus der
Erzählung die Einheit gegeben; für einen Roman, der mehrere Personen und einen größeren Zeitraum umfassen mußte, ließen sich so
einfache Themen nicht verwenden. Ob Čechov diese Schwierigkeit
schon sah, läßt sich nicht erkennen. Zunächst arbeitet er am Roman
weiter, und die Mitteilung eines Details zeigt noch das Bild der zusam-
mengesetzten Phänomene, wenn er am 11.11.1888 an Suvorin schreibt:

„... я написал строк триста о пожаре в деревне: в усадьбе
просыпаются ночью и видят зарево — впечатления, разговоры, стук босых ног о железную крышу, хлопоты...”
(XIV 230).

---

[15] Vgl. XIV 15: „Роман этот захватывает целый уезд (дворянский и
земский), домашнюю жизнь нескольких семейств. ... в романе же взяты
люди обыкновенные, интеллигентные, женщины, любовь, брак, дети —
здесь чувствуешь себя, как дома, и не утомляешься.”

Das Problem, das sich Čechov hinsichtlich des Romans stellte, wird
aber in der zweiten Hälfte des November von ihm deutlich gesehen.
Er bricht die Arbeit am Roman ab und wendet sich einem besonderen
Typ von Erzählung zu. [16] Er teilt den Stoff in einem Brief zwischen
dem 20. und 25.11.1888 Suvorin mit:

> „Пишу на тему о любви... Порядочный человек увез от
> порядочного человека жену и пишет об этом свое мнение:
> живет с ней — мнение; разводится — опять мнение. Мель-
> ком говорю о театре, о предрассудочности „несходства
> убеждений”, о Военно-грузинской дороге, о семейной
> жизни, о неспособности современного интеллигента к этой
> жизни, о Печорине, об Онегине, о Казбеке...” (XIV 239).

Der Akzent ist damit deutlich gesetzt. Čechov spricht die Intention
am 28.11.1888 wieder an Suvorin klar aus:

> „Я учусь писать „рассуждения” и стараюсь уклонятся от
> разговорного языка. Прежде чем приступить к роману,
> надо приучить свою руку свободно передавать мысль в
> повествовательной форме” (XIV 242).

Im Anschluß daran gibt er den Stoff einer Erzählung:

> „Сюжет рассказа таков: я лечу одну молодую даму, зна-
> комлюсь с ее мужем, порядочным человеком, не имеющим
> убеждений и мировоззрения; благодаря своему положению,
> как горожанина, любовника, мужа, мыслящего человека, он
> волей-неволей наталкивается на вопросы, которые волей-
> неволей, во что бы то ни стало должен решать. А как
> решать их, не имея мировоззрения? Как? Знакомство наше
> венчается тем, что он дает мне рукопись — свой „автобио-
> графический очерк”... Рассказ мой... кончается тем, ... что
> осмысленная жизнь без определенного мировоззрения — не
> жизнь, а тягота, ужас.” (XIV 242).

Beiden Stoffen gemeinsam ist die Benutzung von Aufzeichnungen
des Helden als Form der Darstellung der „mysl”. Diese Form erschien
ihm geeignet, Überlegungen, ‚rassuždenie’, in den Erzählungen zu
bringen. [17]

Diesen Rahmen eines Stoffs konnte er für den Roman nicht anwenden und so zeigen die Bemerkungen nach der Wiederaufnahme der
Arbeit am Roman im Frühjahr 1889 keine direkten Spuren dieser Ver-

---

[16] Vermutlich hat ihn auch noch die Anfang November geschriebene Erzählung
Pripadok in die Richtung gebracht.

[17] Beide Erzählungen sind nicht erschienen. Der erste Stoff wurde in der
Arbeit *Duel’* 1891 weitergeführt, der zweite lag sogar ausgeführt vor, ist aber
danach nicht wieder erwähnt worden.

suche. Die Erwähnung eines Kapitels vom 10.3.1889 in einem Brief an
A. M. Evreinova deutet einige Personen des Romans an:

> „Половина действующих лиц говорит: „Я не верую в
> Бога", есть один отец, сын которого помер в каторжные
> работы без срока за вооруженное сопротивление, есть
> исправник, стыдящийся своего полицейского мундира, есть
> предводитель, которого ненавидят, и т.д. . ." (XIV 328).

Am 11.3.1889 teilt er Suvorin den Titel mit:

> „Очертил уже ясно девять физиономий. Какая интрига!
> Назвал я его так: „Рассказы из жизни моих друзей. . ."
> (XIV 330).

Näheres läßt sich auch aus der Mitteilung vom 9.4.1889 an Pleščeev
nicht erkennen, wenn er schreibt:

> „В основу сего романа кладу я жизнь хороших людей, их
> лица, дела, слова, мысли и надежды; цель моя — убить
> сразу двух зайцев: правдиво нарисовать жизнь и кстати
> показать, насколько эта жизнь уклоняется от нормы" (XIV
> 339).

Auch dieser Entwurf war wohl als Stoff allgemein ein Gesellschaftsroman. Die Zeichnung des gewöhnlichen Lebens war das eigentliche
Ziel, die Einheit gebende Idee lag nach der Mitteilung an Pleščeev in
dem Nachweis des Ungewöhnlichen im gewöhnlichen Leben. Tatsächlich war dies die einzige Möglichkeit für Čechov. Angaben über den
Stoff des Romans fehlen in der folgenden Zeit.

Die einzige vollendete größere Arbeit des Jahres 1889, die *Skučnaja
istorija*, schloß im Rahmen des Stoffs an die zwei Erzählungen zu
Ende des Jahres 1888 an. Sie stellen ‚Überlegungen' (rassuždenija) in
der mittelbaren Form der Aufzeichnungen eines alternden Gelehrten.
Angaben über den Stoff fehlen. Das Motiv empfand Čechov als
neu. [18] Ebenso hielt er den Stoff für gewichtig. [19]

Die Bemühung um die größere Form ließ Čechov also erkennen,
daß das Element seiner früheren Arbeiten, die Situation, zu größeren
Organismen zusammengefügt werden mußte und sich nicht einfach
erweitern ließ. Die Suche nach der Form der Organisation brachte
den Begriff der Objektivität in Schwierigkeiten.

6

Die größere Form der Erzählung, die sich Čechov zur Aufgabe gemacht hatte, mußte — wollte sie den intrigenlosen Ansatz behalten —

---

[18] Vergl. XIV 387 und 391.
[19] Vergl. XIV 399 am 13.9.1889 an V. A. Tichonov: „Вещь тяжеловесная,
так что человека убить можно. Тяжеловесны не количеством листов,
а качеством."

als Roman Gesellschaftsroman werden und in der Erzähung welt-
anschauliche Aspekte einführen.

Diese Entwicklung zeigten auch die Stoffe zu den ausgeführten oder
nur geplanten Arbeiten der Jahre 1887/88 und 1889. Ebenso belegten
sie das Festhalten am intrigenlosen Ansatz der Erzählung.

Schon in der Formulierung gegenüber der Kiseleva hatte Čechov den
Begriff der Objektivität gegen den der Subjektivität abgesetzt. Diese
Korrespondenz der Begriffe findet sich auch in den folgenden
Jahren. So kritisiert er die Dichter Korolenko und Leont'ev am 5.2.1888
in einem Brief an Pleščeev:

> „... зачем они оба специализируются? Первый не рас-
> стается со своими арестантами, а второй питает своих чита-
> телей только одними обер-офицерами... Я признаю
> специальность в искусстве, как жанр, пейзаж, историю...
> но не могу помириться с такими специальностями, как
> арестанты, офицеры, попы... Это не специальность, а
> пристрастие" (XIV 32).

Ebenso heißt es in einer Kritik Leont'evs, die Čechov ihm am
22.2.1888 schreibt:

> „Но, к сожалению, Вы субъективны до чортиков. Вам
> не следовало бы описывать себя" (XIV 46).

Eine Erweiterung des Begriffs der Objektivität — verstanden als
Darstellung des Lebens wie es wirklich ist — findet sich in der
Diskussion über den Schluß der Erzählung *Ogni*. Sie stellte gleichsam
als Fazit der Gespräche und Erzählungen der Personen über den Pes-
simismus den Ausspruch ‚Ničego ne razbereš' na ètom svete' an den
Schluß. Gegen diesen Zug in Čechovs Erzählung wandten sich Pleš-
čeev und Suvorin. Daraus entspann sich eine längere grundsätzliche
Diskussion. Čechov antwortet Suvorin am 30.5.1888:

> „Вы пишете, что не разговор о пессимизме, ни повесть
> Кисочки нимало не подвигают и не решают вопроса о
> пессимизме. Мне кажется, что не беллетристы должны
> решать такие вопросы, как Бог, пессимизм и т.п. Дело
> беллетриста изобразить только, кто, как и при каких
> обстоятельствах говорили или думали о Боге или песси-
> мизме. Художник должен быть не судьею своих персонажей
> и того, о чем говорят они, а только беспристрастным свиде-
> телем" (XIV 118).

Schließlich umreißt er die Aufgabe des Dichters mit folgenden
Worten:

> „Мое дело только в том, чтобы быть талантливым, т.е.
> уметь отличать важные показания от неважных, уметь

освещать фигуры и говорить их языком... Если же художник, которому толпа верит, решится заявить, что он ничего не понимает из того, что видит, то уж это одно составит большое знание в области мысли и большой шаг вперед" (XIV 119).

Der Kiseleva gegenüber hatte er 'den Begriff der Objektivität hinsichtlich der Wahl des Themas durch den Künstler gefordert. Damals versuchte er das Thema der Erzählung *Tina* (1886) zu verteidigen. Mit der Diskussion über den Schluß der Erzählung *Ogni* war aber schon die Frage nach der Beantwortung des Themas durch den Künstler gestellt. Für Čechov gab es nur die indirekte Beantwortung: das Eingeständnis, eine Lösung nicht zu wissen. Aber allein das Stellen von Fragen in den Erzählungen oder die erwähnte richtige Auswahl wiesen über den früheren Ansatz hinaus. [20] Damit trieb die Entwicklung zu einer Einschränkung der Objektivität.

In dieser Zeit bemühte sich Čechov, ,mit Richtung' zu schreiben. So kündigt er am 30.9.1888 Pleščeev die Erzählung *Imeniny* an:

„Рассказ вышел немножко длинный (2 листа), немножко скучный, но жизненный и, представьте, с ,направлением' " (XIV 172).

Diese Richtung, die er in seinen Erzählungen jetzt einführt, und das richtige Stellen der Frage setzen ein Programm voraus. Čechov formuliert es am 4.10.1888 an Pleščeev:

„Я боюсь тех, кто между строк ищет тенденций и кто хочет видеть меня непременно либералом или консерватором. Я не либерал, не консерватор, не постепенец, не монах, не индиферентист. Я хотел бы быть свободным художником... Я ненавижу ложь и насилие во всех их видах... Мое святое святых — это человеческое тело, здоровье, ум, талант, вдохновение, любовь и абсолютнейшая свобода, свобода от силы и лжи, в чем бы последние две ни выражались. Вот программа, которой я держался бы, если бы был большим художником" (XIV 177).

Von diesem Programm her läßt sich eine Frage stellen, kann man ihr eine Richtung geben. So versteht er unter Richtung allgemein den Protest gegen die Lüge, wenn er z.B. zwischen dem 7. und 8.10.1888 an Pleščeev schreibt:

„Неужели в последнем рассказе не видно ,направления'?... Но разве в рассказе от начала до конца я не

---

[20] Vergl. die spätere Formulierung vom 27.10.1888 an Suvorin: „Вы смешиваете два понятия: решение вопроса и правильная постановка вопроса" (XIV 28).

протестую против лжи? Разве это не направление?" (XIV
181).

Diese Haltung wird von Čechov an einem Beispiel in einem Brief an
Pleščeev vom 9.10.1888 genauer ausgeführt:

> „Если мне симпатична моя героиня Ольга Михайловна,
> либеральная и бывшая на курсах, то я этого в рассказе не
> скрываю ... Правда, подозрительно в моем рассказе стрем-
> ление к уравновешиванию плюсов и минусов. Но ведь я
> уравновешиваю не консерватизм и либерализм, которые
> не представляют для меня главной сути, а ложь героев с
> их правдой. ... Когда я изображаю подобных субъектов
> или говорю о них, то не думаю ни о консерватизме, ни о
> либерализме, а об их глупости и претензиях" (XIV 184/185).

Allerdings zeigt diese Antwort, wie weit die Objektivität schon in
Frage gestellt ist, denn auch die Lügen eines Helden kann er ja nur an
einem festen Schema erkennen, womit dann ja auch indirekt die poli-
tischen Richtungen beurteilt werden. Freilich bleiben wenigstens in der
Theorie die Intentionen Čechovs unterschieden.

Aufs Ganze gesehen, hat er in dieser Zeit keine Schwierigkeit theoretischer Art, in seinen Arbeiten Stellung zu nehmen. Er blieb aber dabei
unsicher und man erkennt, daß er sich fremden Forderungen gegenüber sah. So schreibt er anläßlich der Arbeit an *Pripadok* am 11.11.1888
an Suvorin:

> „В этом рассказе я сказал свое, никому не нужное мнение
> о таких редких людях, как Гаршин... Говорю много о
> проституции, но ничего не решаю" (XIV 229).

Ebenfalls an Suvorin schreibt er am 18.11.1888:

> „... хочу я в этом сезоне писать рассказы в протестую-
> щем тоне — надо поучиться — но от непривычки скучно, и
> я виляю" (XIV 236).

Dieser Brief beweist doch, wieweit er auf die Forderungen der Zeit
eingegangen war.

Es deutet sich aber schon der Kunstgriff an, mit dem er sich der
Schwierigkeit zu entziehen glaubt: die Darstellung der Meinung seiner
Personen in geschlossener Form. Einen solchen Plan teilt er Suvorin
am 20.-25.11.1888 mit:

> „Пишу на тему о любви. Порядочный человек увез от
> порядочного человека жену и пишет об этом свое мнение,
> живет с ней — мнение; расходится — опять мнение" (XIV
> 239).

Die Meinung wird als Meinung dargestellt.

Als er sich im Jahre 1889 wieder dem Roman zuwendet, glaubt er die

Schwierigkeit durch einen weiteren Kunstgriff zu lösen, den er am 9.4.1889 Pleščeev mitteilt:

> „... цель моя — убить сразу двух зайцев: правдиво нарисовать жизнь и кстати показать, насколько эта жизнь уклоняется от нормы. Норма мне неизвестна, как неизвестна никому из нас. Все мы знаем, что такое бесчестный поступок, но что такое честь — мы не знаем. Буду держаться той рамки, которая ближе сердцу и уже испытана людьми посильнее и умнее меня. Рамка эта — абсолютная свобода человека, свобода от насилия, от предрассудков, невежества, чорта, свобода от страстей и проч." (XIV 339).

Mit dieser Ankündigung glaubt er den Standpunkt der einfachen Darstellung überwunden zu haben. Der Ausgang dieser Ankündigung läßt sich nicht übersehen, da der Roman nicht geschrieben wurde und somit blieb dieser Versuch nur Theorie.

Mit der *Skučnaja istorija* griff er wieder auf die Selbstdarstellung des Helden zurück. Er geht sogar noch weiter, indem die „Langweiligkeit" der Überlegung als charakterisierendes Mittel für den Helden angegeben wird. So schreibt er am 24.9.1889 wieder an Pleščeev:

> „Самое скучное в нем, как увидите, это длинные рассуждения, которых, к сожалению, нельзя выбросить, так как без них не может обойтись мой герой, пишущий записки. Эти рассуждения... характеризуют и героя, и его настроение, и его вилянье перед самим собой" (XIV 405).

Čechov setzt sich aber Suvorin gegenüber von diesen Gedanken — als notwendig seinen eigenen — ab, wenn er am 17.11.1889 schreibt:

> „Если я преподношу Вам профессорские мысли, то верьте мне, и не ищите в них чеховских мыслей" (XIV 417).

Wie ein Schlußstrich unter die Versuche dieser Jahre, seine Anschauung von der Objektivität mit den Erfordernissen der seriösen Themen in Übereinstimmung zu bringen, liest sich eine Mitteilung an Suvorin vom 1.4.1890, kurz vor seiner Abreise nach Sachalin geschrieben. Sie bezieht sich auf die Erzählung *Čerti*. Čechov schreibt:

> „Вы браните меня за объективность, называя ее равнодушием к добру и злу, отсутствием идеалов и идей и проч. Вы хотите, чтобы я, изображая конокрадов, говорил бы: кража лошадей есть зло. Но ведь это и без меня уже давно известно. Пусть судят их присяжные заседатели, а мое дело показать только, какие они есть... Конечно, было бы приятно сочетать художество с проповедью, но для меня лично это чрезвычайно трудно и почти невозможно по условиям техники" (XV 51).

So schließt die Bemühung um den Begriff und den Inhalt der
Objektivität mit einer Rückkehr zur Darstellung einer Situation ...
notwendig verbunden mit der Rückkehr zur kurzen Erzählung. Sie
endet mit dem Eingeständnis Čechovs, unvermögend zu sein, mit der
Sache eine ‚Predigt' zu verbinden. Eigenartig ist die Betonung der
Objektivität und die erneute Abweisung der Subjektivität aus der ange-
nommen Kürze, die die weiteren Züge der Erzählung bestimmt, wenn
er fortfährt:

> „. . . если я подбавлю субъективности, образы расплы-
> вутся и рассказ не будет так компактен, как надлежит быть
> всем коротеньким рассказам."

7

Die Bemühung um die größere literarische Form warf für Čechov
das Problem ihrer Komposition auf. Dabei stand die Gewohnheit der
kurzen Form, die er in seinen bisherigen Arbeiten gepflegt hatte,
einer Lösung von Anfang an im Wege.

Noch während der Arbeit an *Step'*, am 9.1.1888, schreibt er über
diese Schwierigkeiten an V. G. Korolenko:

> „. . . пишется весело, но, к несчастью, от непривычки пи-
> сать дпинно, от страха написать лишнее я впадаю в край-
> ность: каждая страница выходит компактной, как малень-
> кий рассказ, картины громоздятся, теснятся и, заслоняя
> друг друга, губят общее впечатление. В результате полу-
> чается не картина, в которой все частности, как звезды на
> небе, слились в одно общее, а конспект, сухой перечень
> впечатлений" (XIV 11).

Die gleiche Klage ergeht fast wörtlich am 12.1.1888 an Grigorovič,
zugleich findet sich aber auch eine Mitteilung zur Komposition.
Čechov schreibt:

> „Каждая отдельная глава составляет особый рассказ, и
> все главы связаны, как пять фигур в кадрили, близким
> родством. Я стараюсь, чтобы в них был общий запах и
> общий тон, что мне может удаться тем легче, что через все
> главы у меня проходит одно лицо" (XIV 14).

Schließlich kritisiert er seine Arbeit mit folgender Betrachtung:

> „. . . вместо художественного, цельного изображения
> степи я преподношу читателю ‚степную энциклопедию' "
> (XIV 14).

Damit ist die Problematik der Komposition klar gesehen. Die Eindrücke, die Situationen, stehen nebeneinander und geben kein ge-
schlossenes Bild. Das Gewicht der einzelnen Bilder und Situationen

ist zu groß, und so häufen sie sich. In diesem Sinn schreibt Čechov am 18.1.1888 an Ja. P. Polonskij:

„В общем моя повестушка меня не удовлетворяет. Она кажется мне громоздкой, скучной и слишком специальной" (XIV 19).

Freilich stammen diese Urteile noch aus der Zeit der Abfassung der *Step'*. Späterhin äußerte sich Čechov positiver und fand in der Reise des kleinen Helden ein Kompositionsprinzip der Erzählungen und Bilder. Die Problematik der Kürze kommt aber auch späterhin in den Briefen zum Ausdruck. [21] Čechov benutzt eine Formel, die auch bei späteren Arbeiten, nach *Step'*, angewendet wird.

Noch während der Arbeit an *Step'* berichtete er von einem Roman. Das Problem der Komposition deutete sich nur indirekt in einem Brief vom 12.1.1888 an Grigorovič an, wenn er die allgemeinen Züge angibt:

Степь — тема отчасти исключительная и специальная ...; в романе же взяты люди обыкновенные, интеллигентные, женщины, любовь, брак, дети — здесь чувствуешь себя, как дома, и не утомляешься" (XIV 15).

Die Angabe der Elemente des gewöhnlichen Lebens ließ schon wieder die Gefahr der kompakten Einzeldarstellung erkennen. Für diesen Fall blieb Čechov nur der Kompositionsrahmen einer Addition der Einzelteile. Allerdings konnte er ein solch spezielles Prinzip wie in *Step'* nicht anwenden. Eine Lösung wird er in dieser Zeit nicht gehabt haben.

Die Möglichkeiten der Lösung schränkte er in dem Vorschlag eines Romans an Lejkin am 11.5.1888 ein. Er entspricht den Forderungen des intrigenlosen, naturalistischen Romans vollkommen hinsichtlich des Stoffs. [22] Zugleich belegt dieser Brief die theoretische Beschäftigung mit dem Roman für Čechov. Er schreibt:

„Люди в романе живые, но ведь для романа этого недостаточно. Нужно еще знать, как Вы справились с архитектурой... Главное Ваше достоинство в больших вещах — отсутствие претензий и великолепный разговорный язык ... Засим, еще одно достоинство: чем проще фабула, тем лучше, а Ваши фабулы просты, жизненны и не вычурны. На Вашем месте я написал бы маленький роман из купеческой жизни..., описал бы обыкновенную любовь и семейную жизнь без злодеев и ангелов, без адвокатов и

---

[21] Vergl. XIV 19, 23 (am 23.1.1888 an A. N. Pleščeev), 26 (nach Beendigung der *Step'* an Pleščeev) usw.

[22] Vergl. Émile Zola, *Les romanciers naturalistes*, 3. Aufl., Paris 1881. Dort den Abschnitt über Gustave Flaubert.

дьяволиц; взял бы я сюжетом жизнь ровную, гладкую, обыкновенную, какова она есть на самом деле..." (XIV 110).

Damit schied die Verknüpfung der Teile durch ungewöhnliche Ereignisse und durch den Helden aus. Im Mittelpunkt steht die Beschreibung. Die Beschreibung endete aber für Čechov immer in der Kürze. Hier zeigte sich bereits das Zurücktreten der Komposition vor dem Problem der Beschreibung. [23]

Die Gewohnheit der Kürze scheint er nur für einen Augenblick ablegen zu können, als er am 30.3.1888, während der Arbeit an *Ogni*, an K. S. Barancevič schreibt:

„... потерял (не знаю, надолго ли) способность творить мелкие вещи" (XIV 64).

Aber sehr bald kürzt er *Ogni* und schreibt schließlich auf *Ogni* zurückblickend am 30.5.1888 an Suvorin: [24]

„От непривычки писать длинно я мнителен; когда я пишу, меня всякий раз пугает мысль, что моя повесть длинна не по чину, и я стараюсь писать возможно короче" (XIV 118).

Allgemein beschreibt Čechov den Prozeß des Schreibens am 9.10. 1888 an Pleščeev:

„Привыкнув к маленьким рассказам, состоящим только из начала и конца, я скучаю и начинаю зевать, когда чувствую, что пишу середину" (XIV 184).

Gerade in dieser Zeit arbeitet er am Roman. Die Bemerkungen rühren also aus der Praxis her. Am gleichen Tage findet sich in einem Brief an Grigorovič ein Ansatz zur Komposition des Romans. Čechov schreibt:

„В центре уезда две главные фигуры, мужская и женская, около которых группируются другие шашки" (XIV 183).

Am 27.10.1888 schreibt er von seinen Schwierigkeiten an Suvorin. Die Probleme liegen auf zwei Gebieten. Zuerst erwähnt er die Schwierigkeiten aus der Gewohnheit der Kürze beim Schreiben:

„... начало выходит у меня всегда многообещающее, точно я роман начал; середина скомканная, робкая, а конец, как в маленьком рассказе, фейерверочный."

Als Zweites zeigt sich das Fehlen eines Kompositionsprinzips. Die

---

[23] Die Komposition des naturalistischen Romans ergab sich nach der Theorie aus dem Zusammenhang der Gegenstände selbst. Ihr Prinzip mußte im ‚Leben' liegen, man hatte nur die Teile zu beschreiben.

[24] (382) S. 64.

Aufnahme des Paares als Zentrum, die sich schon im Programm von 1886 fand, scheiterte in der Ausführung. Čechov schreibt:

„...из массы героев и полугероев берешь только одно лицо... и рисуешь только его... одна большая луна и вокруг нее масса очень маленьких звезд. Луна же не удается, потому что ее можно понять только тогда, если понятны и другие звезды, а звезды не отделаны. И выходит у меня не литература, а нечто вроде шитья Тришкиного кафтана" (XIV 209).

Es ist offensichtlich, daß die Schwierigkeit für ihn darin bestand, den kompakten Charakter der Teile in Verbindung mit den übrigen Teilen zu bringen. Jede Beschreibung war in sich geschlossen und vollends unmöglich war die Ausführung der geforderten Bevorzugung einzelner Teile oder Helden.

Im November 1888 wandte sich Čechov vom Roman ab, um an der Erzählung Vorarbeiten zum Roman zu leisten. Die Mitteilung des Stoffs an Suvorin, vom 20. bis 25.11. verfaßt, läßt ein neues Kompositionsprinzip erkennen.[25] Der Held der Erzählung schreibt seine Meinung über Situationen seines Lebens. Es handelt sich also um die Form der Aufzeichnungen. Einen weiteren Plan teilt er am 28.11.1888 an Suvorin mit:

„...он дает мне рукопись — свой „автобиографический очерк", состоящий из множества коротких глав. Я выбираю... главы..." (XIV 242).

Damit war immerhin eine spezielle Lösung gefunden, wenn auch vorerst nur für die Erzählung. Im folgenden Jahre versuchte Čechov sie aber auch auf den Roman anzuwenden, wie ein Brief vom 11.3.1889 an Suvorin belegt. Er schreibt über den Roman:

„Назвал я его так: *Рассказы из жизни моих друзей,* и пишу его в форме отдельных, законченных рассказов, тесно связанных между собою общностью интриги, идеи и действующих лиц. У каждого рассказа особое заглавие. Не думайте, что роман будет состоять из клочьев. Нет, он будет настоящий роман, целое тело, где каждое лицо будет органически необходимо" (XIV 330).

Leider findet sich über die Ausführung nichts in den späteren Briefen. Nur am Scheitern des Romans kann man erkennen, daß ihm jene Einheit, dem geschlossenen Charakter der einzelnen Teile oder Erzählungen zum Trotz, nicht gelungen ist.

In der *Skučnaja istorija,* die er im Spätsommer 1889 schrieb, bediente er sich wieder des Kunstgriffs der Aufzeichnungen, aber der

---

[25] Vergl. XIV 239.

Roman blieb ungeschrieben. Zum Ende des Jahres gab er die Versuche die Gewohnheit der Kürze zu überwinden allem Anschein nach ganz auf. Er bittet sich sogar Suvorin um fremde Manuskripte, um sie zu kürzen und so zu verbessern. [26]

Unmittelbar vor seiner Abreise nach Sachalin verteidigt er seine 1890 entstandene kurze Erzählung *Čerti* vor Suvorin. Die Begründung schließt mit der Entwicklung der vergangenen Jahre ab, wenn er am 1.4.1890 schreibt:

> „Конечно, было бы приятно сочетать художество с проповедью, но... почти невозможно по условиям техники. ... если я подбавлю субъективности, образы расплывутся и рассказ не будет так компактен, как надлежит быть всем коротеньким рассказам" (XV 51).

Die kurze, geschlossene Erzählung ist damit wieder der feste Punkt an dem sich die anderen Forderungen orientieren. Offensichtlich konnte er diese Form nicht aufgeben. Diese Grundform seiner Arbeit durch Komposition in die größere Form zu überführen, war ihm nur als die spezielle Lösung der Aufzeichnungen gelungen. So wird die Kürze der Darstellung, die auch die äußere Form der kurzen Erzählung bedingte, wieder zum Zentralbegriff seiner Poetik, nachdem sich einige Zeit ihre Problematik gezeigt hatte.

8.

Von der Problematik der größeren Form unberührt bleiben die übrigen Aspekte der Poetik. Die Briefe enthalten weiterhin die Forderung nach Wahrhaftigkeit, die Ablehnung von Gemeinplätzen, aber auch den Abweis der ‚Kleinigkeiten', die den Charakter der dichterischen Sprache stören und in dieser Form der Forderung der Kürze zuwiderlaufen.

So kritisiert er am 13.2.1888 in einem Brief an N. A. Chlopov:

> „... где Вы видели церковного попечителя Сидоркина? Правда, существуют старосты .., но никакие старосты ... не имеют права и власти переводить дьячка с одного места на другое ... то дело архиерейское ..." (XIV 41).

Es folgt damit ein Aufzählung von weiteren Ungenauigkeiten:

> „Вы знаете, что кто пашет первый раз в жизни, тот не сдвинет плуга с места — это раз; дьячку выгоднее отдать свою землю под скопчину — это два; воробьев никаким калачом не заманишь из деревни в поле — это три ... В конце рассказа дьячок ... поет: „Благослови, душе моя, господи, и возрадуется ...". Такой молитвы нет" (XIV 42).

---

[26] Vergl. die Briefe am 23.10.1889, am 20.11.1889, am 15.3.1890.

Oder Čechov rügt den Dichter Giljarovskij in einem Brief an Plešćeev vom 5.-6.7.1888:

„Ужасно падок до общих мест, жалких слов и трескучих описаннй... Он чует красоту в чужих произведениях, знает, что первая и преглавная прелесть рассказа — это простота и искренность, но быть искренним и простым в своих рассказах не может: нехватает мужества" (XIV 131).

Über den Stil und die Art der Darstellung schreibt er am 20.10.1888 an A. S. Lazarev-Gruzinskij:

„Надо быть мужественным, сильным, а Вы в описаниях медового месяца и т.п. вдаетесь в сентиментально-игриво-старушечий тон ...Описания природы у Вас недурны; Вы хорошо делаете, что боитесь мелочности и казенщины... Женщин нужно описывать так, чтобы читатель чувствовал, что Вы в расстегнутой жилетке и без галстука, природу — то же самое. Дайте себе свободы" (XIV 201/202).

Gegen eine zu ängstliche Beschreibung schreibt er auch am 15.11. 1888 kritisch an Suvorin:

„...Вы несвободны; например: из боязни, что Вы недостаточно точны..., Вы находите нужным мотивировать каждое положение и движение" (XIV 233).

Damit ist freilich noch nichts über den Stil im einzelnen gesagt, sondern vielmehr nur eine Andeutung gemacht. [27] Die Ablehnung der Schablone und die Forderung der Originalität wurden, wie nicht anders zu erwarten, von der Bemühung um die größere Form nicht berührt. So schreibt Čechov, während der Arbeit am Roman, am 11.3.1889 an Suvorin:

„Неверных жеп, самоубийц, кулаков, добродетельных мужиков, преданных рабов, резонирующих старушек, добрых нянюшек, уездных остряков, красноносых капитанов и „новых" людей постараюсь избежать, хотя местами сильно сбиваюсь на шаблон" (XIV 330).

Allerdings scheint es, als seien diese Forderungen vor den Zentralbegriffen zurückgetreten.

9.

Mit dem Scheitern des Romans und den Schwierigkeiten der größeren Erzählung schlägt das Gefühl der Unsicherheit und Unzufriedenheit, das die Jahre nach der Wende begleitet hatte, in Resignation um.

---

[27] Es bliebe zu prüfen, wieweit der Stil sich in der größeren Erzählungen geändert hat.

Am Ende des Jahres 1889 gibt Čechov eine Zusammenfassung seiner
Arbeit, die eine herbe Kritik enthält. Er schreibt am 18.-23.12.1889
an Suvorin:

> „... очерков, фельетонов, глупостей, водевилей, скучных
> историй, многое множество ошибок и несообразностей,
> пуды исписанной бумаги, академическая премия, житие
> Потемкина — и при всем том нет ни одной строчки, которая
> в моих глазах имела бы серьезное литературное значение.
> Была масса форсированной работы, но не было ни одной
> минуты серьезного труда... Мне страстно хочется спря-
> таться куда-нибудь лет на пять и занять себя кропотливым,
> серьезным трудом." [28]

Die Resignation findet ihren Ausdruck auch in einem Verzicht
auf Bemerkungen zur Poetik. Am 12.13.1890 schreibt er Leont'ev seinen Standpunkt mit den knappen Worten:

> „Все произведения я делю на два сорта: те, которые мне
> нравятся, и те, которые мне не нравятся. Другого критериу-
> ма у меня нет..." (XV 42).

Am 21.4. begibt sich Čechov auf die Reise nach Sachalin.

Damit endet die Entwicklung, die 1886 mit der Wende zur literarisch
anspruchsvollen Erzählung begann. In diesem Zeitraum vollzog sich der
Eintritt Čechovs in die große Literatur.

Die Möglichkeiten, die in dem literarischen Ansatz der Jahre vor
1886 lagen, hatten sich an der Aufgabe der größeren Form und dem
anspruchsvollen Inhalt entwickelt und eingegrenzt. Ihr theoretischer
Ausdruck, der sich in den Begriffen einer Poetik im Briefwechsel
fand, ermöglichte den Versuch, diesen Prozeß im theoretischen Bereich
mit seinen Problemen zusammenzustellen. In diesem Prozeß kamen die
Begriffe der Objektivität und Kürze in Schwierigkeiten gegenüber
den Forderungen der traditionellen Ausdrucksformen. Er endete mit
einem Verzicht auf jene Formen der Erzählung. Daß Čechov nach dieser Entwicklung zur Form der kurzen Erzählung kam, war nicht die
einfache Wiederaufnahme einer schon vorher besessenen Form, sondern der Erwerb dieser Form für die große Literatur auf den Be-
dingungen der Begriffe der Objektivität und Kürze. Was für Čechov
aus der Resignation heraus als verlorene Jahre gelten mochte, war in
Wirklichkeit die Geburt einer neuen literarischen Form für die russische Literatur.

---

[28] XIV 454; der Anfang des Briefes ist nicht erhalten.

GEORGE IVASK

ČECHOV AND THE RUSSIAN CLERGY

In popular speech the clergy of the Greek-Orthodox Church are divided into two classes, called *black* and *white*. The black clergy are the monks, from whose ranks are drawn all the higher officials of the church — the bishops, the metropolitans, the patriarchs: the white clergy are the parish priests and deacons, who always serve under the jurisdiction of a bishop. In former times, the black clergy came from all the various classes of Russian society. The white clergy formed a distinct and almost closed class, for the sons of priests usually became priests and a parish was sometimes inherited by the son or the son-in-law of its priest. The white clergy had a bad reputation. Even the pious people often despised the parish priest, and referred to him by the derogatory name *pop* because of his selfishness, ignorance, stupid jokes, and bad manners.

To be sure, the black clergy were not too popular in pre-revolutionary Russia, either. Though the Rev. George Florovskij [1] has shown that among them there were outstanding theologians and historians, they were accused of dull scholastic thinking and duller teaching. The truth was that such learned clergymen had no contact or connection with the intelligentsia. Some black clergymen, the so called elders (*starcy*), were revered as wise men. Thousands made pilgrimages to St. Serafim of Sarov, a practitioner of the new Christianity of the Holy Ghost. Both the ignorant and the enlightened — even such writers as Dostoevskij, Tolstoj, and K. Leont'ev — listened to the elders of the Optina monastery, and the elder Zosima, an idealized monk, was used by Dostoevskij as his mask in "The Brothers Karamazov".

Very few Russian writers have portrayed a parish priest with respect. Perhaps only N. Leskov created vivid characters of clergymen, in his famous novel, "The Cathedral Folk" (1872). There one may read of the righteous and enlightened Father Savelij and his faithful companion, the pure-hearted savage, Deacon Achilla, a triumph of characterization. But in other stories and essays Leskov wrote merciless descriptions of Russian clerical life, and under the influence of Tolstoj and Schopenhauer he almost broke with the Church. [2] In the twentieth century V. Rozanov (1856-1919), a man of indubitable genius as yet

---

[1] Rev. George Florovskij, "A Survey of Russian Theology" (*Puti russkogo bogoslovija*), 1938.

[2] The best summary on Leskov we find in W. Setschkareff's book *N. Leskov. Sein Leben und sein Werk*, 1959.

little known outside Russia, proclaimed his sympathy with all the clergy. His views may be termed eccentric; as an anti-Christian and an adherent to the Hebrew Canon he praised the *popy* for their patriarchal lives and their amazing fecundity, worthy of Jacob himself. [3]

In contrast to the isolation of the black clergy and the low estates of the whites, the *popoviči,* the sons of the priests and deacons, played important roles in the secular life of Russia. They included Speranskij, the great codifier and founder of Russian bureaucracy, and such historical scholars as S. Solov'ev and Ključevskij. Many of the *popoviči* became atheists, materialists, and radicals: such were the critics Černyševskij and Dobroljubov and the writers Pomjalovskij and G. Uspenskij. All these prodigal sons of white clergymen left the Church forever and successfully attempted to shake the foundations of the Russian monarchy.

These are norms by which one may judge the account and descriptions of the pre-Revolutionary clergy by a Russian writer. To deduce a Russian writer's own religious position from the treatment of the Orthodox clergy is not a simple matter. Wih this preamble, one may turn to Čechov.

Anton Čechov's father, Pavel, owned a grocery store in the provincial town of Taganrog. A silly hypocrite and a domestic tyrant, he forced his sons to attend the local church and to sing in its choir. They naturally hated it. In his mature life as a doctor of medicine and a writer, Anton Čechov would have nothing to do with the Church. In this he resembled the majority of the intelligentsia. May one conclude that he was an atheist? The many critics who have affirmed that Čechov believed neither God nor future life may be right; but the matter is more complicated than most of them supposed. Čechov's scepticism deterred him from all absolute statements. In one of his notebooks he wrote: "There lies an immense field between the sayings 'God exists' and 'There is no God' "; [4] in that field he preferred to stay. Certainly Čechov did not seek God, nor was he tortured by God like Dostoevskij; on the other hand he neither dishonored nor sought to disprove the notion of a Deity.

Čechov distrusted the ideological extremism of Russian intellectual life, and was suspicious of abstract ideas. His lack of interest in philo-

---

[3] V. Rozanov, "A Collection of Essays", with an introduction of G. Ivask (in Russian), 1956.

[4] Čechov, "Notebooks" (in Russian), edited by L. Grossman, 1927, p. 37. This text reveals Čechov's dislike of any kind of exaggerations emphasized by W. Gerhardi: "Imagine the revolutionary and the monk both shouting 'Forward!' in the mind of a single man, and you will not be astonished at Čechov's choice of standing still." (*A. Chekhov,* 1949, p. 24).

sophy made it impossible for him to portray an outstanding intellectual. The young philosopher in "The Black Monk" can scarcely be called convincing, for he is obviously ignorant of the philosophical discussions of his day. [5]

It was, I believe, partly through his anti-intellectualism that Čechov appealed to the tired and disappointed British intellectuals after the first World War. John Middleton Murry, a very sensitive represen- tative of that generation, considered Proust and Joyce "antiquarian survivals" but Čechov an "advanced writer"; Čechov knew "where the intellectual conscience was impotent; and he knew it was impotent precisely for the apprehension of the eternal livingness of life." [6] Both Murry and his wife, Catherine Mansfield, the writer of short stories, were attracted by Čechov's "mysterium simplicitatis", [7] his detachment from all complex and pretentious ideas.

Certainly, the anti-intellectualism of Čechov annoyed and irritated the Russian religious philosophers and God-seekers of the early twentieth century. Šestov (1866-1938) condemned him for his lack of philosophical ideas, for his "creation based on nothing", for his nihilistic scepticism. [8] Merežkovskij (1865-1941) discovered a non- existence behind the Čechovian simplicity admired by Murry. [9] And though N. Michajlovskij (1842-1904), the leader of the radical Popu- list Movement (*narodniki*), was far removed from all the modernist God-seekers, he attacked Čechov much as they did, charging him with a lack of general ideas. Of course, in Michajlovskij's mouth, the phrase referred to progressive social ideals. [10]

But to say that Čechov was anti-intellectual does not mean that he trusted in emotions as guides. Both in his life and his art he avoided sentimentality. He was sensitive but not at all sentimental. It is true that everywhere behind the screen of his placid, even prosaic, state- ments and understatements we discover one and the same emotion — the sense of pity, of charity (*caritas, agape*). As V. Rozanov wrote at the end of his notes in *Solitaria* — "Mankind does not deserve respect: it deserves to be pitied." [11] And though Rozanov himself despised Čechov's simplicity, the quotation might serve as an epigraph to

---

[5] L. Šestov, "Works": Čechov is an irreconcilable enemy of any kind of philo- sophy; his characters philosophize in a very unconvincing way (v. V, p. 50).

[6] John Middleton Murry, *John Clare and Other Stories*, 1950, p. 112.

[7] Ibid, p. 109.

[8] L. Šestov, op. cit., p. 31.

[9] D. Merežkovskij, "Complete Works" (in Russian), v. XI, 1911 (*Čechov i Gor'kij*).

[10] N. Michajlovskij, "Essays" (in Russian), 1957, pp. 594-607 ("On Fathers, Sons and Mr. Čechov").

[11] V. Rozanov, op. cit., p. 236 (*Solitaria*).

Čechov's entire works. One may contrast Čechov to Dostoevskij, who preached pity for all the oppressed and the humiliated, and attempted to save them through a humanistic Christianity we find in the monologues of Magdalene-Sonja (Marmeladov) or in the sermons of the wise elder, Zosima. Čechov had doubts about any kind of salvation whatsoever; he avoided alike great hopes based either on religion, or revolution. He was rather an ordinary man with excellent common sense, a doctor of medicine, a typical Russian *intelligent* except that he was devoid of any definite ideology. Finally his hidden sense of pity was more convincing than Dostoevskij's overemphasized Christian love for one's neighbour. Čechov's pose as a cool, indifferent observer of everyday life was no more than a pose: all his matter-of-fact statements prompt compassion for the rich and poor, smart and dull people, for all people except those both smug and mediocre. In this he follows the traditional ethics of Russian literature, which has always been ready to forgive a murderer but never a *pošljak, pošlyj čelovek* (vulgar man). [12] Almost all Čechov's characters are ordinary people, [13] without particular talents or great ideas; but some of them have a deep sensibility. These may be called open-hearted or pure-hearted; they differ very little from other people except in fine curiosity or a wistful compassion. Is it by chance that many of these men belong to the clergy? Čechov was vividly aware of the vices typical of the clergy, for he often portrayed priests with severity. It is enough to mention the incident at the funeral banquet in "The Ravine", where the priest raised to his mouth a fork bearing a salted red mushroom as he said to the sorrowing mother: "Do not mourn your infant. For theirs is the Kingdom of Heaven." [14] Nevertheless, some of Čechov's clergymen were the most sensitive human beings among his characters; he described them with a deep if implicit sympathy.

For example, there is Father Christofor Sirijskij, in "The Steppe" (according to C. Mansfield, this novel is an *Odyssey* of our time!). He could have had a prosperous career if he had entered a Theological Academy, but his parents had objected and refused their permission. He became the priest of a provincial parish. He is no saint; he is actively engaged in the wool-trade. But he only plays the role of a traveling business man; he is an easygoing person, full of aesthetic curiosity and enthusiasm. It is true that Father Christofor "has never in his life been conscious of anything which could like a boa-constrictor

---

[12] The best characteristic of the Russian expression *pošlost'* we find in V. Nabokov's book *Gogol'*, 1947.
[13] "We both like ordinary people," wrote Čechov to A. Suvorin (November 20-25, 1888); XIV 240.
[14] Ibid., XI 411.

coil about his soul and hold it tightly." [15] But he looks at the Lord's creation with interest and amazement. It seems as if his broad smile even embraced the rime of his top-hat. He is a kind of a *homo ludens,* [16] a playing or playful man, like the deacon Pobedov in the novel "The Duel" (1891). One must admit that the deacon has less common sense than Father Christofer, but he shares his aesthetic attitude toward life. He exclaims "My God, how nice it is!... People, rocks, the fire, the twilight, a monstrous tree — nothing more, and yet how fine!" [17] Led by his curiosity, he secretly approaches the site of the duel, and hides behind the bushes. "Though they are infidels they are good people, and will be saved," he says aloud, as he lights his cigarette. [18] These words of the good-hearted simpleton resemble a remark written by Čechov in his notebook: "And everything is forgiven, and it would be strange not to forgive." Murrys comment on the remark may have penetrated to the very heart of Čechov's secret convictions: "This condition which Čechov experienced when he listened to music, we experience when we listen to Čechov. It would be not impossible, not inhuman, not stupid, but simply strange not to forgive." [19]. And so the deacon Pobedov cannot help forgiving the two duellists, the two neurotics, Laevskij and Von Koren. He even promises them that they will enter the Kingdom of Heaven, in which his creator himself did not believe.

Another sensitive spirit in a cassock occurs in Čechov's early story, "Easter Eve" (1886). Father Ieronim (Hieronymus), another wordly, meek monk, acts as a ferryman. While his boat is crossing the river he gazes long at the young and beautiful wife of the merchant; but there is no erotic component in his motive. He sees in the woman's face the soft and tender features of his dead friend, Father Nikolaj. Nikolaj had once compiled some canticles in the most elevated Church-Slavic, and in them Ieronim had particularly admired some *composita* literally translated from the Greek, such as *svetopodatel'nyj* in the sense of radiant. [20] Čechov could scarcely expect his Russian readers to enjoy this stiff and erudite phrasing; but, he tells us, to the etherical Father Ieronim it had sounded like the melody of an angel.

---

[15] Chekhov, *The Bishop and Other Stories,* translated by C. Garnett, 1916, p. 178.

[16] J. Huizinga, *Homo Ludens,* N.Y. 1950.

[17] Chekhov, *The Duel and Other Stories,* translated by C. Garnett, p. 61.

[18] Ibid., p. 147.

[19] J. M. Murry, op. cit., p. 113.

[20] Father Ieronim believed that *svetopodatel'nyj* is an expression invented by Father Nikolaj, i.e. a neologism, but we find this word in I. I. Sreznevskij's "Dictionnary of Old Russian" (new edition of 1958) in the form of свѣтодатель-ный — фотобóлос, Минся 1096 л.

Almost in the same fashion the pious Ol'ga (In "The Peasants", 1897)
responded to the Church-Slavic word *dondeže* (that is, until) ; though
she did not understand this word, she always wept when she heard
it in the liturgy, no doubt because to her it seemed angelic. The
comparison may underline the remark that there is nothing sentimental
in "Easter Eve" : the pathetic monologue of the simple-minded and
pure-hearted monk is not adorned with any lyrical digressions of the
author. Yet we feel that Father Ieronim enjoyed a religious-aesthetic
view of life.

Finally, there are the student and the bishop, in the two stories
named for them (1894; 1901-1902). The first is a young and strong
boy who is studying theology; the second is a dying Prince of the
Church. Though they are both descendents of typical clerical families,
and have been educated in the scholastic mode, they are spiritually close
to the *intelligentsia* of the time. The student has some doubts. The Bishop
believes sincerely in God ; yet he feels some defect in his piety, some
shadow in his comprehension, and he does not wish to die. Neither has
an innate aesthetic sense like that of the clergymen previously described ; neither has the common sense of Father Christofor or the
humility of Deacon Pobedov ; neither is etherical as Ieronim : yet they
both listen to what Rozanov termed the sweet and wistful music of
Christianity. It may be worth while to recount the two stories in a
little more detail.

The student, Ivan Velikopol'skij, the son of a poor sexton, is walking
in the village on Good Friday. The village seems almost deserted, the
day is sombre, his fingers almost freeze. Even Nature seems horrified
by the cold and darkness of the early Russian spring. He sees a
little fire in what is called the Widow's vegetable garden; he approaches
it and finds a woman sitting there with her feeble-minded daughter,
who is also a widow. He tells them the story of that day some 2000
years earlier, of the Last Supper, and the arrest in the Garden of
Gethsemane, and how Peter who loved his Saviour nevertheless be-
trayed him thrice. The older woman weeps, and the younger woman
seems deeply moved; and the student suddenly discovers that there
is a resemblance between the passion of Our Lord on Golgotha and the
sufferings of the Russian peasants ; and at that moment he experiences
a kind of ecstasy, a revelation of eternal happiness.

In the novel called "The Bishop", it is the eve of Palm Sunday. The
invalid bishop has presided over all the long services for Holy Week,
and as he has done so his mind wandered to the past. Sometimes he
remembered his youth, when he was as poor as Ivan Velikopol'skij
and lived in as poor a village. Now his mother has come to visit him
in order to borrow some money for the family of her son-in-law. Once

she nursed him tenderly; how constrained she is now, how uncertain in her speech, since her son is a great man, a Prince of the Church; but her little granddaughter talks some charming childish nonsense, and the Bishop is amused and grateful. The simple incidents are described in the simplest way, yet the story is perhaps one of Čechov's best. In the church, while the divine service proclaims deep mourning for the crucified Saviour, they hear the promise that the Bridegroom shall come at midnight, bringing eternal felicity to all those who have faith. The agnostic Čechov was rather indifferent to poetry, except Puškin's, but he had a fine feeling of Old-Russian hymnology. [21] As a boy he had hated the church choir, because he had been forced to sing there; but the old hymns remained imprinted on his heart.

Both the student and the bishop are rather ordinary people, such as Čechov liked. They are not vulgar; they are, on the contrary, more open-minded and more sensitive than the average man. They have an unusual gift of admiration, and they are aware of some of the obscure mysteries of life.

One of the most penetrating readers of Čechov, the poet I. Annenskij (1856-1909), remarked that many of Čechov's characters are merely *souls;* [22] Virginia Woolf even affirmed that all the characters of both Čechov and Dostoevskij are souls living on earth... [23] Following this line one may suggest that all the clerics we have discussed are souls, and akin to many other languishing or anguished souls in Čechov, such as those of the "Three Sisters", of "The Darling" (*Dušečka*), and even of the lost but faithful dog, *Kaštanka.* No doubts all these souls are rather ordinary than extraordinary; yet one may suggest that some of the clergymen are perhaps closer to the *letzte Dinge der Menschen,* to the mysteries of life and death — the ferryman-monk Ieronim, and the bishop, and the student Ivan Veliko-pol'skij. May one dismiss the circumstance of their origin and status? No; while I do not think the social milieu is of much importance, these men are typical representatives of their social groups.

In contrast to Čechov, other Russian writers may be seen as unable to overcome their social antipathies. Both Tolstoj and Dostoevskij wrote in cold anger about lawyers, and many Russians sneered in writing at the *popy.* Čechov is the most unbiased among the Russian authors: though since his childhood he had known the vices of the class, many of his most sensitive characters are clergymen.

The dynamic God-seeker Dostoevskij was a prophet of a Christian

---

[21] The epigraph to Čechov's story "The Misery" (*Toska*) is a quotation from a psalm (in Church-Slavonic).

[22] I. Annenskij, "The Book of Reflections" (*Kniga Otraženij*), 1906, p. 154.

[23] V. Woolf, *The Common Reader,* 1929, pp. 224-226.

Utopia, like his Father Paisij ("Brothers Karamazov"). Čechov did not
promise anything. As we know, he was not sure either that God
exists, or that He does not. Perhaps he believed that all souls are
worthy of salvation. [24] But did he believe in Salvation promised in the
Gospels? He avoided any kind of intellectual discussion which referred
to the dimensions of the past or the future, or to the Kingdom of
Heaven. He was not interested in history, or traditions, or in utopian
dreams either social or religious. And we cannot take seriously the
melodramatic promises (in the play "Uncle Vanja") that in two or
three hundred years people will live in an earthy paradise. Čechov was
only interested in the fact that the dimension of time being is populated
by unhappy people with different degrees of sensibility. Some of them
are so drawsy that they seldom break away or through the inertia of
everyday life; others awake, and look about them with widely opened
eyes. Čechov pitied both kinds. His writings convey, *not hope for the
future but pity for the present.* [25] We live today; that is the main
belief and message of Čechov. One may note that similarly *today,* now,
nunc, is the central reality of the four Gospels; only the Apocalypse
is directed toward the future, toward the Judgment. If a decision or a
change must be made in our life, it must be made now. The life of
everyday, as Čechov describes it, has its own charm. The deacon in
"The Duel" admired even "an ugly tree", and we cannot forget
the birch rods that appear in the reminiscences of the bishop. Yet it is
at times difficult to accept this unique but sad reality. Čechov himself
had no zeal to fight for a better life as his great predecessors in
Russian literature had done. His charity is after all a passive virtue;
it does not help in the conquest of the vices. True, some readers find
him more sympathetic than the energetic and ambitious God-seekers,
even than Dostoevskij. Čechov is a charitable sceptic without illusions,
a clever physician who knows the bitter truth that he cannot cure the
unhappy people, though they deserve salvation.

As many critics have said, Čechov was a master of Russian prose.
In order to procure him more intelligent praise, and clearer understanding, it may be worth while to mention what foreign students
seldom realize, that throughout the whole period of his literary activity
he made enormous efforts to eliminate bookish and journalistic clichés
from his language of a Russian intelligent. Yet he did not rid himself

[24] See the notes 18 and 19.
[25] The best analysis of pity and hope in Čechov's works is done by Daniel-
Rops, in his essay included into the collection *Carte d'Europe (Antoine Tchekhov)*, pp. 89-120. Also in P. Bitsilli's "The Creative Work of Chekhov" (in Russian), published in *Godišnik* of the University of Sofia, Bulgaria, v. XXXVIII,
1941-1942, pp. 121-122.

completely of such *Schablons*. Three characteristic devices in his prose may be listed:

1 Degrading or lowering similes and metaphors (*snižajuščie metafory*): *e.g.*, the comparison of a poetic phenomenon such as lightning with a prosaic gesture such as the striking of a match; or the roar of thunder to a barefooted man walking on a tin roof ("The Steppe").[26] In "The Student" the wind hoots as if someone were blowing into an empty bottle. In such passages Čechov attempts by wit to ridicule any romantic ennobling of nature.

2 In his best stories Čechov avoided such pathetic similes, and produced amazing effects by the use of some of the simplest sentences conceivable in the language. In "The Student", again, the hero says that the Garden of Gethsemane was "quiet, quiet, dark, dark" ("*tichij-tíchij, temnyj-temnyj sad*").[27] Such a description seems poverty-stricken and feeble; nevertheless we remain convinced that in the situation given and in the narrative under way, anything more elaborate would grate upon us. A similar effect, obtained by similarly modest means, occurs in "The Bishop". The day after his death was Easter Sunday: "the birds sang, the sun shone brightly."[28] The reader knows well that the year was at spring when birds sing everywhere; still, following the climactic passage, the description of the bishop's death, the simple statement seems the most appropriate.

3 Mixed with all such matter-of-fact-statements, Čechov made use of understatements, which have now been discussed by many critics, and have become famous. How was he to describe the grief of a mother, mourning for her son? It is a passage in "The Bishop" again. She used to walk out from the little town where she lived in the evening, to meet her cow. Occasionally she met some other women, and she told them "that she had a son, a bishop, and this she said timidly, afraid that she might not be believed... And indeed, some did not believe her." [29] So Čechov wrote, and that was all he wrote; nevertheless we all know well what the mother felt and sympathize with her in her sorrow. [30]

Such prosaic statements and understatements bring us closer to Čechov's *mysterium simplicitatis* in the phrase of Middleton Murry. They reveal his secret compassion for the creatures, who all deserve

---

[26] D. Merežkovskij was one of the first literary critics who paid attention to these similes in Čechov's writings, op. cit. (see note 9).

[27] Čechov, VIII 347. There is euphony in the quoted passage: *tichij... temnyj...* Nevertheless it is a very simple expression used very often.

[28] Čechov, "The Bishop'"..., p. 25.

[29] Ibid., p. 26.

[30] P. Bitsilli, op. cit. There we find a very fine analysis of Čechov's style.

salvation. Boris Zajcev, when he was trying to discover the ultimate
secret about Čechov, the good godless Christian, remarked: "Maybe
God loved him more than he loved God." [31] Perhaps Zajcev was right,
but I do not think that Čechov would have liked the overstatement.

---

[31] Boris Zajcev, *Čechov* (in Russian), 1954, p. 50.
I slightly changed some of the texts translated by Mrs C. Garnett.

GUNNAR JACOBSSON
DIE NOVELLE „DER STUDENT"
Versuch einer Analyse

Mit allem Recht hat man davor gewarnt, Čechovs eigene Ansichten mit denen, die er seine literarischen Figuren vertreten läßt, zu identifizieren (vergl. neuerdings z.B. G. Dick, *Die deutsche Čechov-Interpretation der Gegenwart, Zeitschrift für Slawistik,* IV, 1959, S. 698). Die diametral entgegengesetzten Auffassungen von Čechovs persönlicher Lebensanschauung, die schon früh bei den Kritikern und den Lesern herrschten, dürften ihren Grund hauptsächlich in dieser fehlerhaften Identifizierung haben. Ivan Bunin, dessen Erinnerungen für die Bewertung von Čechovs Person und Werk äußerst wertvoll sind, hat einmal gesagt:

„В своих работах он почти никогда не говорил о себе, о своих вкусах, о своих взглядах, что и повело, кстати сказать, к тому, что его долго считали человеком беспринципным, необщественным". (*Čechov v vospominanijach sovremennikov.* Vtoroe, dopolnennoe izdanie, 1954, S. 474-475).

Dieselbe Vorsicht bei der Identifizierung muß natürlich auch in Bezug auf die Notizen literarischer Art gelten, die in Čechovs *Zapisnye knižki* enthalten sind (vgl. die Erläuterungen zu diesen in *P.S.SP* XII 362).

Hierzu kommt noch Čechovs eigene Abneigung dagegen, von sich selbst zu reden, seine Scheu, sogar seinen Nächsten Zutritt zu seinem Innersten zu gewähren. Es ist bezeichnend, daß Aleksander Kuprin, der Čechov während seiner Jaltazeit nahestand, folgendes schreiben konnte:

„Думается, что он никому не раскрывал и не отдавал своего сердца вполне. . ." (*Čechov v vospominanijach sovremennikov,* S. 515).

Oder wie Ivan Bunin sagt:

„Но сдержанность осталась; и проявлялась она не только в обращении со мной, но и с людьми самыми близкими ему. . ." (*Op. cit.,* S. 477).

„Я писал, что никогда ни с кем не был он дружен, близок по-настоящему" (*Op. cit.,* S. 484).

Unter den Arbeiten Čechovs befindet sich ein Werk, das trotz seines geringen Umfanges eine Schlüsselstellung in seiner literarischen

Tätigkeit einnimmt. Das ist die kleine Novelle „Der Student", erstmals
unter dem Namen *Večerom* in „Russkie vedomosti", 1894, No 104,
den 16. April veröffentlicht und später unter dem neuen Namen
in *Povesti i rasskazy*, Moskva 1894 in I. Sytins Ausgabe abgedruckt.
Ivan Bunin hat uns Čechovs eigene Worte übermittelt, die uns an-
nehmen lassen, daß gerade „Der Student" die persönlichen Ansichten
des Verfassers widerspiegelt:

> „А какой я нытик? Какой я ‚хмурый человек', какая я
> ‚холодная кровь', как называют меня критики? Какой я
> ‚пессимист'? Ведь из моих вещей самый любимый мой
> рассказ *Студент*" (*Op. cit.*, S. 480).

Es ist bekannt, daß die neunziger Jahre des vorigen Jahrhunderts,
als eine Vertiefung der Lebensauffassung und des Verfassertums
Čechovs stattfand, auch ein Abstandnehmen von der Tolstojschen
Lebensanschauung mitsichbrachten:

> „толстовская мораль перестала меня трогать, в глубине
> души я отношусь к ней недружелюбно. . . . толстовская
> философия сильно трогала меня, владела мною лет 6-7 . . .
> Теперь же во мне что-то протестует",

heißt es in einem Brief im Jahre 1894 an den Herausgeber der *Novoe
vremja* A. S. Suvorin (*PSSP* XVI 132).

Daß Čechov nach dem Bruch mit den Tolstojschen Ansichten nicht
in einem Vakuum lebte, was seine Lebensauffassung betrifft, ist jedoch
vollkommen sicher. Ein Nebeneinanderstellen seiner eigenen, soeben
angeführten Aussage und eines Auszugs aus einem Brief, der schon
1888 an denselben Suvorin gerichtet war,

> „(кончается тем) что давно уже известно, а именно, что
> осмысленная жизнь без определенного мировоззрения — не
> жизнь, а тягота, ужас" (*PSSP* XIV 242),

kann nur zu dem Schluß führen, daß eine optimistische Einstellung
zum Leben eine bestimmte Lebensanschauung voraussetzt.

Der oben angeführte Brief aus dem Jahre 1894 ist am 27. März in
Jalta geschrieben. Daselbst und im selben Monat hat Čechov die Novelle *Večerom* (später *Student*) geschrieben (vgl. N. I. Gitovič, *Leto-
pis' žizni i tvorčestva A. P. Čechova*, Moskva 1955, S. 360, und *PSSP*
XVI 141 und 462). Ist es nur ein Zufall, daß die Abrechnung mit
Tolstoj und das Verfassen des „Studenten" zeitlich so nahe zusammen-
fallen? Sicherlich nicht, denn es ist eine Lebensanschauung, die im
„Studenten" ihren Ausdruck findet, eine Lebensanschauung, die ohne
jeglichen Zweifel Čechovs eigene war, die man in seinen früheren Werken hatte ahnen können und die uns immer wieder in seinen späteren
Arbeiten entgegentritt.

Diejenigen, die es bisher überhaupt der Mühe wert gefunden haben, die Novelle „Der Student" zu kommentieren, haben zwar deren Bedeutung für das Verständnis für Čechov betont, sind aber zu verschiedenen Ergebnissen gekommen, was als das wichtigste Moment in dieser Novelle zu betrachten sei. Z. Papernyj z.B. ist der Ansicht, der Kontakt mit dem einfachen Volk wäre der entscheidende Faktor, der die Bekehrung der Hauptperson zu einem neuen Lebensglauben erkläre, ja, er sieht in dem Glauben an das Volk einen Grundfaktor dieser und anderer Novellen:

> „Именно простые люди из народа выступают в рассказе, как подлинные хранители человечности, помогают герою освободиться от безнадежных мыслей, заражают его верой в торжество правды на земле" (Z. Papernyj, *A. P. Čechov. Očerk tvorčestva*. Moskva 1954, S. 66; vgl. auch S. 89).

M. E. Elizarova meint, das Entscheidende im „Studenten" sei die Frage von der Notwendigkeit „перевернуть жизнь" (*Mirovoe značenie tvorčestva A. P. Čechova*, in: *Tvorčestvo Čechova*. Sbornik statej. Moskva 1956, S. 331; vgl. auch Z. I. Gerson, *Kompozicija i stil' povestvovatel'nych proizvedenij A. P. Čechova*, in: *Op. cit.*, S. 97-98).

M. E. Elizarova betont in einem anderen Zusammenhang das Optimistische beim „Studenten". Infolge einer plötzlichen geistigen Bekehrung, die die Hauptperson mit Freude und der Vorahnung etwas Großen und Bedeutungsvollen erfüllt, findet diese einen neuen Glauben, neue Anschauungen (*Tvorčestvo Čechova i voprosy realizma konca XIX veka*. Moskva 1958, S. 150-151).

Ähnlichen Gedankengängen begegnen wir schon bei Serge Persky, der den „Studenten" der Epoche im Verfassertum Čechovs zuzählt, wo dessen pessimistische Tendenz durch neue Hoffnungen ersetzt wird (Serge Persky, *Les maîtres du roman russe contemporain*, Paris-Lausanne 1912, S. 112).

Sophie Laffitte, die Čechov eine kurze aber wohldokumentierte Studie gewidmet hat, charakterisiert den „Studenten" als eine „courte nouvelle... toute baignée de poésie religieuse" und sieht darin ein Beispiel des Gefühls für kirchliche Bräuche und die religiöse Poesie, das Čechov, trotz seines Rationalismus, seines Glaubens an den Fortschritt und seiner wissenschaftlichen Einstellung zum Leben, bis zu seinem Tode bewahrt hat (Sophie Laffitte, *Tchékhov par lui-même*. Paris 1955, S. 148, 149).

Irène Némirovskys Ansicht nach macht „Der Student" denselben Eindruck wie „un accord musical, extraordinairement tendre et pur". Als Abschluß fügt sie hinzu: „Trois pages à peine, qui ont plus de sens et de résonance qu'un long roman" (Irène Némirovsky, *La vie de Tchekov*, Paris 1946, S. 171).

Von anderer Art, in Hinsicht auf die Erzählungstechnik, ist die Behauptung, „Der Student" sei ein Beispiel von Čechovs Talent, durch ein Anknüpfen der Vergangenheit an die Zukunft Atmosphäre zu schaffen (Ronald Hingley, *Chekhov. A Biographical and Critical Study*. London 1950, S. 208).

Die Bedeutung dieser verschiedenen Ansichten kann selbstverständlich in Frage gestellt werden. Klar ist jedenfalls, daß sie keine alles umfassende Charakteristik des „Studenten" bringen. Sie dürften wohl durch eine Analyse der Novelle selbst als einheitliches Ganzes vervollständigt werden.

Kompositionstechnisch besteht die Novelle aus drei Teilen, von denen jeder von seinem Wortvorrat und seinem Inhalt charakterisiert wird: aus der Einleitung, der zentralen Erzählung, der Auflösung. Selbstverständlich ist diese Dreiteilung nicht als eine Aufteilung in im Verhältnis zu einander isolierte Abschnitte aufzufassen; sie stehen vielmehr in Abhängigkeit von einander, wie es der Fall in einer Kettenreaktion ist, und sind dem Ganzen, d.h. dem Thema untergeordnet.

Die äußere Handlung ist einfach und undramatisch: aus der Abenddunkelheit, an einem Tage der Karwoche [1], taucht ein Student der Geistlichen Akademie auf, tritt an ein Feuer heran, an dem zwei Witwen, Mutter und Tochter, sitzen, redet mit ihnen und verschwindet dann wieder im Dunkeln. Die Novelle macht den Eindruck von einem Szenenbild eines Theaterstückes: dunkele Bühnenseiten, ein dunkeler Fond und im Gegensatz hierzu die von den Flammen beleuchtete Bühnenmitte, wo die Konzentration der vom Feuer bestrahlten Hauptpersonen eine Assoziation zu der Komposition eines Rembrandtgemäldes erweckt.

Die Einfachheit der Handlung steht in umgekehrtem Verhältnis zu dem reichen Thema der Inhaltsebene: die Entwickelung oder Bekehrung der Hauptperson vom Pessimismus infolge der Inhaltlosigkeit des Lebens zu jugendlichem Optimismus, hervorgerufen von der Einsicht von und im Glauben an die Kräfte, die das Leben bestimmen.

Die Einleitung hat zur Aufgabe, Stimmung zu schaffen, sowie den Ausgangspunkt für die eigentliche Handlung darzustellen. Ein kurzer Auftakt optimistischen Charakters: stilles, schönes Wetter, der Schuß eines Jägers, der fröhlich durch die Frühlingsluft hallt, hebt durch seinen Gegensatz die pessimistische Stimmung hervor, die den Studenten Ivan Velikopol'skij erfüllt. Auf der Ausdrucksebene entspricht dieser Stimmung eine Beschreibung der Kälte und Finsternis, die plötz-

---

[1] Es ist vollkommen unverständlich, weshalb Z. Papernyj (*op. cit.*, S. 63) behauptet, die Handlung trage sich an einem Herbstabend zu; gerade der Zeitpunkt — der Karfreitag — erklärt die in der Novelle enthaltene Erzählung.

lich das schöne Wetter ersetzen und die mit Worten und Wendungen
wie

> „стемнело; вечерние потемки сгустились; мрак; подул ...
> холодный пронизывающий ветер; по лужам ... ледяные
> иглы; запахло зимой; у него закоченели пальцы; внезапно
> наступавший холод; все сплошь утопало в холодной вечер-
> ней мгле; пожимаясь от холода" (*PSSP* XVII 345-348)

beschrieben werden.

Zur Kälte und Finsternis gesellen sich auch die Stille, die Öde, die
Ungemütlichkeit, die Ungastlichkeit:

> „все смолкло; стало ... неуютно, глухо и нелюдимо;
> самой природе жутко; кругом было пустынно".

Im Körper des Studenten nagt der Hunger, denn

> „по случаю страстной пятницы дома ничего не варили, и
> мучительно хотелось есть".

Er ist erfüllt von einem Gefühl der Trostlosigkeit über die Unwan-
delbarkeit des traurigen Menschenlebens, das seit ältester Zeit immer
gleich geblieben ist und das noch tausend Jahre bestehen wird:

> „точно такая же лютая бедность, голод; такие же
> дырявые соломенные крыши, невежество, тоска, такая же
> пустыня кругом, мрак, чувство гнета, — все эти ужасы".

Diese dunkele Partie ist es, die die Einleitung ausmacht und etwa ein
Viertel der ganzen Novelle umfasst. Wenn man vom Wortverrat der
Einleitung (etwa 260) alle semantisch unprägnanten Wörter (wie
Bindewörter, Verhältniswörter, Fürwörter u. dgl.) abzählt, machen die
semantischen Kernwörter etwa 160 aus. Von diesen geben ungefähr
ein Fünftel der Stimmung ein Gepräge von Pessimismus und bezeich-
nen negative Begriffe. Selbstverständlich beruht ihre gefühlsmäßige
Ladung jedoch nicht auf ihrer eigenen semantischen Bedeutung verein-
zelt genommen, sondern ist das Resultat der Stimmung des ganzen
Abschnittes oder Bedeutungsfeldes.

Im Gegensatz zu der Finsternis und Kälte der Einleitung steht das
Feuer, an dem die beiden Witwen Vasilisa und Lukerja sitzen und an
das der Student herantritt, um sich zu erwärmen. Die Wärme und das
Licht geben dieser Episode das äußere Gepräge, was durch folgende
Wörter veranschaulicht wird:

> „костер; огонь; горел; жарко; грелся; освещая".

Die Szene mit dem Feuer sowie der äußere Zeitpunkt — die Karwoche — und die Zugehörigkeit des Studenten zu einer Geistlichen
Akademie sind es, die hier eine Aufteilung der Handlung verur-

sachen [2] : die auf der Bühne mit den beiden Frauen und dem Studenten
am Feuer und die in der Erzählung des Studenten von Petri Verleugnung. Diese beiden Handlungen verlaufen parallel aber nicht isoliert
von einander und greifen immer wieder in einander; die Frauen erleben ebenso deutlich wie ihre eigene Situation die Szene mit Petrus,
wie er seine voreiligen Versprechungen Jesus gegenüber äußert und
wie er sich am Feuer im Hof des Hohepriesters erwärmt; sie leben mit
in seiner Verleugnung und seiner verzweifelten Reue mit den bitteren
Tränen. Die Parallelhandlung der Erzählung endigt mit diesem Moment, welches ja das bittere Weinen der alten Vasilisa auslöst und
sozusagen identisch mit ihm wird, und das auch die Gemütsbewegung
der trägeren Tochter hervorruft. Die Parallelhandlungen werden also
zusammengeknüpft und rein äußerlich gesehen dadurch abgeschlossen,
daß die Hintergrundhandlung auf die Vorderbühne verlegt wird:

> „Работники возвращались с реки, и один из них верхом
> на лошади был уже близко, и свет от костра дрожал на
> нем”.

Dieses Auftreten neuer Personen auf dem beleuchteten Teil der
Bühne ist das Zeichen für den Studenten, sich von den Frauen zu
verabschieden und wieder in der Dunkelheit zu verschwinden.

Der Wortvorrat in der Erzählung des Studenten umfasst ein reiches
Register und weist kirchenslawische Wörter und Formen aus der
Bibel auf:

> „петел; исшед; плакася”

neben den eigenen Worten des Studenten mit ihren familiär-stilisti-
schen Zügen, wie

> „вот-вот; горько-горько; тихий-тихий; темный-темный”.

Die strenge Darstellungsweise der Bibel, mehr oder weniger genau
wiedergegeben [3],

> „С тобою я готов и в темницу, и на смерть”;
> „Говорю тебе, Петр, не пропоет сегодня петел, ... как ты
> трижды отречешься, что не знаешь меня”,

steht im Gegensatz zu den eigenen umschriebenen Wendungen des Studenten, beispielsweise als er die Gemütsstimmung Petri schildert:

> „Петр, изнеможенный, замученный тоской и тревогой,

---

[2] Auch ein Hintergrundhandlung spielt sich ab — Knechte tränken Pferde am
Fluß — aber sie ist technischer Natur und hat zur Aufgabe, die Handlung der
Vordergrundbühne plastisch zu gestalten.

[3] Die Auszüge beziehen sich auf das 22. Kapitel des Lucasevangeliums. Es
ist uns nicht möglich gewesen, genau festzustellen, welcher Quelle sie entnommen
worden sind.

понимаешь ли, не выспавшийся, предчувствуя, что вот-вот на земле произойдет что-то ужасное; он страстно, без памяти любил Иисуса".

Die Szene mit den Frauen löst die seelische Verwandlung des Studenten aus, die im letzten Abschnitt der Novelle stattfindet, während er sich auf dem Heimweg befindet. Die Finsternis ist dieselbe:

„И опять наступили потемки";

ebenso die Kälte:

„стали зябнуть руки. Дул жестокий ветер, в самом деле возвращалась зима ...".

Diese Kälte und diese Finsternis haben jedoch nicht mehr dieselbe emotionelle Spannung wie in der Einleitung, denn die Stimmung ist eine ganz andere jetzt, wo der Student versteht, daß die Gemütsbewegung der beiden Frauen andere Gründe hat als nur seine Erzählungskunst. Der Petrus der Erzählung stand ihnen so nahe, seine geistige Unruhe war in solchem Grad ihre eigene geworden, daß die Entfernung in der Zeit weiter von keiner Bedeutung war. Dieselben Prinzipien, die das Leben der Menschen zu Petri Zeit bestimmten, und zwar die *Wahrheit* und die *Schönheit,* haben immer noch dieselbe Aktualität. Und dies Erkenntnis füllte nicht nur seine Seele mit Freude, er hatte auch ein „Gefühl von Jugend, Gesundheit und Kraft; ein unsagbar liebliches Gefühl von Glück, von einem fremden, geheimnisvollen Glück" bemächtigte sich seiner; sein Leben schien ihm nicht bloß „entzückend und wunderbar" sondern auch „erfüllt von tiefem Sinn". Gegen die pessimistische Stimmung der Einleitung kontrastiert also der letzte Abschnitt der Novelle (der auch etwa ein Viertel des Ganzen umfasst) mit seinem Charakter tiefer Glücksverknüpfung positiver Eigenschaften. Typisch für diesen Abschnitt sind Wendungen wie:

„радость вдруг заволновалась в его душе; чувство молодости, здоровья, силы; невыразимо сладкое ожидание счастья; (жизнь казалась ему) восхитительной, чудесной".

Aber der zentrale Ideeninhalt nicht nur des letzten Abschnittes sondern der ganzen Novelle ist in den zwei Worten

„правда" und „красота"

enthalten.

Es sind diese zwei Prinzipien, die, wie in der Novelle ausgesagt wird, allzeit und ununterbrochen das menschliche Leben bestimmt haben, die das Wichtigste im Menschenleben und überhaupt auf der Erde ausmachen sollen. Es sind diese Prinzipien, die dem Leben einen Sinn verleihen.

Aber abgesehen von diesen äußeren Charakteristika, welcher ist der
Sinn dieser beiden Prinzipien an sich? „Wahrheit" und „Schönheit"
sind ja abstrakte Begriffe so allgemeiner Bedeutung, daß eine genauere
Fixierung ihres eigentlichen Sinnes notwendig sein dürfte. Die Novelle
enthält jedoch keine nähere Aussage hierüber. Wenn der Verfasser
diese beiden Begriffe nicht nur zufällig in die Novelle eingeführt hat
in der Voraussetzung, sie wären bekannt — was nicht der Fall sein
dürfte, da sie gerade in dieser Novelle so klar und deutlich als der Ausdruck einer Lebensanschauung auftreten [4] — so muß die Erklärung
ihres Sinnes in der Novelle selbst zu suchen sein. In erster Linie
müßte er in der Schilderung des Studenten von Petri Verleugnung zu
finden sein, da ja diese der Hauptperson die beiden Begriffe offen-
barte.

Es dürfte klar sein, daß unter „Schönheit" hier in erster Hand
ein moralischer und nicht ein ästhetischer Begriff zu verstehen ist. [5]

---

[4] Es ist nicht schwer, die Begriffe „Wahrheit" und „Schönheit" in Werken
Čechovs, die vor dem „Studenten" erschienen sind, nachzuweisen. Aufs Geratewohl
greifen wir aus *Černyj monach,* der im Sommer 1893 verfasst wurde (*PSSP*
VIII 561), heraus:

„Ты служишь вечной правде......; (посвящены они) разумному и
прекрасному, то есть тому, что вечно" (*Op. cit.,* S. 278).

In Werken, die später als „Der Student" entstanden sind, gibt es so zahlreiche
Beispiele, daß es nicht vonnöten sein dürfte, sie hier in größerer Anzahl anzu-
führen:

„Счастье и радость жизни не в деньгах и не в любви, а в правде"
(Čechovs Notizbuch, in Bezug auf *Tri goda, PSSP* XII 217, niedergeschrieben
Ende des Jahres 1894, *PSSP* VIII 596).

„И как ни велико зло, все же ночь тиха и прекрасна, и все же в
божьем мире правда есть и будет, такая же тихая и прекрасная, и все
на земле только ждет, чтобы слиться с правдой..." (*V ovrage, PSSP*
IX 400, niedergeschrieben Ende des Jahres 1899, laut einem Brief des Verfassers
an seine Schwester M. P. Čechova vom 14. [nicht 4. gemäss *PSSP* IX 611]
November 1899, *PSSP* XVIII 259-260).

Alle diese und ähnliche Beispiele von „Wahrheit" und „Schönheit" haben jedoch
bedeutungsgemäß ihren Fokus im „Studenten".

Über die Schönheit der Natur als Ausdruck für die Schönheit, die in einem
künftigen, besseren Leben der Menschheit herrschen wird, vgl. V. A. Kovalev,
*Vzgljady A. P. Čechova na chudožestvennoe masterstvo pisatelja, Vestnik Mos-
kovskogo universiteta* 1959, 4, S. 101-120, besonders S. 110-111.

[5] D.h. wir gehen von dem Sinn aus, der in der Novelle „Der Student" zum
Ausdruck kommt. Daß „Schönheit" für Čechov auch ein ästhetischer Begriff war,
ergibt sich aus anderen seiner Werke. V. Ermilov, *Anton Pavlovič Čechov,* 1860-
1904. Izdanie vtoroe, pererabotannoe. Moskva 1949, S. 315 und *passim* erwähnt die
Begriffe „правда" und „красота" ohne direkt vom „Studenten" auszugehen
und ohne eine klare Definition ihres Sinnes zu geben.

Nach der Niederschrift des vorstehenden Artikels wurde mir diese Arbeit in
ihrer vervollständigten Fassung (Moskau 1959) zugänglich.

Für Petrus muß „Schönheit" das Ideal des Vollendeten, des Vollkommenen, des in moralischem Sinn nicht Defekten repräsentieren. Jede Handlung, die in Übereinstimmung mit diesem Ideal ausgeführt wird, d.h. nicht gegen dies Ideal verstößt, ist somit „schön". Um in dieser Weise handeln zu können, muß man dem Ideal treu bleiben, d.h. eine Handlung darf nicht das Ideal verschatten, so daß es verkleinert oder beschränkt wird, sondern es muß in seiner ganzen Vollkommenheit, in „Wahrheit" dastehen. Während die „Schönheit" also das Statische ist, ist die „Wahrheit" das Dynamische. Eine kann nicht ohne die andere bestehen, denn ohne „Wahrheit" würde die „Schönheit" nicht sichtbar sein, und ohne „Schönheit" hätte die „Wahrheit" keine Berechtigung. Petri Tat der Unwahrheit, d.h. sein Verleugnen des Ideals (der „Schönheit") und seine Reue deswegen sind es, die die beiden Frauen ergreifen, wodurch die Gültigkeit der zwei Prinzipien für alle Zeiten bewiesen wird.

Der Sinn der „Schönheit" und der „Wahrheit" wird auch außerhalb der zentralen Erzählung beleuchtet. Die Worte „невежество", „тоска", „ужасы" der Einleitung sind negative Begriffe, welche die Harmonie der „Schönheit" brechen und deswegen einen Akt von Unwahrheit voraussetzen. Die plötzliche Rückkehr der Kälte (in der Einleitung) die

„нарушил во всем порядок и согласие"

kann symbolisch als ein Verbrechen gegen die „Schönheit" aufgefasst werden. Und im Schlußabschnitt sind es die Treue und die Aufrichtigkeit (die „Wahrheit") der „Schönheit" gegenüber, die die positiven Gefühle von Optimismus bei dem Studenten erwecken.

Da „Der Student" die Phase in Čechovs Leben und Tätigkeit repräsentiert, die mit Recht mit den Worten „на переломе" charakterisiert werden kann (Z. Papernyj, op. cit., S. 62), ist es nur selbstverständlich, daß der Wortvorrat der Novelle den Kontrast zwischen den pessimistischen Erzählungen der achtziger Jahre und den positiven Zügen in der literarischen Tätigkeit Čechovs im Laufe des letzten Jahrzehntes seines Lebens widerspiegeln. Der *Kontrast* ist auch ein technisches

---

In der neuen Auflage hat V. Ermilov seine Gesichtspunkte hinsichtlich der Begriffe „Schönheit" und „Wahrheit" in einem Kapitel weiter dargelegt, das er (S. 317-334) „Мы живем накануне величайшего торжества" bezeichnet. Darin wird „Schönheit" von Ermilov als ein ästhetischer Begriff aufgefasst, der bei Čechov mit dem ethischen Begriff „Wahrheit" in nahem Einklang steht: „красота всегда сливалась в сознании Чехова с правдой, эстетическое — с этическим" (S. 332). Ermilovs Auffassung der beiden Begriffe soll damit für Čechovs gesamtes Werk, auch für den „Studenten" insbesondere seine Gültigkeit haben, was auch aus der Fortsetzung des eben angeführten Zitates hervorgehen mag: „Красота и правда правят миром („Студент")" (S. 332).

Mittel, das die ganze Novelle auszeichnet, ob es sich nun um den Wortvorrat, die Personenwahl oder die Komposition im übrigen handelt. Der *Parallelismus,* von dem das *Symbol* eine Art sein dürfte, ist ein anderes stilistisches Hilfsmittel, dessen sich der Verfasser bedient, um der Inhaltsebene eine doppelte Beleuchtung zu geben. Wenn auch Čechovs technische Meisterschaft in vielen anderen Werken an den Tag tritt (vgl. beispielsweise V. Šklovskij, *Zametki a proze russkich klassikov,* Moskva 1953, S. 289-322; N. I. Pruckov, *K voprosu ob èvoljucii realizma A. P. Čechova,* im Sammelband *Iz istorii russkich literaturnych otnošenij XVIII-XX vekov,* Moskva-Leningrad 1959, S. 266-278; V. V. Golubkov, *Masterstvo A. P. Čechova,* Moskva 1958; vgl. auch V. V. Vinogradov, *O jazyke chudožestvennoj literatury,* Moskva 1959, *passim*), so ist es doch von Interesse zu beachten, welchen Wert der Verfasser auf die Novelle „Der Student" legte. Es ist bekannt, daß sein Bruder I. P. Čechov auf eine Frage, welches von seinen Werken Čechov selbst am höchsten schätze, folgendes antwortete:

„'Студент'. Считал наиболее отделанной" (scilicet вещью) (*PSSP* VIII 564).

Der Schwerpunkt der Inhaltsebene konzentriert sich in den beiden Begriffen „Wahrheit" und „Schönheit". Diese sind es, die mit einer plötzlichen Kraft ein Stück Alltag in eine höhere Dignität heben und von einer Lebensanschauung durchleuchten lassen, die nicht nur der Hauptperson gehört sondern auch Čechovs eigene ist.

R. A. KLOSTERMANN

DIE NOVELLE „DER STUDENT"

EIN DISKUSSIONSBEITRAG

Daß Čechovs Werk schwer verständlich ist und nach ganz verschiedenen Richtungen hin zu deuten ist, darf als allgemein anerkannte Anschauung vorweggenommen werden und ist im Vorigen auch durch G. Jacobsson bei einem Spezialfall erneut aufgewiesen worden. [1] Bei der ausgesprochen dürftigen Quellenlage und fehlenden einschlägigen Auskünften durch den Verfasser selbst wird man immer wieder ohne autoritative Deutungen auskommen müssen und daher die innere Berechtigung besitzen, an den einzelnen literarischen Stücken herumzudeuten, um womöglich auf solche Art zu einem tieferen Verständnis der komplizierten Gedankenwelt Čechovs zu gelangen: Eine Tatsache, die bereits zu Lebzeiten des Dichters nach eigenen Zeugnissen aus dem Briefwechsel zu belegen wäre, ein Umstand, der vielleicht schon von dem Verfasser als wohl überlegtes Kunstmittel bei der Niederschrift seiner Werke mit einkalkuliert worden ist, und eine Situation, wie sie ohne jeden Zweifel auch bei der vorliegenden Novelle vorzuherrschen scheint.

Sicherlich hat G. Jacobsson in seiner Analyse von Čechovs „Student" Recht, wenn er die starke Symbolik der vorgetragenen Gedanken und die weitgehende Parallelität des Geschehens zwischen den verschiedenen Handlungen, dem Evangelienbericht von der Verleugnung Christi durch Petrus, der eigentlichen Erzahlung und einer kulissenhaften weiteren Ausstattung nachdrücklich unterstreicht und damit den Grundstock zu einer variierenden, durchaus diskutabelen Interpretation legt. In Wirklichkeit werden aber die geheimnisvollen symbolischen Elemente und Parallelen, versteckte Andeutungen und Anspielungen vielleicht noch bedeutend weiter gehen. Ohne den Ehrgeiz zu besitzen, hier alles aufzugreifen, sei doch in Bescheidenheit auf einige Möglichkeiten aufmerksam gemacht, die einerseits in der besonderen theologischen Thematik, andererseits in der positiv zu beurteilenden Religiosität des Verfassers liegen, der in betont kirchlicher Umwelt aufgewachsen längere Zeit im Kirchenchor gestanden hat, zahlreiche Theologen persönlich kannte, die Sprache der Bibel gern auch in seinem Briefwechsel anwandte, Kirchen und Klöster mit Fleiß besuchte, andere

---

[1] Da G. Jacobsson bei seiner Analyse dieser Novelle (vgl. S. 93) ein recht umfangreiches Anschauungsmaterial und bibliographische Noten bringt, wird man sich hier auf das Notwendigste beschränken dürfen.

Schriftsteller auf gewisse Verstöße bei religiösen Fragen aufmerksam machte, der für sich, einzelne Familienmitglieder und Freunde Ikonen zu erwerben suchte.

Die im März 1894 in Jalta geschriebene Novelle hat zunächst den Titel *Večerom* getragen. Aber selbst wenn man die Erzählung nunmehr im allgemeinen Gebrauch nach der geänderten Bezeichnung als *Student* namhaft macht und in Rechnung stellt, daß Čechov nach Zeugnissen aus seinem umfassenden Briefwechsel oft genug bei der Namengebung seiner geistigen Kinder in großer Verlegenheit war und gern anderen die letzte Entscheidung überließ, so kann doch der ursprüngliche Titel keineswegs ein Zufallsprodukt oder eine planlose Lösung darstellen, an denen man ohne weiteres vorbeigehen dürfte: Der zunächst gewählte Titel scheint doch rein äußerlich seine Bedeutung schon darin zu haben, daß er die Tageszeit der Handlung gleich eingangs näher zu bestimmen sucht, die zum mindesten aus den ersten drei vollen Sätzen der Erzählung nicht zu erkennen ist und bei der Schilderung der Landschaft wie der seelischen Stimmung der auftretenden Personen garnicht so unwichtig ist, vielleicht sogar den letzten Anstoß zu dem freimütigen Gedankenaustausch in der Haupthandlung bietet. Er erinnert aber auch — zumal wenn man das Kernstück der Erzählung vor Augen hat, doch bereits in den Einleitungssätzen [2] — an die bekannten Oratorienworte und die musikalische Stimmung „Am Abend, als es kühle ward..." und damit an ein religiöses Denken, das gerade in der Karwoche seine besondere Berechtigung hat und von sich aus für feine Ohren, die es heraushören wollen, auf den schwerwiegenden Inhalt in einer verwandten Gedankenrichtung aufmerksam macht. Berücksichtigt man dann die Hauptfigur des Studenten, keines einfachen Seminaristen, sondern des Zöglings einer der vier großen russischen Geistlichen Akademien und damit eines überdurchschnittlich gebildeten und gereiften jungen Theologen, so liegt doch wohl noch eine weitere Verbindungsbrücke zwischen dem ursprünglichen Titel und der Handlung vor. Er weist nicht auf einen völlig beliebigen Abend im Frühjahr hin, sondern erinnert im biblischen Sprachgebrauch an eine Zeitangabe, in der immer wieder Entscheidendes geschieht: etwa an die rührenden Worte: „Bleibe bei uns; denn es will Abend werden" [3], oder an den Abend, an dem des Judas Verrat angekündigt und das Herrenmahl gestiftet wird. [4] Aber auch die Vorhersagung und Verleugnung des Petrus ist nach den Synoptikern [5] abends oder des Nachts gedacht, wobei die Relativität der Zeitbegriffe mit zum Aus-

---

[2] Vgl. Čechovs Worte: холодный пронизивающий ветер!
[3] Vgl. Lk. 24, 29.
[4] Vgl. Mtth. 26, 20 und Parr.
[5] Vgl. Mtth. 26, 36ff.; Mk. 14, 26 ff; Lk. 22, 39.

druck kommen mag. Darüber hinaus wird man noch darauf verweisen dürfen, dass das Wort „вечером" sprachlich wie sachlich mit „вечеря", Abendmahl, mit „вечерня", Vesper, Abendmesse verwandt ist.

Wenn dann im dritten Einleitungssatz von dem Ziehen einer Waldschnepfe die Rede ist, die bald durch einen freudig klingenden Schuß doch wohl getroffen wird, obwohl ein solches Detail charakteristisch genug nicht ausdrücklich erwähnt wird, so kann man — soweit man nicht selber Jäger ist — das Ereignis als Tod eines unschuldigen Wildvogels ansprechen und dahingehend interpretieren: als Motiv unmittelbar mit der Erlegung der Möwe in Čechovs gleichnamiger Komödie aus dem Jahre 1896 verwandt (zwei Jahre liegen lediglich dazwischen) und vielleicht auch mit H. Ibsens „Wildente" (1884) in Zusammenhang zu bringen [6], will doch der russische Dichter in beiden Fällen das unschuldige Opfer der Liebe symbolhaft zum Ausdruck bringen. In der vorliegenden Erzählung wird dann die Waldschnepfe — eine Wildtaube wird der Verfasser aus Furcht, religiöse Gefühle und christliche Symbolik zu verletzen, nicht in Betracht gezogen haben — doch nicht nur das unschuldige Opfer einer vom menschlichen Standpunkt aus gesehen fröhlichen Jagd, sondern auch Parallelen zum unschuldsvollen Leiden und Sterben Christi darzustellen haben.

Der Held der Erzählung, der Student Ivan Velikopol'skij, trägt merkwürdig genug denselben Namen wie ein zweitrangiger Poet, der Satiriker und Dramatiker Ivan Ermolovič Velikopol'skij (1797-1868), [7] was bei der Fülle von neutral klingenden anderen Lösungen, unter Anrechnung der tiefgründigen Schaffensart von Čechov sowie seinem ausgesprochenen Interesse für auffällige Eigennamen keinesfalls ohne Bedeutung sein kann. Ist hiermit nicht ein „typischer klerikaler Name" — wie eine Oxfordedition es will [8] — sondern wirklich ein naher Vorgänger unseres Dichters gemeint, so wird sich die Einführung einer solchen Persönlichkeit auf halb positive, halb negative innere Zusammenhänge zwischen Čechov und dem historischen Velikopol'skij deuten lassen. Auf die vorliegende Erzählung bezogen würde der zweitrangige Charakter des genannten russischen Literaten unserem gleichnamigen Studenten etwa den Anstrich des Unfertigen, aber auch womöglich einiger positiven Entwicklungsmöglichkeiten zu verleihen haben. Aber

---

[6] Hinweis von B. Lundberg, Göteborg; vgl. im übrigen: Nils Åke Nilsson, *Ibsen in Rußland,* Stockholm 1958, S. 221 ff. (Acta universitatis Stockholmiensis, Études de philologie slave 7).

[7] Vgl. *Enc. slovar'* 10, 1892, S. 828. Ein höherer russischer Offizier des gleichen Namens ist um 1827 belegt, vgl. Russkaja Starina 48, 1885, S. 396, 399.

[8] Vgl. G. A. Birkett-G. Struve, *Anton Chekhov, Selected Short Stories,* Oxford 1951, S. 137.

vielleicht darf man nur den Vornamen „Ivan" als typische Kennzeichnung des Russen schlechthin aufgreifen, was dann ähnlich das Durchschnittliche des Helden, vielleicht auch die Alltäglichkeit seiner Erfahrungen und Gedanken betonen soll. Schließlich mag auch der Name „Velikopol'skij" ohne festen Bezug auf die historische Gestalt auf *grosse* Pläne auf weitem *Felde* gedeutet werden.

Der Student, der am Karfreitag oder Karsamstag durch die Felder streift, seinen trübsinnigen Gedanken nachhängt und dann aus Zufall oder Fügung auf zwei ihm bekannte Witwen Vasilisa und Luker'ja, Mutter und Tochter stößt und ihnen die Erzählung von der Verleugnung Christi vorträgt, mag zunächst völlig neutral nur in die vorgeführte Episode, in das gegenwärtige Einzelerlebnis hineinpassen. Bei längerem Nachdenken wird man aber auch hier an biblische Motive erinnert, die mit der Kreuzigung Christi und seiner Auferstehung zu kombinieren wären: etwa an den Gang der beiden Jünger nach Emaus — auch der Student der Theologie darf als „Jünger Christi" angesprochen werden —, oder an die trauernden Frauen am Grabe, wie denn Mutter und Tochter beide Witwen sind, sich am gleichen Platz vereint der Trauer hingeben und der Student in düsterer Gemütsverfassung hinzutritt.

Als der Student von den beiden Witwen nicht sofort wiedererkannt wird, entschuldigen diese das Versäumnis mit dem Hinweis auf ein russisches Sprichwort, das in solchem Fall der verkannten Persönlichkeit Reichtümer zu versprechen scheint: [9] ein Sprichwort, dessen umgehende Erfüllung wir hier an Ort und Stelle selber noch miterleben dürfen: der Student — auch dieser sprichwörtlich arm — erhält die Prophezeiung unter den denkbar ungünstigsten Vorzeichen, wird aber noch vor Ende der Erzählung innerlich beglückt und reich dargestellt, womit eine schöne Umdeutung und Vergeistigung eines an sich banal gedachten geflügelten Wortes erreicht wird. Aber auch der Student selbst tritt in der Erzählung nach den Vorstellungen auf, wie sie etwa das russische Sprichwort an großen Theologen beobachten zu können glaubt. Er ist — auch ironisch betrachtet — ein großer Theologe und kann alle Feiertage an seinen Fingern aufzählen! [10]

An die Namen der beiden Witwen wird sich ebenfalls anknüpfen lassen. Zunächst wird man vermuten dürfen, daß Repräsentanten dieses Namens Vasilisa und Luker'ja Čechov in Jalta wirklich begegnet sind und in seinem Leben eine gewisse Rolle gespielt haben, wie es nach dem

[9] Vgl. die entsprechende Notiz in der bereits genannten Oxfordedition S. 137. In V. Dal', *Poslovicy russkogo naroda,* Moskva 1957 scheinen ähnliche Formulierungen nicht mit aufgenommen zu sein.
[10] Vgl. V. Dal', a.a.O., S. 511: Великий богослов: все праздники знает по перстам (все праздники наизусть, на перечете).

umfangreichen Briefwechsel unseres Dichters durchaus naheliegt. Für die etwas stärker hervortretende Vasilisa könnte Aleksandra Alekseevna Kiseleva Vorbild gewesen sein, die in Čechovs Briefwechsel (XIII und folgende) entgegen ihrem eigentlichen Namen so bezeichnet wird. Vasilisa und Luker'ja scheinen darüber hinaus keine eigentliche Tradition im großrussischen Raum zu besitzen: Heilige dieses Namens hat es dort nicht gegeben, [11] wie überhaupt weibliche Heilige in der russisch-orthodoxen Kirche recht selten sind. Dagegen wird eine Deutung nach griechischer, byzantinischer wie neugriechischer Seite sich im Rahmen der inneren Möglichkeiten bewegen: Vasilisa wird mit dem griechischen „βασιλεύουσα" in der Namensform mit „Βασιλίσσα" (Himmelskönigin) zusammenhängen, was unter Berücksichtigung der neueren Aussprache (β = v) noch näher anklingt. Luker'ja soll — wie, das mögen die Philologen erklären — der griechischen Namensform von Γλυκερία entsprechen. Geht man dann aber der inneren Bedeutung dieser beiden Vornamen nach, so wird doch in dem ersten Fall Regierung und Rechtsprechung nach dem Begriff der Wahrheit, im anderen Fall die Anmut und Schönheit betont: damit käme man dann von ganz anderer Warte aus zu den von G. Jacobsson zuletzt herausgestellten Grundidealen von Wahrheit und Schönheit.

Nimmt man einen moderneren russischen Heiligenkalender zur Hand [12] — bei den griechischen entsprechenden Ausgaben findet man hinsichtlich Vasilisa zum Teil andere Daten [13] — so sind die Gedenktage der griechischen Vasilisa etwa am 10/23. März, am 15/28. April, am 16/29. April sowie am 3/16. September angesetzt, während die entsprechenden Daten für Glykeria nach griechischen wie russischen Belegen am 13/25. Mai, beziehungsweise am 2. Oktober/4. November, also in einer Zeit liegen, die sich zu bedeutenden Teilen mit der üblichen Placierung der Osterwoche deckt. Von hier aus gesehen könnte man auf den Gedanken kommen, daß sich Čechov bei der Namengebung der Heldinnen wenn nicht anders so doch etwa an ein Kalenderblatt gehalten hat, welches derartige Gedenktage immer festgehalten hat: ist doch die Novelle selbst im März 1894 in Jalta geschrieben!

Wenn der Student in der Erzählung so lebenswahr und nachdrücklich die Geschichte von Petri Verleugnung in starker bibelnaher Sprache vorträgt und in dem ganzen mit einander verwachsenen Geschehen der

---

[11] Vgl. etwa N. P. Barsukov, *Istočniki russkoj agiografii*, Peterburg 1882.

[12] Vgl. *Pravoslavnyj cerkovnyj kalendar' na 1956 god*, Moskva o.J.

[13] Tr. E. Euangelides, Οἱ βίοι τῶν ἁγίων, Athen 1895, bringt z.B. S. 61 f. ähnlich wie M. Gedeon, Βυζαντινὸν ἑορτολόγιον, Konstantinopel 1899, S. 55 bereits im Januar die Notizen zu einer Vasilisa. Da sich Čechov jedoch vornehmlich an den russischen Festkalender gehalten haben wird, muß diesem hier auch der Vorzug gegeben werden.

verschiedenen Handlungen eine deutliche Sinnesänderung der Personen vorgezeichnet wird, so soll damit vielleicht auch im Sinne unseres Dichters zusätzlich noch etwas zum Ausdruck kommen. Weit wirkungsvoller als alle menschlichen Betrachtungen und Erwägungen, besser als langatmige Predigten oder theoretische Vorhaltungen ist und bleibt die Bibel mit ihrer stets gültigen Sprache und mit ihren richtungweisenden Exempeln: eine Erkenntnis, der Čechov als Mensch und Dichter recht nahegestanden hat und die keines Kommentares bedarf.

Damit sind einige Möglichkeiten angedeutet, die bei einer Einschätzung von Čechovs Novelle „Der Student" eine Rolle spielen könnten und die — mit der vorstehenden Analyse von G. Jacobsson kombiniert — größere Durchschlagskraft gewinnen würden. Daß es nicht mehr als eben nur Möglichkeiten sind, ist in der Natur der Sache begründet, muß jedem einsichtigen Menschen offenbar sein und kann bei einem liebevollen Nacherleben des dichterischen Stoffes niemandem übel genommen werden.

SOPHIE LAFFITTE

ČECHOV ET TOLSTOJ

> „Mon rôle n'est pas de transformer le monde ni
> l'homme. Mais il est peut-être de servir à ma place
> les quelques valeurs sans lesquelles un monde, même
> transformé, ne vaut pas la peine d'être vécu."
>
> (Albert Camus)

Ils appartenaient à deux générations différentes. Quand le jeune lycéen de Taganrog entendit pour la première fois le nom de Tolstoj, celui-ci était déjà l'auteur fameux d'„Enfance", des „Cosaques", de „Guerre et paix". Immédiatement, Tolstoj devient l'écrivain préféré de Čechov, celui qu'il appellera le No. 1 de la littérature et de l'art russe. Tolstoj, lui, ne lira sérieusement Čechov qu'en 1888, après la publication du recueil „Au crépuscule" (*V sumerkach*) qui avait obtenu l'année précédente le prix Puškin et apporté à Čechov une large notoriété. Ce premier contact avec l'oeuvre čechovienne inspire à Tolstoj des réflexions désabusées. Il note dans son Journal: „Je lis de jolies petites choses de Čechov. Il aime les enfants et les femmes, mais ce n'est pas assez [1]... Ce n'est pas bien, c'est mesquin... Seul, toute la soirée, ai encore lu Čechov. Il a la faculté d'aimer jusqu'à une sorte de voyance artistique, tout cela, pour le moment, en vain". [2]

Mais, les récits suivants de Čechov retiennent de plus en plus l'attention du maître de Jasnaja Poljana. „La steppe" l'enchante, la „Salle No. 6" et le „Moine noir" sont à ses yeux des oeuvres remarquables. Anton Pavlovič recueille de tous côtés les échos des appréciations flatteuses de Tolstoj; les amis et disciples de ce dernier l'invitent à collaborer aux éditions, d'inspiration tolstoïenne, du *Posrednik*; Lev Nikolaevič désire le connaître et s'offre à lui rendre visite le premier. Tout cela, Čechov le ressent d'autant plus vivement qu'il admire, qu'il aime profondément Tolstoj, son „écrivain préféré". [3] „Dans toute ma vie je n'ai respecté personne aussi profondément, aussi, pourrait-on dire, *totalement*, que Lev Nikolaevič..." [4] „Je n'ai aimé aucun homme autant que lui". [5]

---

[1] Tolstoj, „Journal intime", 15 Mars 1889.
[2] Tolstoj, „Journal intime", 17 Mars 1889.
[3] Lettre à V. A. Tichonov, 22 Juin 1892.
[4] Lettre à I. Gorbunov-Posadov, 9 Novembre 1898.
[5] Lettre à M. O. Menšikov, 28 Janvier 1900.

La première rencontre des deux écrivains ne devait avoir lieu, cependant, que le 8 Août 1895 à Jasnaja Poljana (la dernière, le 31 Mars 1902, en Crimée).

A son ami et correspondant habituel, Aleksej Suvorin, Čechov décrit sa première visite à Tolstoj, l'impression „magnifique" qu'il en retire, leurs „conversations faciles et aisées". [6] Et il ajoute : „Les filles de Tolstoj sont très sympathiques, elles adorent leur père et croient fanatiquement en lui. Cela veut dire que Tolstoj représente une grande force morale, car, s'il n'était pas sincère et sans reproche, ses filles, les premières seraient sceptiques à son égard. On peut tromper facilement une fiancée, une maîtresse; aux yeux d'une femme amoureuse, même un âne peut paraître un philosophe; mais pour des filles, il en va tout autrement". [7]

Il est charmé, subjugué par la personnalité de Tolstoj : „Comme cet homme est intéressant! Si on tentait de l'étudier de près, on risquerait de se noyer en lui comme dans un puits sans fond. Et quelle force morale immense! Quand on parle avec lui, on se sent entièrement en son pouvoir. Je n'ai jamais rencontré d'être plus séduisant, plus harmonieusement conçu. C'est un homme presque parfait". [8]

Quant à Tolstoj, il écrit à son fils Lev : „Čechov est venu nous voir et m'a plu. Il est très doué et son coeur me paraît excellent; mais il n'a pas encore de vision du monde bien définie". [9]

Dès cette première rencontre, apparaissent avec évidence les différences de tempérament des deux hommes, ainsi que des buts qu'ils se proposent en tant qu'artistes. Un dédoublement constant caractérise leur attitude réciproque. Tolstoj oscille entre des appréciations enthousiastes, dès qu'il consent à n'être qu'un simple lecteur et à se laisser subjuguer par la finesse, la vérité et la poésie de l'art čechovien, et la plus vive réprobation aussitôt qu'il reprend son attitude de critique et de juge. Réprobation du „vide", de l'inutilité, du manque de „fond" [10] de cet art qui sert d'excellente illustration à sa condamnation si sévère de toute la littérature contemporaine.

Chez Čechov, admiration illimitée et fidèle envers l'homme et l'artiste; attrait passager envers les idées du philosophe et du moraliste; enfin, divorce absolu d'avec le „tolstoïsme".

---

[6] Lettre à A. Suvorin, 21 Octobre 1895.
[7] Lettre à A. Suvorin, 26 Octobre 1895.
[8] Paroles de Čechov citées par B. A. Ščetinin, „Dans la fourmillière littéraire" (*Istoričeskij Vestnik* 1911, No. 33, p. 881).
[9] Tolstoj, lettre à son fils Lev, 4 Septembre 1895.
[10] Tolstoj, lettre à V. G. Čertkov, 30 Nov. 1901; „Journal intime", 17 Mars 1889.

Ce „dédoublement" se manifeste dès les 2 jours, passés ensemble, d'Août 1895. [11] Tolstoj écrit à ce moment là „Résurrection". Il en fait lire quelques passages à Čechov. Anton Pavlovič admire, mais fait des réserves. Il les exprimera, plus tard, une fois le roman terminé, dans une lettre à M. O. Menšikov:

„J'ai lu „Résurrection" d'un seul coup, avec passion. C'est une remarquable oeuvre d'art. Le moins intéressant sont les rapports de Nechljudov et de Katjuša; le plus intéressant — les princes, les généraux, les vieilles tantes, les moujiks, les prisonniers, les gardiens de prison. La scène chez le général, commandant de la forteresse St Pierre et Paul, je l'ai lue, le souffle coupé, tellement c'est beau... Mais le roman n'a pas de dénouement, ce qui en tient lieu ne peut pas être considéré comme tel. Ecrire, écrire, et puis, tout à coup, tout rejeter sur un texte de l'Évangile, c'est vraiment par trop le fait d'un théologien. Il est aussi arbitraire de tout trancher avec un passage de l'Évangile que de classer les prisonniers en 5 catégories. Pourquoi cinq et pas dix? Pourquoi un texte de l'Évangile et pas du Coran? Il faudrait d'abord nous faire croire à l'Évangile, nous faire croire qu'en lui seul est la vérité, et seulement après tout trancher par un texte tiré de lui..." [12] „Résurrection" est un remarquable roman. Je l'ai beaucoup aimé ... Mais la fin est sans intérêt et fausse". [13]

Ce jugement rejoint en quelque sorte celui que Čechov avait émis sur la „Sonate à Kreutzer" et, surtout, sur la „Postface" de Tolstoj à cette même oeuvre:

„Est-ce possible que vous n'aimiez pas la „Sonate à Kreutzer"? Je ne dirais pas que c'est une oeuvre géniale, éternelle, pour celà je ne suis pas juge; mais, à mon sens, dans la masse de tout ce que l'on écrit maintenant chez nous et à l'étranger, il est douteux qu'on puisse trouver quoi que ce soit qui l'égale par la grandeur de la conception et la beauté de l'exécution. Sans parler des qualités artistiques qui, par endroit, sont étonnantes, on peut dire merci à ce livre de stimuler à un tel degré la pensée. En le lisant, on se retient à peine de crier: „C'est vrai!" ou: „C'est inepte!". Il est vrai que le récit a des défauts agaçants... Il y a quelque chose qu'on n'a pas envie de pardonner à l'auteur, c'est l'audace avec laquelle il traite des choses qu'il ne connaît pas et que, par entêtement, il refuse de connaître. Ainsi, ses jugements sur la syphilis, les maisons de redressement, sur l'horreur de la femme envers l'acte sexuel, etc... peuvent non seulement être contestés mais révèlent un homme ignorant, n'ayant pas fait, durant sa longue vie, l'effort de lire deux ou trois ouvrages

---

[11] 8-9 Août.
[12] Lettre à M. O. Menšikov, 28 Janv. 1900.
[13] Lettre à A. Suvorin, 12 Févr. 1900.

écrits par des spécialistes. Et pourtant, ces défauts s'envolent comme plumes au vent; étant données les qualités du récit, ou bien on ne les remarque pas, ou bien, les ayant remarqués, on déplore que cette oeuvre n'ait pas évité le sort de toutes les oeuvre humaines, imparfaites et non exemptes de souillures." [14]

Quant à la „Postface" à la „Sonate à Kreutzer", elle a le don d'irriter profondément Čechov :

„Avant-hier j'ai lu la „Postface". Dites ce que vous voulez, mais c'est plus bête et plus étouffant que les „Lettres à la femme du Gouverneur" [15] que je méprise. Que le diable emporte la philosophie des grands de ce monde! Tous les grands sages sont aussi despotiques que des généraux et aussi impolis et indélicats qu'eux, car ils sont sûrs de leur impunité. Diogène crachait à la figure des gens, sachant qu'il ne risquait rien en le faisant; Tolstoj traite les médecins de scélérats et fait preuve d'insolence envers les grands problèmes, car il est, lui aussi, un Diogène qu'on ne peut ni conduire au poste de police, ni attaquer dans les journaux. Donc, au diable la philosophie des grands de ce monde! Elle ne vaut pas, toute entière ... une seule des juments de *Cholstomer*". [16] [17]

Il critique l'assurance du philosophe, et, tout en admirant le génie de l'artiste, voit clairement ses faiblesses, son absence d'objectivité historique, ses irrésistibles parti-pris :

„Chaque nuit, je me réveille et relis „La Guerre et la paix". Je lis avec autant de curiosité et de naïf étonnement que la première fois. C'est remarquablement bien. Les seuls passages que je n'aime pas sont ceux où apparaît Napoléon. Dès qu'il est en scène, un malaise se fait jour ainsi que différents trucs tendant à le montrer plus bête qu'il n'était en réalité. Tout ce que font et disent Pierre, le prince André et même le totalement médiocre Nicolas Rostov, tout cela est bien, intelligent, naturel; tandis que ce que pense et fait Napoléon n'est ni naturel ni intelligent, mais boursouflé et d'un intérêt médiocre". [18]

Mais la plupart du temps, l'admiration envers l'artiste immense qu'est Tolstoj l'emporte : „Je relis Turgenev. C'est ravissant mais combien moins dense que Tolstoj! Tolstoj, à mon avis, ne vieillira jamais. Sa langue vieillira, mais lui restera toujours jeune". [19]

[14] Lettre à A. N. Pleščeev, 15 Février 1890.
[15] Allusion à un passage du livre de Gogol', „Morceaux choisis de ma correspondance avec mes amis".
[16] Titre d'une nouvelle de Tolstoj.
[17] Lettre à A. Suvorin, 8 Septembre 1891.
[18] Lettre à A. Suvorin, 25 Octobre 1891.
[19] Lettre à A. Suvorin, 13 Février 1893.

Quant à Tolstoj, sa dualité personnelle influe constamment sur ses jugements :

> „La littérature contemporaine est toute entière basée sur une beauté formelle et une absence totale de nouveauté dans les sujets ... Lisez, par exemple, Anton Čechov. La forme est parfaite. Mais de quelle utilité peut être tout ce qu'il écrit ! ... Où est chez lui cet élément *nouveau* qui doit faire progresser la société, lui montrer ses erreurs, lui ouvrir les yeux sur des phénomènes nouveaux du monde spirituel, sur une voie nouvelle de perfectionnement moral ? Cet élément là est absent [chez Čechov] ! ... Où est l'idée directrice de ses oeuvres ? On les lit et on se demande : „Pourquoi les a-t-il écrites, perdu tant de temps, travaillé ?''... Où est chez lui cette pensée qui spiritualise, qui rend immortelles les oeuvres vraiment grandes de l'esprit et du coeur humain, comme, par exemple, l'Évangile ?'' [20]

Et dans une lettre à sa femme, il se plaint que „tous ceux qui écrivent, tous ces Čechov, Zola et Maupassant ne savent même pas ce qui est bien et ce qui est mal. La plupart du temps, ils considèrent comme bien ce qui est mal, l'offrent sous les apparences de l'art au public et le pervertissent''. [21]

Mais après avoir lu „Une morne histoire'', Tolstoj parle avec enthousiasme de l'art et de l'intelligence de Čechov. „Quel étrange écrivain ! Il jette les mots de ci, de là comme par hasard et, cependant, tout chez lui vit. Et que d'intelligence ! Jamais il n'y a de détails superflus, chacun est, ou bien indispensable, ou bien plein de beauté''. Et il ajoutait que la langue de Čechov était, peut-être, la plus belle de toute la littérature russe. [22]

Au moment de sa première rencontre avec Tolstoj, en 1895, Čechov était déjà presque entièrement libéré de l'emprise, de „l'hypnose'' des doctrines tolstoïennes. Cette „hypnose'' avait, cependant, pendant près de 7 ans, fortement marqué son oeuvre.

Au fond, rien n'était plus opposé à la nature profonde de Čechov que le tolstoïsme. La raison de cette emprise doit, semble-t-il, être cherchée dans une certaine vacuité, une certaine disponibilité intérieure qui, pendant longtemps, caractérisa Čechov. Il n'était pas croyant, n'avait pas de convictions politiques fermes, ne possédait aucune „Weltanschauung'' bien établie, sans laquelle peut difficilement vivre un homme pensant, surtout s'il est Russe et s'il possède une nature aussi

---

[20] Paroles de Tolstoj rapportées par A. V. Jirkevič, „Rencontres avec Tolstoj'', 1890 (Dans *Literaturnoe nasledstvo,* 37/38, pp. 421-422-424).
[21] Tolstoj, Lettre à sa femme, 20 Octobre 1893.
[22] Paroles de Tolstoj raportées par A. B. Gol'denvajzer, „Près de Tolstoj'' — Moscou, Goslitizdat, 1959 ; pp. 98 et 393.

réfléchie, aussi avide de vérité que celle de Čechov. „Une vie consciente, sans une conception du monde bien définie, n'est pas une vie, mais un fardeau, une horreur", écrit-il à Suvorin le 28 Novembre 1888. Et il note dans ses *Carnets*: „Le bonheur et la joie de la vie ne sont ni dans l'argent, ni dans l'amour, mais dans la vérité". Mais qu'entend-il par vérité? Jusqu'ici, Čechov n'avait su la définir que par la négative: „La norme m'est inconnue, comme elle est inconnue de nous tous. Tous, nous savons ce qu'est une action malhonnête, mais nous ignorons ce qu'est l'honnêtete", écrit-il à Pleščeev. [23] À cette époque, dans les années 80, années où justement commence pour lui l'envoûtement tolstoïen, les mobiles qui règlent sa conduite sont effectivement d'essence négative.

Il n'a pas encore rompu à cette époque avec ce qu'il appelle son *héritage d'esclave*, [24] cette somme de mensonge, d'oppression, d'hypocrisie, d'envie, de grossièreté et d'ignorance qui forme le décor familier de son enfance et de son adolescence. Mais toutes les négations, tous les refus qu'il lui oppose se résument essentiellement en ceci: sa haine de toute injustice, partant, de toute autorité abusive. Pour lui, cette haïssable notion d'autorité se trouve à la source de tout mal. C'est l'autorité, quelle qu'elle soit, qui est génératrice de mensonge, d'hypocrisie et de violence. Et Čechov entend la rejeter, comme il rejette tout ce qui est inertie, oppression ou despotisme: „Je ne suis ni un libéral, ni un conservateur. Mon saint des saints, c'est le corps humain, la santé, l'intelligence, le talent, l'inspiration, l'amour de la liberté la plus absolue, la libération de toute force brutale et de tout mensonge, de quelque manière qu'ils s'expriment: voilà ce qui serait mon programme si j'étais un grand artiste". [25] Onze ans plus tard, une lettre de Maksim Gor'kij semble confirmer que ce programme a été réalisé: „Je suis formidablement heureux de vous avoir rencontré! Vous êtes, je crois, le premier homme *libre* que j'aie connu, *le premier qui n'adore*

---

[23] Lettre du 9 Avril 1889.
[24] Lettre à A. Suvorin, Janv. 1889. „Ce que les écrivains de la noblesse reçoivent „gratuitement", par droit de naissance, les roturiers l'achètent au prix de leur jeunesse. Essayez donc d'écrire l'histoire d'un jeune homme, fils d'un serf, ancien boutiquier, chantre à l'église, lycéen, puis étudiant. Dressé à courber l'échine, à baiser les mains des popes; soumis aux idées d'autrui; reconnaissant pour chaque morceau de pain; cent fois rossé; courant, misérablement chaussé, donner quelques leçons; bagarreur; aimant torturer les animaux; acceptant avec gratitude les dîners des parents riches; hypocrite devant Dieu et devant les hommes, sans besoin aucun, simplement par conscience de sa propre nullité. Racontez donc comment ce jeune homme essaye de se libérer, goutte à goutte, de l'esclave qui est en lui et comment, se réveillant un beau matin, il se rend compte que ce n'est plus un *sang d'esclave* qui coule dans ses veines, mais le sang d'un être humain". — Cette lettre célèbre figure, à juste titre, dans toutes les biographies de Čechov.
[25] Lettre à A. Pleščeev, 4 Oct. 1888.

rien". [26] Et quand son ami Ivan Ščeglov lui demande ce qu'il aime et ce qu'il déteste par dessus tout, Čechov répond: „J'aime la nature et la littérature, j'aime les jolies femmes et je hais la routine et le despotisme. — Le despotisme politique? — Tout despotisme, où qu'il se manifeste".

Mais on ne saurait vivre dans le seul négatif. Parfaitement conscient de ce qu'il méprise et de ce qu'il hait, Čechov cherche passionnément ce qu'il pourrait admirer et aimer. Et c'est ainsi qu'il succombe, vers 1886, à l'envoûtement, à l'hypnose du génie tolstoïen. Ce génie puissant, fort de ses certitudes, affirmant *sa* vérité, subjugue, aussi paradoxal que cela puisse paraître, le contempteur de toute autorité qu'est le jeune Čechov. Il croit avoir trouvé dans l'utopie sociale de Tolstoj une conception du monde harmonieuse et cohérente. Cette morale sociale, basée sur des principes de perfectionnement intime, offrait à chaque individu une série de recettes permettant de lutter contre les injustices et les inégalités de l'ordre établi: limitation des besoins, ascétisme, travail manuel, retour à la terre et à la vie naturelle.

Attaché par toutes les forces de son être à l'idée de justice; de par son activité de journaliste, puis de médecin, observateur quotidien des pires iniquités sociales; incrédule par tempérament, et étranger aux milieux où se préparait la Révolution, Čechov met en doute l'éventualité même d'un bouleversement social. „Il n'y aura jamais de révolution en Russie", écrit-il à Pleščeev. [27] L'utopie tolstoïenne reste pour lui la seule issue concrète, en cette période de l'histoire de Russie où la réaction politique paraissait particulièrement pesante et où l'individu se sentait écrasé par une morne et accablante inertie. Exprimée en termes simples et exaltants, la doctrine monolithique de Tolstoj séduisit Čechov par son caractère à la fois anticlérical, individualiste et foncièrement idéaliste.

Mais, nouvelle Arcadie, cette conception du monde reste par trop simpliste et féodale pour pouvoir satisfaire pendant longtemps un esprit aussi rigoureux, aussi précis, aussi scientifique que le sien. Tolstoj, riche aristocrate, disciple de Rousseau, cherche à renoncer aux biens de ce monde, à se „simplifier" (*oprostit'sja*), à descendre au niveau de ses paysans. Čechov, petit-fils de serf, [28] lutte pied à pied pour s'élever, pour se libérer du „sang d'esclave" qui est en lui. Il éprouve un attachement passionné pour le progrès et la culture. La

---

[26] Gor'kij, Lettre à Čechov, 22/25 Avril 1899.

[27] Lettre du 9 Février 1888.

[28] Détail curieux: le grand-père paternel de Čechov, Egor Michajlovič Čech, avait été serf du propriétaire foncier Čertkov, père du fameux ami et disciple de Tolstoj, Vladimir Grigor'evič Čertkov.

conjonction de deux esprits aussi dissemblables, de deux sensibilités aussi opposées ne pouvait évidemment qu'être éphémère.

Dès 1891, Čechov écrit à Suvorin: „J'aurais envie maintenant de tapis, d'une cheminée, de bronzes, de discussions savantes! Hélas, je ne serai jamais un disciple de Tolstoj...! Chez les femmes, j'aime avant tout la beauté, dans l'histoire de l'humanité, la culture qui s'exprime dans les tapis, les équipages à ressorts et l'acuité de la pensée". [29] „L'hypnose" tolstoïenne s'était dissipée sous l'influence directe de la réalité, de celle, par exemple, que Čechov avait pu observer pendant son voyage à Sachalin (1890). Voyage trop peu connu et d'où il rapporte une extraordinaire moisson d'expériences, une maturité nouvelle et un document d'une valeur unique, „L'Ile de Sachalin". „Je l'ai écrit en 1893 ... c'est un travail académique ... La médecine ne peut plus m'accuser de trahison et j'ai ainsi payé mon tribut à la science. Je suis heureux que dans ma garde-robe d'écrivain ait aussi sa place ce dur vêtement de condamné". [30]

Le 27 Mars 1894, une lettre à Suvorin devait faire le bilan de l'unique grande passion intellectuelle de Čechov:

> „La morale tolstoïenne a cessé de me toucher jusqu'au fond de mon âme, je n'ai plus de sympathie pour elle, ce qui, sans doute, est injuste. Mais c'est parce que le sang qui coule dans mes veines est un sang de moujik et qu'on ne peut guère m'étonner avec des vertus de moujik. Dès mon enfance, j'ai appris à croire au progrès et n'aurais pas pu ne pas y croire car la différence entre l'époque où l'on me fouettait et celle où l'on a cessé de le faire, était terrible. J'aime les hommes intelligents, la sensibilité, la politesse, l'esprit ... Quant à la philosophie tolstoïenne, elle m'a touché profondément, j'ai été subjugué par elle pendant environ 6-7 ans, et ce qui agissait sur moi, *ce ne sont pas ses préceptes fondamentaux* ... mais la manière tolstoïenne de s'exprimer, son haut bon sens et, sans doute, *une sorte d'hypnose*. Mais maintenant, quelque chose en moi proteste. *Le raisonnement et le sens de la justice me disent que dans l'électricité et la vapeur il y a plus d'amour du prochain que dans la chasteté et le refus de manger de la viande".

Si l'électricité et la vapeur sont plus valables que la chasteté et l'abstinence, c'est qu'elles représentent le progrès, tandis que l'ascétisme tolstoïen renferme au contraire un obscur ferment réactionnaire, implique le retour à un idéal rétrograde et médiéval. Čechov croit au progrès, aime la civilisation et la science. Tolstoj les condamne, comme il condamne la musique, le théâtre, les arts, si chers à Čechov.

[29] Lettre à A. Suvorin, 30 Août 1891.
[30] Lettre à A. Suvorin, 1894.

Et, cependant, profonde et durable fut l'influence tolstoïenne sur l'oeuvre de Čechov. Dès 1886, cette influence est très nette dans une nouvelle telle que „Les braves gens" (*Chorošie ljudi*) et, l'année suivante, dans une série de courts récits, „Le mendiant", „La rencontre", „Le cosaque", „La lettre". Il est frappant de constater que le plus tolstoïen de ces récits, celui qui ressemble à une illustration pure et simple de la thèse tolstoïenne de non-résistance au mal par la violence, „La rencontre", soit aussi le plus faible au point de vue artistique, le plus puéril, le plus naïf. On a l'impression très nette que l'influence du maître de Jasnaja Poljana reste superficielle, comme plaquée, et ne pénètre à aucun moment les couches profondes de la création čechovienne. Artiste exceptionnellement personnel et indépendant, Čechov ne pouvait pas se soumettre à des canons esthétiques, aussi originaux fussent-ils, autres que les siens. Envoûté, entraîné par le souffle grandiose de celui qui fut à la fois le Rousseau et le Luther de la Russie, Čechov ne fut jamais vraiment pénétré par le puritanisme et l'absolutisme si contraires à sa nature qui sont à la base de la *doctrine* de Tolstoj. [31] Et ce produit si typiquement „tolstoïen", „La rencontre", est une oeuvre ratée, à laquelle manque tout ce qui rend inimitable l'art de Čechov: son extrême laconisme, son sens du détail typique et frappant, sa simplicité, sa poésie, son naturel souverain. Conscient de ce „ratage", Čechov refusa d'inclure „La rencontre" dans la 1ère édition complète de ses oeuvres.

Mais, par contre, les oeuvres dans lesquelles Čechov s'oppose à Tolstoj ont une portée et un intérêt profond. Les plus frappantes sont „Une morne histoire" (1889), „La salle No. 6" (1892), „Ma vie" (1896) et „Groseilles à maquereaux" (1898).

Quand parut „Une morne histoire", la majorité de la critique l'accueillit comme une réplique à la „Mort d'Ivan Il'ič" [32] (1884). Cette assertion est fausse car, malgré un parallélisme certain de situations, la pensée qui anime les deux récits et les conclusions divergentes auxquelles ils aboutissent reflètent l'opposition fondamentale entre les natures profondes de leurs auteurs. Rien n'est plus intéressant que de voir la manière dont Tolstoj et Čechov traitent le même thème: celui d'un homme arrivé au terme de sa vie et qui se trouve placé, du fait de l'âge et de la maladie, face à la solitude et à la mort. Le Nikolaj

---

[31] Les plus grandes oeuvres artistiques de Tolstoj lui-même sont justement celles où ses conceptions philosophiques et morales sont le moins apparentes, celles où, d'après le mot de Turgenev, tel Antée, il touche à la terre (Lettre de Turgenev à P. Annenkov, 13/25 avril 1868).

[32] Récit que Tolstoj écrivit sous l'impression de la mort de quelqu'un qu'il avait bien connu, le frère d'Il'ja Mečnikov, Ivan Il'ič Mečnikov (1836-1881), atteint d'un cancer à l'estomac.

Stepanovič de Čechov, l'Ivan Il'ič de Tolstoj refont, dans cette ultime
solitude, le bilan de leur vie passée, revoient leurs erreurs, procèdent
à un vaste examen de conscience.

Qu'en résulte-t-il? Pour Tolstoj, la préoccupation morale est et reste
la fin dernière. Il juge et condamne sévèrement l'égoïste et falot Ivan
Il'ič qui, durant toute son existence, a ignoré ce qui doit régir la vraie
vie, c'est-à-dire la loi morale, la loi d'amour.

Cette loi fondamentale qu'il avait toujours ignorée, ce n'est qu'aux
portes de la mort qu'Ivan Il'ič apprendra à la connaître, grâce au
dévouement, à la pitié, à l'amour du simple Gerasim. Et cette mort lui
apportera en définitive une merveilleuse lumière, une fulgurante révélation :

> „Soudain, le problème qui l'obsédait s'éclaira de deux côtés, de
> dix côtés, sous toutes ses faces... Il n'avait plus peur, car il n'y
> avait plus de mort. Au lieu de la mort, il voyait la lumière. „Ah,
> voilà donc ce que c'est", prononça-t-il à haute voix. „Quelle joie!"
> Tout celà ne dura qu'un instant. *Mais l'importance de cet instant fut
> définitive.* — „C'est fini!" dit quelqu'un derrière son chevet. Il en-
> tendit ces paroles et se les répéta pour lui-même. „Finie la mort...
> La mort n'existe plus!" dit-il. Il fit un mouvement d'aspiration qui
> demeura inachevé, se raidit et mourut."

Dans une suprême révélation, Tolstoj fait comprendre à son héros ce
qu'est la vie et son indispensable corollaire, cette autre et sublime réalité
qu'est la mort.

Partant d'un point de vue tout différent, Čechov condamne son
Nikolaj Stepanovič à un scepticisme sans issue. Bon, intelligent, dés-
intéressé, passionnément attaché aux choses de l'esprit, le professeur
Nikolaj Stepanovič est, dans toute l'acception du terme, un homme de
bien. Mais, malgré sa façade glorieuse et brillante, la vie de cet homme
de bien est un échec. Pourquoi? Parce qu'aucune pensée synthétique,
aucune „idée générale", ne viennent cimenter, ordonner, diriger cette
activité intellectuelle vers un but supérieur et clairement défini. Rappelons encore une fois ce qu'écrivait Čechov à Suvorin au moment même
où il composait „Une morne histoire" : „Une vie consciente sans une
conception du monde bien définie, n'est pas une vie, mais un fardeau,
une horreur". [33]

Nikolaj Stepanovič est un médecin-poète, fanatique de la science,
mais en même temps amoureux de toute beauté; amateur de parfums,
de romans français et d'élégance ; conférencier de talent, véritable chef
d'orchestre lorsqu'il est en chaire; capable d'introduire dans ses
démonstrations scientifiques des éléments d'humour et de fantaisie; et

[33] Lettre à Aleksej Suvorin, 28 Nov. 1888.

qui, en vrai poète, croit profondément à l'inspiration, à l'intuition, à l'esprit de synthèse, à tout ce qui différencie un grand scientifique des ternes artisans de la science, pour lesquels et lui et Čechov n'ont qu'éloignement et mépris. Mais ... Mais, s'il continue à croire „que la science est la chose la plus importante, la plus belle et la plus nécessaire dans la vie humaine; qu'elle a toujours été et sera toujours la plus haute manifestation d'amour et que c'est grâce à elle que l'homme parviendra à triompher et de la matière et de lui-même", [34] cette croyance, cette certitude restent, chez lui, toutes théoriques, toutes passives. Dans la vie, il est plus désarmé qu'un enfant, ses méditations, ses pensées, ses rêves restent désincarnés et ne deviennent à aucun moment un outil pratique, efficace, concret, lui permettant d'être secourable et utile. Étrangement privé, malgré sa noblesse native, de ce que Čechov appelait le „talent humain" ou faculté d'amour agissant. Étrangement incapable, malgré son intelligence et sa science, de bâtir une conception du monde qui canaliserait vers un but précis tant d'aspirations éparses et de velléités inemployées. Aussi, reste-t-il impuissant devant les drames qui se jouent autour de lui. Impuissant, désemparé et, en fin de compte, vaincu et stérile.

Tolstoj s'élève avec véhémence, juge, condamne, et absout. Avec l'infaillible sûreté d'un démiurge, il conduit sa créature à travers une suite de circonstances inexorables vers une fin, connue de lui seul, et qu'il impose avec une force souveraine.

Čechov ne domine pas, n'impose pas, ne conduit pas. Il dialogue avec lui-même et ce dialogue est poignant parce que, dissimulé avec son habituelle pudeur derrière le personnage de Nikolaj Stepanovič, l'auteur nous dit ses propres dégoûts, ses propres attachements passionnés. Il observe, il critique, il hésite, il souffre. Mais rien de positif ne découle de ce long soliloque. Que faire?, demande Katja, Nikolaj Stepanovič, dites-moi, que faire? Et Nikolaj Stepanovič répond avec Čechov: je ne sais pas, Katja, je ne sais pas! [35] „Je la regardais, dit Nikolaj Stepanovič, et j'avais honte d'être plus heureux qu'elle. L'absence de ce que mes amis les philosophes appellent idée générale, cette absence, je ne l'ai constatée chez moi que peu de temps avant ma mort tandis que l'âme de cette pauvrette ne trouvera jamais de repos, ne le connaîtra pas durant toute sa vie... Il est clair que dans mes désirs, ... dans ma passion de la science, dans mon désir de vivre... dans toutes mes pensées, aspirations et conceptions, il manque ce quelque chose de

---

[34] „Une morne histoire".

[35] „Aidez-moi, sanglote Katja,... Vous êtes mon père, mon seul ami! Vous êtes intelligent, instruit, vous avez derrière vous une longue vie! Vous avez été un maître... Dites-moi, dites: que dois-je faire?" — „Sur mon honneur, Katja, je ne le sais pas..."

général, de commun qui leur servirait de lien. Chaque sentiment et chaque pensée vivent en moi isolément et [dans tout celà] ... même l'analyste le plus adroit ne pourrait trouver rien qui ressemble à une idée générale ou au Dieu d'un homme vivant."

Et quand, quelques années plus tard, Suvorin critique la „Salle No. 6", Čechov semble commenter dans sa réponse les pensées mêmes de son Nikolaj Stepanovič:

„Il n'est pas difficile de vous comprendre... Vous êtes un sombre ivrogne et moi, je vous ai offert de la limonade sucrée! Tout en rendant justice à la limonade, vous remarquez à bon droit qu'elle manque d'alcool. Dans nos oeuvres, il manque précisément cet alcool qui enivre et subjugue, et çà, vous me le faites très bien comprendre. Pourquoi manque-t-il? ... Nous manquons de „quelque chose", c'est exact, et cela veut dire que si vous soulevez la robe de notre muse, vous y verrez un vide. Rappelez-vous que les écrivains que nous appelons éternels ou simplement grands et qui nous enivrent, ont tous un trait commun et très important: *ils se dirigent quelque part et nous appellent avec eux* et vous sentez, non avec votre esprit, mais avec tout votre être, qu'ils ont un but déterminé... Les meilleurs d'entre eux sont réalistes et décrivent la vie telle qu'elle est, mais, parce que chacune de leurs lignes est imprégnée, comme d'un suc, de la conscience de leur but, vous sentez, en plus de la vie, telle qu'elle est, encore la vie comme elle devrait être, et c'est celà qui vous séduit. Mais nous, nous! Nous peignons la vie telle qu'elle est et après, plus rien, rien, même si vous vouliez nous stimuler avec des verges. Nous n'avons de buts ni proches, ni lointains et notre âme est vide, totalement vide. Nous n'avons pas de vues politiques, nous ne croyons pas à la révolution, Dieu n'existe pas, nous n'avons pas peur des revenants, et, personnellement, je ne crains ni la mort ni la cécité. Celui qui ne veut rien, n'espère en rien et n'a peur de rien, ne peut pas être un artiste... Oui, je suis assez intelligent pour au moins ne pas me cacher à moi-même mon mal et ne pas me mentir en masquant mon vide intérieur avec des haillons empruntés à autrui". [36]

Ces „haillons", empruntés à celui qui, lui, savait où il allait et dispensait généreusement cet „alcool" dont parle Čechov, ces „haillons" tolstoïens, Anton Pavlovič les avait déjà résolument rejetés dans „La Salle No. 6", une de ses créations les plus profondes et les plus sombres. Quelqu'un qu'on peut difficilement soupçonner de sensiblerie, Lénine, a écrit: „Quand j'ai eu fini de lire cette nouvelle, j'ai eu peur. Je ne pouvais plus rester seul dans ma chambre et sortis: tellement j'avais la sentation d'être emprisonné moi-même dans la Salle No. 6". Effective-

[36] Lettre à Aleksej Suvorin, 25 Novembre 1892.

ment, la force de ces pages est hallucinante. Le doux Dr Ragin, âme délicate et pure, qui, à toute science médicale, préfère Marc-Aurèle, Epictète et d'interminables discussions philosophiques, est un disciple de Tolstoj : „Je sers une cause nuisible, néfaste et suis payé par des gens que je trompe; je ne suis donc pas honnête. Mais, par moi-même, je ne suis rien qu'une parcelle d'un mal social inévitable : tous les fonctionnaires du district sont nuisibles et touchent leur traitement pour rien. Ce n'est donc pas moi qui suis responsable de ma malhonnêteté, mais l'époque où je vis. Si j'étais né 200 ans plus tard, j'aurais été tout autre". Et puis, à quoi sert la médecine en général :

„Pourquoi empêcher les hommes de mourir puisque la mort est la fin normale et légitime de chacun? A quoi cela avancerait-il si un quelconque boutiquier ou fonctionnaire voyait sa vie prolongée de 10, de 20 années? Et si l'on voit le but de la médecine dans le fait que les remèdes soulagent les souffrances, involontairement la question se pose : à quoi bon les soulager? Premièrement, on dit que les souffrances conduisent l'homme vers le perfection; deuxièmement, si l'humanité apprend à soulager ses souffrances avec des pilules et des gouttes, elle laissera fatalement de côté religion et philosophie dans lesquelles elle avait trouvé jusqu'ici non seulement un réconfort à tous ses maux mais aussi le bonheur. Puškin a éprouvé avant de mourir d'atroces souffrances; le pauvre Heine est resté plusieurs années paralysé. Pourquoi donc un quelconque X ou Y ne seraient-ils pas malades eux aussi, eux dont la vie est si médiocre que, privée de souffrances, elle serait totalement vide et semblable à la vie d'une amibe?"

Le bon, le doux Dr Ragin, qui, personnellement, ne ferait pas de mal à une mouche, se forge un système philosophique qui lui permet d'accepter les conditions atroces dans lesquelles vivent les malades de l'hôpital dont il a la charge, en particulier les malades de la salle No. 6, sous la férule du sinistre infirmier Nikita.

Mais voilà qu'il se lie d'une sorte d'étrange amitié avec l'un des pensionnaires de la salle No. 6, Gromov, interné pour maladie mentale. Ce malade est fin, sensible, passionné; il souffre atrocement de son internement.

„Quelle différence y a-t-il, lui dit le Dr Ragin, entre cette chambrée et un bureau tiède et confortable? La paix et la satisfaction, l'homme les trouve non en dehors de lui mais uniquement en lui-même ... Marc-Aurèle a dit que la douleur n'est autre chose que la représentation vivante que l'on se fait de la douleur. Faites un effort de volonté pour transformer cette représentation, rejetez-là, cessez de vous plaindre et la douleur disparaîtra. C'est juste. Le sage, ou, tout simplement l'homme qui pense, se distingue justement par son mépris de la souffrance; il est toujours content et ne s'étonne de rien...

Une pensée profonde et libre, qui s'efforce de comprendre les phé-
nomènes de la vie, et un mépris total de la stupide agitation du
monde, — voilà les deux plus grands bienfaits que l'homme ait connus. Et vous pouvez les acquérir tout en vivant derrière de triples
barreaux".

Cette paraphrase du précepte tolstoïen, „le Royaume de Dieu est
en nous", a le don de mettre Gromov en fureur:

„Je sais que Dieu m'a donné du sang chaud et des nerfs; tout tissu
organique vivant doit réagir à ce qui l'irrite. Et voilà, je réagis! À
la douleur, je réponds par des cris et des pleurs; à la bassesse, par
le mépris; à l'ignominie, par le dégoût. A mon avis, c'est justement
celà qu'on appelle vivre... Ici, on nous enferme, on nous torture, mais
c'est bien, c'est sage, car entre cette salle et un tiède et confortable
bureau, il n'y a aucune différence! Quelle plate et commode philosophie! On n'a besoin de rien faire, on a une conscience pure et on
se considère en plus comme un sage! Non, monsieur, celà ne
s'appelle ni philosophie, ni raisonnement, ni largeur de vue, mais
simplement paresse, immobilisme, abrutissement... Oui, vous mépri-
sez la souffrance, mais si on vous pinçait seulement un doigt dans
une porte, vous vous mettriez à hurler à pleins poumons!"

A cause de ses visites trop fréquentes et trop prolongées à un malade
mental, le Dr Ragin est, lui aussi, suspecté de dérangement cérébral et
finalement interné dans la salle No. 6. A son tour, il subit les bruta-
lités de Nikita et toute l'horreur de la privation de liberté. Sa philosophie quiétiste ne résiste pas un seul jour à l'injustice et à la souffrance.
Son calme intérieur, sa sérénité, son acceptation passive de la vie, se
muent en une révolte farouche au premier coup de poing de l'infirmier
Nikita. Sans théories, sans vaines paroles, à sa manière sobre, concrète
et irréfutable, Čechov montre l'inconsistance, la fausseté, face aux bru-
tales réalités de la vie, de la prédication tolstoïenne.
Mais ces problèmes continueront néanmoins à le hanter. Il y revien-
dra dans „Ma vie" (1896) et, avec plus de profondeur encore, dans
„Groseilles à maquereaux" (*Kryžovnik*) (1898). Comme toujours,
les résultats de ses méditations, il les livre sous le couvert d'une oeuvre
d'art, en se dissimulant derrière le masque de l'un de ses personnages,
ne parlant jamais à la première personne (à l'encontre de Tolstoj):
„On a l'habitude de dire qu'un homme n'a besoin que de 3 archines [37]
de terre. Mais c'est un cadavre qui n'a besoin que de 3 archines et non
un homme vivant. Et on dit encore que si notre intelliguentzia se sent
attirée par la terre et désire s'installer à la campagne, que c'est là une
bonne chose. Mais ces propriétés de campagne, c'est justement l'équi-

[37] Archine = 0,71 m.

valent des 3 archines de terre. Quitter la ville, la lutte, les remous de
l'existence et se cacher dans ses propriétés, çà ne s'appelle pas une vie,
mais de l'égoïsme, de la paresse, une sorte de retraite monacale,
exempte toutefois de tout ce qui en fait l'héroïsme. L'homme a besoin
non de 3 archines de terre, non de retraite à la campagne, mais du globe
terrestre tout entier, de la nature toute entière, où, libre et indépendant,
il pourra extérioriser tout ce qu'il a au fond de lui-même''.

C'est là la réponse de Čechov au célèbre conte de Tolstoj „De combien de terre l'homme a-t-il besoin?'' Tolstoj disait: 3 archines suffi-
sent. Cette philosophie de l'ascétisme, de refus de vivre, fait horreur à
Čechov. Les joies de ce monde, Tolstoj les avait toutes goûtées et s'en
détournait maintenant avec l'aversion et le mépris du moraliste et du
puritain qui vivaient en lui depuis toujours. Čechov, le malade, l'éternel
condamné reste attaché à la vie par toutes les fibres de son être. Il
éprouve une joie d'enfant à acheter de beaux objets, une montre en or,
une pelisse neuve. Sa table de travail est chargée de bibelots. Il aime
les objets bien faits, parce qu'à ses yeux le travail accompli avec amour,
intelligence et perfection est la suprême noblesse de l'homme. „Je
méprise la paresse, de même que je méprise la faiblesse et l'apathie des
mouvements de l'âme. Pour vivre bien, en homme digne de ce nom,
il faut travailler, travailler avec amour, avec foi''. [38] Malade, retiré à
Jalta, ayant renoncé à la médecine et à la vie active, il s'efforce de
créer autour de lui de la beauté. „Voyez-vous, dit-il à Aleksandr
Kuprin, c'est moi qui ai planté ici chaque arbre et, bien entendu, ils
me sont chers. Mais ce qui importe, ce n'est pas çà, c'est le fait
qu'avant moi il n'y avait ici que des terrains vagues et de stériles ravins,
remplis de pierrailles et de chardons savages. Puis je suis venu
et j'ai transformé ce coin perdu en un lieu de civilisation et de beauté.
Savez-vous? Dans trois, quatre cents ans toute la terre se transformera
en un jardin florissant. Et la vie sera alors étonnamment légère et
facile.'' [39] Cet espoir d'une vie meilleure coexiste bizarrement en lui
avec une parfaite lucidité quant à la condition actuelle de l'homme. Il
aime la vie, mais telle qu'elle devrait être, telle qu'elle serait si „les
hommes n'oubliaient pas les buts supérieurs de la vie et leur dignité
humaine''. [40] („Chez l'homme tout doit être beau, le visage, les vête-
ments, l'âme et les pensées''. [41]) Mais la vie russe qui l'entoure le
remplit d'amertume et de dégoût. Il lutte contre l'injustice et la misère
en soignant des malades, en créant des écoles, en alimentant des
bibliothèques, en aidant ceux quit font appel à lui. Tout cela à sa

---

[38] Lettre à A. Suvorin, 7 Avril 1897.

[39] A. Kuprin (cf. *Čechov v vospominanijach sovremennikov*, Moscou 1952,
p. 401).

[40] „La dame au petit chien'', 1899.

[41] „Oncle Vanja'', 1899.

manière silencieuse, modeste et efficace. Mais jamais il ne s'érige
en maître, jamais il ne se permet de prêcher ou d'enseigner. En toute
humilité, il avoue „ne pas comprendre": „Nous n'essayerons pas de
jouer aux charlatans et dirons très nettement qu'on ne peut rien comprendre en ce monde. Seuls les imbéciles et les charlatans comprennent
et savent tout". [42] Et trois mois avant sa mort, il écrit à sa femme:
„Tu me demandes: qu'est-ce que la vie? C'est comme si tu me deman-
dais: Qu'est-ce qu'une carotte? Une carotte est une carotte et on ne sait
rien d'autre". [43]

L'auteur le plus lu, le plus abondamment annoté de sa bibliothèque,
c'est Marc-Aurèle: „Ce qui nous sauve dans la vie, c'est de voir ce
qu'est *exactement* chaque objet, dans sa matière comme dans sa
forme". Que ces lignes sont conformes à l'esprit précis, pénétrant et
avide de connaissance de Čechov! De tous les grands écrivains russes,
il est celui qui se rapproche le plus du scientifique aussi bien par sa
structure intellectuelle que par ses procédés littéraires. Il en est lui-
même parfaitement conscient: „La pratique des sciences naturelles et
des méthodes scientifiques m'a rendu prudent et je me suis toujours
efforcé, chaque fois que c'était possible, de prendre en considération
les données de la science; lorsque c'était impossible, je préférais ne
pas écrire du tout". [44] Le but de l'artiste, c'est la vérité absolue,
l'homme ne pouvant „devenir meilleur que lorsqu'on le lui aura
montré à lui-même tel qu'il est". [45] Čechov entend se servir dans
son oeuvre de cet instrument de vérité qu'est la science, dont les
méthodes positives et efficaces ne sont nullement en contradiction avec
celles de la création artistique: „Celui qui possède la méthode scientifique, celui-là sent avec son âme qu'un morceau de musique et un arbre
ont quelque chose de commun, que l'un et l'autre sont créés d'après
des lois également logiques et simples". [46] Autant qu'un homme de
science, l'artiste doit savoir être objectif, „aussi objectif qu'un
chimiste". [47]

Tolstoj disait que Čechov aurait été un écrivain encore plus
grand s'il n'avait pas été médecin: „la médecine le gênait". Tolstoj
disait aussi: „La science est un lingot d'or fabriqué par un alchimiste
charlatan. Vous voulez la simplifier, la rendre accessible au peuple,
autrement dit, frapper une quantité de *fausse monnaie*. Le jour où le

---

[42] Lettre à Ivan Ščeglov, Juin 1888.
[43] Lettre à sa femme, Avril 1904.
[44] Čechov, Note autobiographique envoyée au Dr Rossolimo, le 11 Octobre
1899.
[45] Carnets.
[46] Lettre à A. Suvorin, 3 Novembre 1888.
[47] Lettre à M. Kiseleva, 15 Janvier 1887.

peuple s'apercevra de la valeur réelle de cette monnaie, il ne vous dira pas merci". [48]

Là encore, l'esprit concret, scientifique, objectif de l'un se heurtait à l'intelligence impérieuse, dogmatique et personnelle de l'autre.

La visite tant de fois décrite que Tolstoj fera à Čechov le 28 Mars 1897 ne changera rien à leur attitude respective: amitié et affection personnelles, divergence totale de pensée.

Se relevant à peine des suites d'une violente hémoptysie, Anton Pavlovič était en traitement dans la clinique moscovite du Dr Ostroumov. Il est très typique pour Tolstoj d'avoir aussitôt attaqué, au chevet d'un grand malade, un sujet que tout autre aurait soigneusement évité: celui de la mort et de l'immortalité de l'âme. Il avait intuitivement senti que le plus grand témoignage d'estime est, à l'égard de certains êtres nobles et forts, une parfaite et même brutale sincérité. Le thème de la mort avait toujours été l'un de ses thèmes majeurs et l'on pourrait presque dire que toute l'oeuvre tolstoïenne est un immense diptyque dont l'un des volets constitue l'hymne le plus exaltant à la gloire de la vie, l'autre — une glorification sans précédent de la mort (il suffit de rappeler ici les extraordinaires descriptions de la mort tout au long de cette oeuvre: la mère („Enfance"); le prince Andrej et le vieux prince Bolkonskij, dans „Guerre et paix"; Dmitrij Levin dans „Anna Karenina"; „Trois morts"; „La mort d'Ivan Il'ič"; etc, etc... Et aussi ces paroles énigmatiques, après la mort de son fils Vanečka: „Qu'est-ce que çà veut dire: il est mort? La mort n'existe pas, la mort n'existe pas!" [49]

L'idée de la mort poursuivra constamment Tolstoj. Dans les notes de son „Journal intime", très souvent, après la date, on trouve les trois mystérieuses lettres: c. b. ž. (*esli budu živ* — si je vis encore), sorte de formule magique destinée à écarter celle qu'il prétend ne pas craindre.[50]

Lors de sa longue visite à la clinique Ostroumov, Tolstoj expose à Čechov ses idées sur l'immortalité:

„Lev Nikolaevič est venu me voir et nous avons eu une très intéressante conversation, intéressante surtout pour moi qui écoutais plus que je ne parlais. Nous avons parlé de l'immortalité. Il croit à

---

[48] Paroles de Tolstoj rapportées par Gor'kij, *L. N. Tolstoj* (cf. Maxime Gorki, *Trois Russes,* Paris, Gallimard, 1935, p. 21).

[49] Paroles rapportées par Ivan Bunin, *Tolstoj* (Dans *Vospominanija,* Paris, Vozroždenie, 1950; pp. 76-77. — A rapprocher des dernières phrases de „la Mort d'Ivan Il'ič".

[50] Dans une lettre à Gor'kij du 15 févr. 1900, Čechov écrit, en parlant de „Résurrection": „Tout m'a frappé dans ce roman, et sa force, et sa richesse, et son envergure, et aussi l'absence de sincérité d'un homme *qui craint la mort, ne veut pas l'avouer* et se raccroche à des textes de l'Évangile".

l'immortalité dans un sens kantien : il pense que nous tous (hommes et animaux) survivrons au sein d'un principe (raison, amour) dont l'essence et le but constituent pour nous un mystère. Pour ce qui est de moi, ce principe ou élément m'apparaît sous la forme d'une masse informe et gélatineuse; que mon moi, ma personnalité, ma conscience se fondent avec cette masse, non, je ne le veux pas, je n'ai pas besoin d'une telle immortalité, je ne la comprends pas et Lev Niko-laevič s'étonne que je ne la comprenne pas". [51]

Tolstoj disait : „Toute la vie humaine m'apparaît sous la forme de ce dessin :

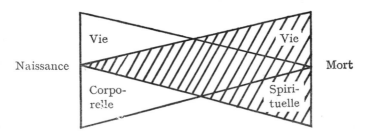

En naissant, nous sommes le plus fort physiquement, tout est devant nous. Spirituellement, nous sommes infiniment petits. La vie, elle, est une mort physique progressive et une croissance spirituelle, une libéra-tion. Cette infinie libération du „moi" spirituel est le sens même de la vie. C'est cela, la vie". [52] Et la mort, la libération suprême.

Là encore, sur cette question si grave, primordiale pour Tolstoj, Čechov n'est pas d'accord. Son esprit positif évite de penser à ce qui lui apparaît comme une horreur, un néant, un noir abîme. Quelques semaines après sa conversation avec Tolstoj, Čechov dit à Aleksej Suvorin :

„La mort est une cruauté, un affreux supplice... Je ne peux pas me consoler en pensant qu'après larmes et souffrances, je me fondrai dans la vie universelle qui a, dit-on, un but. Ce but, je ne le connais même pas. *La mort provoque en moi quelque chose de plus grand que la terreur.* Mais tant qu'on vit, on pense peu à elle, moi, tout au moins. Quand je mourrai, je verrai bien ce qu'il en est. C'est effrayant d'être réduit à néant. On vous porte au cimetière, puis on rentre chez soi, et on se met à boire du thé et à tenir des discours hypocrites. Cà me dégoûte, rien que d'y penser". [53]

Et il fait dire au Dr Ragin de „La salle No. 6" :

---

[51] Lettre à M. O. Menšikov, 16 Avril 1897.
[52] A. B. Gol'denvajzer, „Près de Tolstoj", Moscou, Goslitizdat, 1959; p. 153.
[53] Paroles de Čechov, notées par A. Suvorin dans son „Journal", le 23 Juin 1897.

„Oh, pourquoi l'homme n'est-il pas immortel? ... A quoi bon, la vue, la parole, la conscience, le génie, s'il est prescrit à tout cela de retourner à la terre, de se refroidir avec l'écorce terrestre et d'être ensuite emporté, sans but et sans pensée autour du soleil, en même temps que la terre, durant des millions et des millions d'années?... Les transformations de la matière! Quelle lâcheté de se consoler avec ce succédané de l'immortalité! ... Placer son immortalité dans l'évolution de la matière est aussi étrange que de prédire un brillant avenir à un écrin, quand le violon précieux qu'il contenait est brisé et hors d'usage".

C'est un aveu bien čechovien: on ne sait rien, on ne sait pas davantage ce qu'est la vie que ce qu'est la mort. Il note dans ses Carnets: „Il m'est affreux de penser que lorsqu'on inaugurera un monument à ma mémoire, il y aura des chambellans dans l'assistance".

Parler de sa propre mort avec cette sorte d'humour macabre est très caractéristique de Čechov. Il est non moins caractéristique pour son esprit positif d'écarter la pensée même d'une chose à la fois inaccessible à la raison et tragiquement inévitable. Et il est également caractéristique pour Tolstoj de s'élever par la pensée vers des régions éternelles et infinies, tout en se refusant, au fond de soi-même, de croire pleinement à la *réalité* de la mort, de *sa* mort. Car si la pensée de Tolstoj est foncièrement idéaliste, celle de Čechov se voudrait matérialiste. Pour lui,

„la tendance matérialiste n'est ni une école, ni une tendance... Ce n'est pas quelque chose de fortuit, de passager; c'est quelque chose de nécessaire, d'inévitable et qui échappe au pouvoir de l'homme. Tout ce qui vit sur la terre est nécessairement matérialiste... Les êtres supérieurs, les hommes qui pensent, *sont, eux aussi, matérialistes par nécessité. Ils cherchent la vérité dans la matière* et ne peuvent la chercher ailleurs, car ils ne voient, n'entendent et ne perçoivent que la matière seule... Interdire à l'homme d'être matérialiste équivaut à lui défendre de rechercher la vérité. En dehors de la matière, il n'y a ni expérience, ni connaissance possible, par conséquent il n'y a pas non plus de vérité". [54]

Mais, tout en affirmant son incroyance („je crains la religion", „je regarde avec étonnement tout intellectuel croyant"), Čechov avoue son respect profond pour „la foi, cette aptitude de l'âme qui n'est accessible qu'aux organismes supérieurs". [55] Et, si malgré tout ce qui les sépare, il se sent parfois si proche de Tolstoj, de sa soif, de sa quête perpétuelle de Dieu, c'est parce qu'il lui est arrivé à lui aussi d'écrire:

---

[54] Lettre à A. Suvorin, 7 Mai 1889.
[55] Carnets.

„Entre „Dieu existe" et „Dieu n'existe pas" s'étend tout un champ immense que traverse à grand' peine le vrai sage". [56]

Čechov a mis longtemps à traverser ce „champ", mais même définitivement devenu ce „rationaliste qui aime encore le son des cloches", [57] il transcrira cet aveu étrange pour un „rationaliste" convaincu: „Je méprise mon enveloppe matérielle et tout ce qui s'y rapporte". [57] Et, fait non moins paradoxal, il ne renoncera pas, jusqu'à la fin de sa vie, à terminer ses lettres par les formules de son enfance, „que Dieu soit avec toi", „que Dieu te garde", sans que cela puisse jamais être, chez ce grand styliste, un lieu commun banal.

Et ne le rapproche-t-il pas aussi de Tolstoj et de ses aspirations ascétiques, ce vieux rêve caressé tant de fois, „devenir un vagabond, un pélerin, aller visiter les lieux saints, s'installer dans un couvent, au milieu d'une forêt, au bord d'un lac. Etre assis, les soirs d'été, sur un banc, près de la porte du monastère". [58]

La dernière période des relations personnelles entre Čechov et Tolstoj a pour décor la Crimée. Gravement malade, Tolstoj séjourne pendant l'automne et l'hiver 1901-1902 à Gaspra, propriété mise à sa disposition par la comtesse Panina. Čechov, lui, habite à 10 Km de là, à Jalta, où il est installé depuis la grave hémoptysie de 1897 qui a fait de lui un grand malade, un condamné. Il habite, aux portes de la ville, une maison toute blanche, toute simple, mais qu'il aime parce que, contigu au mur de son jardin, il y a un antique cimetière tatare, toujours vert, silencieux et désert, avec les humbles pierres de ses tombes abandonnées; parce que, par la fenêtre de son bureau, il voit les terrains en pente qui descendent vers la mer, puis la mer elle-même, cernée par des maisons qui s'étagent en gradins.

Mais cette beauté qui l'entoure ne l'empêche pas de s'ennuyer, de regretter Moscou et ces paysages du centre de la Russie qui sont le véritable „lieu de son âme". „Je m'ennuie. Pas dans le sens de la Weltschmerz, pas dans le sens de la nostalgie de la vie, mais, simplement, je m'ennuie sans hommes intelligents, sans la musique que j'aime et sans femmes qui n'existent pas à Jalta. Je m'ennuie sans caviar et sans choucroute". [59]

Cet homme fatigué, malade, désenchanté, aime profondément la vie, l'aime pour les petites joies passagères qu'elle donne, mais aussi pour ce qu'elle apporte de grand, pour ses merveilleuses promesses :

---

[56] Čechov, Journal, 1897.

[57] Carnets.

[58] Paroles de Čechov rapportées par Ivan Bunin dans ses „Souvenirs" (*Vospominanija*), Paris, Vozroždenie, 1950; p. 101.

[59] Lettre à Maksim Gor'kij, 15 Févr. 1900.

„Tolstoj dit qu'un homme n'a besoin que de trois pieds de terre. Erreur! Ce sont les morts qui n'ont besoin que de trois pieds; le vivant, lui, veut le globe terrestre tout entier. Et surtout, l'écrivain". [60]

Tolstoj, lui, se plaît beaucoup en Crimée dont il découvre les beautés avec „une joie purement enfantine." [61] Dès le 12 septembre 1901, Čechov lui rend visite. Il est aussitôt question de sa nouvelle „Dans le ravin" que Tolstoj aime beaucoup et de ses pièces, que Lev Nikolaevič déteste:

„Celles de Shakespeare sont mauvaises, mais les vôtres bien pires encore. Shakespeare, lui, prend malgré tout le spectateur au collet et le conduit vers un but déterminé, sans lui permettre de s'en écarter d'un côté ou d'un autre. Tandis que vos personnages à vous, où nous mènent-ils? Du divan, sur lequel ils sont couchés et jusqu'au cabinet de débarras, aller et retour". [62]

L'instrument littéraire [62] de Čechov que Tolstoj qualifiait de „musical", [62] ne convenait pas, d'après lui, aux exigences de la scène. Il trouvait que les procédés novateurs de Čechov étaient erronés; que les „drames d'atmosphère" qu'il avait crée usurpaient le rôle de la poésie lyrique. Le drame doit servir, selon lui, à d'autres buts:

„Une oeuvre dramatique doit poser un problème non encore résolu par l'humanité et le faire résoudre par chacun des personnages de la pièce conformément à sa nature propre. Ce sont là, en somme, des expériences de laboratoire. Or, chez Čechov, il n'en va pas ainsi. Il attire l'attention des spectateurs par exemple sur le destin de ces malheureux que sont l'Oncle Vanja, ou le Dr Astrov. Mais il ne s'apitoie sur eux que parce qu'ils sont malheureux, en omettant de nous *montrer s'ils sont dignes ou non de pitié*. Il leur fait dire qu'ils sont les hommes les meilleurs de leur canton sans montrer en quoi ils sont les meilleurs. Moi, par exemple, je crois qu'ils ont toujours été mauvais et médiocres et c'est pourquoi leurs souffrances ne peuvent pas être dignes d'intérêt". [63]

---

[60] Paroles de Čechov rapportées par Ivan Bunin dans *Op. cit.* p. 87.
[61] Lettre de Čechov à Gor'kij, 24 sept. 1901.
[62] S. L. Tolstoj, *Očerki bylogo*, 1955, p. 206; — „Un médecin ivre étendu sur un divan, la pluie derrière les carreaux: pour Čechov, c'est une pièce; pour Stanislavskij, — une atmosphère. Mais pour moi, un affreux ennui. Rester couché sur un divan ne constitue pas une action dramatique" (Paroles de Tolstoj citées par P. Gnedič dans une lettre à sa femme, datée de Paris, 1903).
[63] S. T. Semenov, „Rencontres avec A. P. Čechov", 1895 (Cf. *Put'*, 1913, No. 2, pp. 36-38). Cité également par P. Sergeenko dans „Tolstoj et ses contemporains", Moscou 1911; p. 231.

Anton Čechov

Tolstoj avait déjà sévèrement condamné „La mouette". [64] „Les trois soeurs", il ne pouvait se forcer à les lire, et „Oncle Vanja" le révoltait. Cependant, c'est en revenant de la représentation d'„Oncle Vanja" qu'il écrit un résumé du „Cadavre vivant" : „Je suis allé voir „Oncle Vanja" et m'indignais. J'ai voulu alors écrire un drame, „Le cadavre", et jetais sur le papier un résumé". [65] De toute évidence, „Le cadavre vivant" (1900) est une oeuvre où flotte comme une atmosphère čechovienne. Exceptionnelle chez Tostoj, cette note de sympathie humaine, libre de tout dogmatisme moralisant. Exceptionnelle, cette pitié pour le „pauvre coeur des hommes", pour ses faiblesses et ses souffrances. Dernière expression (avec „Hadži-Murat") du génie tolstoïen, „Le cadavre vivant" doit, semble-t-il, beaucoup au „drame d'atmosphère" de Čechov, auquel Tolstoj avait tellement reproché ce même manque d'action qui caractérise la plus belle de ses propres pièces.

„Anton Pavlovič écoutait mon père en silence et manifestait envers ses paroles un intérêt respectueux mais sceptique. Lui-même parlait peu et évitait de discuter. Mon père sentait qu'Anton Pavlovič, tout en lui témoignant une profonde sympathie, ne partageait pas ses opinions… Je crois qu'il aurait voulu se lier davantage avec Čechov et le soumettre à son influence, mais il sentait chez Anton Pavlovič une résistance inexprimée et quelque chose qui empêchait un plus intime rapprochement. „Čechov n'est pas un homme religieux", disait mon père"… [66] „Convertir Gor'kij serait encore possible, mais pas Čechov, un „agnostique" fini" [67] … „un parfait athée". [68]

C'est l'incroyance, le scepticisme de Čechov qui rendent si sévères certains jugements de Tolstoj : „Un si grand talent ! Mais au nom de quoi écrit-il ? Il ne s'agit pas seulement chez lui d'une absence de conception du monde mais bien plus d'une conception du monde erronée, basse, matérialiste, contente d'elle même". [69] Car l'être de passion et de démesure qu'est Tolstoj ne peut pas pardonner à Čechov cette

---

[64] Il avait dit à Aleksej Suvorin que „La mouette" „était un galimatias, sans aucune valeur, écrit à la manière d'Ibsen. Čechov a accumulé Dieu sait quoi et Dieu sait dans quel but. Et l'Europe crie : „excellent" ! Čechov est le plus doué de tous mais sa „Mouette" ne vaut rien" (cf. A. Suvorin, Journal — 11 Février 1897).

[65] Tolstoj, Journal, 27 Janvier 1900. (La représentation au Théâtre artistique de Moscou d'„Oncle Vanja", le 24 Janvier 1900, donna à Tolstoj l'impulsion de travailler au „Cadavre vivant" auquel il songeait depuis 1897. — La pièce, dans sa première rédaction, s'appelait „Le cadavre").

[66] Sergej Tolstoj, Očerki bylogo, Moscou, 1955, pp. 206-207.

[67] K. V. Volkov, „Souvenirs sur L. N. Tolstoj" (cf. N. Apostolov, „Tolstoj vivant", Moscou 1928, p. 422).

[68] Tolstoj, Lettre à V. Čertkov, 30 Novembre 1901.

[69] Paroles de Tolstoj rapportées par N. Gusev dans „Deux ans avec L. N. Tolstoj" (Note du 23 Juin 1908, p. 183).

suprême honnêteté qui est la sienne : ne jamais conclure et savoir de-
meurer négatif parce que n'estimant pas avoir une foi ou une raison
suffisante pour pouvoir être positif et affirmer :

> „Les gens qui écrivent, surtout s'ils sont artistes, doivent enfin
> avouer qu'en ce monde tout est incompréhensible. La foule pense
> qu'elle sait et comprend tout. Plus elle est bête, plus large est son
> horizon. Mais si l'artiste, en qui cette foule croit, a le courage de dé-
> clarer qu'il ne comprend rien à tout ce qu'il voit, cela seul constituera
> déjà un grand pas en avant... Ce ne sont pas les écrivains qui doi-
> vent résoudre des problèmes tels que celui de Dieu, du pessimisme,
> etc., etc... L'artiste ne doit être le juge ni de ses personnages, ni de
> ce qu'ils disent, mais seulement un témoin impartial". [70]

Il appartient à ce „témoin impartial" qu'est l'artiste de talent, „de
savoir distinguer les témoignages importants de ceux qui ne le sont pas,
de savoir régler l'éclairage de ses héros et de savoir parler leur langue
propre". [71] C'est exactement ce que fait Čechov. Prenons, par exemple,
deux de ses nouvelles ayant pour thème les femmes et l'amour, dont
l'une provoque la colère et l'indignation de Tolstoj, l'autre — sa plus
fervente admiration.

„La dame au petit chien" (1899) est un des chefs-d'oeuvre de
Čechov. L'auteur reste, comme toujours, dans la coulisse. Mais, de par
le ton, le nostalgie, le profond lyrisme qui le baigne, ce récit, qui aurait
pu n'être qu'une banale histoire d'adultère, s'élève miraculeusement
vers les sommets de l'art, de la vérité humaine et de la poésie.

Or, voici l'opinion de Tolstoj : „Je viens de lire la „Dame au petit
chien" de Čechov. Encore du Nietzsche. Des êtres qui n'ont pas encore
élaboré en eux-mêmes une conception du monde bien définie, séparant
nettement le bien et le mal. Autrefois, ils hésitaient, cherchaient ; à présent, croyant être par delà le bien et le mal, restent de ce côté-ci,
c'est-à-dire sont presque des animaux". [72]

Par contre, la deuxième de ces nouvelles, intitulée *Dušečka,* [73]
devient immédiatement l'oeuvre favorite de Tolstoj :

> „C'est une véritable perle ! Comme la nature même de l'amour
> féminin y est finement saisie et dessinée ! Et quelle langue ! Per-
> sonne d'entre nous, ni Dostoevskij, ni Turgenev, ni Gončarov, ni
> moi-même n'aurions pu écrire comme cela..." [74] „C'est semblable

[70] Lettre à A. Suvorin, 1888.
[71] Lettre à A. Suvorin, 1888.
[72] Tolstoj, Journal, 16 Janvier 1900.
[73] Publiée le 3 janv. 1899, dans la revue *Sem'ja* et apportée par P. Sergeenko
à Tolstoj le 14 Janvier 1899.
[74] Paroles de Tolstoj rapportées par P. Sergeenko dans „Tolstoj et ses
contemporains", Moscou, 1911.

à une dentelle tissée par une vierge. Il y avait autrefois des dente-
lières, des vieilles filles qui mettaient dans leurs broderies toute leur
vie, tous leurs rêves. Elles traduisaient leurs rêves en dessins, tout
ce qui leur était cher, tout leur pur et vague amour qu'elles entre-
laçaient dans leur dentelle". [75]

Chaque soir, Lev Nikolaevič relisait *Dušečka* à haute voix et préten-
dait „qu'elle l'avait rendu plus intelligent". [76] Certes, il appréciait la
perfection artistique de ce petit chef-d'oeuvre d'humour et d'humanité,
mais il est incontestable que ce qui le séduisait surtout, c'est d'y trouver la confirmation de ses propres idées sur le rôle de la femme et sur
l'amour en général. En 1905, ayant décidé d'inclure *Dušečka* dans son
„Cercle de lecture", il lui adjoint une „Postface" dans laquelle il sou-
ligne que l'héroïne de Čechov est „un exemple incomparable de ce que
doit être une femme pour être heureuse elle-même et rendre heureux
ceux en présence de qui l'a met le destin". Dušečka est pour lui l'incarnation de cet acte sublime et qui rapproche le plus l'être humain
de Dieu, — l'acte d'amour —, qui consiste à se donner entièrement à
celui qu'on aime et que savent si bien et si naturellement accomplir les
meilleures parmi les femmes... Non, elle n'est pas ridicule, elle est
étonnante, elle est sainte, l'âme de *Dušečka*.

Or, l'interprétation de Čechov est toute autre : l'histoire de Dušečka,
qui se soumet entièrement à ceux qu'elle aime et répète aveuglément les
opinions de ses maris successifs, puis de son fils adoptif, est racontée
sur un ton à la fois ironique et tendre, parfaitement čechovien. L'auteur
constate, s'apitoie, déplore le vide, la monotonie, la dépersonalisation
de cette vie. La profonde humanité de Čechov et son incomparable
„talent humain" s'y manifestent à chaque page. Mais en aucune
façon, la pitoyable histoire de la pitoyable Dušečka ne peut être consi-
dérée comme l'idéal de l'auteur et comme sa conception personelle de
l'amour.

Bien au contraire. Dans ses Carnets, il avait écrit : „Il ne faut aimer
que ses égaux". L'opinion de Tolstoj : „Dans *Dušečka* est représenté
le véritable amour féminin" n'est aucunement celle de Čechov. Non,
ce qu'il admire bien plus, c'est la passion d'Anna Karenina, c'est l'amour
libre et irrésistible qui lie Gurov et Anna Sergeevna dans la „Dame au
petit chien", justement tout ce que Tolstoj moraliste condamne avec
tant de rigueur.

„Anna Sergeevna et Gurov s'aimaient comme des êtres très
proches, comme des époux, comme des amis très tendres. Il leur

[75] Paroles de Tolstoj rapportées par M. Gor'kij, *Anton Čechov* (Dans Gor'kij,
Trois Russes. — P., Gallimard, 1935).
[76] Lettre de Tat'jana L'vovna Tolstaja à Čechov, 1899.

semblait que la destinée les avaient créés l'un pour l'autre et il leur paraissait incompréhensible qu'elle fût mariée de son côté, lui — du sien. Ils étaient comme un couple d'oiseaux migrateurs, le mâle et la femelle, qu'on aurait capturés et obligés à vivre dans des cages séparées. Ils avaient mutuellement pardonné l'un à l'autre tout ce qui pouvait leur faire honte dans le passé, ils se pardonnaient tout l'un à l'autre dans le présent et sentaient que leur amour réciproque les avait transformés tous deux''.

La conception du rôle de la femme et de la nature profonde de l'amour peinte dans le „Dame au petit chien" est diamétralement opposée à celle qui enchantait Tostoj dans *Dušečka*. Là encore, on ne peut que constater une fois de plus, la profonde divergence de nature de Čechov et de Tolstoj.

La femme soumise, la femme totalement dévouée à l'homme, épouse et mère avant tout, cet idéal tolstoïen n'a guère varié depuis sa jeunesse, depuis „Guerre et paix" et Nataša, depuis „Anna Karenina", Kitty et cette apothéose de la femme selon Tolstoj qu'est Dolly, symbole même du renoncement à soi et de la maternité triomphante. Grand peintre de la cellule familiale, Tolstoj a toujours rejeté et condamné l'amour qui n'avait pas pour but la procréation. Au contraire, de toutes les héroïnes de Tolstoj, Čechov préfèrera Anna Karenina, [77] celle justement dont son créateur avait si durement châtié la passion extra-conjuguale et coupable. Pour Čechov, la femme est l'égale, la compagne, l'amie. Ce qui l'intéresse avant tout, ce n'est pas l'accomplissement d'un devoir social et moral, le mariage, la procréation. Mais c'est l'intimité, la parenté d'âme, la tendresse et la compréhension mutuelle entre deux êtres dont aucun ne domine l'autre, mais où tous les deux sont, au contraire, égaux. Là encore, il se montre aussi „moderne", aussi progressiste, que Tolstoj reste patriarcal, moralisateur et, disons le mot, rétrograde.

Et si, par delà l'oeuvre, on se tourne vers la vie des deux écrivains, on constate que dans leur propre mariage ils ont chacun tenté de réaliser leur conception personnelle de l'amour et de ce que doit être l'union d'un homme et d'une femme.

La dernière rencontre de Čechov et de Tolstoj eut lieu à Gaspra, le 31 Mars 1902. Tolstoj était encore malade, couché. Čechov resta un long moment à son chevet. Ils parlèrent de littérature. Lev Nikolaevič écrivait alors „Hadži-Murat", son ultime chef-d'oeuvre. Čechov note „son air d'extrême vieillesse", son esprit resté si alerte, „ses yeux si étonnamment intelligents". [78]

---

[77] Voir ses lettres à Michail Čechov, 10 mars 1887 et à A. Suvorin, 24 février 1893.
[78] Lettre à N. P. Kondakov, 2 avril 1902.

Ils ne devaient plus se revoir. Deux ans après, Anton Pavlovič mourait à Badenweiler. Et, en Juillet 1904, un correspondant du journal *Rus'* allait recueillir à Jasnaja Poljana les paroles d'adieu de Tolstoj à Čechov:

„Il fut un artiste incomparable, ... un artiste de la vie. Et la grande qualité de son oeuvre c'est qu'elle est accessible à tous et proche non seulement de chaque Russe, mais de chaque être humain en général. Et c'est là l'essentiel... Il était sincère et vrai et grâce à cette sincérité, il créa des formes d'art nouvelles, entièrement nouvelles pour l'univers entier, des formes littéraires dont je n'ai rencontré d'égales nulle part ailleurs. Sa langue est une langue extraordinaire. Je me souviens qu'à la première lecture, elle m'avait paru bizarre, „maladroite"; mais dès que je me mis à lire attentivement, cette langue m'empoigna... Ces formes nouvelles ont été créées par Čechov et, en rejetant toute fausse modestie, j'affirme qu'au point de vue de la technique, Čechov m'est très supérieur... Et il y a en lui un autre grand signe caractéristique: il est un de ces écrivains qui, comme Dickens, Puškin et quelques très rares autres, peuvent être relus maintes et maintes fois — je le sais par ma propre expérience". [79]

Quant à Čechov, ses sentiments profonds, il les avait exprimés 4 ans avant sa mort:

„Je crains la mort de Tolstoj. S'il mourait, il se formerait dans ma vie un grand vide. En premier lieu, *je n'ai aimé aucun homme autant que lui*... En second lieu, quand dans le monde des lettres il existe un Tolstoj, il devient facile et agréable d'être homme de lettres. Et même si l'on a conscience de n'avoir rien fait, de ne rien faire encore, ce n'est pas vraiment terrible, car Tolstoj, lui, fait pour tous. Son oeuvre sert de justification pour les espoirs et les croyances qu'on met dans la littérature. En troisième lieu, la situation de Tolstoj est solide, son autorité, immense, et tant qu'il vivra, le mauvais goût en littérature, tout ce qui est vulgarité insolente et larmoyante, tous les amours-propres aigris resteront loin, enfouis dans l'ombre. Seul, son ascendant moral peut élever à un certain niveau les divers courants et tendances littéraires. Sans lui, il ne resterait plus qu'un troupeau sans berger..." [80]

[79] A. Zenger, „Souvenirs sur une visite à L. N. Tolstoj" (dans *Rus'* No. 212, 15 Juillet 1904); cité aussi par *P. Sergeenko* dans „Tolstoj et ses contemporains", Moscou 1911, p. 226.
[80] Lettre à M. O. Menšikov, 28 Janvier 1900.

Voici les 30 nouvelles de Čechov que Tolstoj préférait et qu'il avait rangées en 2 catégories:
1ère catégorie: Detvora; Choristka; Drama; Doma; Toska; Beglec; V

sude; Van'ka; Damy; Zloumyšlennik; Mal'čiki; Temnota; Spat' chočetsja; Supruga; Dušečka.

2ème catégorie: Bezzakonie; Gore; Ved'ma; Veročka; Na čužbine; Kucharka ženitsja; Kanitel'; Perepoloch; Nu, publika!; Maska; Ženskoe sčast'e; Nervy; Svad'ba; Bezzaščitnoe suščestvo; Baby.

On remarquera que n'entrent dans cette liste ni „La steppe", ni „Une morne histoire", ni „Dans le ravin", ni la „Salle No. 6", ni „l'Évêque", ni „l'Étudiant", ni „Les moujiks', ni tant d'autres chef-d'oeuvres!

ВЛАДИМИР МАРКОВ

О СТИХАХ ЧЕХОВА

Крупные прозаики, не писавшие стихов, в русской литературе редкость, даже если прибавить имена знаменитых драматургов и критиков. Одни писали стихи в юности (Гоголь, Белинский, Гончаров, Салтыков-Щедрин), другие прибегали к стихотворной форме под давлением обстоятельств (Достоевский), но были и такие, кто продолжал заниматься стихотворством в течение жизни, как правило, не относясь к этому слишком серьезно (С. Аксаков, Л. Толстой, Горький, возможно и Чернышевский). Редко кто из них достигал уровня, позволяющего назвать их поэтами (Аксаков, Тургенев, Бунин, в наши дни — В. Набоков); но даже и в этих случаях некий „потолок" мешал им достигнуть пределов, за которыми начинается подлинная поэзия. Интересно тут же отметить, что попытки поэтов писать прозу, напротив, обычно увенчивались успехом, а некоторые из этих поэтов даже оказывали большое влияние на развитие русской прозы.

Взглянув на стихи прозаиков с жанровой точки зрения, можно заметить, что среди них преобладает шутка. Полуэкспромтной, короткой шуткой, часто оброненной в дружеском письме, пользовались чуть ли не все русские прозаики 19-го века от Гоголя и Аксакова до Максима Горького. Шутка позволяет обыграть поэтическую неумелость, превращая технические дефекты в достоинства. На том же принципе строятся стихи, которые можно назвать „подкидышами" и которые являются типичными только для прозаиков. Стихотворения авторской юности приписываются позже действующему лицу. При этом нередко недостатки первоначальной версии заостряются, а число их сознательно умножается. Примером могут служить стихи Адуева младшего в *Обыкновенной истории* Гончарова. Наконец, следующим шагом вперед является писание стихов „в образе", т.е. прямо от лица героя. Это используется и в поэтических произведениях (например, стихи Ленского перед дуэлью в *Евгении Онегине*), однако только в прозе этот жанр приобретает ясные очертания. Иногда „стихи в образе" подаются „серьезно" (*Дворянское гнездо* и *Новь* Тургенева), иногда бывают блестящими образцами юмора, сатиры или пародии. Может быть, гениальнейший образец такого использования — стихи Лебядкина в *Бесах* Достоевского. [1]

Иные прозаики высказывались иронически о сложении стихов вообще (Салтыков-Шедрин), большинство же направляли иронию против самих себя. Чехов в этом не составляет исключения. Вспоминая шуточную басню, написанную несколькими годами раньше, он писал в письме к А. Авиловой от 29 апреля 1892: „... сам я, покорный общему закону, изображаю из себя старую литературную собаку, смотрящую на стихоплетство свысока и с зевотой" (XV 375). За год до этого, в другом письме, к М. В. Киселевой от 20 июля 1891, в ответ на получение стихов от дочери адресата, он говорит: „... хотел бы ответить ей стихами, целый месяц напрягал мозги, но голова треснула от натуги и все-таки стихов не вышло. Поневоле позавидуешь талантам" (XV 223).

В уже цитированном письме к Авиловой Чехов также говорит: „Отродясь я не писал стихов, впрочем только раз написал в альбом одной девочке басню, но это было очень давно". На самом деле, басня была написана всего за пять лет до этого письма, а фраза о неповинности в стихотворстве так же далека от истины, как и утверждение другого прозаика-стихотворца, Л. Н. Толстого, который в 1872 г., в стихотворном послании к А. Фету, заявлял: „Итак, пишу впервой стихами", уже будучи автором, по крайней мере, десятка стихотворений. [2] Чехов также шутил, что „перепробовал все, кроме стихов и доносов". [3] В отношении доносов это сущая правда.

Первые известные нам стихи А. П. Чехова были написаны мелом на заборе в ответ на другие стихи, тоже написанные мелом на том же заборе гимназисткой Ираидой Савич. Ираида жила с матерью в флигеле, который они снимали у Чеховых в Таганроге, и четырнадцатилетний стихотворец был в нее влюблен, по свидетельству его брата М. П. Чехова. [4] М. П. Чехов приводит эти стихи:

> О, поэт заборный в юбке,
> Оботри себе ты губки.

---

[1] См. об этом подробнее в моей статье „Стихи русских прозаиков," *Воздушные пути. Альманах* (Нью Йорк, 1960), стр. 135-178.

[2] А. А. Фет, *Мои воспоминания, 1848-1889* (М., 1890), т. 2, стр. 257.

[3] А. Роскин, *Антоша Чехонте* (М., Советский писатель, 1940), стр. 90.

[4] М. П. Чехов, *Вокруг Чехова. Встречи и впечатления* (М.-Л., Academia, 1933), стр. 43.

> Чем стихи тебе писать,
> Лучше в куколки играть.

По другим свидетельствам, будучи в гимназии, Чехов писал сказку в стихах под *Конька-горбунка,* начало которой приведено в т. XII ПССП. В этом отрывке есть погрешности не только против метрики, но и против русского языка:

> Эй, вы хлопцы, где вы, эй!
> Вот идет старик Агей.
> Он вам будет сказать сказку
> Про Ивана и Савраску.

Следующие по времени написания стихотворные попытки Чехова относятся уже к 80-м гг., когда он жил с семьей в Москве. Стихотворение „Прости меня, мой ангел белоснежный," написанное, опять-таки по свидетельству М. П. Чехова, в студенческие года А. П., предназначалось для несохранившегося водевиля *Бритый секретарь с пистолетом.* В нем для комического эффекта шесть раз повторяется слово „стремглав". Стихотворение приводится по ПССП (т. II), но оно существует и в ином варианте, с незначительными разночтениями.

> Прости меня, мой ангел белоснежный,
> Подруга дней моих и идеал мой нежный,
> Что я, забыв любовь, *стремглав* туда бросаюсь,
> Где смерти пасть ... О, ужасаюсь!
> В могильный склеп с груди горячей,
> Убитый, раненый, лежачий,
> *Стремглав* я падаю ... Не плачь, прости,
> Все птицы будут петь и розаны цвести
> Над свеже-вырытой могилой,
> Куда меня злой рок *стремглав* опустит.
> Тогда поймешь, как я страдал,
> Как я любил свой идеал ...
> Над ней *стремглав* взойдет моя идея
> Во образе цветов, ландышей, роз приятных;
> Тогда по повеленью таинств непонятных
> Из гроба буду я вставать *стремглав* ночами
> И, отравясь цветов благоуханьем,
> Как чудной девицы лобзаньем,
> Уйду обратно в гроб *стремглав* с прослезенными
>   глазами.

Другое стихотворение этого времени датировано автором

и представляет собой шуточное письмо. По утверждению
М. П. Чехова оно было включено в тот же водевиль. [5]

Последнее прости
(Е. И. Ю . . . . .й)

Как дым мечтательной сигары,
Носилась ты в моих мечтах,
Неся с собой любви удары
С улыбкой пламенной в устах.
Но я — увы! — погиб уж для мечтаний,
Тебя любя, я веру потерял . . .
И средь моих мечтательных скитаний
Я изнывал и угасал! . .
Прости меня . . . Зачем тревожить
Заснувшего в гробу навеки мертвеца?
Иди вперед! Не унывай! Быть может,
Найдешь другого . . . подлеца!!

Известный

Москва. 1883 года. 2 ноября. Полночь.

Письмо это обращено к подруге сестры Чехова, Е. И.
Юношевой, за которой писатель, как утверждает его брат,
„кажется, ухаживал". [6]

Первые четыре строки каждого из этих двух стихотворений
(из первого — с одним незначительным разночтением) были
в следующем, 1884 г. помещены в рассказ *О, женщины,
женщины! . . .*, напечатанный в газете *Новости Дня* (см.
ПССП Т. III). Таким образом, второе четверостишие попадает
в группу „стихов-подкидышей". От других „подкидышей"
его отличает лишь то, что первоначально оно тоже было
написано невсерьез. Сам рассказ типичен для периода
Антоши Чехонте, и приведенные в нем два четверостишия
служат примером начала одного бездарного стихотворения,
присланного поэтом, князем Прочуханцевым, редактору
газеты *Кукиш с маслом* Почитаеву. Редактор возмущается
ошибками в версификации, но в приведенных строчках эти
ошибки не продемонстрированы и имеются только в первоначальной, „водевильной" версии первого стихотворения;
рифму же „лошадь: ношей" нельзя найти ни в одной из
первоначальных версий.

Годы 1886-87 можно считать „расцветом поэтического твор-

---

[5] М. П. Чехов, *Антон Чехов. Театр, актеры и „Татьяна Репина"* (П.
1924), стр. 8-9.
[6] *Вокруг Чехова*, стр. 70.

чества" Чехова. Именно к этому времени относятся самые известные из его стихотворных шуток. Как и прежде, эти стихи биографически связаны с женщинами. Правда, первая из них, Саша Киселева, была в то время еще девочкой. Чехов, как известно, провел три лета (1885, 1886 и 1887 гг.) в Бабкине у ее родителей, причем именно эти годы можно считать временем превращения Антоши Чехонте в Антона Чехова. Чехов любил дурачиться с Сашей, которую звал „Василисой Пантелевной", и ее братом Сережей. Он написал для них рассказ „Сапоги всмятку", куда, в виде иллюстрации, вклеил рисунки из юмористических журналов. Саша сама была не чужда стихописания (см. выше отрывок из письма Чехова к ее матери), и, видимо, намекая на это, он в абсурдно-пародийном письме к ней посылает „два пера для писания стихов: одно перо для плохих стихов, а другое для хороших" (XIII 254). В другом письме Чехов называет Сашу „моя будущая супруга" (XV 11).

Первые стихотворные строки, посвященные Саше Киселевой, были вписаны в ее альбом за подписью „А. Чехонте" 12 мая 1886 г.

> Милого Бабкина яркая звездочка!
> Юность по нотам allegro промчится:
> От свеженькой вишни останется косточка,
> От скучного пира — угар и горчица.

Повидимому, в том же альбоме, за подписью „Индейкин и Петухов" и датированные 3-м июня 1887 г., помещены стихотворение

> *Битва*
> (Рассказ старого солдата)
>
> Василиса Пантелевна!
> Когда взята была Плевна,
> Так солдаты отличались,
> Что даже турки удивлялись,

недатированное четверостишие, очевидно, относящееся к тем же годам:

> Пошел с визитом потолок
> Как-то раз к соседке
> И сказал ей: „ангелок,
> Посидим в беседке!"

а также четыре абсурдных четверостишия, объединенных названием

Элегия

1

Купила лошадь сапоги,
Протянула ноги,
Поскакали утюги
В царские чертоги.

2

Ехал груздь верхом на палке,
Споткнулся и упал
И тотчас пошел к гадалке,
Там случился с ним скандал.

3

В метлу влюбился Сатана,
И сделал ей он предложенье;
К нему любви она полна,
Пошла в Сибирь на поселенье.

4

Сказал карась своей мамаше:
„Мамаша, дайте мне деньжат"
И побежал тотчас к Наташе
Купить всех уток и телят.

Другие образцы шуточной поэзии Чехова этих лет связаны
с другой Сашей, — Александрой Львовной Селивановой. Она
была племянница Г. П. Селиванова, который так не по-
свойски завладел чеховским домом в Таганроге. В 1875 г. она
поселилась пансионеркой у Чеховых, потом жила в том же
доме уже у дяди, а Чехов давал ей уроки; потом же учитель-
ствовала и часто навещала Чеховых в Москве. Впоследствии
она вышла замуж, но скоро стала „очаровательной вдовой"
(XVI 255). М. П. Чехов пишет, что А. П. „приударял" за ней, [7]
и эта „бедовая, шумная и гремучая девка" (XIII 405), видимо,
создавала вокруг себя атмосферу непринужденности и весе-
лости. Письма Чехова к ней всегда шутливы по тону, а среди
стихов, написанных ей в альбом в 1887 г., [8] находится самая
известная из чеховских стихотворных шуток:

---

[7] Ibid., стр. 57.

[8] Н. И. Гитович в *Летописи жизни и творчества А. П. Чехова* (М. 1955),
стр. 160, датирует эту басню 19-м июня 1887 г. и утверждает, что она
написана в альбом Саши *Киселевой* (!), хотя в ПССП, т. V, она помещена
среди произведений 1886 г., а в списке адресатов к т. XIV после ее упоминания стоит даже 1895 г., и оба раза она считается написанной для
Саши Селивановой. С другой стороны, в письмах И. А. Бунина Г. Ада-

Басня

Шли однажды через мостик жирные китайцы,
Впереди них, задрав хвостик, торопились зайцы.
Вдруг китайцы закричали: „Стой! Лови! Ах, ах!”
Зайцы выше хвост задрали и попрятались в кустах.

Мораль сей басни так ясна:
Кто хочет зайцев кушать,
Тот ежедневно, встав со сна,
Папашу должен слушать.

В уже цитированном письме к А. Авиловой Чехов пишет:
Басня жива еще до сих пор, многие знают ее наизусть”.
Еще забавнее, что, как сообщается в комментариях к пятому
тому ПССП, „стихотворение летом 1921 г. было записано
этнографом Л. А. Мерварт со слов крестьянки в деревне
Петроково Старицкого уезда Тверской губернии”.

Два других стихотворения в альбом А. Л. Селивановой
намекают, одно на ее занятия акушерством, другое на ее
выход замуж за инженера А. К. Краузе. Оба датированы 24-м
декабря 1887 г. и подписаны „Чехонте”.

Я полюбил Вас, о ангел обаятельный,
И с тех пор ежедневно я, ей-ей,
Таскаю в Воспитательный
Своих незаконнорожденных детей...

Признание

Упоенный любви нектаром,
Я хотел бы быть директором!
(примечание: без жалованья).

Вот, кажется, и все имеющиеся в нашем распоряжении
факты о стихах Чехова. К ним можно еще добавить про

мовичу, в отрывках, опубликованных в журнале *Опыты* № 6 (Нью Йорк,
1956), стр. 27, сообщается, что Чехов надписал Бунину на подаренной
книге: „Я тоже когда-то писал стихи” и подарил ему два своих стихотворения, текст которых приводится полностью. Это *Битва* (начинающа-
яся словами *„Акулина* Пантелевна”) и *Басня,* но без „морали”. В текстах
есть незначительные разночтения, очевидно по вине Бунина (он сообщает это по памяти). Так, например, Чехов вряд ли ошибся бы в имени
„Василиса Пантелевна”, т.к. в одних только письмах десятки раз называет так Сашу Киселеву. Впрочем, может быть, Чехов намеренно заме-
тает следы, тем более что Бунин также говорит, что, даря книгу, Чехов
сказал со смехом: „Честное слово, это мои стихи, написанные *в Таганроге, когда мне было восемь лет”* (курсив мой. В. М.). Наиболее интересно во всем этом то, что Чехов, видимо, ценил свою басню, если дарил
ее не раз и разным лицам. Бунин, впрочем, находит ее „плохой шуткой”,
в которой нет „ровно ничего смешного”.

встречу композитора П. И. Чайковского с Чеховым в октябре
1889 г., во время которой обсуждалось либретто оперы
Бэла по Лермонтову. Чайковский будто бы хотел, чтобы
либретто написал Чехов. [9] Это звучит не совсем правдо-
подобно.

Итак, до нас дошло с десяток стихотворений Чехова. Все
они шуточного характера, и Чехов не считал их литературным
фактом, не печатал их и даже два раза отрицал их существование. Как факт биографический, они могут возбудить неко-
торый интерес. Это лишняя краска к уже известному облику
Чехова. Они еще раз подчеркивают его беспретенциозность,
человечность и скромность, доходящую до самонедооценки.
Однако и в этом отношении нового света они не проливают.
Если коллекционировать стихи русских прозаиков, то чеховские и тогда займут далеко не первое место в этом
забавном собрании.

И тем не менее нельзя согласиться с суровым суждением,
высказанным недавно советским литературоведом С.
Машинским: „в полное собрание сочинений Чехова, вышед-
шее тиражом в 53 тыс. экземпляров, включены вещи, явно
необязательные для такого типа изданий, например,
альбомные стихи, не имеющие ни малейшей художественной
ценности." [10] Во-первых, если собрание сочинений названо
полным, то странно было бы не помещать этих десяти с
половиной стихотворений, потому что все написанное Чеховым интересно теперь не только для науки, но и для читателя.
Во-вторых, если сам Чехов с удовольствием писал такие
стихи в альбомы, а две Саши громко хохотали, то не исклю-
чена возможность, что и другие читатели с удовольствием
посмеются, читая их. Может улыбнуться даже исследователь
литературы, давно потерявший способность воспринимать
шутки. В-третьих, отрицать художественное значение, не
говоря уже об историко-литературном, за некоторыми из
этих шуток просто неверно. При внимательном рассмотрении
может оказаться, что не одна чеховская подпись делает их
интересными.

Прежде всего, *Басня, Элегия* и *Пошел с визитом потолок* являются неплохими образцами русской абсурдной
поэзии. Этот жанр, столь популярный в англосаксонских

⁹ *Вокруг Чехова,* стр. 135.
¹⁰ С. Машинский, „В борьбе за классическое наследие," *Новый Мир,*
№ 3, 1958, стр. 220.

литературах под названием „поэзия нонсенса", в России обычно влачил периферийное существование, а критики почти не обращали на него внимания, занимаясь более важными вещами. Объяснение этому завело бы нас слишком далеко.

Тем не менее, абсурдная поэзия в России не только существовала, но и оставила вещи достойные внимания. Д. Святополк-Мирский в своей знаменитой истории русской литературы называет крупнейшими русскими абсурдными поэтами А. К. Толстого, Владимира Соловьева и графа Федора Соллогуба. [11] Нужно заметить, что абсурдный элемент у А. К. Толстого теперь часто затушевывается и преподносится как составная часть его сатиры и пародии. Однако, сатира, по существу, чужда „поэзии нонсенса", хотя последняя и часто связана с пародией. [12] Но и пародия не обязательно должна соприсутствовать абсурду. Например, в английской поэзии пародия имеется в некоторых стихах в „Алисе в стране чудес" Льюиса Кэрролла, но она отсутствует у величайшего абсурдного поэта Англии Эдуарда Лира. В стихах Козьмы Пруткова, одним из создателей которого был А. К. Толстой, абсурд вполне отделим от пародии. Именно абсурд вызывает наслаждение при чтении этих стихов, а не то, что некоторые из них являются пародией, скажем, на Щербину. Однако литературные исследователи всегда делают преувеличенное ударение на пародии, да еще не совсем правильно рассматривают и пародию как выражение только литературной борьбы того времени. У А. К. Толстого имеются также образцы чистого нонсенса, как, например, его маленький шедевр *В берестовой сидя будочке*. Следует также добавить, что А. К. Толстого можно считать одним из величайших абсурдных драматургов мира за его пьесы Козьмы Пруткова.

У В. Соловьева чистого нонсенса, пожалуй, нет, так как он связан с вышучиванием себя (внутреннее раздвоение) или других (пародии на символистов). Тем не менее, как литературный элемент, абсурд ясно ощутим как в его стихах, так и в письмах, а пьеса *Белая лилия* стоит в одном ряду с пьесами Козьмы Пруткова.

Но к этим поэтам русская абсурдная традиция не сводится. В русском фольклоре, — в прибаутках, перевертнях, непри-

---

[11] D. S. Mirsky, *A History of Russian Literature* (New York, 1955), pp. 223, 352-53.
[12] Emile Cammaerts, *The Poetry of Nonsense* (London, 1925), p. 9.

личных частушках, — можно наблюдать целое царство нонсенса, на которое фольклористы редко обращают внимание, потому что фольклор продолжает изучаться под определенным углом, абсурда не предусматривающим. Элементы нонсенса можно также найти у Пушкина (например, в *Домике в Коломне*), а в поэзии ХХ-го века нонсенс встречается в поэмах Хлебникова (особенно в „Шамане и Венере"), в ранних вещах Николая Заболоцкого и в стихах Даниила Хармса, а также в детской поэзии К. Чуковского и С. Маршака, на которую традиция английского нонсенса оказала сильнейшее влияние.

Английский исследователь поэзии абсурда выводит ее из „стихов для детей (nursery rhymes)" [13] и подчеркивает, что основной ее чертой является „ненаправленность", иррациональность и алогичность (15). Эта поэзия создает свой особый мир наизнанку, Topsy-turvydom, die verkehrte Welt (27). Создается такая поэзия часто под влиянием детей или пишется прямо для них (33). Она имеет большой успех в народе (55). Даже прозаики, вроде Киплинга или Честертона, рассказывая свои абсурдные истории, часто прибегают к стиховой форме (39). С чисто формальной точки зрения, абсурдные стихи часто характеризуются особой ролью рифмы, которая как бы творит из себя стихотворение (42). Отмечается также склонность абсурдных поэтов и писателей иллюстрировать собственные произведения (59). Кроме алогичности и фантастики, в нонсенсе констатируется еще один аспект, idiotic obviousness, т.е. преподнесение очевидных вещей с таким видом, как будто это открытие.

Из краткого изложения ясно видно, с какой легкостью Чехов становится в этот контекст. Алогичный мир встает во всей своей красе в четверостишиях *Элегии*, в то время как *Битва* рассказана с „идиотской очевидностью". Во всех этих стихах с полнейшей свободой, детской непосредственностью и даже литературной безответственностью (что может возмутить серьезных людей) царит нереальная реальность — не этого мира и не „того света", а мира никакого, вольно творимого из свободного соединения слов и предметов. Стихи 1887 г. написаны для девочки Саши Киселевой или для подруги детства Чехова Саши Селивановой, непосредственной натуры, болтушки и певуньи, в общении с которой у

---

[13] Op. cit., p. 3. В дальнейшем ссылки на страницы даются в тексте статьи.

Чехова преобладала радостная детскость. Абсурдная рифма особенно хорошо видна в четверостишии *Пошел с визитом потолок*. Некоторые начала („Шли однажды...", „Пошел однажды") звучат совсем как в абсурдных английских лимериках. Наконец, Чехов иллюстрировал свой абсурдный рассказ *Сапоги всмятку* весьма абсурдным образом (см. факсимиле в ПССП V). „Басню" Чехова (содержащую пародический элемент, но самого общего характера) [14] принял простой народ и превратил в фольклор.

Как создания чистого воображения, *Басня, Битва, Элегия* и другие стихи 1887 г. возвышаются над более ранними просто шуточными стихами и без труда занимают место не только в русской абсурдной традиции, но и в поэзии нонсенса вообще. В этом контексте они сразу становятся интересным литературным фактом и несомненным обьектом эстетического наслаждения. Нельзя, конечно, запретить более „серьезные" подходы. Например, фрейдист мог бы сделать неожиданные заключения из *Битвы*, а в некоторых литературных кругах могли бы обнаружить „критику царского режима" или „продолжение декабристской традиции" в последней строке 3-его четверостишия *Элегии*. Однако все это было бы не столько интерпретацией, сколько абсурдом в своем роде, и хорошо, что, по крайней мере, эти произведения Чехова не так легко поддаются фальсификации, может быть, в силу их предельной чистоты.

Есть в чеховских стихах еще одна деталь, достойная интереса, и ее легче всего наблюдать на четверостишии *Я полюбил Вас, о ангел обаятельный*. В этой шутке комизм достигается тем, что на едва уловимой канве пятистопного ямба повествование ведется в обычной прозе при сохранении рифмы, отчего получается впечатление метрической беспомощности. [15] Чехов вряд ли предполагал, что включение прозы в стих [16] будет

---

[14] Пародийность Чехова в его нонсенсах вообще „ненаправленная", почти бессознательная. Так *Я полюбил Вас, о ангел*... содержит отголосок известных строк Пушкина, *Битва* звучит как пародия на *Бородино* Лермонтова, а *Прости меня, мой ангел белоснежный* выглядит сводной пародией на романтическую лирику первой четверти 19-го века, хотя это наверняка не входило в авторское задание.

[15] Ср. в этой связи последнюю строку *Прости меня, мой ангел белоснежный*. Об этой строке ее автор, герой водевиля, говорит: „Последняя строчка несколько тяжела, — но главное — это нужно уметь прочесть" (Комментарии к *Вокруг Чехова*, стр. 267-68).

[16] В известном примере у Пушкина, в *Послании Дельвигу* (1827), проза прерывает стих, но не располагается строчками.

потом развиваться русскими поэтами-примитивистами 20-го века и даст особенно интересные результаты в „сдвигах" поэмы В. Хлебникова *Шаман и Венера* (1912) и у Николая Заболоцкого — в отдельных стихах сборника *Столбцы* (1929), например, в стихотворении *Цирк*, и в поэме *Торжество земледелия* (1929-30). Еще ближе к Чехову в этом отношении популярный американский поэт-юморист Огден Нэш, достигающий комического эффекта также рифмовкой длинных прозаических строк. Как часто и справедливо указывали русские формалисты, некоторые явления, прежде чем войти в литературный обиход, долго ведут окололитературное существование.

Целью этой статьи было только указать на контексты, в которых „случайные" стихи Чехова приобретают значение, с такой легкостью у них отбираемое. Можно было бы повести исследование в ином направлении и попытаться установить, например, как предрасположенность к нонсенсу отразилась на юморе Чехова вообще и на отдельных элементах его зрелого творчества. Например, образ Шарлотты и монолог Гаева к шкафу могли бы заиграть новыми красками при таком подходе. Господствующее „психологическо-реалистическое" толкование, если и не до конца искажает, то часто обедняет и как-то „осеряет" Чехова. Не сводим Чехов и к критике, сатире, „разоблачению", „борьбе с" и „протесту против".

Есть у всего этого и другая сторона. В уголках русской литературы имеются вещи незамечаемые и обходимые, хотя даже при минимуме литературоведческого внимания и воображения их можно представить в новом, более истинном свете и обогатить этим наше представление о русской литературе. Изредка такие реабилитации предпринимаются. Так, например, А. Бем перевернул ходячее представление о *Хозяйке* Достоевского,[17] а А. М. Ремизов спас от забвения *Скверный анекдот* того же писателя.[18] Но это единичные попытки. Большинство, по словам поэта Георгия Иванова, предпочитает

> Шагать со всеми — рядом, в ногу,
> По пустякам не волноваться
> И правилам повиноваться.

---

[17] А. Л. Бем, *Достоевский. Психоаналитические этюды* (Берлин, „Петрополис", 1938), стр. 77-141.
[18] Алексей Ремизов, *Огонь вещей. Сны и предсонье* (Париж, „Оплешник", 1954), стр. 187-202.

RALPH E. MATLAW

ČECHOV AND THE NOVEL

Čechov's narrative production so uniformly utilizes the shorter forms of fiction, that an inquiry into "Čechov and the Novel" seems at first glance to be an anomaly. Yet at the very beginning of his literary career and intermittently thereafter Čechov was intrigued by the prospect of writing a novel, and at least one of his early works, *Drama na ochote* (1884-5) (translated as "The Shooting Party") represents an unsuccessful attempt in that form. Čechov's attitudes toward the novel were remarkably consistent — whether expressed in his correspondence, in his early works (frequently parodies of novels and novelists then in vogue) or in his remarks about his later stories. Coupled with Čechov's effort to broaden the range of his work, and the absence from his mature works of elements he considered "novelistic", they offer an unusual opportunity to assess all Čechov's achievements as well as the continuity that underlies his work.

The very terms for Russian fiction, *rasskaz, povest', roman,* cannot be satisfactorily translated into English. Like their German and French counterparts, the first two are etymologically related to the retelling of something (*conte — Erzählung — rasskaz*) and the reporting of "news" (*nouvelle — povest'*). The term for novel, *roman,* is borrowed from French, and significantly also has a second meaning: "romance" — a love story or amatory intrigue. A number of Čechov's early stories are subtitled *"roman"* but are "love stories" rather than novels. However, for Čechov, as for other Russian novelists, the "romance" is an important ingredient of the novel. To translate the three terms as short story, short novel and novel is unsatisfactory, as the English "short novel" begs the question of genre. The Russian *povest',* moreover, is much closer to the German *Novella* and its attendant concepts of the *"unerhörte Begebenheit"* than to the short story, and like it has tended to minimize the action or event on which it is founded in order to emphasize other elements as, for example, characterization, setting, and the like.

A distinction is sometimes made among the three forms on the basis of length or, more meaningfully, on the manner in which each treats its material. Paul Bourget formulated the following progression:

"Le conte n'est pas plus une courte nouvelle que la nouvelle n'est pas un court roman.... Le conte est un épisode rapporté sans analyse des caractères; la nouvelle, un épisode avec analyse des caractères;

le roman...... une suite d'épisodes avec analyse des caractères et des causes". [1]

Even this useful conceptual distinction is not satisfactory for Russian because the first two categories, *rasskaz* and *povest'*, are usually grouped together, without regard for length or complexity, and together are isolated from the novel. Čechov's first collection, *Pestrye rasskazy* ("Motley Stories"), were simply what we would today call short stories or even that refinement of the genre, "short shorts." Ultimately (but not consistently), Čechov distinguished the *rasskaz* from the *povest'* according to the point of view taken in the work, subtitling first person narrations *rasskazy* regardless of their length ("My Life", "House with Mezzanine"). He thereby approximates German usage, where purists will not consider a first person narration, even when it is set in a frame, a true *Novella*. [2]

Russian writers use all three terms flexibly and idiosyncratically. Dostoevskij considered much of his production novels, including such short works as "Poor Folk" and "The Gambler", and subtitled them so. On the other hand Turgenev, a writer with whom Čechov has much more in common, originally called only one of his works a "novel" (*Virgin Soil*, 1876), though subsequently he put six works in that category. In his correspondence Turgenev refers to these interchangeably as "novels" or "long tales" (*bol'šie povesti*), as Čechov will refer to "long stories" and "tales." At best we can assume that the novel has a greater number of characters, more complex or deeper characterization, a fuller background and frequently, in Russia, some political or social significance. So, at least, Čechov conceives it in his correspondence. Size is but a result of fulness: "Oh, if only you knew what a subject for a novel sits in my brain! What wonderful women! What funerals, what weddings!" [3]

It has frequently been remarked that Čechov's skirmishes with the novel at the beginning of his career (1880-1885) resulted in parodies and that his attempts to write novels stem from the notion of parody. Unfortunately, the question has never been sufficiently investigated, and the attempt to do so soon discloses unexpected complexities. Čechov's reactions to the novel can be grouped under two headings.

---

[1] Quoted from W. T. Secor, *Paul Bourget and the Nouvelle* (New York, King's Crown Press, 1948), p. 25.

[2] Reinhold Trautmann, *Zu Form und Gehalt der Novellen Turgenjews* (Leipzig, Hirzel, 1942), p. 21.

[3] Letter to A. N. Pleščeev, February 9, 1888, PSSP XIV 36 and *passim*, particularly the letters to Suvorin and Grigorovič. References in the text and notes will be to this edition, except for the first volume, where I have had to use, and cite, the 1930 twelve volume edition of Lunačarskij and Baluchatyj.

The first contains parodies and farcial distortions of literary works. It depends directly upon these models and clearly indicates Čechov's criticism of their shortcomings. The second contains Čechov's own attempts to write in these forms, sometimes as a stylization, sometimes in a more elaborate attempt to comment on, or improve upon, current novels. The first group can further be subdivided into two categories. The first, directed against novels of so-called Russian life, consists entirely of clichés, as in "A Life in Questions and Exclamations" (1882) where a brief, six-phase biography — childhood, youth, and so on — is compiled by the simple expedient of accumulating, without connectives, the bromides, clichés, and commonplaces appropriate to each age. A similar catalogue of situational platitudes appears in the brief list "What do Novels, Tales, etc. Most Frequently Contain?" (1880) :

A count, a countess with traces of former beauty, a neighboring baron, a literary man who is a liberal, an impoverished landowner, a foreign musician, dull-witted servants, nurses, governesses, a German stewart, an esquire and heir from America. Plain, but congenial and attractive characters. The hero, who rescues the heroine from a horse driven mad, is strong spirited and can demonstrate the power of his fists on any convenient occasion.

The heights of the firmament, the impenetrable, immeasurable ... unfathomable distance, in short — Nature!!!

Fair friends and swarthy foes.

A rich uncle, liberal or conservative, depending upon the circumstances. His guidance is not as useful to the hero as his death.

An aunt in Tambov.

A doctor with a worried face, who holds out hope for the crisis; frequently he has a cane with a cane-head and a baldspot. And where there is a doctor you also find rheumatism from righteous work, migraines, cephalitis, attendance on those wounded at a duel and the inevitable advice to take the waters.

A servant who had already served the old masters, who is ready to crawl anywhere, even into the fire, for his masters. A remarkable wag.

A dog who can do everything but speak, a parrot and a nightingale.

A cottage on the outskirts of Moscow and a mortgaged estate in the South.

Electricity, which is usually completely out of place.

A briefcase of Russian leather, Chinese porcelain, an English saddle, a revolver that never misses fire, a medal on one's chest, pineapples, champagne, truffles and oysters.

Accidental eavesdropping as the cause of great discoveries.

An endless quantity of interjections and attempts to use technical terminology where suitable.

Delicate observations on quite gross circumstances.

Very frequently a missing ending.
Seven deadly sins at the beginning and a wedding at the end.
The End. 4

The second type of parody is directed against the adventure novel,
the roman-boulevard, based on foreign models and frequently utilizing
exotic settings in order to mask poverty of invention and stylistic in-
competence no less glaring than that found in novels of Russian life.
Here Čechov's parodies consist of wild agglomerations of improbable
and incomprehensible events expressed outlandishly. The three-page
"A Thousand and One Passions, or A Terrible Night (A novel in one
part with an epilogue) dedicated to Victor Hugo" (1880) begins at
midnight during a fearful storm, contains a mysterious carriage ride,
curses and imprecations, murders, wine at the hotel "The Purple
Hippopotamus," demonic revenge by the light of the moon, that
"impartial, silent witness of the sweet moments of love and vengeance"
(I 117), marriage, a trip to America, the return three years later accom-
panied by a child and a negro retainer, the whole work punctuated
by farcical reflections and inept metaphors at every pretext. Thus "a
coachman is brother to the wind," "the sky was dark as printer's ink. It
was dark as the inside of a hat that has been put on one's head. A dark
night is a day inside a nutshell." The action is suited to the style: "I
looked at her demonically. She noticed my look. Reason left her. I
killed her. It is better to die than to live without reason."

Occasionally a parody of an adventure novel is based on real material.
Čechov acted as reporter during the Rykov Trial of 1884, and evidently
shortly thereafter wrote his "Mysteries of a Hundred Forty-four Cata-
strophes, or A Russian Rocambole (An enormous novel in abbreviated
form) translated from the French," which was not published in
Čechov's lifetime. Again there is much incomprehensible, unmotivated,
disconnected action, the more striking as much of the parody consists of
telegrams that necessarily have to be discreet. But more frequently
Čechov uses exotic settings to parody by grotesque distortion the
improbable events and passions of popular fiction. Thus "Artists'
Wives (translated from the Portuguese)" (1882) is set in a Lisbon
hotel and treats the shortcomings of popular fiction in Russia. In "The
Sinner from Toledo (translated from the Spanish)" (1881) the hero
finds a solution to his problem by poisoning his wife — a witch — and
delivering her body to the Inquisition, for while he would like to have
his sins remitted by denouncing her, he cannot out of love for her
bring himself to do so while she is alive. "Flying Islands. By Jules
Verne. A Parody" (1883) clearly is directed at another fashionable

---

4 *Soč.* (1930), I 105.

genre. The stage, too, is subjected to similar treatment — a popular melodrama is parodied in 1884 in "Unclean Tragedians and Leprous Dramatists (A terribly, horribly, disgustingly desperate trrragedy)".

It would probably be a kindness to Čechov's reputation to dismiss the puerile humor of these works and to relegate them to the undistinguished sketches and stories he produced at that time in order to support his family. Nevertheless, they reflect his concern with action, with plot, with "the faculty of rapid, passionate, almost reckless improvisation" which Henry James at one time thought the most important aspect of a storyteller's art. [5] Thus at one extreme his parodies are directed against the commonplace in art and life [6] and at the other at the distortion of reality in literature that results from a failure to deal meaningfully with life. Nor is it surprising that these attacks recur in Čechov, for surely the essence of his greatness lies in dealing with the ordinary and commonplace imaginatively and sympathetically.

Among Čechov's early attempts to write a novel *Nenužnaja Pobeda* ("An Unnecessary Triumph") was undertaken in 1882 as a result of a bet that he could produce a work in a foreign setting as good as the material being translated. Its power of invention is in no way inferior to that shown in Čechov's models. As it is set in Hungary and patterned after Mór Jókai's style (Jókai enjoyed a vogue not only in Russia but elsewhere, including the United States), it was taken by many to be another of Jókai's works. Like them, its action is rapid and variegated, the scenes and effects sensational, its characters flat. It is an adventure novel, or simply a potboiler, about an itinerant musician and his beautiful daughter. The plot hinges on the daughter's desire to avenge her insulted father, on the rapid decline of two noble families, the machinations of sanctimonious in-laws, on unrequited love and in the end, reconciliation and death. A gentle and well-intentioned, though bankrupt, nobleman falls in love with the musician's daughter Il'ka and promises to marry her if she will bring him a dowry of a million. Her rise in the theatre is spectacular, and she so manages her affairs that when she finally agrees to sell herself for 120,000 francs the offer comes at the height of a Parisian orgy and eight people draw lots for her. A Lyon manufacturer "who paid in his hundred twenty thousand 'in jest' and who could profit from it only by a kiss!" (I 276) wins the

---

[5] Henry James, *French Novels and Novelists* (New York, 1904), p. 212.

[6] In a letter of March 11, 1889 to Suvorin (XIV 330) he writes apropos of a novel he never finished: "I still cannot manage the technique. I am still weak on that score, and I feel that I am making a lot of crude mistakes. There will be overlong passages and stupidities. I will try to avoid unfaithful wives, suicides, kulaks, virtuous peasants, devoted slaves, moralizing old ladies, kind nurses, provincial wits, red-nosed captains and "new" people, though in places I badly fall into platitudes."

drawing. Baron Artur von Sainitz accepts the money after ruefully commenting that he had meant a million thalers, not francs (the 40,000 needed in addition to the lottery money presumably come from other sources), but shortly thereafter he is deprived of his nobility through a false accusation. Il'ka poisons herself after discovering she has misjudged her father's insultor.

As an imitation of someone else's style and setting "An Unnecessary Victory" has little in common even with Čechov's early work. The descriptions are quite conventional and superficial ("The sun reached the midpoint of its journey to the east" (215)), the characterization perfunctory, the psychology practically absent. Events are explained by author's comments rather than presented through action. Yet Čechov makes a fair bid for the unsophisticated reader's attention until the pace of events is accelerated even beyond the norms of the adventure novel. Čechov was to complain later that he could not adequately develop his material within the limits the editor Lejkin had set him, and then repeatedly complained that he rushed all his endings and thereby spoiled his work, but one cannot help feeling that this time he was relieved when the editor Kičeev, feeling that the novel had occupied a sufficient number of issues, suggested that Čechov dispose of it in two more episodes — "one in Paris, the second the conclusion, and *punctum*. Henceforth we had better publish short stories." [7]

Even in his early, derivative, conventional work, however, Čechov achieved some balance between the literary hack and the sensitive artist. In an article of 1884 describing current reading tastes, he writes:

There are and have been terrible things in this world, beginning with Polyphemus and ending with rural liberals, but such horrors (I am speaking of the novels our Moscow paper-devourers like *Evil Spirit*, *Domino* (of all colors) and others treat the public with) have never occurred before. Panic strikes you when you read them. You become terrified at the thought that there exist such terrible minds from which such "Patricides," "Dramas," etc. can crawl out. Murder, cannibalism, the loss of millions, visions, false nobility, castle ruins, owls, skeletons, somnambulists and the devil only knows what there is in these convulsions of imprisoned and drunken thought!... Psychology takes the leading place in it. Our novelists are specialists in it. Their heroes even spit with a tremor in their voice and clenching their "beating" temples. The public's hair stands on end, their stomachs turn, but nevertheless they devour it and praise it. They like our scribbling. *Suum cuique*. [8]

He had to produce material for popular consumption, and he knew

---

[7] *Soč.* (1930), I 573. Letter to Čechov dated July 29, 1882.
[8] *Oskolki moskovskoj žizni* quoted in *A. P. Čechov o literature* (Moscow, 1955), p. 25-26.

what was expected. But he also sought to endow this material with greater significance. In one of his first successes based on the parody, "The Safety Match (The Story of a Crime)" (1884), the devices of the popular detective story, with its excessive ingenuity in finding and interpreting clues, its dependence upon highly refined psychological analysis, its reticent witnesses and dubious alibis are employed only in order to reach a ludicrous conclusion. The murdered man turns out to be very much alive, being kept by another man's wife — an ending that is far from romantic, if not even somewhat sordid. Extravagant leaps from appearance to gory interpretation satisfy the sensation-seeking penchant of the public. But beyond the literary parody Čechov deals with the repeated refusal on the part of the investigator and others to evaluate facts realistically, to accept the commonplace and humdrum as such. The attempt to seek more appealing explanations, like the unquestioning acceptance of everything by the police superintendent, is rooted in the failure to seek significance and meaning in life. "The Safety Match" states it humorously.

That this trend was already important in Čechov's mind can be gathered from his other attempts to extend the scope of the story and to write a longer work with a broad background, profounder characterization, and richer thematic development. One such work is the story *Cvety zapozdalye* ("Belated Blossom") (1882), interesting despite its schematic presentation. Here the major chord of Čechov is adumbrated, for the story deals with the theme of wasted lives, of the inability of people to communicate with each other; it exposes the amoral, inconsiderate, dissipated, purblind nobility and the rigorously efficient, if unimaginative and narrow, life of a doctor (who speaks almost exclusively in infinitives!) and who formerly was a serf of this decaying family. Technically too, the story is significant, as Čechov already uses the repeated incident where, because communication is at a standstill, "nothing happens," though each episode contributes to the cumulative effect. The ending and the unmotivated realization to which the doctor comes are beyond the limits of credibility and seriously damage the story.

But the central item in Čechov's early attempts at the novel is *Drama na ochote* ("A True Event"), in length and complexity unique among Čechov's works. It too started as a parody of the detective novel, with frequent references to popular writers, to what is expected from fiction, to the differences between fiction and life, and it contains many of the props of the detective story. The interesting innovation here is that the author and leading character of this first-person narrative is also the murderer, though of course this cannot be stated in the work. Consequently an elaborate framework is designed for the central por-

tion, which is subtitled "From the Notes of an Examining Magistrate."
An editor receives a manuscript and makes certain observations about
the personality of the man who offers it to him. After the end of the
manuscript the author returns and the editor confronts him with
internal evidence (which he had previously signaled to the reader by
footnotes, pointing out discrepancies and incorrect procedures), that the
author is the murderer.

In the narrative Čechov has provided precisely what the reading
public wants and has done so with considerable technical competence.
It begins with the effective "A husband has killed his wife! Oh, how
stupid you are! Do finally give me some sugar!" (III 308) which
wakes the narrator and introduces a conversation on crimes and local
heat. Only after several exchanges does it become clear that these are
phrases repeated by a parrot. Less shocking, but as traditional, is the
remainder of the manuscript, which consists of two very different
sections. The first is devoted to the life and events of the moody narrator Kamyšev, an educated, intelligent man, indifferent to his surroundings, serving as examining magistrate in a rural retreat. It
describes Kamyšev's friend, a dissipated, cirrhotic, sensuous nobleman,
a beautiful but vain and shallow young lady who marries the nobleman's
elderly overseer and then becomes the nobleman's and narrator's
mistress, her insane father, a mysterious Pole who exerts great influence over the nobleman, and other interesting folk. Similar material,
and the crudest, most cynical portions of the narrative were omitted
according to the editor's note (470-1), despite his earlier assurance that
he has published the complete work.

The second section begins immediately after a "large gap" in the
manuscript and contains numerous erasures and gaps, also quite common in the tradition of the "found manuscript." It differs greatly from
the first and is devoted primarily to the investigation of the murder, a
second crime, and the trial. It is mechanical in its undramatic trans-
cription of the investigation. This section is later described by the
editor as "having everything a crime novel needs — crime, witnesses,
investigation, a sentence of 15 years at hard labor......" (472) though
he has incessantly pointed out its shortcomings in the text, and the
absence of the real culprit in the conclusion. The second part, then,
is essentially a report. The editor comments on the falseness of the
action committed, rather than on its literary statement. In the first
part, on the other hand, the narrator constantly referred to the difference between novels and reality: "Husbands only kill wives in
novels, and then in the tropics, where African passions boil" (308).
"The bride got up from the table and left — what an effective and
theatrical section for a provincial novel of 'high society'!" (386) Kamy-

šev's servant Polikarp, like Gogol's Petruška, reads everything that comes within his purvey, but acknowledges "only terrible, strongly affecting novels with noble gentlemen, poisons and underground passages, and dubs all the rest 'nonsense' " (313). The narrator repeatedly refers to Polikarp in order to emphasize the difference between the use of objects and devices in these books and their use here. The servant himself ("my civilized fool" [312]), for all his attraction to sensational novels, has a very strict moral sense. He constantly berates Kamyšev for misconduct, threatens to leave him, will not confuse fiction with life on important issues. He thereby makes a distinction some of Čechov's later intellectual characters — Laevskij in "The Duel," Treplev in "The Seagull" — do not make.

Such remarks on the novel are essentially the appurtenances of irony. Through them Čechov invites the reader to consider more carefully the matter before him. The very form of the novel indicates Čechov's desire to overcome the limitations of the adventure novel, [9] and he uses it to emphasize important issues. The narrator maintains that his story is not fictional but true, that its events are unlike those in novels and conclude differently. The editor at first is interested in the work only from a professional point of view. He does not care whether it is true or not, so long as it pleases his readers. But as he reads the story, he is repelled by the narrator's moral coarseness and by his falseness during the investigation. The editor now emphasizes the inaccuracy of the manuscript and subordinates narrative interest to truth. When, at the end, he again meets the author, he is appalled at his indifference, his refusal to admit his guilt publicly and assume its burden. The editor is overcome by a feeling of horror and terror, not for himself, but rather for the murderer and for man in general (373). Kamyšev points out that few readers will guess the identity of the true culprit, that they will be amazed at Kamyšev's skill as an investigator and will curse the putative murderer. They will thus have been seduced by the novel form into condoning the narrator's behavior, of which his crime is a logical result. Kamyšev will have employed the form to make a veiled confession and to rid himself of the oppressive torture that for eight years people have been looking upon him without suspecting his crimes. Even for Kamyšev the strain of this burden is too great. The editor is left alone in his office thinking bitter (but unspecified) thoughts, and feeling depressed.

---

[9] Shortly before this, of course, Dostoevskij had used the form in "The Brothers Karamazov". There are some interesting purely external similarities: the shift in the center of each work from the question of what will happen to the search for the murderer, the discussion of aberrations (affekty) as justification for the act, the fact that the murderer is not legally punished, the orgies, etc.

Thus Čechov uses the form itself to introduce more important issues than those customarily dealt with in the detective story. Čechov touches upon many subjects and approximates his conception of the novel: a long work well populated by different kinds of characters, full of movement, excitement and passion. But perhaps the form itself makes it impossible for Čechov to write this novel successfully. There is too much editorial guidance and warning, unmotivated action, gaps, heavy-handed and excessive foreshadowing. Its most striking feature is the large amount of dialogue utilized in order to communicate its events. This tends to make the work appear more dramatic than it in fact is, for the dialogue, while not unskillful, does not communicate economically its required material. Čechov seems very conscious of balancing his effects, of creating an essentially "literary" work. Hence there is a great deal of doubling: two orgies, two storms, two murders, two rejections of the other lady involved and other doublets. Each presumably casts new light on its mate, but unfortunately the device is used mechanically. From one point of view these shortcomings can be attributed to the *persona* of Kamyšev who, after all, is an amateur, but when compared with other works of the period, it becomes clear that they are Čechov's.

The smaller units support this contention. Kamyšev's narrative and his attitudes toward life are distinguished neither by originality nor depth. His assumptions frequently do not correspond to the reality, in part because he prefers the "light genre" in description [10] and is quite aware that he has a limited understanding of himself and others (314). One of Čechov's earlier critics maintained that the descriptions of nature in *The Shooting Party* indicated considerable care and revision on Čechov's part. [11] Yet they are trite and literary:

> We got out of the carriage. The rain had already stopped. The thunder cloud that sparked with lightning and emitted an angry grumbling, sped to the northeast, more and more disclosing the blue starry sky. It seemed as though a heavily armed force, that had wreaked havoc and taken a terrible toll, hurried toward new victories. The remaining clouds pursued it and rushed, as though they were afraid of not catching up with it. Nature received its world back (337).

Particularly in view of the beauty and function that descriptions of similar phenomena have later in Čechov's work, this example is strikingly weak. It is possible that the description is designed to characterize

---

[10] *Cf.* III 313-314, 352.

[11] A. A. Izmajlov, *Pervye šagi Antoši Čechonte,* in A. P. Čechov, *Sobranie sočinenij* (St. Petersburg, A. F. Marks, 1911), XXII 134.

Kamyšev by showing us the operation of his mind. But this is unlikely
from the rest of Čechov's portrait.

In presenting the main character, Čechov is from the first concerned
to show a man whose inner impulses are at variance with his outer
appearance. In the introductory section he presents a man who is not
only tall, powerful, handsome and well-dressed — as a hero of a
popular novel should be — but also decisive, forceful, and apparently
incapable of deceit. This view is offered by the editor as an interpretation the reader may well find contradicted later in the text. As soon
as Kamyšev's narrative begins, we find that the man is impulsive in
his actions and undecisive when confronted with personal decisions or
the duties of his office, who is indifferent to his physical surroundings
and possessions, and who, in fact, at the count's invitation at the beginning of the story returns, without much vacillation, to the riotous
living he had renounced only a year before. Čechov efficiently discloses
these defects through Kamyšev's remarks about others and by his own
volatility. Other characters disclose what Kamyšev no longer remembers: the results of Kamyšev's violence which followed in the wake of
physical or psychological stimulation. Čechov even tries to indicate
through these abulia or lapses and through the opinion of Kamyšev's
friend, a doctor, that Kamyšev is a "psychopath" whose behavior may
be the result of psychological malfunction. However, Čechov is much
more interested in the moral meaning of the act. Kamyšev is decisive
and swift when his concern is self-preservation. At the end of "The
Shooting Party" he will not surrender himself and asks the editor to
look at the decrepit count of whom he has taken complete charge.
Čechov thereby stresses the ineradicable tie between the two and indicates the physical counterpart to Kamyšev's moral degeneration.

In going beyond the confines of the detective novel, Čechov begins
to utilize the themes he will later exploit more fully. He touches
briefly on the degeneration of the landed gentry and on the corruption
of their retainers, and the theme of unequal marriage and superficiality treated here is later expanded in "Anna on the Neck" and
"The Grasshopper". He deals with provinciality and its expectations
and the desire to move to a more stimulating setting. Most important, he
writes about men of ability who cannot attune themselves to the life
around them and who consequently turn their natural gifts against
themselves, as with the narrator Kamyšev, or who waste them as
Kamyšev's friend the doctor does, by failing to create a meaningful
existence with these gifts.

To the end of the 1880's Čechov seriously considered writing a novel.
The idea recurs in his correspondence, both apropos of his first mature
attempts in the longer forms for the "respectable" literary periodicals

(the so-called "thick journals") such as "The Steppe" and "The Name-Day Party" (*Imeniny*) and of incomplete or unrealized projects. [12] In 1887 the idea of writing a novel occurred to him, and when he abandoned it to write "The Steppe," he described it as follows to Grigorovič: "I will continue the interrupted novel in the summer. That novel encompasses a whole district (nobility and territorial), the private lives of several families. ... the novel will deal with ordinary people, intelligent people, women, love, marriage, children — here you'll feel at home and won't be bored." [13] Later that year he again writes Grigorovič about the novel, indicating that until it ripens in his mind he will write shorter things, but that he will not waste on these shorter compositions the material he has already gathered and in part written. He amplifies the content by noting that "my novel encompasses several families and a whole district with forests, rivers, ferries, railroads. In the center of the district there are two main figures, male and female, around whom the others are grouped. I still don't have a political, religious and philosophical world-view. I change it every month, and therefore I have to limit myself to describing how my heroes love, marry, beget children, die and how they speak." [14] The following year he writes to A. M. Evrejnova that the censor will find a great deal of work in his forthcoming novel, for "half the characters in it say 'I don't believe in God,' there is a father whose son was sentenced to life at hard labor for armed resistance, there is a police inspector who is ashamed of his uniform, a marshall of nobility whom everyone hates, etc." [15] More detail about it is given in a letter to Suvorin the following day: "I call it "Stories from my Friend's Lives," and am writing it in the form of separate, complete stories, closely connected to each other by a common plot, ideas and characters. Each story has its own title. Don't think that the novel will consist of fragments. No, it will be a real novel, a whole torso, where each character will be organically necessary. Grigorovič, to whom you communicated the content of the first chapter, was afraid that I used a student who died and therefore won't go through the novel, that is, will be superfluous. But the student is only a nail in a big shoe — a detail." [16]

---

[12] Towards the end of 1887, Čechov sought to escape from financial straits by publishing "a work of 1500 lines" (approximately fifteen times his usual length), that he had finished (III 373, 378). As he never produced it although the publisher was willing to take it, this was clearly a hoax. Early that year he had conceived a novel and frequently returned to the idea (see the letter to Suvorin of March 11, 1889 cited above), but nothing came of it.

[13] Letter to Grigorovič, January 12, 1888. XIV 15.

[14] Letter to Grigorovič, October 9, 1888. XIV 183.

[15] March 10, 1889. XIV 328.

[16] XIV 330.

Although this novel was never written, another that Čechov embarked on around that time was. At the end of 1888 he writes to Suvorin: "Oh what a story I have begun!...... I am writing on the theme of love. I chose the feuilleton-belletristic form. A decent man carries off a decent man's wife and writes his opinion about it. He lives with her — an opinion. He leaves her — again an opinion. In passing I touch on the theatre, on the prejudices of differing convictions, on the Georgian Military Highway, about family life, on the incapacity of the contemporary intellectual to live such a life, about Pečorin, about Onegin, about the Kazbek......" [17] The work stems from Čechov's two-fold concern with the love story and with the current social scene. It was subjected to similar considerations of form that Čechov had to solve in connection with another story he was engaged on at the time. Of this story — which may ultimately have contributed to "The Duel" — Čechov writes that "It is turning out boring. I am learning to write 'comments' and am trying to avoid conversational language. Before I can begin the novel ["The Duel"], I have to teach myself to convey my thoughts freely in narrative form. I am busy with that training now ... the husband gives me a manuscript, his 'autobiographical sketch' consisting of a mass of short chapters. I choose the chapters that seem most interesting to me ... my story starts directly from the seventh chapter ... It is turning out as a feuilleton rather than as a story." [18] At least until March he is still troubled by the technical problems of the novel. [19]

"The Duel" was interrupted for the play "Ivanov" and the trip to Sachalin. When Čechov returned in 1891 he finished the work, without undue complaints of formal difficulties, except that he was becoming bored with it and thought it lacked movement. [20]

Čechov never came closer to the "traditional" novel than in "The Duel" (1891). It is unquestionably the most "literary" of Čechov's works, constantly referring as it does to literary types and situations, and in that sense may perhaps be considered as a late example of the literary proces that impelled Čechov to attempt novels that are essentially anti-novels. "The Duel" is set in the Caucasus, or more exactly on the Eastern shores of the Black Sea. This traditionally romantic and exotic setting affords Čechov an opportunity to assert the contrast between expectation and reality. He thus follows in the footsteps of Tolstoj, who had already in his early work and in "The Cossacks" (1862) attempted to de-romanticize this picturesque staple of Russian

---

[17] November 20-25, 1888. XIV 239.
[18] November 28, 1888. XIV 242.
[19] See note 6 *supra*.
[20] Letter to Suvorin, February 23, 1891. XV 163-164.

literature. The locale is not far removed from that used in Lermontov's novel, for which Čechov's admiration is well known, and this novel provides Čechov with both the figure of the good-natured Samojlenko, who is clearly based on Maksim Maksimyč, the inarticulate but compassionate military man, and Laevskij, who patterns himself after "the superflous man" so frequently deemed to be in Pečorin. Von Koren is patterned after Turgenev's Bazarov, and the duel itself is based on the similar episode in "Fathers and Children." At the novel's center is a human relationship that is an almost programmatic reply to "The Kreutzer Sonata" and to that of Tolstoj's Vronskij and Anna Karenina. The love affair, as in a Turgenev novel, is projected against a background of more or less contemporary social and intellectual problems afflicting Russia. As in a Turgenev novel, again, these themes are developed quite obviously and even somewhat too neatly.

"The Duel" begins at the unusual and novelistically very difficult point when a man has fallen out of love with a woman and seeks to part from her. The protagonist, Laevskij, is a weak charakter who must not be made into a villain since he is to be partially rehabilitated at the end. Čechov presents this man in the larger context of the issues with which his society struggles. To Laevskij, Čechov contrasts the ambitious zoologist von Koren, who very adequately points out Laevskij's shortcomings, but who is even more unacceptable to the reader in his pedantic rationality, his fanatic belief in science, and his lack of tolerance for human failings. Von Koren condemns Laevskij out of hand not on moral grounds but because he views him is an unproductive, corrupting, pernicious member of society, and as such one unfit for survival. While Laevskij blames his plight on civilization and its debilitating effect on man, von Koren finds an explanation for everything in the natural world and by analogy has sanguine hopes for civilization. His explanations for man, however, are inadequate until he understands compassionately the imperfection of man, and this he can only do — and then only partially — after the struggle between him and Laevskij has changed the course of both their lives.

Laevskij constantly compares himself to outdated literary prototypes. He is the latest incarnation of the "superfluous man," the sensitive man of the 1880's crippled by civilization. He is hampered by neurotic anxiety and "Hamlet-like indecision" when action is called for, yet he interminably ponders his neurosis and superfluity. Laevskij assumes this pose for it serves his personality and interests in many ways. It has a physical counterpart in Laevskij's gesture following his attack of hysteria, when he tries to attribute the onset of the attack to a stitch in his side. Gesture and pose both betray Laevskij's weakness, but they do not prove him false: Čechov objected to Suvorin's suggestion that he change the name to "The Lie (*Lož*), as such a title "is appropriate only when one treats a conscious lie. An unconscious lie is a mistake rather than a lie. Tolstoj calls our having money and eating meat a lie — that's going too far." [21] Čechov uses this falseness to communicate Laevkij's ineffectual dealing with his life, and to indicate his increasing desperation that leads to the hysterical fit and the duel. Laevskij does not entirely belong within the tradition he claims he continues. [22] Unlike its members, he rarely speaks and then almost exclusively about himself. On other topics he limits himself to fragmentary, brief communications. Čechov frequently indicates Laevskij's conflicts and tribulations (as he does that of the female lead) through an inner monologue that verbally formulates the deepest level of his misery, and by the outer sign of his discomfort, the abrupt cruelty of his actions.

Von Koren, his opposite, is never given an inner monologue, just as though he were not concerned with such notions. All that he thinks is uttered, usually in lengthy set pieces, whether the subject is science, Laevskij or civilization. In one way he too is an artificial figure, who patterns himself after Bazarov. His scientific observations and pedantic explanations of natural phenomena characterize the rigor of his mind and the firmness of his principles. Unlike Bazarov, however, whose grandeur stems from his devotion to these tasks, von Koren is also a self-appointed arbiter of society and social ills. His venomous opposition to Laevskij is grounded on more than the scientific principle that a weak specimen can corrupt the whole species. Laevskij himself points out von Koren's overriding ambition and his need to conquer the world single-handedly (VII 370-1), while he recognizes the likelihood of von Koren's achieving something out of the ordinary. Laevskij at first considers civilization a corrupting influence; von Koren accepts it as a regulatory organism that must not be threatened. Von Koren quickly judges Laevskij as unfit for life, and then maintains that Laevskij should be eliminated from society just as the insufficiently fit in nature are destroyed by their enemies. During the discussion with Dr. Samojlenko, von Koren talks about animals' protective devices and expatiates particularly on the mole. These animals have the curious habit of beginning to clear a platform as soon as two of them meet underground. They then begin to fight until the weaker drops (381). Precisely this image comes to the reader's mind when von Koren duels

---

[21] Letter to Suvorin, September 8, 1891. XV 240.

[22] See the interesting article on the basic characteristics of this vexing "personage" in F. F. Seeley's *The Heyday of the 'Superfluous Man' in Russia, SEER* (December, 1952), particularly pp. 108-110.

with Laevskij, and what he finds admirable in moles becomes a repulsive destructiveness in man. Von Koren is intrigued by the mole's extraordinarily powerful chest and jaws, and he rather ineptly claims that if a mole were the size of an elephant it would be invincible. He neglects to mention that when nature provides animals with a particular weapon it usually does so at the expense of a weakness. The mole is blind, and the mole-like duel of the two protagonists is based on blind hatred. A mole may not tolerate another of its species because the balance of nature demands it, but such intolerance is unthinkable in human society.

Laevskij's hostility toward his mistress is based on their fundamental similarity. His self-torments about leaving Nadežda Fedorovna are balanced by her guilt at her recent unfaithfulness to him; his intellectual superficiality by her pretensions; his chimerical hopes of a new life in Petersburg by her daydream of a self-sacrificing life devoted to supporting Laevskij anonymously. Laevskij finds a sympathetic listener in Dr. Samojlenko, Nadežda in the townswoman Mar'ja Konstantinovna. These friends emphasize the need to make the relationship permanent in both the legal and personal sense, for Laevskij and Nadežda Fedorovna love and depend upon each other, even if they do not fully recognize it. Von Koren also finds a sounding board in a deacon of limited perception, whom he tries to spur to greater deeds at the sacrifice of his family life.

Čechov uses these pairings to illuminate various aspects of the central theme, which is nothing less than to lead as many of the characters as possible to a profounder conception or clearer articulation of the meaning of human love and thereby to understand more clearly the universe around them. This he accomplishes at different levels. Samojlenko, friend to both Laevskij and von Koren, attempts to moderate quarrels but fails to formulate sucessfully his understanding of human nature. His role in human affairs is rather less successful than his exertions in the kitchen. Samojlenko can only appeal to what he considers obvious human responses. He accepts all life without differentiating moral from other phenomena, as can be seen in his reaction at dinner when von Koren claims that Laevskij should be executed or sent to hard labor: " 'What are you saying?' Samojlenko said, terrified. 'With pepper, with pepper,' he shouted with despair in his voice, when he noticed that the deacon was eating stuffed eggplant without pepper."(348). Nadežda Fedorovna's confidante is far more practical and realistic in her appraisal of the relationship and has an eye for domestic detail and for decorum. But even she cannot close her house to Nadežda Fedorovna for her moral and physical laxity. Her good nature and her sympathy for the suffering creature prevail over her stricter intentions. Finally the deacon, who at first is merely a foolish giggler, under the pressure of von Koren's exhortations becomes increasingly aware of his love for his newly-wedded wife. By the end of the story he has found a new dimension to his life. It is the deacon who saves Laevskij's life by shouting at the crucial moment in the duel, and it is also the deacon who first notices that Laevskij now walks like an old man. He signals to the reader the change that Laevskij has undergone during the night preceding the duel, in the course of which Laevskij assessed all the falseness of his former existence. As the extent of his attachment to Nadežda Fedorovna becomes clear, so he gains a purpose in life which leads him to a wondrous reëvaluation of everything he previously had taken for granted.

Everything in the work points toward that climactic night — the antagonism of Laevskij and von Koren, the consequences of Nadežda Fedorovna's infidelity, even nature which plays a striking symbolic role. At the very beginning of the story when the characters swim in order to escape from the oppressive heat, a wave covers Samojlenko and Laevskij and interrupts their reflections about the proper way of ordering one's life. The heat does not abate, and the internal stresses of the characters increase. On the eve of the duel, the rumblings that have sporadically sounded erupt into a fearful squall — clearly designed as a counterpart to the development within Laevskij. On the morning of the duel the sun's rays shine with an unusual green tinge that must as clearly herald a new era. These rays are first noticed by von Koren, who marvels at their beauty. Since he had previously insisted on explaining scientifically the phosphorescent beauty of the sea, this also signals a change within von Koren. These details are part of a larger scheme that constantly supports the themes of the work.

The arid, hot, provincial town does not correspond to Laevskij's and Nadežda Fedorovna's expectations of the Caucasian setting. Quickly they become disenchanted and abandon their dreams of a productive life. Samojlenko, who has lived in the town for eighteen years and has a different point of view, cannot understand why Laevskij does not like the Caucasus: "He thought that the boulevard was very well laid out, that the young cypress trees, the eucalyptuses and the ugly, anemic palm trees were pretty and would in time give much shade" (333). Laevskij is far from insensitive to nature, but his enjoyment depends upon his state of mind. To Samojlenko's exclamations on the beauty of the scenery on the way to the picnic, Laevskij replies: "I see nothing good in that. To be ecstatic about nature all the time shows the poverty of one's imagination. In comparison with what my imagination can do for me, all these rivulets and rocks are junk and nothing more" (357). Čechov follows this remark with a splendid description of the mountains and rivers. When Laevskij returns from the duel he remembers "how oppressive it was for him to drive at dawn, when the road, the rocks and the mountains were wet and dark and the uncertain future seemed terrible, like a bottomless abyss, and now the rain drops that hung on the grass and rocks shone like diamonds, nature smiled gaily, and the fearful future was left behind . . . 'It's all over,' he thought of his past (424)."

Laevskij and Nadežda renounce their former life. Instead of running away, they stay behind to begin a difficult existence and quotidian routine in order to repay their debts. The abrupt change in their mode of life, which has frequently been criticized as artistically unjustifiable, is actually an ambiguous ending. Their triumph over the inner selves, noted by the deacon, is achieved at the cost of a pitiful dehumanization, noted by von Koren. They have become aged and diffident, their day-dreams have ceded to a humbler reality, and in the act of accepting this life they have lost their former attraction and illusory distinction as literary characters. The undistinguished reality of life is mirrored in the windy, rainy, cold final day, and by the drizzle that ends the story. As a counterpart to human change, summer heat at the beginning of the novel is now replaced by the onset of winter. A new storm is brewing at sea, perhaps destined for von Koren, who has admitted his erroneous estimate of Laevskij's potential and the fallibility of his kind of truth. But the storm is also part of a larger picture. Near the novel's end, the incessantly pulsating sea which had been introduced on the first page and reëmphasized on the morning of the duel during the deacon's walk to the scene, is equated by Laevskij with life, and the determined effort of the boatmen to reach the ship with man's effort to find truth. This is no longer merely a moody observation on Laevskij's part, but a summary of experiences within the work.

Čechov's increasing penetration into life's complexities and the fragility of human aspirations accounts for the compassionate view he took of the situation in "The Duel." That he was able to give its main lines and themes so rich an elaboration can be attributed in large part to the enormous technical advances he had made since "The Shooting Party." While there is much narrative plot in "The Duel," the highly variegated material it encompasses is really organized around the disintegrating relationship of two people. Other figures are introduced in such a way that they contribute to the plot and at the same time expand the theme. Čechov now marshals topical allusions and natural phenomena to underscore his meaning rather than to make comments that bear only mechanically on the work. At crucial points in the novel, characters launch into extended monologues on the intellectual topics they consider most important, and only secondarily comment on their personal involvement in the situation. The reader is thus almost made to feel that he is dealing with literary stereotypes, and he turns gratefully to the skillful use of other kinds of dialogue that shed light on the characters and their thoughts. The dialogue conveys, frequently without direct statement, the evanescent feelings and moods of the characters, as Čechov's brilliant descriptions (which support and enhance the mood of the novel) convey a scene by a few striking details. The plot development is perhaps too obvious and mechanical, and leads to a physical climax that is unusual in Čechov's late works. But the plot and the content of the speeches are surely not what distinguishes "The Duel." The skill with which Čechov conveys the desperation of the two main characters, the bunglings of the samaritan Samojlenko, the way Čechov subordinates setting to his purpose, the dogged reality of the ending, the glimpse of the ineffable in human relations — these are its achievements. Eventually, these were precisely the things Čechov conveyed so well in his dramatic works, where similar thematic development can also be observed.

"The Duel" is the last of Čechov's extended works to assume a traditional form of the novel. He never again wrote a work of such length, and among his longer prose works in later years he developed different techniques and concentrated on other subjects. The novel he had begun earlier may have had bearing on some of the works he wrote later (1895-1901) like "Three Years," "My Life," "Peasants," "In the Ravine" — which bear the mark of a general similarity in theme, treatment and attitude. Yet to speak of them as "novels" is not accurate. Even if they are taken as a unit, [23] they have less claim to the designation "novel" than a work like "A Hero of Our Time," for they lack central focus. They are, however, an expansion of a method that begins with Čechov's first important long works, "The Steppe" and "The Name-Day Party," whose fundamental approach is cumulative impressionism. Čechov refers to "The Steppe" as "An encyclopedia of the steppe" [24] unified by the single character of a nine-year-old boy who goes through a series of experiences in a journey. Because the story ends with the journey's end, Čechov felt it gave the impression of an unfinished story, and he never took it up again. But in fact it has its own kind of unity. Similarly, "The Name-Day Party" presents various characters to the main figure, so that gradually a full canvas unfolds before the reader. The later works can be considered larger units for a larger canvas, but one cannot find a central conception that would weld them into a whole. Indeed, the stories ap-

---

[23] See Anton Chekhov, *Peasants and other stories,* selected and with a preface by Edmund Wilson (Garden City, N.Y., Doubleday Anchor Books, 1956).
[24] Letter to Grigorovič, January 12, 1888. XIV 14.

peared with less and less frequency as Čechov's interests turned increasingly to the stage.

While Čechov keenly appreciated other writers' achievements in the novel, the form always remained somewhat foreign to his talents and his attemps in it are somewhat artificial. Early in his career the impetus toward the novel had been primarily that of financial gain. As his techniques improved and his vision deepened, he found more and more that the rigorous structure novels required did not suit his essentially miniaturist skills. He could better present these by concentrating on a more restricted subject, as for example the development of a single trait or feeling or mood that he could communicate by ever increasing dependence upon narrative and description. The dialogue that had earlier played so important a role in his longer work now also found its appropriate function in Čechov's theatre. There his radical innovations ennabled him finally to present the rich complexities of life, the passions, the excitement, the "larger considerations" he had sought unsuccessfully to embody in the novel.

NILS ÅKE NILSSON

INTONATION AND RHYTHM IN ČECHOV'S PLAYS

I.

"This was an important step in my work for the theatre. I had my own scenic aims... The play had no hero, the main parts were intended for character actors. More hazardous still was the fact that the love intrigue played a completely subordinate part, it hardly existed even. Finally there was not a single outward effect, no shots, no fainting fits, no hysteria, no slap, no trick or, as it was then called, deus ex machina... I wanted to find an interest in the scenic form itself and capture the secret of comedy by simple means." [1]

These words are about a Russian play from the end of the last century, and if one does not already know who wrote them one might be tempted to guess at Čechov. At the end of the 1880's and during the 90's he worked on the drama, trying to find new forms, dissatisfied as he was with the stereotyped patterns dominating the Russian drama of the times. It was not Čechov who wrote the above words, however, but Vladimir Nemirovič-Dančenko, Stanislavskij's co-worker and co-producer at the Moscow Art Theatre, who was also no unknown dramatist in his time.

The play he talks about was called "A New Project" (*Novoe delo*) and was performed in 1890 at the Little Theatre (Malyj teatr) in Moscow. Even if the author's views on his play are of later date and perhaps a little coloured by historical perspective, "A New Project" differed very considerably from the domestic plays which were performed on the Russian stage about 1890. A play without love, without any exciting plot, with the interest wholly centred on the psychological characterisation of the main figures, with very laconic exchanges written in simply everyday language — this was certainly something new.

Čechov followed Nemirovič-Dančenko's authorship with interest. "It seems to me," he wrote in a letter dated 1899, "that this Nemirovič is a very likeable man and that gradually he will develop into a real dramatist. In any case he writes better and better every year." [2] To him Nemirovič-Dančenko's plays were one of several signs that new dramatic forms were slowly working their way forward on the Russian stage. The opposition towards the conventionality of the theatre and the drama which had been raised since the beginning of the 1880's gradually began to give practical results.

---

[1] V. I. Nemirovič-Dančenko, *Iz prošlogo, Leningrad* 1936, p. 37.
[2] A. P. Čechov, *PSSP* XIV 443.

It seems clear to me that one must look on the novelty of Čechov's plays not only against the background of Turgenev's, as always occurs nowadays. It is often considered that Čechov, in his opposition towards the set forms of the times, allied himself to Turgenev's dramatic experiments. In this way one is able to find a certain continuity in the development of the Russian drama and Čechov's plays do not stand so isolated as at first glance might be supposed. Nemirovič-Dančenko had already felt that there was a certain similarity here, [3] as also Mejerchol'd was later to do. [4] It is known that Čechov saw at least one performance of Turgenev's plays; his opinion was, however, negative: he thought them old-fashioned (PSSP XX 73).

It seems to be that certain outer similarities have prompted too close a parallel. But these similarities can be explained in part by Turgenev's dramatic art, like Čechov's, having its roots in an opposition towards the prevailing conventionality of the theatre of his times, the result of which was a search for new, simpler, more natural means of expression. And further, those qualities in Turgenev which are considered to presage Čechov is that his plot is simple and realistic, his characters are everyday people, their actions natural, the dialogues smooth and colloquial but at the same time full of hidden dramatic tension. [5] Just these qualities, however, may be found in some few of Čechov's contemporary playwrights who understood, as he did, that a renovation was necessary. It is therefore not surprising that they are evident in the above-mentioned play by Nemirovič-Dančenko. It is thus quite clear that one must regard Čechov's plays also against a background of these tendencies — weak as they may be — towards new forms which are to be found in several playwrights now quite forgotten who were active just those years around 1890. Of course I by no means wish to say that they give a complete explanation of certain original innovations in Čechov's dramatic technique which belong to him alone, but they can give a certain background to some of them. This is a question which still awaits deeper investigation. [6]

There is one special thing in Nemirovič-Dančenko's play that I should like to dwell on here. One of the main characters, A. Kalguev, says at one stage: "When someone speaks to me I hardly understand the

---

[3] M. Stroeva, *Čechov i chudožestvennyj teatr*, Moskva 1955, p. 156.

[4] V. Mejerchol'd, *O teatre*, S.-Peterburg 1912, p. 112.

[5] *Teatr* 1954, 7, p. 41.

[6] There is some material on this subject in a paper by V. B. Chalizov, *Russkaja dramaturgija nakanune "Ivanova" i "Čajki"*, in: *Naučnye doklady vysšej školy. Filologičeskie nauki*, 1959, 1, p. 20 f. See also N. P. Ljul'ko, *A. P. Čechov i russkij teatr 80-90-ch godov XIX v.*, in: *Vestnik Leningradskogo universiteta*, 1955, 6, p. 82.

words he pronounces at all. To be quite honest the words don't exist for me. I disown them completely. They never show me what the human soul in reality wants. But the sounds — they affect me. Do you follow me? The sounds of the voice. By them I am always able, like a prophet, to discern whether a man is happy at heart or not." [7]

The author demonstrates his thesis in different ways in the play. When Stolbcov, the main character, explains at one point that he is really satisfied with his life and that there is no reason for him to work at the new project he had spoken so much of, his tone of voice belies the fact, and one of the characters does point this out. And when Stolbcov is promised money to start on his project he becomes so joyful that he wanders around humming a tune, and without words those present gradually understand that he has succeeded and is to be congratulated.

This idea that the intonation, the voice often better than the words can unveil what is happening inside a person is of course no new discovery in Russian literature. The man who had propounded this thesis earlier with much emphasis was Lev Tolstoj, as is well known. It is constantly expressed in his novels. Speaking of Nataša in "War and Peace" for example he says that "she could not write because she found it impossible in writing to express even a thousandth part of what she was used to expressing with her voice, her smile and her gaze." The same contrast between the communicative content of the words and the emotionally charged delivery of them which Nemirovič-Dančenko uses in his play had already been made use of by Tolstoj, in the following example from "War and Peace", for instance: " — What? What? How dare you! said Teljamin. But the words sounded like a piteous, desparing cry, begging for forgiveness. As soon as Rostov heard their sound an enormous stone of doubt fell from his breast." [8]

This technique, new for the novel, of describing what is going on inside a person originated with Tolstoj in a demand for greater realism. What he was against was that the novel expressed feelings solely in words. The characters gave long descriptions of how they thought and felt. In reality, Tolstoj asserted, they did not. People intimate their feelings to each other less by the words themselves than by mime, the gestures and movements that accompany the words and — of no less importance — by the intonation itself.

2.

Similar demands for greater realism in the reproduction of human

---

[7] V. I. Nemirovič-Dančenko, *Povesti i p'esy,* Moskva 1958, p. 359.

[8] See V. Vinogradov, *O jazyke Tolstogo* (50-60-e gody), in: *Literaturnoe nasledstvo* 35/36, p. 196 ff.

feelings must sooner or later be made for the stage. We have seen how one of the main characters in Nemirovič-Dančenko's play rejects the value of words as evidence of what a man thinks and feels. He sets the voice in place of the words. Čechov goes further on this path. For him there is also a demand for realism in background: on stage everything must be "as in real life", this he never tires of stressing.

But on the other hand, the modern drama — as Čechov himself often points out — shifts the interest more and more from the main action to the inner man, from the outward intrigue to the psychological conflict. How to combine scenic realism with "the drama of souls"? How is the realistic playwright to reproduce feeling, the innermost thoughts of man on the stage? How much can words express? How far can he use everyday words without their losing their dramatic tension and — on the other hand — how far can he "dramatise" words without their ceasing to appear natural?

"No, not that. It was not that I wanted to say" (*ne to, ne to*) Čechov's characters are often forced to say. They cannot find the right words for their thoughts and feelings, noticing suddenly that the words they are using do not express what they are really thinking. In the third act of "Uncle Vanja", Sonja tries to explain to her father how difficult a time she and uncle Vanja have had, but the words do not suffice: "That was not what I wanted to say (*ja govorju ne to, ne to ja govorju*), but you must understand us, Papa". "I am a gull. No, not that", Nina reiterates in conversation with Trigorin in the final scene of "The Seagull". In the third act of "Uncle Vanja", Elena Andreevna thinks of Sonja and her love for Astrov: "He is not in love with her — that is clear, but why should he not be able to marry her? She is not beautiful, but for a country practitioner, of his age, she would make an excellent wife. She is intelligent, so good and pure... No, it is not that, not that" (*Net, éto ne to, ne to*). Her words do not express her inner thoughts: she is herself interested in Astrov. "Why am I saying these words?", Maša exclaims in despair in the first act of "Three Sisters", abstractedly repeating a line from a poem by Puškin.

Like Tolstoj, Čechov had to find other means of expressing feelings and thoughts outside of the words. The most important of these were to be: first of all the voice, then different sounds (from the night-watchman's hammering, from guitar playing to the snapping string in "The Cherry Orchard"), associatively charged objects (from the symbolic gull to Nataša's belt in "Three Sisters"), the pauses, used very frequently and with great variation, silent scenes (the last scene in "Uncle Vanja" where Marija Vasilevna sits writing and Marina knits stockings; the last scene in "Three Sisters", where Kulygin and Andrej appear in the background during the three sisters' monologue as a reminder of commonplace life), and lastly the language itself, the structure of the sentences.

These devices are not used only to create a background atmosphere on the stage. The aim is also to communicate to the audience things which concern the characters or the setting or the action, things which the realistic drama according to Čechov neither could nor should express in words.

Research in Čechov's dramatic technique ought to tackle this system of devices as a whole and study it in its opposition towards or co-operation with the dramatic diction. No other dramatic writer, I think, is so interesting from this special point of view as Čechov. Lack of space will not allow of it here; I shall only attempt to give some remarks on a component of this system which as far as I know has received rather little attention: the intonation and its rhythm.

For Čechov intonation was one of the realistic playwright's most important aids. In a letter to Ol'ga Knipper dated 2nd January 1900 he wrote: "I have written to Mejerchol'd and recommended him not to be so exaggerated when representing a nervous person. The greater majority of people are nervous, the majority suffer, only a very few feel a sharp pain, but where, outdoors or indoors, do you see people running about, hopping and holding their heads in their hands? Suffering must be shown as it is shown in life, i.e. not with feet and hands but with tone of voice, and eyes, not with gesticulation but with grace. The subtler emotions characteristic of cultured people must also be given subtle outward expression. Conditions on the stage do not allow of this, you will say, but no conditions justify a lie" (XVIII 292).

This was advice given to an actor as to how he should express emotions on the stage. Yet it was also advice to the playwright. If an actor's voice was going to be of such great importance, then it was essential for the author to intimate carefully how the lines were to be spoken. And it is in fact so that no playwright before Čechov, hardly anyone after him either, lays such great importance on directions for intonation. His four great plays overflow with them, culminating in his last play "The Cherry Orchard". In this play one can find about 175 directions as to how the lines are to be spoken. And here it is important to note that these directions are by no means stereotype or trivial. On the contrary, they are notable for an abundance of variation, in actual fact each rarely occurs more than once. It is thus possible to find some 80 d i f f e r e n t directions for speaking. They are often complicated, sometimes being composed of wholly opposing parts, for instance: "cheerfully, in tears" (*radostno, skvoz' slezy*), "happily, disturbed" (*veselo, vozbuždenno*), "angrily and mockingly" (*serdito i nasmešlivo*), "impatiently, with tears" (*neterpelivo, so slezami*).

It is also possible to see that certain characters or scenes in Čechov's plays are acoustically thought out, that a certain tone of voice or certain sounds are a dominating and characteristic element of them. When "Uncle Vanja" was to be performed at the Moscow Art Theatre, Čechov wrote to Stanislavskij about the last scene: "He [Astrov] whistles, you know... Whistles. Uncle Vanja is crying but Astrov whistles." [9] Stanislavskij understood what Čechov wanted to say with this laconic note. Here he found something characteristic of the doctor Astrov, fighting with his own despair, who is outwardly trying to appear unmoved. He thus included this detail in the first act as well. As soon as Astrov shows himself he starts whistling, it becomes a sort of signature-tune which characterises an important part of him much more clearly than any words.

Čechov wrote to Ol'ga Knipper about Ranevskaja in "The Cherry Orchard": "It is not difficult to play Ranevskaja, only one has to find the right key from the very beginning; one has to find a smile and way of laughing, one must be able to dress" (XX 164). Just as whistling is something characteristic for Astrov so is the laugh something important for the picture of Ranevskaja. With his words Čechov wanted to point out her limitations, an emotionally static person who lives through the sale of the property and the cherry orchard without being affected. Her unchanged laugh and smile tell her story more clearly than words.

Against this background of the careful directions for intonation one understands better why Čechov sometimes so energetically maintained that it was necessary to follow the author's directions on the stage, that the author really ought to have more to say on the stage even than the producer. On one occasion he was thus able to say that "I really do believe that no play can be set up by even the most talented producer without the author's personal guidance and directions... There are different interpretations, but the author has the right to demand that his play is performed and the parts played wholly according to his own interpretation... It is necessary that the particular atmosphere intended by the author is created." [10]

These intonational directions show how important the emotional key was for Čechov, but they also show one more important thing: the rhythm of the emotional key. The Čechov mood was, and perhaps still often is, interpreted as a dominating, all-pervading atmosphere of elegy and despair, an interpretation which threatens to make Čechov's plays boring and monotonous. But what Čechov did want was to give

---

[9] K. S. Stanislavskij, *Sobranie sočinenij*, T. 1, Moskva 1954, p. 232.

[10] *Teatr i istkusstvo* 1904, nr. 28, p. 522.

an illusion of life on the stage, and life was for him both laughter and tears, both hope and despair, both longing and triviality. It is certainly true that the emotional scale Čechov works with is of no very broad register. The poles do not lie very far from each other. But in the middle register he uses, Čechov has been able to capture very subtle nuances — the hasty glance we had at the intonation in "The Cherry Orchard" above clearly shows this.

And in this middle register he works with perpetual changes and contrasts. It is as if he were keen that no one key become too dominating or last too long. There must be change and rhythm if his plays are really to give a picture of everyday life. His striving towards this is most obvious in "The Cherry Orchard". Here Čechov marks it very clearly, underlines it, presumably because he thought that not sufficient attention had been paid to it in his previous plays. As I said before, there are not many intonational directions in "The Cherry Orchard" that appear more than once. The only ones that occur more often are those that intimate that a line is to be spoken "happily" and "laughingly" or "sorrowfully" and "in tears". In the play there are some 15 of each type which in its own way thus shows how he tries to keep a balance between the contrasting keys.

Some of Čechov's most usual contrasts are the contrast between a lyrical or elated and a banal, everyday atmosphere, the contrast between a sad, serious and a comic atmosphere, the contrast between a lively, active and a resting, pensive atmosphere. It is characteristic for Čechov that these keys not only succeed each other but are also to be found in balance in the same scene.

It is often said that there are many "indifferent" lines in Čechov's plays. Apart from the self-characterising monologues so typical of him, monologues whose syntactic construction — often without directions from the author — intimate their lyrical key, there are long passages with markedly colloquial lines. But these are only indifferent in that the semantic content of the words is at this point transferred to the background. Instead it is the way the words are intoned that is functional, the voice expressing what a person thinks or feels.

These indifferent remarks, I think, give the most obvious examples of how intonation and rhythm work in Čechov's plays. I will use some of them here to clarify what I mean.

There are several types of indifferent remarks in Čechov's plays. Let us begin with Gaev's billiard terms in "The Cherry Orchard". The real meaning of the words has no relevance in the context where they are used. Gaev resorts to them on occasions when he is disturbed or embarrassed and does not know what to say. Čechov always gives clear directions for intonation. The words are either to be spoken "disconcerted" (*skonfuženno*) or "in deep thought" (*v glubokom razdum'e*) or "despondently" (*unylo*).

Thus the semantic content is of no interest here, what matters is the intonation: it reveals the emotional state of mind behind the words. Čechov works this type of "indifferent" words to the limit in "Three Sisters" where Maša and Veršinin hold their strange dialogue:

Maša. *Tram-tam-tam…*
Veršinin. *Tam-tam…*
Maša. *Tra-ra-ta…*
Veršinin. *Tra-ta-ta…*

And the second time:

Veršinin. *Tram-tam-tam.*
Maša. *Tram-tam.*

The third time, Veršinin's voice is heard offstage: *Tram-tam-tam.* And Maša answers him with a: *Tra-ta-ta.*

It is understandable that a "dialogue" such as this would puzzle the actors: what was its function in the context, what intonation was one to use here? Ol'ga Knipper wrote to Čechov and asked about the passage. Čechov replied: „Veršinin speaks his ‚*Tram-tam-tam*' as a question and you as an answer, and you think that it is such an original joke that you speak this ‚*tram-tam*' with a smile" (XIX 24).

It is clear that these lines together form a dialogue of mutual understanding between Maša and Veršinin, a sort of love duet without words. One is reminded of the well-known scene in *Anna Karenina* where Levin and Kitty declare their love for each other without words, using only letters of the alphabet which they are able to interpret with the peculiar intuition of lovers.

And here another type of "indifferent" exchange. In the second act of "The Cherry Orchard", Epichodov crosses backstage playing on his guitar.

Ljubov' Andreevna (pensively). Epichodov is coming.
Anja (pensively). Epichodov is coming.

Ljubov' Andreevna thus states that she hears and sees her bookkeeper pass by. It is a statement, i.e. the semantic content of the words is not completely to be disregarded as in the above examples. But it is no normal statement; if such were the case Čechov would not have marked that the line were to be said "pensively". It must therefore have a different contextual function. If this function is to be looked for in the semantic content of the words, a possible interpretation to these lines may be given with reference to the earlier conversation between Trofimov and Lopachin, Lopachin saying that giants would be necessary to solve the problems in Russia. Now when Epichodov appears on the scene perhaps Ljubov' Andreevna and Anja come to think that there are no giants to be found in Russia but all the more such tragi-comical figures as Epichodov, "thousand and one misfortunes" as he is called.

But I think it is of no use here to stress the semantic content of these words, trying to find some hidden meaning behind them. The scene is first of all conditioned by the rhythm in the emotional key. After the serious conversation between Trofimov and Lopachin the appearance of Epichodov comes in marked contrast, as a change in the emotional key. It communicates something comic and trivial, concepts connected with the figure of Epichodov. And further, after the lively, active conversation, a contrast of rest: Ljubov' Andreevna's and Anja's pensive, abstracted lines.

In this connection it is worth remembering some words which Čechov wrote to Ol'ga Knipper in 1901 while rehearsals for "Three Sisters" were in progress. "Do not look sad in any of the acts", he wrote. "Angry, certainly, but not sad. People who have long borne grief inside them and have become used to it only whistle a little and often become lost in thought (*zadumyvajutsja často*). So you too must now and again lose yourself in thought on the stage" (XIX 10). Most of Čechov's characters are certainly such people who have long borne a grief or a longing within them. They often shut themselves from the outside world for a moment, letting some indifferent words communicate their abstracted state of mind.

There is another similar passage in "Three Sisters". Čebutykin, who usually sits reading the paper, noting down the various curiosities he finds there, suddenly reads aloud: "Balzac was married in Berdičev". And Irina meditatively repeats his words as she plays patience: "Balzac was married in Berdičev".

Čebutykin's words follow on a conversation between Veršinin and Tuzenbach where Veršinin propounds his favourite theory that life in two or three hundred years will be better and happier but that the generations living now have not the right to think of happiness. Čebutykin's words come when the discussion has reached a dead point and Tuzenbach says that "it is difficult to argue with you both."

Some scholars have chosen to give Irina's repetition of Čebutykin's words a special meaning. That Balzac, a great poet, marries in Berdičev, a little village in the country which no one might have heard of before, perhaps starts Irina thinking that happiness is possibly to be found where one least expects it. Perhaps their Moscow dream, their great dream of finding happiness in the city, is only an illusion? It may be that happiness is also to be found in the small town where they now live?

But I am very doubtful about this interpretation. If Čechov had wished to include this idea in his play it would have needed further support, and one can hardly say that the thought is developed in other passages in "Three Sisters". In fact this scene is a direct parallel to the scene in "The Cherry Orchard" which we have already looked at. It is above all an example of the rhythm which Čechov works with in the intonation and the emotional key. After the serious conversation between Veršinin and Tuzenbach, Čebutykin's trivial line follows as a marked contrast, a return to everyday life. And afterwards, a moment of rest and meditation: Irina's abstracted, dreamy repetition of Čebutykin's indifferent words.

In the last act of "Uncle Vanja", Astrov goes over to a map of Africa hanging on the wall and says a few words about how terribly hot it must be in Africa just then, to which Vojnickij replies: "Yes, I suppose so." This remark about Africa is like the one we have just spoken of; its effect is also abrupt, unexpected, without any visible function in the context. As with other indifferent lines, a hidden meaning has been sought in it.

Stanislavskij, who played Astrov in the first performance at the Moscow Art Theatre, for instance, gave it a definite emotional content, let his voice give meaning to the words. Ol'ga Knipper told of this: "How much bitterness and experience of life he put into this phrase. And how he pronounced these words with a sort of bravura, challenging almost." [11] It appears as if one ought to understand by Ol'ga Knipper's remark that Astrov, with his words, brought out a sort of contrast to Russian life where everything is indifferent, dull and apathetic; in other countries, far away, there is heat, there is something that burns and consumes.

Yet it is characteristic that the words may be interpreted in many other ways. A Soviet scholar, Prof. Ermilov, for instance, writes thus: "Astrov is ready to leave, his carriage is waiting for him at the door. And this remark about Africa conclusively transports everything that has happened here a moment before far far away: Africa, it is a sort of scale, it is the impossibility of being able to measure the distance which now separates the heroes in the play from the dramas they took part in not long ago... After the remark on Africa everything that has taken place on the property becomes conclusively as distant as Africa is distant from here." [12]

As Čechov himself said: "There are different interpretations..." But if one is to judge by the author's own words, this was not at all his intention with the remark. In a letter to Ol'ga Knipper he wrote about this scene: "You write that Astrov in this scene turns to Elena as a passionate lover, clutches for the emotion as a drowning man clutches

[11] O Stanislavskom, Moskva 1948, p. 266.
[12] V. Ermilov, Izbrannye raboty v trech tomach, T. 3, Moskva 1956, p. 175.

for a straw. But this is wrong, absolutely wrong. Astrov likes Elena, she appeals to him strongly because of her beauty, but in the last act he knows already that nothing will come of it, that Elena is going away from him for ever — and he speaks to her in this scene in the same tone as he speaks of the heat in Africa, and he kisses her simply like this, because he has nothing else to do" (XVIII 235).

Thus we see that according to Čechov himself there is no use of seeking a hidden meaning behind these words. What matters here is the intonation, the words merely form a backcloth for Astrov's resigned tone of voice.

Another illuminating example of how Čechov tries to create rhythmic variation in the emotional key is to be found in the scene between Ljubov' Andreevna and Trofimov in Act III of "The Cherry Orchard", a disturbed scene full of emotion which is unexpectedly and abruptly turned into something comic when Trofimov, rushing in agitation from Ljubov' Andreevna, falls downstairs with a crash. Here, as in several of the earlier examples, a contrasting note comes in afterwards, breaking the foregoing serious atmosphere of the scene. Čechov is also capable of the opposite. In Act III of "The Cherry Orchard" Lopachin has his great scene, a dramatic entrance and monologue similar to the climax which the drama before Čechov usually worked up to in the third or fourth act. When Lopachin does make his expected and prepared entrance, however, it is in by no means the same effective way as it would have been made with one of Čechov's predecessors. Varja thinks it is Epichodov who had just been teasing her who has returned. She waits at the door with a stick and smites Lopachin when he comes in. The new owner of the cherry orchard thus makes rather a ridiculous entrance. It is clear that Čechov inserted this mode of entry to contrast with the coming monologue, that it might not be too "dramatic" in the old meaning of the word.

But Čechov also works with rhythmic variations in the middle of a monologue or a scene. An obvious example of this is to be found at the beginning of "Three Sisters". Ol'ga's and Irina's lyrical scene, where the atmosphere of the house as it was a year ago at their father's death is brought back, is interrupted in the middle by a conversation between Solenyj, Čebutykin and Tuzenbach in the background. Only a few words are heard: "Čebutykin: Damned silly (*Čerta s dva*). Tuzenbach: Utter nonsense, of course (*Konečno, vzdor*)". It is clear that Solenyj has said something to make them indignant. These short exchanges occur just in the middle of the lyrical conversation between the sisters. It is obvious that they are intended to break the lyrical atmosphere, that it shall not become too monotonous, by introducing a more trivial one.

The final monologue of the three sisters is also constructed in a similar way. Right at the very end Maša's husband appears, in company with Andrej, pushing a pram at the same time as Čebutykin is humming his everlasting "Ta...ra...ra... boomdee-ay, nothing matters". Against the lyrical atmosphere, against the poetic structure of the sentences, Čechov inserts the mute appearance of Andrej and Kulygin in contrast, a reminder of everyday life (compare Epichodov's appearance in "The Cherry Orchard") and Čebutykin's philosophy of hopelessness. He is anxious about the monologue, that the lyrical intonation shall not become too dominant and thus brings in contrasting tones.

It is characteristic of today's Čechov scholars that they look for new meanings in the "indifferent" remarks. "It is said that Čechov taught us scenic simplicity, but his words are not simple", Nemirovič-Dančenko said during rehearsals for "Three Sisters" in 1939. [13] His words seem to have left their mark on the modern scenic interpretation of Čechov's play in the Soviet Union and on Čechov's research as well. It is, of course, quite right to say that Čechov's simple words are not simple in that they are not inserted at random; there is always a reason for them in the context. But I think that one may often go too far in seeking hidden meanings behind the "indifferent" lines. I do not believe that Čechov tried to fill his plays with secret connotations which must be pieced together like a jig-saw puzzle. The most obvious reason for the indifferent remarks is always the rhythm, the variation in the intonation, in the emotional key. Certainly in their context these remarks at the same time often evoke certain associations, but these associations are always of a general character. I consider it difficult to narrow them down by indicating one of them as being that which Čechov intended.

3.

The problem of the insufficiency of words was a problem of the times. In comparison we can refer to Mejerchol'd and his attempts to solve this problem on the stage. At one point Mejerchol'd quotes Wagner as an example. He says that for Wagner recitativo lines were not enough to express a singer's inner feelings, so he brings in the orchestra to help; the orchestra could express the unutterable. It is the same thing in a play: "The word is not a sufficient means of revealing the inner dialogue". [14]

Thus here the intonation becomes as valuable an accessory for Mejer-

---

[13] M. Stroeva, *Čechov i chudožestvennyj teatr*, p. 270.
[14] *Teatr. Kniga o novom teatre*. Sanktpeterburg 1908, p. 166.

chol'd as for Čechov, yet he makes use of it in quite a different way. In his opposition towards the declamatory style of the old theatre Mejerchol'd wishes to liberate the actor's voice from every pathos and vibrato. He goes even further: he wants a cold, clear diction (*cholodnaja čekanka slov*). But in it there is also to be a "mysterious tremble" (*mističeskij trepet*) which can better hint at what goes on inside a person than the bursts of temperament of the old actors.

"In the rhythm of the monotonously uttered words, behind the outer spoken dialogue, one feels an inner, hidden dialogue of sensation and impression which cannot be expressed by the words", as a reviewer described his impressions of Mejerchol'd's performance of Ibsen's *Hedda Gabler* in 1906. "The playgoer may forget the words that Hedda and Lövborg say to each other, but he must not forget the suggestivity of them." [15]

Mejerchol'd did not produce Čechov in the same radical manner. [16] But he certainly had another interpretation of his plays than the Moscow Art Theatre. After the first performance of "The Cherry Orchard" he wrote a letter to Čechov in which he criticized Stanislavskij. It is interesting to note that also here he was looking for the key to the play in precisely its rhythmical-acoustic character. He compared it with a symphony by Čajkovskij, a comparison many were to make after him. But he had in mind not so much its melancholic mood as its structure, abstract as a musical work; especially pointed out the rhythmical contrasts in the third act. "The producer", he concludes, "must first of all understand it [the play] with his hearing." [17]

---

[15] V. Mejerchol'd, *O teatre*, p. 190. But apart from the diction, Mejerchol'd also laid great stress on an actor's movements. Gesture, pose, gaze and silence were of great importance for him. The producer was to work out a plan for the actor's movements on the stage where every change had to have a definite function and meaning and together with light and decorations help to express what the words could not.

[16] *Literaturnoe nasledstvo*, Vol. 68, 1960, pp. 430-34.

[17] S. D. Baluchatyj & N. V. Petrov, *Dramaturgija Čechova*, Char'kov 1935, p. 120.

З. ПАПЕРНЫЙ

ПРАВДА И ВЕРА ЧЕХОВА

В записной книжке Чехова мы находим строки, которые помогают многое понять в самом его подходе к изображению человека:

„Тогда человек станет лучше, когда вы покажете ему, каков он есть" (*Зап. кн.* I, стр. 126, № 5).

Видеть то, что есть, а не то, что хотелось бы увидеть; не подгонять факты под заранее заданные решения и схемы; смотреть в лицо жизни бесстрашно и свободно, — вот, что означала чеховская правда. Было в ней что-то суровое и самоотверженное. И слышалась в ней печаль: груба жизнь, и до счастья еще далеко.

Но всем этим не исчерпывается содержание чеховской записи. Мысль о верности правде слита здесь с верой в человека.

Одно дело изображать героя, как он есть, не веря в то, что он может стать лучше. И совсем другое — изобразить человека, каков он есть, запечатлеть существующее именно для того, чтобы помочь человеку преодолеть настоящее, оттолкнуться от него, устремиться в будущее.

Вера здесь не соседствует с правдой, но проникает в нее. Чеховский реализм строится не на правде добросовестного воспроизведения, но на правде преодоления.

Один из рассказов Чехова — *Весной* (1886 г.) открывается словами:

„С земли еще не сошел снег, а в душу уже просится весна".

Когда думаешь об этих словах, на память приходит картина Левитана, любимого художника Чехова — „Март" (1894). Земля еще покрыта снегом, но уже дрогнуло царство зимы, и все в природе полно скрытого ожидания.

Изобразить приближающуюся весну — не значит делать вид, что уже нет снега; надо так изобразить снег — рыхлый, влажный, потемневший, чтобы читатель или зритель почувствовал: недолго уже осталось ждать.

Думается, что чеховские слова о несошедшем с земли снеге, о весне, которая просится в душу, характеризуют не только его общий взгляд на жизнь, но и поэтический угол видения действительности.

Изображение у Чехова возникает в результате скрытой,

но напряженной, драматической борьбы существующего и ожидаемого, человека, каков он есть и каким может и должен быть. Отсюда, как в *Чайке*, столкновение двух мотивов:,,Груба жизнь"! — с горечью восклицает Нина Заречная и она же говорит: ,,Не боюсь жизни". Смысл пьесы и — шире — смысл творчества Чехова несводим к какому-то одному из этих сталкивающихся друг с другом мотивов. Вне этого мы не сможем оценить и роль чеховской детали, которая не просто оживляет картину или характер, но всегда участвует в столкновении двух планов, ,,двух сюжетов", связанных с сущим и должным. Чеховский подтекст тоже глубоко связан с поэтикой преодоления ,,данного", с верой в то, что ,,человек станет лучше".

Попробуем проследить это на примере рассказа *Панихиды* (1886).

Герой рассказа — лавочник Андрей Андреич. Верный своей манере, Чехов отказывается от прямой отрицательной характеристики этого глубоко неприятного ему человека: относит его к ,,людям положительным, рассудительным и религиозно-убежденным", подчеркивает его солидность, ,,торжественно-панихидное выражение лица", ,,выражение важности и степенства".

Но за этой торжественной ,,положительностью" мы различаем тупость, ханжеское смирение перед ,,неисповедимыми судьбами" и презрение к простонародью. Лавочник пришел в церковь с просьбой помянуть за упокой ,,блудницу Марию", как он называет свою дочь актрису, скончавшуюся от болезни.

Безразличие, какая-то душевная запущенность Андрея Андреича, может быть, сильнее всего раскрывается в разговоре с дочкой, о котором он теперь вспоминает с тяжелым чувством:

,,Как ни жутко ему было гулять среди бела дня, на глазах всего честного народа с дочкой актрисой, но он уступил ее просьбам ...

— Какие чудные у вас места! — восхищалась она, гуляя. Что за овраги и болота! Боже, как хороша моя родина!

И она заплакала.

,,Эти места только место занимают ... — думал Андрей Андреич, тупо глядя на овраги и не понимая восторга дочери. — От них корысти, как от козла молока".

А она плакала, плакала и жадно дышала всей грудью, словно чувствовала, что ей недолго еще осталось дышать ..."

Однако он не безнадежен, этот лавочник. Под печальные напевы и слова панихиды с его лица медленно сползает выражение степенства, он погружается в грусть, ему все больней вспоминать, и он встряхивает головой, как укушенная лошадь — неотвязные мысли о прошлом, о дочери, как будто жалят его. Он видит ее маленькой девочкой, с белокурой головкой, с большими задумчивыми глазами. И хотя он по-прежнему, по неистребимой привычке, молясь, называет ее „блудницей", что-то человеческое, живое шевельнулось в его черствой, заскорузлой душе.

Кончается рассказ так:

„Из кадила струится синеватый дымок и купается в широком, косом луче, пересекающем мрачную, безжизненную пустоту церкви. И кажется, вместе с дымом носится в луче душа самой усопшей. Струйки дыма, похожие на кудри ребенка, кружатся, несутся вверх к окну и словно сторонятся уныния и скорби, которыми полна эта бедная душа".

Можно ли назвать случайным это увенчивающее весь рассказ сравнение струек дыма с кудрями ребенка? Оно несет в себе живую и важную частицу общего идейно-образного замысла произведения. Сравнение это напоминает другой образ, тоже на первый взгляд непритязательный, неприметный. В рассказе *Агафья* (1886) — рассказе о грубых человеческих отношениях — миру людей с „глухими" голосами, „душной" любовью противостоит нечто другое, светлое, чистое. Рассказчик говорит: „Я тихо побрел в рощу, а оттуда спустился к реке, где стояли наши рыболовные снасти. Река спала. Какой-то мягкий махровый цветок на высоком стебле коснулся моей щеки, как ребенок, который хочет дать понять, что не спит." [1]

Агафья и *Панихида* — два разные рассказа, с разными темами и замыслами. Отмечая перекличку отдельных деталей, вовсе не нужно стремиться к тому, чтобы искусственно уподоблять одно другому. И все же, как ни различны эти два произведения, в обоих дает себя знать тонкая, едва различимая нота: миру людей с их грубой чувственностью, душевной ленью, ханжеским степенством противостоит „тихий", лирический образ.

Стоит только убрать из рассказа *Панихида* эти „струйки дыма, похожие на кудри ребенка" — и сразу произведение бледнеет, мы уже не чувствуем с такой силой, что в черствой

---

[1] См. мой разбор этого рассказа в *Литературной газете,* 26 янв. 1960 г., стр. 4.

душе героя, собственника и ханжи, вдруг зашевелилось человеческое чувство.

Еще отчетливей выражена эта роль детали как важного средства, помогающего преодолеть неизменность и непререкаемость „грубой жизни”, в рассказе *Припадок* (1888). Исследователи не раз обращали внимание на описание первого снега. Но дело не только в одном этом описании — сквозь всю повесть как некая музыкальная тема проходит один мотив. Сначала это строки о первом снеге, с которым в душу „просилось чувство, похожее на белый, молодой, пушистый снег”. Как чистая, тревожно звенящая мелодия звучат они в мире грязных „заведений”, лакеев с собачьими лицами, пошлой безвкусицы платьев, картин, обстановки, непристойных фраз „барышень”, привычно совершающегося разврата. И далее с каждым новым поворотом в драматическом развитии сюжета в новом образном преломлении раскрывается этот мотив.

Приятели студента Васильева — веселые, пошлые циники. Медик учит жить без „философии”: „Водка дана, чтобы пить ее, осетрина — чтобы есть, женщины — чтобы бывать у них, снег — чтобы ходить по нем . . .”

Так открываются нам два мира, два видения действительности, и это воплощено в двух образных поворотах сквозного мотива: молодой снег, с которым в душу просится радостное, чистое чувство и — обыкновенный снег, по которому ходят, оставляя следы.

И далее все время внутренняя борьба, происходящая в душе героя, связывается с этим мотивом. Он ненадолго развеселился, вдруг захотел быть как все — и ему нравится снег, „редкие, черные следы, какие оставляли по первому снегу подошвы прохожих”.

Но вот он с ужасом думает о публичных домах, о женщинах, которых продают и покупают. И его мысли соединяются с картиной темного вечера, лениво кружащихся хлопьев снега.

„И как может снег падать в этот переулок!” — думает он. „Будь прокляты эти дома!”

Все ближе подступает отчаяние — и ему уже „страшно потёмок, страшно снега, который хлопьями валил на землю и, казалось, хотел засыпать весь мир”. Он выходит на мост и, содрогаясь от ужаса, смотрит на „черную воду, потемки, пустынные берега, покрытые снегом”.

Можно ли сказать, что деталь у Чехова только оживляет

картину, делает ее зримой, наглядной? Да, конечно, это так, но все дело в том, что чеховская деталь как бы заостряет борьбу двух планов; художник рисует жизнь как она есть и настойчиво напоминает о том, какой она могла бы стать, какой должна быть. В безотрадную казалось бы картину врываются светлые краски. Начинается борьба мотивов: как в рассказе *Припадок*: сумерки, потемки, черная вода, грязные следы прохожих на снегу и — белый, молодой пушистый снег. И все это дано не в статическом противостоянии, но в движении, в развивающемся конфликте. Тема молодого снега оказывается не простой художественной подробностью, не фоном, не „пейзажем” — она сливается с главной мыслью произведения.

Известно, что Чехов был глубоко огорчен тем, что строки о первом снеге не были замечены читающей публикой. И дело не только в том, что не обратили внимания на яркую художественную деталь. Читая чеховское письмо, мы видим, что для писателя упомянутая деталь связана с общим замыслом произведения, больше того, — с вопросом о том, для кого и для чего он творит:

„Бывают минуты, когда я положительно падаю духом. Для кого и для чего я пишу? — ... Литературное общество, студенты, Евреинова, Плещеев, девицы и проч. расхвалили мой *Припадок* во-всю, а описание первого снега заметил один только Григорович. И т.д. и т.д. Будь же у нас критика, тогда бы я знал, что я составляю материал — хороший или дурной, все равно, — что для людей, посвятивших себя изучению жизни, я так же нужен, как для астронома звезда” (А. Суворину, 23 декабря 1888 г.).

Вот, оказывается, как важно для самого Чехова на первый взгляд „частное” описание, как неразрывно связано оно с коренными вопросами о цели и смысле творчества.

И становится ясным, как неразделимо целостно чеховское мастерство, где тончайшие детали соединены с общей мыслью произведения, где нельзя прямолинейно делить поэтику на „форму” и „содержание”.

Запись Чехова: „Тогда человек станет лучше, когда вы покажете ему, каков он есть” открывает важную особенность взгляда писателя на жизнь, его раскрытия образа героев. В самом изображении человека мы находим у Чехова просветляющее начало, противостоящее, противодействующее тому, что есть. Чеховская деталь входит в самую сердцевину произведения, связывается с существом конфликта, борьбы двух начал — сущего и должного.

Глубоко человечно чеховское мастерство, в котором нераздельны суровая, бесстрашная правда и вера в человека.

AD. STENDER-PETERSEN

ZUR TECHNIK DER PAUSE BEI ČECHOV

Kaum bei irgendeinem anderen Dramatiker des bürgerlichen Realismus kommt die Regiebemerkung *Pause* so überaus oft vor wie bei Čechov. Weder Henrik Ibsen noch Bernard Shaw — um nur zwei der bedeutendsten Dramatiker der Epoche zu nennen — machen so fleißig Gebrauch von dieser Regieanweisung. Es liegt hier zweifellos ein bedeutungsvoller dramatischer Stilunterschied vor. Bernard Shaw ist der Dichter der logischen Replikenfolgen, wo die Äußerungen der sprechenden Personen antithetisch ineinander oder gegeneinander eingreifen und folgerichtige Ketten bilden, in denen Pausen in der Regel nur störend wirken würden. Bei Henrik Ibsen liegt das ganze psychologische Spiel entblößt und offen in den Fragen und Antworten, Aussagen und Gegenaussagen vor den Augen und Ohren des Zuschauers. Die eigentliche dramatische Spannung ist bei beiden fast ausschließlich im mündlichen Wortwechsel begründet, der unaufhaltsam weitergeht, bis die Lösung des psychischen oder logischen Knotens klar vor aller Augen liegt. Ganz anders bei Čechov, bei dem die Pausen eine mit den mündlichen Repliken fast gleichwertige Rolle spielen. Was bei Ibsen und Shaw gesagt wird, wird bei Čechov verschwiegen, das Verschwiegene schwingt aber im Spiele bedeutsam mit, und es entsteht ein dramatischer Stil, der dadurch gekennzeichnet ist, daß der Wortwechsel immer wieder und wieder unterbrochen wird. Die Pausen, die etwas verschweigen, dienen im Allgemeinen dazu, den Leser, den Zuschauer oder den Zuhörer am Gange der Handlung mitarbeiten zu lassen. Im Gegensatz zu dem beschleunigten Wechseln der Dramatik Ibsens und Shaws ist Čechovs Stil zögernd, zurückhaltend, andeutend.

An sich sagt die Regieanweisung *Pause* anscheinend nichts aus. Sie ist neutral und objektiv, sie konstatiert nur und ist technisch indifferent inbezug auf das äußere Verhalten und das innere Erleben der Auftretenden. Čechov überläßt es dem Schauspieler oder Regisseur, die sich auf das aktive Verhalten der Zuschauer stützen, die Pausen als Bestandteile des Dramas zu deuten. Es gibt dabei auch Pausen bei Čechov, die durch Punkte (...) angedeutet sind, aber diese spielen nicht die Rolle von bedeutsamen Umbrüchen im Dialog, sondern dienen nur zur Angabe einer unvollständigen Rede, eines Suchens nach dem rechten Ausdruck. Es verlohnt sich der Mühe, die verschiedenen Funk-

tionsmöglichkeiten der eigentlichen Pausen bei Čechov näher zu er-
forschen, um ihren Anteil an der Handlung irgendwie zu präzisieren.
Die Schauspieltexte, die hier in die Untersuchung einbezogen werden
sollen, sind die fünf großen vieraktigen Stücke „Ivanov" (1887-1889),
„Die Möwe" (1896), „Onkel Vanja" (1897), „Drei Schwestern"
(1900-1901) und „Der Kirschgarten" (1903-1904). Es sei jedoch ausdrücklich bemerkt, daß ich mir nicht die Aufgabe stelle, sie im Rahmen
dieses Aufsatzes erschöpfend zu analysieren, sondern nur auf einige
charkteristische Erscheinungen in der Čechovschen Pausentechnik
aufmerksam zu machen.

I.

Es ist auffallend, daß Čechov, der Realist, keineswegs das aus dem
klassizistischen Drama übernommene Mittel des M o n o l o g s ver-
schmäht, um den Geisteszustand oder den Gedankengang der gegebenen
Person deutlichzumachen. Dabei ist der Monolog bei ihm von Pausen
durchsetzt. Vielleicht kann hier davon gesprochen werden, daß Čechov
das in Tolstojs Romanen so häufig vorkommende unterbrochene innere
Selbstgespräch der Figuren in direkte, lautgesprochene Rede umsetzt.
In der „Möwe" (Akt I) kommt ein Monolog ganz besonderer Art
vor: es ist die Deklamation der jungen Nina, die als weiße Fee
auftritt und den Anfang des dekadenten Stückes des jungen Dichters
Treplëv im Garten bei Mondschein von einer improvisierten Bühne
vorträgt. Es handelt sich hier somit um ein Spiel im Spiel, und die drei
Pausen, die die Deklamation unterbrechen, sind nicht für Čechov
charakteristisch, sondern für den im Stück auftretenden Dichter, der
bewußt nach neuen Formen und Wegen sucht. Wir können hier von
diesem Beispiel ganz absehen.
Ein typischer Čechovscher Pausenmonolog kommt dagegen im 3.
Akt des „Ivanov" vor. Die Situation ist hier die, daß der Titelheld,
der von seiner totkranken Frau bei einer Liebesszene mit der jungen
Saša im Hause ihrer Nachbarn überrascht worden ist, daheim in seinem Arbeitszimmer über seine unwürdige Haltung meditiert. Der Monolog kann folgendermaßen schematisiert werden:

Ivanov klagt sich selber wegen seiner apathischen Stimmung an,
die ihn seit einem Jahr befallen hat, weint und macht sich Selbstvor-
würfe wegen seiner veränderten Haltung seiner unglücklichen und
kranken Frau gegenüber (*Motiv I*).

Pause I.

Er denkt an die junge Saša, deren unverhohlene Liebe er genieße,
und macht sich neue Verwürfe (*Motiv II*).

Pause II.

Er versteht sich selber nicht und denkt zum ersten Mal an Selbstmord (*Konklusion*).

Die ersten zwei Motive dienen hier, von Pausen unterstrichen und unterstützt, als Prämissen zur Konklusion. Der Monolog führt den Titelhelden durch zwei Etappen, die gewissermaßen antithetisch aufgestellt sind, zum Thema der Konklusion, das den Ausgang des ganzen Schauspiels, den Selbstmord Ivanovs auf offener Bühne am Ende des 4. Aktes, vorausgreifend andeutet und vorbereitet.

Ganz ähnlich ist ein anderer Monolog in demselben Stück aufgebaut, nämlich das Selbstgespräch des jungen Arztes am Anfang des 4. Aktes. Die Situation ist hier die, daß der Arzt, der über den Tod der ersten Frau Ivanovs und seine bevorstehende Verheiratung mit der jungen Saša empört ist, in den Salon ihrer Eltern eintritt. Sein Monolog ist folgendermaßen zu schematisieren:

L'vov tritt auf die Bühne, sieht auf die Uhr und gibt seiner Empörung Luft: er ist überzeugt, daß Ivanov bald auch seine zweite Frau an den Rand des Grabes bringen wird (*Motiv I*).

Pause I.

Er nimmt sich vor, Ivanov öffentlich die Wahrheit ins Gesicht zu schleudern (*Motiv II*).

Pause II.

(angegeben mit den Worten: *Er denkt nach*).

Er erkennt seine Ratlosigkeit dieser Situation gegenüber und denkt an ein Duell mit Ivanov (*Konklusion*).

Auch hier sind die beiden ersten Motive, von Pausen unterstützt, Prämissen zu der Konklusion der dritten Etappe. Die Regiebemerkung *Er denkt nach* ist hier gleichwertig mit der Regiebemerkung *Pause*. In einem Monolog wird jede Pause natürlich durch ein Nachdenken des Sprechenden zu erklären sein. L'vovs Monolog verläuft ganz parallel mit demjenigen Ivanovs, und gerade der negative Ausgang des Monologes des Arztes unterstreicht die Unumgänglichkeit der Konklusion, zu der Ivanov gelangt: nur Ivanov, nicht der Arzt, kann sein Problem lösen und löst es durch die Tat: den Selbstmord. Die Monologpausen dienen in beiden Fällen dazu, die Prämissen voneinander und von der Konklusion nachdrücklich zu trennen. Sie stehen wie Paragraphenzeichen da. Wenn Čechov in seinen ersten Stücken die veraltete Methode des Monologes anwendet, hängt das mit einer konstitutiven Besonderheit seiner dramatischen Kunst zusammen, mit der Idee der Einsamkeit des Menschen. Die Selbstgespräche Ivanovs und

L'vovs sind, jedes in seiner Weise, Einsamkeitsausdrücke, und die Pausen in den Monologen dienen dazu, die Einzelmotive derselben ungehört und unbeantwortet im Raum verklingen zu lassen.

Ebenso kann Ivan Vojnickijs Monolog im 2. Akt des „Onkel Vanja" analysiert werden. Die Situation ist hier die, daß der etwas betrunkene Vojnickij der Jelena, der Frau des alten Professors, seines Schwagers, zum zweiten Mal seine Liebe erklärt. Jelena verlässt erzürnt die Bühne und Vojnickij bleibt allein:

Vojnickij konstatiert etwas verdutzt, daß sie weggegangen sei (*Motiv I*).

Pause I.

Er beklagt, daß er nicht schon vor 10 Jahren der Elena einen Heiratsantrag gemacht habe, er würde sie jetzt in seinen Armen halten und ihre Angst vor dem Gewitter beschwichtigt haben können (*Motiv II*).

Pause II.

Sein Zorn richtet sich gegen den alten Professor, den auch er sinnlos bewundert habe, und dessen Talentlosigkeit er erst jetzt zu seinem Schrecken erkannt habe. Er fühlt sich belogen und betrogen (*Konklusion*).

Und in derselben Weise baut Čechov im 3. Akt den Monolog Elenas auf. Sie hat sich vorgenommen, Sonja in ihrem Verhältnis zu Astrov, in den sie verliebt ist, zu helfen und eine Verlobung zwischen ihnen herbeizuführen. Sie wartet auf ihn und ergeht sich in einem Selbstgespräch:

Sie sagt sich selber, daß nichts schwieriger sei als die geheime Herzensangelegenheit einer anderen Person zu kennen, ohne helfen zu können (*Motiv I*).

Pause I.

(durch die Worte angedeutet: *Sie denkt nach*).

Sie führt Vernunftgründe an für eine Verbindung zwischen dem jungen Mädchen und dem Arzt Astrov (*Motiv II*).

Pause II.

Sie erkennt sich selber gegenüber, daß auch sie sich für den interessanten und tätigen Mann gewonnen fühlt und daher Sonja gegenüber Gewissensbisse hat (*Konklusion*).

So unterstreicht Čechov mit seiner Pausentechnik den dramatischen Aufbau seiner Monologe. Zuweilen kommen doch auch pausenlose Monologe (so Ninas kurzer Monolog im 2. Akt der „Möwe" oder

Sonjas gleichfalls kurzer Monolog im 2. Akt von „Onkel Vanja") oder Monologe mit nur einer ausdrücklich angegebenen Pause (so Treplëvs Monolog vor der letzten Begegnung mit Nina in der „Möwe") vor. Gewöhnlich können aber auch sie ohne Mühe in drei Etappen eingeteilt werden.

Čechov gab in seinen späteren Stücken das Mittel des einsamen Monologes grundsätzlich auf, und zwar in der Weise, daß er zuweilen das Selbstgespräch einer im Dialog vorherrschenden Person in Repliken aufteilte, die entweder von einer anderen Person sekundiert wurden oder unbeantwortet im Raum verklangen. So fängt z.B. das Schauspiel „Drei Schwestern" mit einem zerstückelten Monolog der ältesten Schwester Ol'ga an. Bezeichnenderweise spielen hier die Pausen wieder die Rolle von Paragraphenzeichen. Die Situation ist hier die, daß die Schwestern Ol'ga, Maša und Irina am Namenstag der letzteren auf der Bühne sind.

Ol'ga erinnert ihre Schwestern daran, daß ihr Vater vor einem Jahre gestorben sei (*Motiv I*).

Pause I.

(durch die Regiebemerkung *Es schlägt zwölf* markiert).

Ol'ga bemerkt, daß auch damals die Uhr zwölf schlug (*Motiv II*).

Pause II.

Ol'ga spricht vom Begräbnis ihres Vaters (*Konklusion*).

Gleich darauf setzt Ol'ga ihr Selbstgespräch in Gegenwart ihrer Schwestern fort. Es ist eine neue Folge von monologischen Repliken:

Ol'ga spricht vom Umzug der Familie aus dem frühlingswarmen und blumenreichen Moskau vor 11 Jahren und vom Frühling, der auch jetzt eingetreten sei (*Motiv 1*).

Pause 1.

(durch die Regiebemerkung *Maša, über ein Buch gebeugt, pfeift leise eine Melodie*).

Ol'ga verbittet sich das Pfeifen (*Motiv II*).

Pause II.

Ol'ga klagt über ihre als Provinzlehrerin vergeudete Jugend und wünscht, von Irina unterstützt, nach Moskau zurückzukehren (*Konklusion*).

Diese beiden Stücke sind ihrer Struktur nach wesentlich ein Monolog Ol'gas, aber nur so aufgelöst, daß ein Scheingespräch an seine Stelle tritt. Irinas Bemerkungen, die in den Text eingemischt sind,

haben nur sekundäre Bedeutung, indem sie das folgende Stück vor-
bereiten, wo Ol'ga und Irina parallele Monologe, wieder als Dialog
getarnt, vortragen. Dabei spielen die beiden obenbehandelten Textstücke die Rolle von Prämissen, zu denen das dritte Stück die Konklusion geben soll:

> Irina und Ol'ga stellen sich vor, wie ihr Bruder Andrej auch nach
> Moskau umziehen werde, während Maša die Sommerferien bei ihnen
> zubringen könne (*Motiv I*).

Pause I.

(die durch die Regiebemerkung *Maša pfeift leise eine Melodie* markiert erscheint).

> Irina freut sich über das schöne Wetter und erinnert sich an
> ihre Kindheit, während Ol'ga darüber klagt, daß sie in ihrem
> Schulamt altere und ein Familienleben vorziehen würde (*Motiv II*).

Pause II.

> Ol'ga glaubt, sie würde ihren Mann lieben (*Konklusion*).

Damit ist das Thema der Einsamkeit der Schwestern und besonders
Ol'gas erschüpft. Die drei Offiziere, die sich im Hintergrunde aufge-
halten und Bemerkungen miteinander gewechselt haben, treten ein, und
es entspinnt sich ein allgemeines Gespräch zwischen ihnen und den
Schwestern. Bemerkenswert ist es, daß die drei Stücke, die eben
analysiert worden sind, durch die Hintergrundrepliken der Offiziere
auseinandergehalten werden, die somit auch wieder als Pausen im
Vordergrundspiel dienen.

2.

Sehr oft benutzt Čechov das Mittel der Pause, um die K o n t a k t-
l o s i g k e i t zwischen zwei Menschen zu illustrieren. In primitivster
Weise kommt eine solche Pausenfolge im ersten Akt der „Möwe" vor,
im Gespräch zwischen Maša, die hoffnungslos in den jungen Dichter
Treplëv verliebt ist, und dem sie hoffnungslos liebenden Schullehrer
Medvedenko, der immer wieder von seinen unbefriedigenden wirt-
schaftlichen Verhältnissen spricht:

> Medvedenko klagt in etwas naiver Weise über den Mangel an see-
> lischen Berührungspunkten zwischen ihnen und über die Aussichts-
> losigkeit seiner Liebe zu ihr (*Motiv I*).

Pause I.

(angedeutet durch die Regiebemerkung *Sie nimmt eine Prise aus
ihrer Tabaksdose*).

Maša sagt, seine Liebe rühre sie, aber sie liebe ihn nicht, worauf sie ihm vergebens ihre Tabaksdose reicht (*Motiv II*).

Pause II.

Maša spricht von dem nahenden Gewitter und wirft ihm die Kleinlichkeit seiner Klagen über seine Armut vor (*Konklusion*).

Dieser Szene entspricht im vierten Akt aufs genaueste eine Parallelszene. Es sind viele Jahre vergangen, und Maša und Medvedenko sind miteinander verheiratet und haben ein Kind. Der Abstand zwischen ihnen aber ist nur noch größer geworden. Der Parallelismus ist durch ein nahendes Gewitter unterstrichen.

Medvedenko ist wegen des Gewitters beunruhigt und sagt, daß man im Garten auf dem alten Theater gleichsam jemanden weinen höre, was Maša sinnlos findet (*Motiv I*).

Pause I.

Medvedenko bittet seine Frau, mit ihm nachhause zu fahren, ihr Kind müsse hungrig sein. Sie antwortet, daß die Magd es schon füttern werde (*Motiv II*).

Pause II.

Als er sie wieder bittet, nachhause zu fahren, fordert sie ihn auf, allein heimzukehren. Er fragt sie, ob sie dann am nächsten Tage heimkommen werde.

Pause III.

(angedeutet durch die Regiebemerkung: *Maša nimmt eine Prise*).

Sie sagt ihm, er solle sie in Ruhe lassen, sie werde schon kommen (*Konklusion*).

Wie das letzte Beispiel dartut, ist die Anzahl der Pausen durchaus nicht obligatorisch auf zwei begrenzt, es können drei und mehr Pausen vorkommen. Eine ganze Serie von Pausen durchzieht, mit immer kürzeren Abständen, das Gespräch Varjas und Lopachins im „Kirschgarten". Es handelt sich hier um eine von der Ranevskaja künstlich geschaffene Situation, wo der Käufer des Kirschgartens, der Kaufmann Lopachin, und die Pflegetochter der Ranevskaja, Varja, die einander zugetan sind, sich ihre gegenseitige Sympathie erklären sollen, aber keinen wirklichen Kontakt miteinander herstellen können.

Varja kommt ins Zimmer und tut, als ob sie etwas suche, Lopachin fragt sie, was sie suche, sie weicht einer direkten Antwort aus.

Pause I.

Lopachin fragt, wohin sie sich jetzt nach der Aufhebung des Heimes begeben werde, und sie antwortet ihm.

Pause II.

Lopachin erzählt von seinen Plänen und spricht von dem Frost, der draußen herrsche.

Pause III.

Varja sagt, daß das Thermometer entzweigegangen sei.

Pause IV.

Man ruft Lopachin, und er verläßt schnell die Bühne, als ob er nur auf diesen Ruf gewartet habe.

Pause V.

(dadurch markiert, daß Varja still dasitzt und weint).

Die Ranevskaja kommt herein und fragt, was geschehen sei.

Pause VI.

Sie stellen fest, daß sie fahren müssen.

Die ganze Szene ist tragisch in ihrem Verlauf und besiegelt die Ratlosigkeit und Unfähigkeit der beiden Menschen, Kontakt miteinander zu gewinnen. Während in den oben analysierten Szenen die Pausen die Tatsache illustrieren, daß Medvedenko und Maša einander nichts zu sagen haben, dienen sie hier dazu, die Unfähigkeit der Menschen zu betonen, das entscheidende Wort zu sagen. Die Pausen, die wir verzeichnet haben, tragen in keiner Weise zur Weiterführung der Handlung bei. Sie dienen nur zur Retardierung derselben. Sie unterstreichen die Tragik der Situation.

Komisch interpretiert kommt die Pausenretardierung im „Kirschgarten" vor, und zwar in zwei parallelen Szenen, im Gespräch zwischen dem Kontoristen Epichodov und dem Stubenmädchen Dunjaša, und im Gespräch zwischen dem Diener Jaša und ihr.

Epichodov spricht von seinen vielen Mißgeschicken und Wiederwärtigkeiten.

Pause I.

Er fragt, ob sie Buckle gelesen habe.

Pause II.

Er bitte sie um ein Gespräch unter vier Augen und wird von ihr weggeschickt, um ihren Mantel zu holen. Er entfernt sich mit den Worten, daß er jetzt wisse, was er mit seinem Revolver zu tun habe.

Im folgenden Gespräch zwischen dem Diener und dem Stubenmädchen sind die Rolle umgetauscht.

Dunjaša fürchtet, daß Epichodov sich wirklich erschießen werde.

Pause I.

Dunjaša spricht davon, daß sie zu einem feineren Leben erzogen sei, und gar nicht wisse, wie ihre Nerven eine eventuelle Treulosigkeit seitens des Dieners ertragen würden, sie sei leidenschaftlich in ihn verliebt.

Pause II.

Jaša gähnt und sagt, daß in seinen Augen ein junges Mädchen, daß iemanden liebe, unsittlich sei.

Pause III.

Jaša bemerkt, daß es angenehm sei, in der freien Luft eine Zigarre zu rauchen. Er hört jemanden kommen und bittet sie schnell zu verschwinden.

In diesen beiden Szenen sind die Pausen benutzt, um die einzelnen Repliken in komischer Weise zu unterstreichen. Prinzipiell sind sie aber von der tragischen Szene zwischen Varja und Lopachin nicht verschieden. Sie sind Beispiele einer K a r r i k a t u r d e r K o n t a k t - l o s i g k e i t zwischen den Menschen. In komischer Weise, aber nicht als Karrikatur, sondern als Wirklichkeitscharakteristik liegt diese Pausentechnik im zweiten Akt des „Ivanov" vor. Hier sind viele jungen und alten Gäste im Hause der Lebedevs versammelt, einige spielen im Hintergrund Karten, und Bruchstücke ihrer Meldungen mengen sich in das Vordergrundgespräch, ganz wie das Hintergrundgespräch der Offiziere in den „Drei Schwestern" sich in das Vordergrundgespräch der Schwestern mischt.

Die ihres Geizes wegen bekannte Hausfrau empfängt die heiratslustige Witwe Babakina und läßt ihr vom Diener Tee bringen. Sie dankt.

Pause I.

Während die Spielenden im Hintergrund ihre Karten melden, entspinnt sich im Vordergrund zwischen den beiden Damen ein Gespräch über vorteilhafte Kapitalanbringung.

Pause II.

(markiert durch die Regiebemerkung *Ein Gast gähnt*).

Die Babakina findet das Gähnen unpassend.

Pause III.

(markiert durch die Regiebemerkung *Ein langwieriges Schweigen tritt ein*).

Im Hintergrund hört man wieder die Spielenden ihre Meldungen machen.

Hier haben sich die Leute überhaupt nichts zu sagen und die Pausen und das Gähnen veranschaulichen die tiefe Langeweile, die auf der Bühne herrscht.

3.

Bei weitem charakteristischer für Čechov ist aber die Meisterschaft, mit der er die Pausen als d r a m a t i s c h e B e s t a n d t e i l e einer Szene benutzt: die Pausen dienen dazu, die Spannung des Zuschauers langsam anwachsen zu lassen.

Als ein Musterbeispiel dieser Technik kann hier gleich eine Szene im ersten Akt des „Ivanov" analysiert werden. Die Situation ist hier die, daß Ivanov selbst, sein leichtsinniger und muntrer Onkel Šabel'skij und sein zynischer Gutsverwalter Borkin auf der Terrasse des Gutshauses versammelt sind und auf das Resultat der Untersuchung der Frau Ivanovs durch den Arzt L'vov warten. Die Etappen des Gesprächs, das sich nach dem Erscheinen L'vovs auf der Terrasse entwickelt, seien hier mit Buchstaben bezeichnet:

A. L'vov erklärt, daß Anna, die Frau Ivanovs, unverzüglich nach der Krim reisen müsse, bestätigt aber auf die Frage Ivanovs, daß sie sich weigere zu reisen.

Pause I.

B. Auf die Frage Borkins erklärt der Arzt, daß sie an der Schwindsucht leide, und bittet ihn, leiser zu sprechen.

Pause II.

C. Während Ivanov schweigt, wechseln Šabel'skij und Borkin einige banale Bemerkungen miteinander.

Pause III.

D. Šabel'skij und Borkin ergehen sich in Bemerkungen über die Möglichkeit einer schnellen Bereicherung, während Ivanov weiter schweigt. Sie verlassen die Bühne.

Pause IV.

E. Ivanov klagt über seinen reizbaren Gemütszustand, und der Arzt erklärt, seine Frau würde nach der Krim reisen, wenn Ivanov sie begleiten würde.

Pause V.

F. Ivanov bringt Gründe vor, warum die Reise nicht verwirklicht werden könne, und L'vov sagt erregt, daß Ivanovs Verhalten der Frau gegenüber sie töte.

Pause VI.

G. L'vov gibt seiner Empörung Ausdruck, und Ivanov bekennt, daß er seine Frau nicht mehr liebe, und daß die Möglichkeit ihres Todes ihn nicht berühre.

Von dem Auftakt A bis zur Konklusion G werden wir von Čechov Schritt für Schritt (B>C>D>E>F) von Pause zu Pause (I>II>III>IV>V>VI) geführt. Die Pausen bedeuten, daß man von Ivanov eine Antwort auf die Frage, was tun, erwarte. Es wird allmählich immer deutlicher, daß die Hoffnungslosigkeit ihrer Krankheit, die der Arzt deutlich angibt, nur dadurch behoben werden kann, daß Ivanov sich bereit erklärt, mit seiner Frau, die ihn liebt, nach dem Süden zu fahren, und als Ivanov endlich sein Schweigen bricht, wird es klar, daß er nicht gewillt ist, seine Frau vor dem Tode an der Schwindsucht zu retten. Die ganze Tragik der Situation wird so veranschaulicht, und die retardierenden Pausen vertiefen aufs äußerste den Eindruck der Unabwendbarkeit des Schicksals.

Dieser Szene entsprechen die 6. und 7. Szene desselben Aktes. Anna ist jetzt auch auf der Bühne und hört, daß ihr Mann zusammen mit dem Onkel zu den Lebedevs zu fahren beschließt.

A. Ivanov bittet Anna, ihn fahren zu lassen, und nicht nach dem Grunde seiner Gemütsverfassung zu fragen, aber sie bittet ihn, zuhause zu bleiben, den Abend mit ihr auf alte Weise zu verbringen.

Pause I.

B. Anna fragt ihn vergebens nach dem Grunde seines veränderten Benehmens, und warum sie nicht mit ihm fahren dürfe. Er spricht wieder von seiner Schwermut und eilt weg. Šabel'skij folgt ihm nach. Anna und der Arzt bleiben allein zurück.

Pause II.

C. Anna fühlt sich verlassen und bittet den Arzt, der erregt auf und ab geht, sich zu ihr zu setzen, aber er weigert sich.

Pause III.

D. Anna singt ein Liedchen, dessen Melodie in der Küche gespielt wird.

Pause IV.

E. Sie fragt ihn nach seinen Eltern, er antwortet kurz.

Pause V.

(durch die Bemerkung markiert: *Sie lauscht*).

F. Sie hört eine Eule schreien und spricht in einem längeren Gespräch von ihrem Bruch mit den Eltern und ihrer Liebe zu Ivanov.

Pause VI.

G. Sie sagt, daß jetzt alles verändert sei, und daß sie zuhause sitze und der Eule lausche, während er zu den Nachbarn fährt.

Pause VII

(durch die Regiebemerkung angedeutet: *Man hört den Wächter klopfen*).

H. Sie fragt den Arzt, ob er Brüder habe.

Pause VII .

(durch die Regiebemerkung angegeben: *Anna weint*).

I. Sie beschließt plötzlich, auch zu den Lebedevs zu fahren.

Wieder führen uns die vielen Pausen (I>II>III>IV>V>VI> VII) unerbittlich von der Ausgangsposition A (über B>C>D>E> F>G>H) zur Konklusion I. Die retardierenden Pausen dienen dazu, das spezifische Gewicht der einzelnen Repliken und Replikenfolgen zu unterstreichen und den Eindruck der völligen Verlassenheit Annas nachdrücklich zu vertiefen. Immer wieder klingen die Äußerungen Annas tragisch im leeren Raum aus, und der Zuschauer wird durch die Pausen darauf vorbereitet, daß etwas Unabwendbares eintreffen muß. Die Pausen schwingen bedeutsam mit. Das Unausgesprochene ist nicht weniger wichtig als das Ausgesprochene. In ihrer Wechselseitigkeit offenbaren sie die psychische Entwicklung.

Erschütternd wirkt diese Pausentechnik in der letzten Szene des dritten Aktes, nachdem die junge Saša Ivanov in seinem eigenen Hause besucht hat. Anna erfährt davon und erscheint auf der Bühne, wo Ivanov allein an seinem Tisch mit gesenktem Haupt dasteht.

A. Anna tritt ein.

Pause I.

B. Sie fragt ihn, warum Saša dagewesen sei.

Pause II.

C. Sie wiederholt die Frage, und er bittet sie, ihn nicht danach zu fragen.

Pause III.

D. Ivanov erkennt seine Schuld an, aber bittet sie abermals, ihn nicht zu fragen. Sie wiederholt abermals die Frage.

Pause IV.

E. Ein häßliches und empörtes Gespräch findet zwischen ihnen statt, sie klagen einander an, er schleudert ihr die rohe Wahrheit ins Gesicht, daß der Arzt gesagt habe, sie werde bald sterben.

Pause V.

(durch die Regiebemerkung angedeutet: *Anna setzt sich nieder*).

F. Sie fragt ihn mit gedämpfter Stimme, wann er es gesagt habe.

Pause VI.

G. Ivanov klagt sich selber an und weint.

Die Pausen deuten immer wieder an, daß das tragische Schwergewicht dieser Szene gar nicht so sehr in der Ebene des Gesagten, als vielmehr in der Ebene des Nichtgesagten liegt. Man hat den Eindruck, daß Čechov die Repliken nur dazu benutzt, um die Pausen vorzubereiten. Andrerseits motivieren die gesprochenen Repliken gleichsam nur die Pausen. Wir haben hier ein eklatantes Beispiel von der Wechselseitigkeit der beiden Mittel.

4.

Eine ebenso tragische Funktion haben die Pausen bei Čechov, wenn sie das Gespräch zwischen einem jungen Mädchen, das in einen älteren Mann verliebt ist, und diesem Manne, der ihrer Annäherung zögernd gegenübersteht, begleiten. Dieses Motiv liegt bei Čechov häufig vor. Wir finden es schon im „Ivanov", wo die junge Saša Ivanov ihre Liebe offenbart.

Bedeutend tragischer ist die Situation der jungen Nina in der „Möwe", weil der Mann hier den naiven Idealismus des Mädchens in gröbster Weise mißbraucht. Das erste zögernde Gespräch zwischen Nina und dem schon berühmten Dichter Trigorin, dem Liebhaber der gefeierten Schauspielerin Irina Arkadina, findet gleich im 1. Akt statt. Nina verläßt nach dem Fiasko des Treplëvschen Stückes die improvisierte Bühne und wird Trigorin vorgestellt. Sie träumt davon, Schauspielerin zu werden, und ist durch die erste Begegnung mit einem wirklichen Künstler verwirrt und benommen.

Nina fragt ihn, ob er nicht Treplëvs Stück merkwürdig finde, er antwortet, daß er das Stück nicht verstanden habe, aber daß ihr Spiel und die Dekoration ihm gefallen habe.

Pause.

Trigorin sagt, daß er zu angeln liebe und daran Genuß fühle, aber Nina meint, daß künstlerisches Schaffen ihm einen weit größeren Genuß bereiten müsse.

Durch diese Pause, die deutlich die Erwartung Ninas, er werde ihr etwas Bedeutendes sagen, symbolisiert, wird hier zum ersten Mal der himmelweite Unterschied zwischen dem Enthusiasmus der Nina und den irdischen Freuden Trigorins betont. Dieser Unterschied wird im

weiteren Verlauf immer stärker hervorgehoben. Das zweite Gespräch
zwischen ihnen findet am Ende des zweiten Aktes statt. Die Situation
ist hier die, daß der junge Treplëv, der Nina liebt, ihr eine von ihm
getötete Möwe zu Füßen legt. Die Möwe ist von Čechov symbolisch
als Sinnbild Ninas gedeutet. Gleich darauf tritt Trigorin auf die
Bühne.

Sie begrüßen sich. Er bedauert, daß er und die Arkadina den
Landsitz heute schon verlassen werden, und daß er sie gern näher
kennenlernen wollte, um zu erfahren, wie junge Mädchen fühlen
und denken. Sie dagegen möchte gern an seiner Stelle sein, um zu
erfahren, wie berühmte Dichter fühlen und denken. Er sagt, er habe
nie darüber nachgedacht.

Pause I.

Trigorin meint, ihre Vorstellung von seinem Ruhme sei über-
trieben, sie aber findet sein Dasein bedeutungsvoll und schön. Er
bezeichnet ihre Worte als Marmelade, und er esse sie nie. Doch
erklärt er sich bereit, ihr über sein Leben zu erzählen.

Pause II

(angedeutet durch die Regiebemerkung: *Nach einigem Nachdenken*).

Trigorin spricht in einer langen Replik von dem Zwange seiner
Profession und verrät dadurch seine innere Kälte. Nina unterbricht
ihn immer wieder mit idealistischen und enthusiastischen Bemerkungen über die Erhabenheit der Kunst, für die man alles opfern
könne.

Pause III

(ihr Gespräch wird dadurch unterbrochen daß die Arkadina ihn
Haus ruft).

Er sagt, er wolle am liebsten bleiben, und entdeckt die getötete
Möwe.

Pause IV

(dadurch markiert, dass Trigorin etwas in sein Notizbuch schreibt).

Auf die Frage der Nina sagt er, er notiere ein Sujet für eine
kleinere Novelle, das Sujet von einem Mann, der aus lauter Langeweile ein junges Mädchen zugrunde richtet.

Pause V.

Im Fenster erscheint die Arkadina und teilt ihm mit, daß sie
bleiben würden. Trigorin eilt ins Haus.

Pause VI

(durch die Anweisung *Nach einigem Nachdenken* markiert).

Nina tritt an die Rampe und spricht nur die Worte „Es ist ein
Traum" aus.

Alle diese Pausen dienen dazu, um die Entfernung zwischen dem verhärteten und kalten Dichter, der seine Kunst als eine beschwerliche Profession auffaßt, und dem jungen Mädchen, das Schauspielerin werden will, hervorzuheben. Je mehr Nina vom Ideal des Künstlertums ergriffen erscheint, desto deutlicher wird Trigorins Zynismus. Zuletzt steht es dem Zuschauer klar, daß Nina dazu ausersehn ist, seinem Egoismus und seiner Laune geopfert zu werden. Wie ein Schmetterling fliegt Nina unaufhaltsam dem verderblichen Feuer entgegen. Die Pausen markieren das Wachsen ihrer Gefühle für den hervorragenden Dichter, dessen Wesen nur sie nicht erkennt.

Eine weitere Etappe in der Entwicklung des Verhältnisses zwischen den beiden ist das dritte Gespräch, das im 3. Akt stattfindet. Die Arkadina hat nach dem Selbstmordversuch ihres Sohnes beschlossen, mit Trigorin wegzureisen. Nina und Trigorin treffen sich allein auf der Bühne.

Nina streckt ihm ihre Hand entgegen, in der sie eine Erbse hält, und fragt ihn wie im Spiele: „Paar oder Unpaar"? Er antwortet unrichtig. Nina hat es von seiner Antwort abhängen lassen wollen, ob sie Schauspielerin werden solle oder nicht.

Pause I.

Nina schenkt ihm zur Erinnerung ein Medaillon, in das sie seine Anfangsbuchstaben und einen Hinweis auf eine Seite in einem seiner Bücher hat eingravieren lassen. Er verspricht ihr, sie in Erinnerung zu behalten, wie sie an jenem Tage aussah, als sie die Möwe fanden.

Pause II.

Sie bittet ihn schnell, noch vor der Abreise mit ihr zu sprechen.

Die erste Pause unterstreicht hier das geringe Interesse, das Trigorin für Ninas eigenes Problem hat. Er weigert sich, ihr einen guten Rat zu geben, und es entsteht eine Pause. Die zweite Pause unterstreicht bedeutungsvoll, daß sie ihn nur als novellistisches Thema interessiert. Sie zeigt auch, dass Nina immer noch etwas Entscheidendes von ihm erwartet.

Das vierte Gespräch zwischen ihnen bildet den Schluß des 4. Aktes. Die Arkadina ist schon dabei, den Landsitz zu verlassen, aber Trigorin kommt noch einmal zurück, nicht etwa weil er Ninas Bitte um ein letztes Gespräch erfüllen will, sondern um seinen vergessenen Spazierstock zu holen. Er und Nina treffen sich zufällig.

Nina teilt Trigorin mit, daß sie jetzt den Beschluß getroffen hat, am nächsten Tage das Haus ihres Vaters zu verlassen und nach Moskau zu reisen, um Schauspielerin zu werden. Er gibt ihr seine Adresse und nennt ein Hotel, in dem sie absteigen solle.

Pause.

Nina bittet ihn noch einen Augenblick zu bleiben, er läßt sie verstehen, daß er sich auf ein Wiedersehen freue, und als sie willenlos an seine Brust sinkt, umarmt und küsst er sie.

Eine zweite Pause tritt hier eigentlich nicht ein, aber der Vorhang fällt erst nach *dem langwierigen Kuß,* wie Čechov in einer letzten Regiebemerkung mitteilt. Er vertritt so eine Pause, die das Schicksal Ninas, der Möwe, besiegelt. Erst im letzten Akt erfahren wir aus dem Bericht Treplěvs, wie schnöde Trigorin später in Moskau ihre Liebe zu einem flüchtigen Genuß ausgenutzt habe, um sie dann mit ihrem und seinem Kinde sitzen zu lassen. So begleiten die Pausen ausdrucksvoll das Spiel zwischen dem erfahrenen Schriftsteller und seinem Opfer. Sie dienen immer wieder als Signale der Erwartung Ninas, etwas Wunderbares, etwas Traumhaftes mit ihm zu erleben, während er nicht imstande ist, ihrer Erwartung entgegenzukommen, sondern nur ihre jugendlichen Gefühle zu eigenem Vorteil ausnutzt.

Auch im „Onkel Vanja" finden wir das Motiv von dem jungen Mädchen, das in einen reifen Mann unglücklich verliebt ist. Sonja, die Tochter des alten Professors und Nichte Vanjas, blickt mit Bewunderung und Liebe zu dem tatkräftigen und ideenreichen Arzt Astrov auf und nähert sich ihm vorsichtig und naiv. Im zweiten Akt findet ein Gespräch unter vier Augen zwischen ihnen statt. Es ist Nacht, und das Unwohlsein des Professors hindert die anderen im Hause am Schlafen.

Sonja, die allein auf der Bühne ist, klopft an die Tür des Zimmers, wo Astrov wohnt, und bittet ihn um ein Gespräch. Sie bittet ihn, den Onkel nicht zum Trinken zu verführen. Er verspricht es. Während sie am Buffet stehen und essen, entspinnt sich ein Gespräch zwischen ihnen, in dem Astrov sowohl ihren verwöhnten alten Vater wie auch seine schöne, aber untätige zweite Frau scharf verurteilt. Ein untätiges Leben könne nicht rein sein.

Pause I.

Astrov bekennt, daß er so streng sei, weil er selbst mit dem Leben unzufrieden sei. Er sehe kein Ziel, liebe niemanden, habe kein unmittelbares Verhältnis zu den Menschen oder zur Natur, doch liebe er den Wald. Sonja verhindert ihn am Trinken, und er verspricht ihr niemals mehr zu trinken.

Pause II

(durch die Bemerkung markiert: *Er sieht auf die Uhr*).

Astrov spricht von der jungen Frau des Professors, die ihn bezaubern könnte, aber ihm nicht die rechte Liebe einflößen würde.

Pause III

(durch die Regiebemerkung markiert: *Er deckt mit der Hand seine Augen zu und zuckt zusammen*).

Sonja fragt ihn warum er zusammenzucke, und er erzählt ihr, daß ihm neulich ein Patient unter der Narkose gestorben sei. Sie meint, es sei an der Zeit, daß er es vergesse.

Pause IV.

Sonja fragt, wie er sich verhalten werde, wenn sie eine Freundin oder Schwester hätte, die sich in ihn verliebte, und er antwortet, daß er nicht imstande sei zu lieben. Er nimmt Abschied und eilt fort.

Gleich darauf findet ein pausenreiches Gespräch statt zwischen der schönen Elena und Sonja, sie versöhnen sich, trinken Bruderschaft miteinander, sprechen über Astrov, und der Zuschauer versteht, daß sich auch Elena für ihn interessiert. Im nächsten Akt erbietet sich Elena, mit Astrov von Sonjas Liebe zu sprechen. Der Monolog Elenas vor dem Gespräch mit Astrov, der oben analysiert worden ist, dient als Übergang zum dramatischen Dialog zwischen ihr und Astrov, der mit einer Liebesszene zwischen den beiden endet.

Der ganze Akt ist von Pausen durchzogen, die jede bedeutsame Etappe im Spiel unterstreichen. Aber sie haben eine andre Funktion als die Pausen, die Sonjas Versuch, Astrov ihre Liebe zu verstehen zu geben, begleiten. Während die anderen Pausen wieder mit Paragraphenzeichen verglichen werden können, dienen sie im Gespräch Sonjas mit Astrov dazu, durch ihre retardierende Wirkung die zögernd-erwartungsvolle Haltung Sonjas zu symbolisieren. Die Technik der Pause ist hier insofern mit der in der „Möwe" in den Gesprächen Ninas mit Trigorin verwandt, als es sich in beiden Fällen darum handelt, die Annäherung eines jungen unberührten Mädchens zum bewunderten Mann zu veranschaulichen. Sie bilden somit einen Bestandteil des psychologischen Spiels.

5.

In keinem der Schauspiele Čechovs spielen die Pausen eine so große Rolle wie in den „Drei Schwestern". Die erste Szene, die oben als ein aufgelöster Monolog der Ol'ga analysiert worden ist, gibt mit ihren Pausen den Kammerton des ganzen Stückes an. Es ist dabei bezeichnend, daß, während man in den anderen Schauspielen die Pausen in der Regel als eine Begleitungsmelodie einzelner Auftritte verstehen kann, sie in den „Drei Schwestern" gleichmäßig über den ganzen Text verstreut sind. Man kann freilich Textstücke aussondern, wo die Anwendung der Pausen an die schon oben festgestellte Technik erinnert, aber damit ist ihre Rolle nicht erschüpft. Etwas Neues tritt in diesem Schauspiel hinzu.

Einen Paragraphencharakter haben die Pausen bisweilen auch in den „Drei Schwestern". Besonders deutlich ist das der Fall in der Rede, mit der der Bruder Andrej seinen Schwestern gegenüber seine Frau verteidigt. Das geschieht am Ende des dritten Aktes: die Rede ist deutlich in drei Abschnitte geteilt, indem Andrej sie selber mit den Worten *Erstens, Zweitens* und *Drittens* paragraphiert. Nach jedem Abschnitt steht die Regiebemerkung *Pause.* Hier tritt diese uns schon bekannte Technik ganz nackt und schematisch hervor.

Etwas anders verhält es sich mit den Pausen, die die wortreichen philosophischen Betrachtungen und Aussagen des Batteriechefs Veršinin begleiten. Schon gleich nach der Präsentation im ersten Akt kommen in seinen Reden, vor ihnen und nach ihnen, Pausen vor, die die vermeintliche B e d e u t s a m k e i t des von ihm Gesagten unterstreichen sollen. Er sagt, daß man wehmütig werde, wenn man einsam auf einer bestimmten Brücke in Moskau steht und das Wasser des Flusses rauschen hört, und gleich tritt eine Pause ein. Er sagt, daß alles, was uns jetzt wichtig erscheine, nach Jahren vergessen sein oder unwichtig erscheinen würde, und wieder hebt eine Pause die Bedeutung des Gedankens hervor. Er spricht davon, wie man sich verhalten würde, wenn man sein Leben aufs neue erleben könnte, und eine vorhergehende Pause bereitet die Anwesenden darauf vor, daß dieser Gedanke bedeutsam sei. Im zweiten Akt klagt er im Gespräch mit Maša, seiner Gewohnheit treu, über die Kleinlichkeit seiner zänkischen Frau, und es folgt eine Pause. Er sagt ihr, daß sie sein einziger Trost sei, und wieder tritt eine Pause ein. Nach einer Pause, die wieder auf etwas Bedeutsames vorbereitet, spricht er später beim philosophischen Gespräch, zu dem er selbst auffordert, davon, daß die Aufgabe der Lebenden darin bestehe, ein glücklicheres Dasein auf Erden vorzubereiten. Und als er dann den Gedanken entwickelt, daß es nicht darauf ankomme, glücklich zu werden, sondern für die Zukunft zu arbeiten, tritt eine bedeutungsvolle Pause ein, bevor er die Konklusion zieht: „nicht für mich, sondern für die Nachkommen meiner Nachkommen". Auch im dritten Akt, während des Brandes, philosophiert er wieder über das, was um ihm geschieht, über die Zukunft seiner kleinen Töchter, über die Nichtigkeit der Gegenwart und die Schönheit des Lebens nach 200-300 Jahren, und jeder Abschnitt seiner Rede, jeder Gedanke ist von einer Pause unterstrichen und hervorgehoben. Ebenso arten sich seine Abschiedsreden im letzten Akt. Čechov trägt dabei mit der häufig vorkommenden Regiebemerkung *Er lacht* zur Charakteristik des redelustigen und nicht sehr gefühlswarmen Brigadechefs bei.

Im Allgemeinen aber kann gesagt werden, daß Čechov bewußt die Pausen in seinen Text einstreut, um einen e l e g i s c h e n, nachsinnenden Ton hervorzuzaubern. Immer wieder und wieder treten solche stumme Augenblicke ein, in denen die eben gesagten Worte wie Fragen, die keine Antwort erhalten und sie vielleicht nicht einmal wünschen oder erwarten, im Raume verklingen. Sehr bezeichnend in dieser Beziehung ist die letzte Szene, die im dritten Akt der „Drei Schwestern" in Ol'gas und Irinas gemeinsamem Schlafzimmer vorgeht. Die drei Schwestern sind allein im Zimmer versammelt.

Ol'ga sagt zu Maša, sie sei die unvernüftigste unter ihnen.

Pause I.

Maša will ihren Schwestern beichten.

Pause II.

Maša bekennt, daß sie Veršinin liebe.

Pause III.

Maša sagt, er sei ihr zuerst merkwürdig vorgekommen, dann habe sie mit ihm Mitleid gehabt, schließlich habe sie sich in ihn verliebt.

Pause IV.

Maša schmiegt sich an Irina an und bekennt, daß sie sich vor der Zukunft fürchte.

Pause V.

In diesem Stück sind nur die Pausen I und II als solche ausdrücklich angegeben. Statt der Pause III bemerkt Čechov, daß Ol'ga sich hinter ihrem Bettschirm versteckt habe und nichts hören wolle. Das gleiche ist mit der Pause IV der Fall. Als Pause V sind die letzten Worte in Mašas Beichte: „Schweigen... Schweigen..." zu deuten. Alle dienen dazu, um die ungehörte oder unbeantwortete Beichte, die wie eine Frage wirkt, im leeren Raum verklingen zu lassen. Gleich nach dieser Szene kommt Andrej auf die Bühne, und seine Repliken sind auch von Pausen begleitet. Daran schließt sich sein oben analysierter paragraphierter Monolog. Und endlich, als Ol'ga und Irina allein geblieben sind, erfolgt nach einem kurzen, von einer Pause unterbrochenen Gespräch, der Notschrei Irinas: nur nach Moskau flüchten, um jeden Preis nach Moskau flüchten! Darauf fällt der Vorhang.

6.

Eine einfache Statistik über das Vorkommen der Regieanweisung *Pause* oder gleichwertiger Anweisungen (*Schweigen, Stille, nach einigem Nachdenken* u.s.w.) in den hier behandelten fünf Stücken bestätigt rein quantitativ, daß die „Drei Schwestern" das elegischste von allen Čechovschen Stücken ist. Im nachfolgenden Schema nehmen wir auch die Seitenanzahl der einzelnen Stücke (nach der Ausgabe von 1950) und die Verteilung der Pausen auf die einzelnen Akte mit in Betracht:

„Ivanov" (53 Seiten)   30 (13 + 2 + 15 + 0) Pausen
„Die Möwe" (42 Seiten)   36 (9 + 5 + 9 + 13) Pausen
„Onkel Vanja" (38 Seiten)   44 (6 + 14 + 13 + 11) Pausen
„Drei Schwestern" (51 Seiten) 66 (9 + 15 + 18 + 24) Pausen
„Der Kirschgarten" (42 Seiten) 35 (8 + 16 + 1 + 10) Pausen.

Wir sehen in den 4 ersten Stücken das stetige Anwachsen der Pausen. Im „Onkel Vanja" und in den „Drei Schwestern" übersteigt die Anzahl der Pausen sogar die Anzahl der Seiten dieser beiden Stücke. Im „Kirschgarten" aber findet ein bemerkenswerter Niedergang in der Pausenanzahl statt. Man könnte vielleicht von einer Rückkehr zur Technik der beiden Erstlingsstücke sprechen. Doch würde das sicher kaum richtig sein. Dagegen kann kein Zweifel darüber vorliegen, daß „Onkel Vanja" und besonders die „Drei Schwestern" durchgehends auf dem Thema des Unausgesprochenen, des Angedeuteten, des Zögerns aufgebaut sind. Es ist dabei bemerkenswert, daß sich die Pausen in diesen Stücken recht gleichmäßig auf die vier Akte verteilen, während sich ihre Zahl in den vier Akten der andren Schauspiele, besonders des „Ivanov" und des „Kirschgartens", gleichsam im Zickzack hin und her bewegt. Besonders interessant ist es, daß die Pausen in den „Drei Schwestern" von Akt zu Akt anwachsen, um im letzten zu kulminieren. Das kommt in keinem der anderen Schauspiele vor.

ГЛЕБ СТРУВЕ

ЧЕХОВ И ГРИГОРОВИЧ

Их личные и литературные отношения

Роль Д. В. Григоровича в литературной судьбе Чехова в общем хорошо известна. Один из немногих живых еще в то время представителей того великого поколения, которое дало русской литературе Тургенева, Достоевского, Толстого и Некрасова, связанный со всеми ими узами личной дружбы, вместе с Некрасовым открывший Достоевского как писателя и лансировавший его в литературе (рассказ о посещении ими Белинского с рукописью *Бедных людей* всем известен), в восьмидесятые годы имевший несомненное право смотреть на себя как на старейшину русской литературы (Толстой давно уже отошел от литературных кругов и в литературной жизни участия не принимал), Григорович и по отношению к Чехову сыграл роль „открывателя”: один из первых в большой литературе он обратил внимание на рассказы Чехонте в газетах, привлек к ним внимание А. С. Суворина и А. Н. Плещеева, способствовал превращению Антоши Чехонте в Антона Чехова и открыл ему дорогу в большую литературу.

Всякому поклоннику Чехова, знакомому в общих чертах с его биографией, известны эти основные факты. Но как именно сложились личные отношения Чехова и Григоровича, и можно ли говорить в какой-нибудь мере о литературном влиянии второго на первого? Настоящая статья преследует двойную цель: во-первых, проследить в деталях развитие отношений между Чеховым и Григоровичем па основании их переписки и других источников и на этих отношениях иллюстрировать общую картину отношения Чехова к людям; и во-вторых, установить, сыграл ли Григорович какую-нибудь прямую роль в литературном творчестве Чехова.

1.

Когда произошло личное знакомство Чехова с Григоровичем — до или после знаменитого письма, адресованного последним первому? Н. И. Гитович, составительница недавней детальной *Летописи жизни и творчества Чехова,* относит

это знакомство ко второй поездке Чехова в Петербург в
апреле 1886 г., то есть считает письмо Григоровича от 25
марта 1886 г. написанным *до* личного знакомства. [1] Этому,
однако, противоречит как будто следующее место в письме
Чехова брату Александру от 4 января 1886 г., по возвращении
из первой поездки в Петербург. Чехов писал:

> Я был поражен приемом, который оказали мне питерцы.
> Суворин, Григорович, Буренин... все это приглашало,
> воспевало... и мне жутко стало, что я писал небрежно,
> спустя рукава. (XIII 157). [2]

Надлежит допустить поэтому, что первая встреча Чехова с
Григоровичем произошла еще в декабре 1885 года, когда он
в первый раз побывал в Петербурге. Может быть, он видел
Григоровича на приеме у Суворина или еще у кого-нибудь.
Близких отношений на этот раз во всяком случае не завяза-
лось. В первом письме Григоровича ничто не указывает на
предшествовавшую ему встречу; обращение в письме чисто
официальное: „Милостивый   государь   Антон   Павлович!”
Сближение Чехова с Григоровичем во всяком случае надо
относить к апрелю-маю 1886 г.. Между 27 апреля и 2 мая
Чехов писал брату Ивану: „Сегодня я буду на вечере у Суворина, где будут ‚все’ с Григоровичем во главе” (XIII 213).
А 10 мая он уже пишет брату Александру, что „как нельзя
ближе сошелся с Сувориным и Григоровичем” (XIII 214).

Чехова могли впоследствии раздражать (см. об этом подробности ниже) разговоры о том, что Григорович „открыл”
его талант, но не подлежит сомнению, что Григорович первый
в литературном мире обратил на него всерьез внимание.
Внимание самого Григоровича было привлечено напечатан-
ным в *Петербургской Газете* в июле 1885 г. рассказом *Егерь*.
По словам А. А. Плещеева, сына поэта, Григорович сам ему
рассказывал, что, прочтя этот рассказ, он отправился с ним к
А. С. Суворину — „и о Чехонте заговорили”. Еще до первого

---

[1] Н. И. Гитович, *Летопись жизни и творчества А. П. Чехова,* М. 1955,
стр. 135.

[2] Все цитаты даются по ПССП. Это самое до сих пор полное собрание
чеховских писем, хотя в нем и имеются существенные пробелы,
объясняемые купюрами „идеологического” характера, в которых
оказались повинны советские редакторы издания. Об этих купюрах см.
мою статью „Chekhov in Communist Censorship," *Slavonic & East European
Review,* Dec. 1955. По этому же изданию даются ссылки на некоторые
письма к Чехову, цитируемые в комментариях и часто неопубликован-
ные.

письма Григоровича Чехову Н. А. Лейкин писал последнему: „Григорович просто влюблен в Ваши рассказы” (XIII 471). Хотя первое письмо Григоровича (от 25 марта 1886 г.) очень хорошо известно всем, кто читал биографию Чехова, приведем наиболее существенные места из него:

Около года тому назад я случайно прочел в Петербургской Газете Ваш рассказ; названия его теперь не помню; помню только, что меня поразили в нем черты особенной своеобразности, а главное, — замечательная верность, правдивость в изображении действующих лиц и также при описании природы. С тех пор я читал все, что было подписано *Чехонте*, хотя внутренно сердился за человека, который так еще мало себя ценит, что считает нужным прибегать к псевдониму. Читая Вас, я постоянно советовал Суворину и Буренину следовать моему примеру. Они меня послушались и теперь, вместе со мною, не сомневаются, что у Вас *настоящий* талант — талант, выдвигающий Вас далеко из круга литераторов нового поколенья. Я не журналист, не издатель, пользоваться Вами я могу только читая Вас; если я говорю о Вашем таланте, говорю по убеждению. Мне минуло уже 65 лет; но я сохранил еще столько любви к литературе, с такою горячностью слежу за ее успехом, так радуюсь всегда, когда встречаю в ней что-нибудь живое, даровитое, что не мог, — как видите, — утерпеть и протягиваю Вам обе руки. Но это еще не все; вот что хочу прибавить: по разнообразным свойствам Вашего несомненного таланта, верному чувству внутреннего анализа, мастерству в описательном роде (мятель, ночь, местность в *Агафье* и т.д.), чувству пластичности, где в нескольких строчках является полная картина: тучки на угасающей заре *„как пепел на потухающих угольях . . .”* и т.д., — вы, я уверен, призваны к тому, чтобы написать несколько превосходных, истинно художественных произведений. Вы совершите великий нравственный грех, если не оправдаете таких ожиданий. Для этого вот что нужно: уважение к таланту, который дается так редко. Бросьте срочную работу . . . (199-201). [3]

[3] Цитаты из писем Григоровича к Чехову или ссылки на них даются здесь и дальше, с указанием только страниц, по сборнику *Слово*, II (М. 1914), где напечатаны письма разных лиц, в том числе Григоровича и Плещеева. Адрес Чехова Григорович узнал у Суворина, которому писал в тот же день: „Спасибо за адрес Чехова. Я сегодня же написал ему длинное письмо. Думаю, что оно будет ему приятно и не совсем бесполезно”. См. *Письма русских писателей к А. С. Суворину.* Подготовил к печати проф. Д. И. Абрамович. Государственная Публичная Библиотека в Ленинграде. Серия II: *Материалы по истории русской науки, литературы и общественности,* под общей редакцией проф. Н С.

Григорович дальше укоряет Чехова за вторгающийся иногда в его описания излишний натурализм и еще раз убеждает отказаться от псевдонима.

Если сделать скидку на свойственный Григоровичу слегка экзальтированный тон, на его — как позднее выражался Чехов — „велеречивость", нет никаких оснований сомневаться в искренности его восторгов перед талантом молодого и неизвестного писателя. Это отношение к литературному таланту Чехова осталось у него до конца дней, хотя личные отношения между ними и сошли почти на нет.

Не менее известное ответное письмо Чехова, если принять во внимание прирожденную сдержанность Чехова, благодаря которой он часто свои истинные чувства маскировал шуточкой, производит местами впечатление почти чрезмерного нажима педали. В начале письма особенно бросается в глаза несвойственный Чехову гиперболический тон. Письмо датировано 28 марта 1886 г. Вот главные выдержки из него:

Ваше письмо, мой добрый, горячо любимый благовеститель, поразило меня, как молния. Я едва не заплакал, разволновался и теперь чувствую, что оно оставило глубокий след в моей душе. Как Вы приласкали мою молодость, так пусть Бог успокоит Вашу старость, я же не найду ни слов, ни дел, чтобы благодарить Вас. Вы знаете, какими глазами обыкновенные люди глядят на таких избранников как Вы; можете поэтому судить, что составляет для моего самолюбия Ваше письмо. Оно выше всякого диплома для начинающего писателя, оно — гонорар за настоящее и будущее. Я как в чаду. Нет у меня сил судить, заслужена мною эта высокая награда или нет. Повторяю только, что она меня поразила.

Если у меня есть дар, который следует уважать, то, каюсь перед чистотою Вашего сердца, я доселе не уважал его. Я чувствовал, что он у меня есть, но привык считать его ничтожным.

... Доселе относился я к своей литературной работе крайне легкомысленно, небрежно, зря. Не помню я *ни одного* своего рассказа, над которым я работал бы более суток, а *Егеря,* который Вам понравился, я писал в купальне ...

Державина. Ленинград 1927, стр. 26. Это небрежно редактированное и слишком скупо прокомментированное издание содержит ряд интересных писательских писем к Суворину, в том числе И. С. Аксакова, Гаршина, Гончарова, Григоровича, Достоевского, Лескова, Некрасова, Никитина, Островского, Плещеева, Полонского, Розанова, Салтыкова-Щедрина, Вл. Соловьева и Л. Н. Толстого.

Дальше Чехов указывает, что письмо Суворина было первое, что толкнуло его к самокритике, и продолжает:

> Но вот нежданно-негаданно явилось ко мне Ваше письмо. Простите за сравнение, оно подействовало на меня, как губернаторский приказ „выехать из города в 24 часа!", то есть я вдруг почувствовал обязательную потребность спешить, скорее выбраться оттуда, куда завяз.

Чехов соглашается далее с упреками в натурализме и „циничости", пишет, что сам заметил это в *Ведьме,* обещает избавиться от срочной работы („но не скоро. Выбиться из колеи, в которую я попал, невозможно..."), указывает, что заменить псевдоним уже невозможно, отзывается отрицательно о своей книжке *Пестрые рассказы* („Это винегрет..."), просит Григоровича прислать ему свою карточку и, впадая снова в гиперболический тон, просит не вменять ему в вину, что он „в первый раз в жизни дерзнул себя побаловать таким наслаждением, как письмо к Григоровичу" (XIII 191-94).

О том, какое действительно сильное впечатление произвело на Чехова получение письма Григоровича, свидетельствует то, что на протяжении ближайших недель он пишет об этом событии брату Александру, дяде М. Г. Чехову („В России есть большой писатель. Личность Григоровича настолько почтенна и популярна, что Вы можете представить мое приятное изумление..."), редактору *Осколков* Н. А. Лейкину и литератору В. И. Билибину (XIII 198, 199, 203, 206). Билибину Чехов писал:

> Нечаянно, вдруг, наподобие deus ex machina, пришло ко мне письмо от Григоровича. Я ответил и вскоре получил другое письмо с карточкой. Письмо в полтора листа каждое: почерк неразборчивый, старческий; старик требует, чтобы я написал что-нибудь крупное и бросил срочную работу. Он доказывает, что у меня настоящий талант (у него подчеркнуто) и в доказательство моей художественности делает выписки из моих рассказов. Пишет тепло и искренно. Я, конечно, рад, хотя и чувствую, что Григорович перехватил через край...

Григорович почти сразу же (2-го апреля) отозвался на письмо Чехова. Он писал:

> ...читая Ваши рассказы, я не сразу себе поверил. Как опытная гончая собака, почуяв за кустами дупеля, — я на него не бросился, подобрался тихонько ближе, прочел еще раз, подчеркивая то, что остановило мое внимание, и тогда

уже, сделав конечное заключение, отправился к Суворину, к Полонскому, Потехину и Буренину — которые вполне согласились со мной.

Григорович далее советовал Чехову покончить с срочной работой по мелочам:

> Если к свойствам Вашего таланта не подходит повесть или роман, — пишите мелкие рассказы, — но обделывайте их до тонкости. Тургенев одними записками охотника сделал бы себе громкое имя! ...

Образцом повести Григорович называл *Тамань* Лермонтова, прибавляя:

> Пусть все литераторы соберутся и ни один не найдет слова, которое можно было бы прибавить или убавить; там все как цельный музыкальный аккорд. [4]

---

[4] Часто цитируется мнение Чехова о *Тамани*, как о лучшем „рассказе" в русской литературе. Как видим, оно было высказано Чехову еще в 1886 году Григоровичем. У самого Чехова ни в письмах ни в записных книжках мы такого недвусмысленного высказывания не находим. Есть, правда, близкие к нему высказывания в показаниях мемуаристов. Так, А. Н. Серебров (Тихонов) передает, например, свой разговор с Чеховым в 1902 году о Горьком. Чехов сердито говорил ему, что он ценит в Горьком не то, что надо, тогда как „у него есть действительно прекрасные вещи. *На плотах,* например. Помните? Плывут в тумане... ночью... по Волге ... Чудесный рассказ! Во всей нашей литературе я знаю только еще один такой, это *Тамань* Лермонтова..." (*Чехов в воспоминаниях современников,* 2-е, дополн. изд., М. 1954, стр. 560). Есть аналогичное показание И. А. Бунина, которому Чехов, говоря о *Тамани,* сказал: „Вот бы написать такую вещь да еще водевиль хороший, тогда бы и умереть можно" (*Сборник памяти А П. Чехова,* М. 1906, стр. 71). Высокий общий отзыв Чехова о лермонтовском стиле приводит в своих воспоминаниях о. Сергий Щукин, ялтинский священник и церковный учитель, который советовался с Чеховым относительно своих собственных литературных произведений. Отзыв этот хорошо известен (см. *Чехов в воспоминаниях современников,* 1954 , стр. 542). Есть, однако, в переписке Чехова одно специфическое упоминание *Тамани*: в письме Я. П. Полонскому от 18 января 1888 г. он говорит о *Тамани* и *Капитанской дочке,* как о тех прозаических произведениях в русской литературе, которые „прямо доказывают тесное родство сочного русского стиха с изящной прозой" (XIV 18). Покойный П. М. Бицилли в своей работе *Творчество Чехова. Опыт стилистического анализа* (Годишник на Университета св. Климент Охридски, София, Историко-Филологически Факултет, том XXXVIII, 6. София 1942), говоря о влиянии Лермонтова на Чехова и в частности о параллелях между *Таманью* и чеховским рассказом *Воры,* задает вопрос: „Не Григорович ли сблизил Чехова с Лермонтовым?" (стр. 40). Работа Бицилли представляет обстоятельную (в ней 138 страниц) попытку рассмотреть связи писательской манеры Чехова с различными течениями

Прося Чехова присылать ему свои вещи, Григорович опять
восторгался его описаниями природы и вместе с тем крити-
ковал ненужные грубые подробности во внешних описаниях:

> По любви Вашей к природе и замечательному чувству,
> с каким Вы ее описываете, — Вы еще поэт вдобавок. Это
> драгоценное свойство, столь редкое теперь в литераторах
> новой формации — вынесет Вас как на крыльях. Правди-
> вость передачи внешних впечатлений, — нимало не требует
> подробностей грубо матерьяльного оттенка. Это между
> прочим недостаток Золя — а уж на что талант!

В заключение Григорович спрашивал, читал ли Чехов
Записки Пиквикского клуба Диккенса, и прибавлял:

> Если нет, — непременно прочтите. Такая картина из рус-
> ских нравов давно ждет своего Диккенса. Россия велика, и
> *Мертвые души* далеко еще не все исчерпали (201-03).

При этом письме Григорович послал Чехову свой портрет
с надписью: „От старого писателя молодому таланту”.

На это письмо Чехов уже не отвечал: вскоре после этого
он поехал снова в Петербург и именно тогда, как мы видели,
сошелся близко и с Сувориным и с Григоровичем. Есть все
основания думать, что они разговаривали на темы, затро-
нутые Григоровичем в его обоих письмах.

Следующий обмен письмами произошел в начале 1887 года.
Почин принадлежал Чехову, который 12 февраля написал
Григоровичу длинное письмо по поводу только что прочитан-
ного им рассказа Григоровича *Сон Карелина* — к этому ин-
тересному письму мы еще вернемся во второй части насто-
ящей статьи.

Мы не знаем, сразу ли ответил Григорович на это письмо.
Ответ его без даты, рукой Чехова помечено на нем „Март
87 г.”. Из-за участившихся припадков грудной жабы Григорович не успел закончить и отослать письмо и передал его
прямо в руки Чехову, когда тот приехал в марте в Петербург.
14 марта в письме к М. В. Киселевой Чехов писал:

> Приезжаю к Григоровичу. Старичина поцеловал меня в
> лоб, обнял, заплакал от умиления и . . . от волнения у него

___

и традициями в русской (а отчасти и мировой) литературе. Об этой
„книге”, как он ее называет, очень резко отозвался И. А. Бунин (в своей
незаконченной книге *О Чехове*, Нью Иорк 1955). Этот резкий отзыв
несправедлив: в работе Бицилли, хотя там многое и притянуто за волосы
(Бицилли часто видит параллели и даже заимствования там, где их вовсе
нет), есть много ценного.

приключился припадок грудной жабы. Он невыносимо страдал, метался, стонал, а я 2½ часа сидел возле него, браня во все лопатки свою бессильную медицину. К счастью, приехал Бертенсон, и я мог бежать. Старик серьезно болен и, вероятно, скоро умрет. Для меня это незаменимая потеря. С собой я привез его письмо, которое он начал писать ко мне: описывает подробно свою болезнь и проч.

Каковы впечатления? Право, запить можно. Впрочем, говорят, для беллетристов все полезно (XIII 293).

В этом письме Чехова звучат заслуживающие внимания нотки, к которым мы еще вернемся. Привезенное Чеховым письмо действительно начинается описанием недавнего припадка грудной жабы. Что касается „и проч", то оно состоит из ответа Григоровича на замечания Чехова по поводу *Сна Карелина* — об этом будет речь ниже, во второй части статьи.

Вскоре после своего возвращения в Москву Чехов писал Суворину, что думает посвятить свою готовящуюся книгу рассказов Григоровичу. Эту мысль он осуществил: Григоровичу был посвящен сборник *В сумерках*, за который в следующем году Чехов получил от Академии Наук половину Пушкинской премии. Когда сборник печатался, Чехов напоминал своему брату Александру, наблюдавшему в Петербурге за печатанием, чтобы он не забыл о посвящении. [5]

2.

После этого в переписке между Чеховым и Григоровичем наступил довольно длительный перерыв. Возобновил ее Григорович, который в то время ради здоровья жил в Ницце. Оттуда он написал 30 декабря 1887 г. (ст. ст.) длинное письмо Чехову. Дав ему короткий отчет о своей болезни, он еще более высоко, чем раньше, отозвался о рассказах Чехова („такое мастерство в передаче наблюдений встречается только у Тургенева и Толстого (описания такие в *Анне Карени-*

---

[5] Чехов очень рассердился на своего брата за то, что в присланной тем корректуре Григорович в посвящении оказался названным „кавалером русских и иностранных орденов". Александр объяснил это шуткой (XIII 341 и 510). Происхождение этой шутки надо искать в том, что, обещая Александру познакомить его с Григоровичем, Чехов подчеркивал, что Григорович — „действительный статский советник и кавалер" (XIII 204). Между маем и октябрем 1887 года Чехов три раза запрашивал своего брата о местопребывании и адресе Григоровича (XIII 335, 347, 378).

ной)"). Рассказ *Недоброе дело* он назвал образцовым „по целости аккорда, по выдержке общего сумрачного тона". Он снова советовал Чехову „бросить писание наскоро и исключительно мелких рассказов". Почему бы Чехову не написать роман, спрашивал он. „Дело вовсе не в сюжете, не в том, *что̀*, а *как*, — это великая истина". В подтверждение этого Григорович ссылался на *Горе от ума*, *Ревизора*, *Мертвые души* и *Шинель*. Он даже предлагал Чехову сюжет для романа: самоубийство 17-летнего мальчика на чердаке. Снова и снова заклинал он Чехова не работать наспех: „Утопайте в большой неспешной работе". Письмо кончалось так:

> Не знаю, чего только я не прочел в мой долгий век; читал я всегда внимательно, стараясь всегда угадать прием писателя и как у него что сделано; у меня несравненно больше литературного чутья и такта, чем собственно дарования. Мне Вы можете вполне довериться как литератору и столько же как человеку, который полюбил Вас сердечно и искренно мимо Вашего таланта. За посвящение мне книги спасибо (206-10).

Чехов сразу же (12 января 1888 г.) отозвался на это, как он назвал его, „великолепное" письмо довольно длинным письмом — интересным тем, что в нем дан самоанализ *Степи*, над которой Чехов в то время работал. Это была, как известно, его первая длинная вещь. Чехов писал:

> Не стану объяснять Вам, уважаемый Дмитрий Васильевич, как дорого и какое значение имеет для меня Ваш последнее великолепное письмо. Каюсь, я не выдержал впечатления и копию с письма послал Короленко — кстати говоря, очень хорошему человеку. По прочтении письма мне стало не особенно стыдно, так как оно застало меня за работой для толстого журнала... я принялся за большую вещь...

И дальше Чехов так описывает свою работу над *Степью*:

> Каждая отдельная глава составляет особый рассказ, и все главы связаны, как пять фигур в кадрили, близким родством. Я стараюсь, чтобы у них был общий запах и общий тон, что мне может удаться тем легче, что через все главы у меня проходит одно лицо... в общем выходит у меня нечто странное и не в меру оригинальное. От непривычки писать длинно, из постоянного, привычного страха [не] написать лишнее [6] я впадаю в крайность. Все страницы выходят у меня компактными, как бы прессованными; впечатления теснятся, громоздятся, выдавливают

---

[6] В печатном тексте: „*не* написать лишнее". Это — либо описка Чехова, либо опечатка.

друг друга; картинки, или, как Вы называете, блестки, тесно жмутся друг к другу, идут непрерывной цепью и поэтому утомляют. В общем получается не картина, а сухой, подробный перечень впечатлений, что-то вроде конспекта; вместо художественного, цельного изображения степи я преподношу читателю „степную энциклопедию". Первый блин комом. Но я не робею. И энциклопедия, авось, сгодится. Быть может, она раскроет глаза моим сверстникам и покажет им, какое богатство, какие залежи красоты остаются еще нетронутыми, и как еще не тесно русскому художнику ... Вы, я знаю, поймете мою степь и ради нее простите мне невольные прегрешения. А грешу я невольно, потому что, как теперь оказывается, *не умею* еще писать большие вещи ...

Упомянув дальше, что будет летом продолжать „прерванный роман", Чехов откликается затем на предложенную Григоровичем тему для романа:

Самоубийство 17-летнего мальчика — тема очень благодарная и заманчивая, но ведь за нее страшно браться! На измучивший всех вопрос нужен и мучительно-сильный ответ, а хватит ли у нашего брата внутреннего содержания? Нет. Обещая успех этой теме, Вы судите по себе, но ведь у людей Вашего поколения, кроме таланта, есть эрудиция, школа, фосфор и железо, а у современных талантов нет ничего подобного, и, откровенно говоря, надо радоваться, что они не трогают серьезных вопросов (XIV 14-16).

И Чехов зло гадает, как эту тему испортили бы его современники X, Y и Z. Письмо заканчивается новыми комплиментами адресату: он-де прочно вошел в русскую литературу, и его не забудут, как не забудут Тургенева, Толстого и Гоголя.

Об отношении Чехова к „великолепному" письму Григоровича говорит и то, что он отдал его переписать и послал в копии В. Г. Короленко, которому писал при этом:

... Ценю я его [письмо] по многим причинам на вес золота и боюсь прочесть во второй раз, чтобы не потерять первого впечатления. Из него Вы увидите, что литературная известность и хороший гонорар нисколько не спасают от такой мещанской прозы, как болезни, холод и одиночество: старик кончает жизнь. Из письма Вам станет также известно, что не Вы один от чистого сердца наставляли меня на путь истинный, и поймете, как мне стыдно. Когда я прочел письмо Григоровича, я вспомнил Вас, и мне стало совестно. Мне стало очевидно, что я неправ. Пишу это именно Вам, потому что около меня нет людей, которым нужна моя искренность и которые имеют право на нее, а с Вами я, не спрашивая Вас, заключил в душе своей союз... (XIV 11).

Что касается Григоровича, то он, повидимому, не ответил на письмо Чехова от 12 января. Во всяком случае уже 5 февраля Чехов снова пишет ему и, коснувшись опять *Степи* („...Я знаю, Гоголь на том свете на меня рассердится. В нашей литературе он степной царь. Я залез в его владения с добрыми намерениями, но наерундил немало. Три четверти повести не удались мне...”), спрашивает, получил ли Григорович его январское письмо, одновременно с которым он послал также письмо В. Н. Давыдова. Упомянув, что в этом письме он писал по поводу сюжета о самоубийстве, Чехов снова возвращается к этой теме. Григорович писал о 17-летнем мальчике, которого он предлагал в герои романа:

...Вся его обстановка, все доводы, которые могли довести его до самоубийства, на мои глаза гораздо важнее и глубже причин, заставивших Вертера наложить на себя руки. Такой сюжет заключает в себе вопрос дня; возьмите его, не упускайте случая коснуться наболевшей общественной раны; успех громадный ждет Вас с первого же дня появления такой книги... (209-10).

Чехов теперь писал Григоровичу:

...Я писал в своем письме о Вашем сюжете — самоубийстве 17-летнего мальчика. Я сделал слабую попытку воспользоваться им. В своей *Степи* через все восемь глав я провожу девятилетнего мальчика, который, попав в будущем в Питер или в Москву, кончит непременно плохим. Если *Степь* будет иметь хоть маленький успех, то я буду продолжать ее. Я нарочно писал ее так, чтобы она давала впечатление незаконченного труда. Она, как Вы увидите, похожа на первую часть большой повести. Что касается мальчугана, то почему я изобразил его так, а не иначе, я расскажу Вам, когда Вы прочтете *Степь*...

Возвращаясь к вопросу о самоубийстве, Чехов продолжал:

Не знаю, понял ли я Вас. Самоубийство русского юноши есть явление специфическое, Европе незнакомое. Вся энергия художника должна быть обращена на две силы: человек и природа. С одной стороны, физическая слабость, нервы, ранняя половая зрелость, страстная жажда жизни и правды, мечты о широкой, как степь, деятельности, беспокойный анализ, бедность знаний рядом с широким полетом мысли; с другой — необъятная равнина, суровый климат, серый, суровый народ со своей тяжелой, холодной историей, татарщина, чиновничество, бедность, невежество, сырость столиц и проч. Русская жизнь бьет русского чело-

века так, что мокрого места не остается, бьет на манер
тысячепудового камня. В Западной Европе люди погибают
оттого, что жить тесно и душно, у нас же оттого, что жить
просторно ... Простора так много, что маленькому чело-
вечку нет сил ориентироваться ...

Вот что я думаю о русских самоубийцах ...

Так ли я Вас понял? Впрочем, об этом говорить в письме
невозможно, потому что тесно. Эта тема хороша для раз-
говора. Как жаль, что Вы не в России! (XIV 33-34).

Несмотря на то, что *Степь* имела более чем „маленький"
успех, Чехов не стал ее продолжать, и сделать из Егорушки
„русского самоубийцу" ему не пришлось. Покойный П. М.
Бицилли в своей интересной работе о творчестве Чехова
высказывает предположение, что предложенная Григоровичем
чем Чехову тема могла послужить стимулом к написанию
рассказа *Володя*. [7]

Затем в переписке опять большой перерыв. 7 октября 1888 г.
Академия Наук присудила Чехову половнуи Пушкинской
премии (500 рублей) за его сборник *В сумерках*. Григорович
был членом комитета, присуждавшего премии, и на другой
же день письмом известил Чехова об этом событии. При этом
он снова советовал Чехову ценить больше свой талант и
печатать сразу несколько рассказов в хороших журналах,
бросив писание для газет. О *Степи* он отзывался так: „рама
велика для картины, величина холста не пропорциональна
сюжету. Видение Иезекиля Рафаеля изображено на 10-верш-
ковой доске и кажется громадной картиной". В этом подходе
сказался художественный критик — Григоровичу приходилось много писать об искусстве, и он считался знатоком в
живописи. Заканчивал свое письмо Григорович советом
общего характера, в котором Чехов едва ли нуждался — он
и без того практиковал то, что ему рекомендовал Григорович,
и сам давал сходные советы начинающим писателям:

Когда является содержания на 10 печатных листов, надо
стараться вогнать его в три листа, — в этом вся штука;
тогда только статья или повесть бьет обухом и как свайка
вбивается не в землю, — а в мозг читателя (211-13).

Чехов немедленно ответил на письмо Григоровича —
письмом от 9 октября, выражая радость по случаю выздо-
ровления Григоровича и получения от него письма:

Мне весело, дорогой Дмитрий Васильевич, что Вы нако-

---

[7] Бицилли, цит. соч., стр. 10. Об этом еще будет речь ниже.

нец выздоровели и вернулись в Россию. Те, кто Вас видел, писали мне, что Вы уже совершенно здоровы, попрежнему бодры и читали даже свою новую повесть. Что у Вас теперь большая борода...

Я рад и тому, что получил от Вас письмо. Письма Ваши коротки, как хорошие стихи, видаюсь я с Вами редко, но мне кажется, и даже я почти уверен, что если в Петербурге не будет Вас и Суворина, то я потеряю равновесие и понесу ужасную чепуху...

Мы увидим дальше, что Чехов в последний раз пишет Григоровичу в таком тоне. В присуждении премии ему видится немалая роль Григоровича:

Премия для меня, конечно, счастье, и если бы я сказал, что она не волнует меня, то солгал бы... Конечно, — и это вне всякого сомнения — премией этой я обязан не себе... Мысль о премии подал Я. П. Полонский, Суворин подчеркнул эту мысль и послал книгу в Академию. Вы же были в Академии и стояли горой за меня. Согласитесь, что если бы не Вы трое, то не видать бы мне премии, как ушей своих. Я не хочу скромничать и уверять Вас, что я не стою премии и проч. — это было бы старо и скучно; я хочу только сказать, что своим счастьем я обязан не себе. Благодарю тысячу раз и буду всю жизнь благодарить.

Дальше Чехов пишет о том, что не работает больше в малой прессе (*Новое Время,* говорит он, не малая пресса, и от Суворина уходить он не хочет, так как привязан к нему). Сообщает о своих планах:

Хочется писать роман, есть чудесный сюжет... потрачу на него несколько лет —

и прибавляет:

Политического, религиозного и философского мировоззрения у меня еще нет; я меняю его ежемесячно, а потому придется ограничиться только описанием, как мои герои любят, женятся, родят, умирают и как говорят.

Пока не пробил час для романа, буду продолжать писать то, что люблю, то есть мелкие рассказы в 1-1½ листа и менее... (XIV 181-83).

В конце 1888 года между Чеховым и Григоровичем как будто пробежала первая черная кошка. Чехов был в Петербурге, где должно было состояться чтение его рассказа *Припадок* (Чехов сам начал читать рассказ, но закончил чтение знаменитый артист Александринского театра В. Н.

Давыдов). Григорович, как он сам писал Суворину (13 декабря 1888 г.), „горько сожалел", что не мог из-за сильного мороза присутствовать на чтении. Чехов же, повидимому, не нашел времени побывать у Григоровича. [8] Тот был огорчен, а на Сувориных это произвело неприятное впечатление, о чем сообщила Чехову его сестра, Мария Павловна. В сочельник 1888 года Чехов написал Григоровичу следующее объяснительное письмо:

Моя сестра, вернувшись из Петербурга, сказала мне: „на Сувориных неприятно подействовало, что ты перед отъездом не побывал у Григоровича. Ты этим огорчил его". Уверяю Вас, милый мой, что у меня и в мыслях не было сделать Вам что-нибудь неприятное, а тем более оскорблять Вас своим невниманием. Правда, в моих жилах течет ленивая хохлацкая кровь, я тяжел на подъем и не люблю выходить из дому, но моя любовь к Вам пересилила бы всякую лень. Видеть Вас и говорить с Вами для меня такое удовольствие, какое мне приходится испытывать не часто. Говорю я *искренно*. Не был же я у Вас благодаря одному обстоятельству, которое я считаю просто недоразумением. Прошу Вас припомнить тот вечер, когда Вы, Алексей Сергеевич [Суворин] и я шли из музея в магазин Цинзерлинга. Мы разговаривали. Я, между прочим, сказал:

— Я к Вам на днях приду.

— Дома Вы его не застанете, — сказал Суворин.

Вы промолчали. Ваше молчание я понял не так, как нужно, — отсюда и мое невежество. Всетаки я виноват. Если Вы напишете мне, что не сердитесь на меня, то я буду очень рад и за это, когда приеду в Петербург, обещаю Вам сопровождать Вас по улицам в качестве вожатого доктора сколько Вам угодно.

Пригласив Григоровича приехать в Москву смотреть пьесу Суворина *Татьяна Репина,* которую дают там лучше, чем в Петербурге, Чехов заканчивает:

Так напишите же мне, что Вы не сердитесь. Честное слово, я был далек от мысли огорчить Вас. Пришлите фотографию с подобающей надписью (XIV 261-62).

Несмотря на все заверения Чехова, на подчеркивание слова „искренно", его изъяснения в любви к Григоровичу и в удовольствии, испытываемом от общения со старым писателем, звучат не вполне искренне. И не пройдет и года, как Чехов будет говорить о Григоровиче с нескрываемым

---

[8] См. Гитович, цит. соч., стр 214.

недоброжелательством. Это, конечно, не значит, что Чехов намеренно огорчил Григоровича своим невниманием. Он просто не подумал о том, что его неприход может огорчить того. [9]

Григорович отвечал ему 27 декабря. Отрицая, что он чувствовал какую-то обиду, он писал:

Мне показалось, Вы почему-то вдруг ко мне охладели ... Надо мне простить мою недоверчивость к чувствам ближнего; виною всему безрассудочная горячность моего сердца, слишком часто получавшая щелчки в ответ на ее порывы.

В пример этого Григорович приводил эпизод из своих отношений с Достоевским, с которым, как известно, он был дружен в молодости (они вместе учились в Инженерном Училище).

И Григорович не в первый раз писал Чехову о том, что он горячо полюбил его.

В том же письме Григорович высказывал свое мнение о Припадке Чехова, напечатанном в сборнике памяти В. М. Гаршина. Он не соглашался с теми, кто „возмущался" цинизмом темы. Гоголь, говорил он, был много откровеннее в Невском проспекте. В Припадке все освещается и оправдывается „высоким человеческим чувством". Как всегда, восторгался он мастерством Чехова в передаче „впечатлений природы":

... вечер с сумрачным небом, с только что выпавшим и падающим мокрым снегом ... несколько строк всего, — но все так глубоко прочувствовано, так мастерски передано, — что точно сам переживаешь впечатление. Страница 296, — строки от 6-ой до 11-ой — просто прелесть! Я бесился, что никто не оценил строчку 6-ую на 308 странице, — и были, говорили мне, — еще поэты при чтении в литературном обществе (213-15). [10]

Ответа Чехова на это письмо нет в его переписке. Возможно, что ответное письмо не сохранилось, а может быть, Чехов ответил на словах, когда они встретились в начале

[9] Возможно, что с этим же эпизодом связана фраза в письме Чехова Суворину от 10 декабря 1888 года: „Григорович говорил Вам, что я стал горд и возвышаюсь? Не потому ли это, что моего Медведя играют у министров?" (XIV 252).

[10] Строчка, о которой говорит Григорович, в первоначальной версии читалась так: „И как не стыдно снегу падать в этот переулок!" Впоследствии Чехов переделал ее на „И как может снег падать в этот переулок!" (см. XIV 540).

следующего года и Григорович подарил ему свою фотографию с надписью „Дорогому другу моему Антону Павловичу Чехову почитатель Григорович, 20 января 1889", исполнив таким образом просьбу Чехова в письме от 24 декабря.

4.

Если не считать одной небольшой записки Григоровича от 11 февраля 1891 года [11] по поводу его пьесы *Заноза,* которую Чехов предложил напечатать в редактировавшемся Ф. А. Куманиным журнале *Артист,* на этом переписка между Чеховым и Григоровичем и оборвалась; во всяком случае среди напечатанных писем более поздних не имеется; нет указаний на них и в *Летописи,* составленной Н. И. Гитович. Личные встречи между ними продолжались. В переписке Чехова и других источниках есть указания на такие встречи в феврале 1890 г., в январе, марте и декабре 1891 г., в январе 1893 г. и в октябре 1896 г. Даже если этих встреч и не было больше (а такая возможность есть), редкость их может быть объяснена отъездом Чехова на Сахалин (он отсутствовал с апреля до декабря 1890 г.), а потом его уединением в Мелихове и переездом в Крым. Подробностей о встречах сохранилось мало. В марте 1891 г. Чехов был в Петербурге, и они вместе ходили на выставку передвижников. Чехов писал своей сестре: „... по выставке чичеронствовал мне Григорович, объясняя достоинства и недостатки всякой картины; от левитановского пейзажа он в восторге" (XV 173). В декабре следующего года Чехов был посредником по высылке Григоровичу для его музея каких-то гончарных изделий из Полтавской губернии (Григорович был учредителем и директором Музея художественной промышленности при Обществе Поощрения Художеств). Чехов писал своему приятелю А. И. Смагину: „Недавно у меня был Григорович. Я сказал ему, что хомутецких гончарных изделий в его музей будет выслано наложенным платежом на 25 рублей. Он поблагодарил и продолжал говорить о женщинах" (XV 454). 12 января 1893 г. по случаю Татьянина дня по инициативе Чехова в Петербурге состоялся в ресторане „обед беллетристов". Чехову было поручено пригласить Григоровича, и последний присутствовал на обеде (XVI 9 и 10). В октябре 1896 г. Чехов писал Т. Л. Толстой (Сухотиной): „В Петербурге я виделся с Д. В. Григоровичем. Он поразил меня своим мертвенным

---

[11] В сборнике *Слово* это письмо ошибочно отнесено к 1888 году.

видом. Лицо желто-зеленого цвета, как у раковых больных. Говорит, что замучился на нижегородской выставке" (XVI 387). В этих словах чувствуется какая-то бесстрастность и холодность: когда в 1887 г. Чехов ожидал близкой смерти Григоровича (тот прожил после того еще 12 лет), он писал о том, что эта смерть будет для него незаменимой потерей. В письме к Т. Л. Толстой — никакого выражения чувств, только медицинская констатация.

В том же месяце октябре 1896 г. Чехов, очевидно, разговаривал о болезни Григоровича с Сувориным, и последний записал у себя в дневнике:

В четверг, 17-го [октября], был Д. В. Григорович. Он совсем умирающий. Чехов, который с ним говорил о болезни, по тем лекарствам, которые он принимает, судит, что у него рак и что он скоро умрет. Сам он не подозревает этого. Заболел он на Нижегородской выставке, где работал как вол. Он вдруг почувствовал отвращение к пище. Затем еще у него был злокачественный насморк, и ему делали операцию в носу . . . (стр. 122).

Здесь в издании *Дневника* явная ошибка: либо запись надо датировать 22-го октября вместо 12-го, либо визит Григоровича — раньше. Чехов приехал в Петербург 7 октября, 17 октября в Александринском театре шла и провалилась *Чайка,* а на другой день Чехов „бежал" в Москву. Был ли Григорович на премьере *Чайки* и что о ней думал, мы не знаем. И от более ранних упоминаний Григоровича в письмах Чехова, начиная с 1889 г., веет какой-то холодностью и даже недоброжелательством. Уже в 1889 г. он открывает в Григоровиче „неискренность". В связи с тем, что Григорович якобы обиделся на него (см. выше), он пишет Суворину 6 января 1889 г.:

Я Григоровича очень люблю, но не верю тому, что он за меня боится. Сам он тенденциозный писатель и только прикидывается врагом тенденции. Мне кажется, что его одолевает постоянный страх потерять расположение людей, которых он любит — отсюда и его внутренняя неискренность (XIV 289).

Выше мы видели, что о своей недоверчивости к людям, о боязни „щелчков" от них Чехову до того писал сам Григорович. В чем состояла боязнь Григоровича за Чехова, к сожалению нельзя сказать: как известно, письма Суворина к Чехову были после смерти Суворина изъяты из чеховского архива, и местопребывание их неизвестно.

5.

В течение 1889 года имели место два сравнительно незначительных сами по себе эпизода, из которых один как бы подчеркнул контраст взаимных отношений Чехова и Григоровича, а другой способствовал дальнейшему охлаждению между ними.

В мае 1889 г. Суворин гостил у Чехова в Сумах. Собираясь летом заграницу, в частности в Тироль, он уговаривал Чехова поехать с ним и его семьей, причем в Вене они должны были прихватить Григоровича, который жил в Вейдлингау, под Веной. Чехов в это лето был в каком-то возбужденном, нервном состоянии. 17 июня умер его брат Николай (Суворину Чехов написал об этом лаконически из Сум в письме от 2 июля: „Бедняга Николай умер” — XIV 381). Эта нервная раздерганность его особенно сказалась в письме Плещееву от 26 июня:

... Вероятно, я уеду куда-нибудь. Куда? Не вем. Суворин зовет заграницу. Очень возможно, что поеду и заграницу, хотя меня туда вовсе не тянет. Я не расположен теперь к физическому труду, хочу отдыха, а ведь шатанье по музеям и Эйфелевым башням, прыганье с поезда на поезд, ежедневные встречи с велеречивым Дмитрием Васильевичем [Григоровичем], обеды впроголодь, винопийство и погоня за сильными ощущениями, — все это тяжелый физический труд. Я бы охотнее пожил где-нибудь в Крыму, на одном месте, чтоб можно было работать (XIV 380).

Через несколько дней (2 июля) Чехов писал Суворину, который уже был к тому времени в Тироле:

Сейчас я получил от Вас письмо. Вы пишете, что пробудете в Тироле целый месяц. Времени достаточно, чтобы я мог съездить до заграницы в Одессу, куда влечет меня неведомая сила. Значит, я выеду из Киева не во вторник, как телеграфировал, а позже. Из Волочиска буду телеграфировать.
Из Одессы тоже буду телеграфировать (XIV 381).

Из этого письма следует, что даже день отъезда Чехова заграницу был сговорен между ним и Сувориным, но только Чехов решил немного отложить отъезд и сначала съездить в Одессу. Из Одессы, однако, вместо того, чтобы ехать в Вену, он отправился пароходом в Ялту, о чем извещал брата Ивана. Тон письма опять какой-то взбудораженный, неестественный:

Я еду в Ялту и положительно не знаю, зачем я туда еду. Надо ехать и в Тироль, и в Константинополь, и в

Сумы; все страны света перепутались у меня в голове, фантазия кишмя-кишит городами, и я не знаю, на чем остановить свой выбор. А тут еще лень, нежелание ехать куда бы то ни было, равнодушие и банкротство. Живу машинально, не рассуждая... (XIV 381-82). [12]

Тем временем Григорович, которого Суворин, очевидно, держал в курсе их планов, у себя в Вейдлингау с волнением поджидал Чехова. 2-го июля, в тот самый день, когда Чехов уведомил Суворина об отсрочке своего отъезда, Григорович писал Суворину:

... Проживите в Инспруке до 1-го Августа нашего стиля (лучше будет, чем в Швейцарии), я явлюсь тогда к Вам и мы огулом с Чеховым — совершим ту чудную прогулку через Тироль до Базеля, о которой я говорил Вам. До 1-го Сентября Швейцария гадость: жара невыносимая — разве захотите забраться на вершины, где холодно и где все Вы перепростудитесь. Послушайте хоть раз меня, старого туриста. Обрадовался я весьма приезду Чехова. Адрес мой я ему дал, но вероятно по свойству русской неаккуратности он давно затерял его. (У Вас он был записан в книжке — и то не так написали). Вот что надо сделать, чтобы не вышло путаницы: прежде чем Чехов выедет из Сум, — напишите ему немедленно и сообщите мой адрес; мне же телеграфируйте о дне выезда его из Сум; я узнаю на ж.д. о поездах и рассчитав дни и часы, буду ждать его на платформе в каком бы часу ни было. Затем прямо повезу его к себе на дачу, дам ему отдохнуть и пошлю Вам телеграмму в Зальцбург или Инспрук о нашем выезде из Вены; оставьте только Ваш адрес в Инспруке или Зальцбурге на почте. Мне необходимо только знать, *где Вы будете наверное*, и потому убедительно прошу, не теряя минуты, дать мне обстоятельный ответ; иначе Чехов — не знающий языка и заграничных порядков — все перепутает и Бог весть куда попадет; и я с ним — (если только сойдусь с ним в Вене), — никак не найдем Вас. Итак, мой дорогой, прежде всего жду письма

[12] Автор недавней обстоятельной, хотя и не очень хорошей, английской биографии Чехова, останавливаясь довольно подробно на поездке Чехова в Одессу и Ялту, связывает неестественно-взвинченное состояние Чехова с его влюбленностью в Л. А. Авилову, от которой Чехов, по его мнению, тщетно пробовал „излечиться" (см. David M a g a r s h a c k, Chekhov: A Life, London 1952, pp. 182-83). Магаршак склонен и поездку на Сахалин рассматривать как бегство от любви к Авиловой. Здесь не место касаться этого эпизода в жизни Чехова, но мнение Магаршака, а также И. А. Бунина о том, что любовь к Авиловой была единственной серьезной и глубокой любовью в жизни Чехова, не кажется мне убедительным. Не убедителен и рассказ самой Авиловой.

о том, где Вы решились нас ждать: в Зальцбурге или
Инспруке или другом месте, но другое место было бы в
стороне от пути и повлекло бы меня и Чехова к лишним
расходам . . . [13]

Уведомленный, очевидно, Сувориным после этого, что
Чехов выедет из Киева во вторник 4-го июля, Григорович в
пятницу 7-го (письмо датировано: „Пятница 7-19 VII" — без
года) пишет Суворину:

> Дорогой друг, я в ужасном беспокойстве! Я со вчераш-
> него дня (четверг) был в 5 час. утра на Nordbahnhof, в 7½
> — затем вечером в 5 час. 5 мин., — ночевал Бог весть как,
> снова ждал в 5 утра и 7½. Чехова нет как нет. Что делать?
> Ради Бога, будьте терпеливы, уговорите Анну Ив. еще
> подождать, иначе вся поездка Чехова пропала; меня эти
> два дня ожидания ни свет ни заря на сквозном ветру и
> холоду — совсем уходили. Подождите, умоляю Вас, ради
> Чехова еще два дня; я буду спокойнее и завтра же еще
> Вам телеграфирую. Через 2 часа снова отправлюсь в Вену
> на ж.д. Есть ли у него мой адрес? Я ему дал его еще в
> Петербурге. О Российская неаккуратность и спустя рукава.
> Просто беда! Беда! Главное, ждите его ради самого Бога.
> Завтра телеграмму пошлю Вам и письмо. В таком волнении,
> что не могу писать.
>
>   Обнимаю всех.
>
> Эх, если бы меня послушали и потерпели бы в Haal —
> ничего бы этого не было! А то где теперь Чехову искать
> Вас, если Вы уедете??!!! [14]

Но на этом волнительные переживания и передряги для
Григоровича не кончились, и в тот же вечер (письмо помечено
просто „Пятница вечером") он писал Суворину:

> . . . я в истинном горе; сегодня, в пятницу, несмотря на
> усталость и нервное возбуждение, — я не утерпел и снова
> отправился в Вену на вечерний (последний) поезд Северн.
> дороги; на нем Чехова опять нет! Я распорядился таким
> образом: на большом листе написал его имя по-немецки и,
> дав на пиво, — упросил завтра в 5 ч. утра и 7½ также
> утра орать во все горло его фамилию в то время, как будут
> обирать билеты у выхода. Сам же я больше не в силах

---

[13] *Письма русских писателей...*, стр. 36-37. Вся эта серия писем Григоровича ошибочно дана в этом издании под *1897* годом, хотя ни
обстоятельства жизни Чехова ни обстоятельства жизни Суворина такой
датировки не оправдывают. Между тем у редактора издания была возможность проверить первые по дореволюционному изданию писем
Чехова, а вторые по *Дневнику* А. С. Суворина, вышедшему в 1923 году.
[14] Там же, стр. 37-38.

ждать его; на бумаге написал и свой адрес и просьбу непременно хоть на час заехать в Вейдлингау. Он очевидно [не] выехал во вторник. Не случилось ли чего? Во всяком случае убедительно прошу Вас обстоятельно написать мне, где Вы намерены пробыть несколько времени, дабы я смог его направить, когда он приедет. Он положительно без языка и привычки путешествовать заграницей, — не может угоняться за Вами не путешествующими, но стремящимися как вихри. Ну что бы стоило отовсюду бросить слово на почту, слово одно; я бы успокоился тогда и по отношению Чехова да и Вас самих; ведь Вы все мне не чужие. Вернувшись сегодня в 11 час., я был в таком волнении, что насилу мог писать; руки дрожали как у 100-летнего старца; эти возбуждения мне крайне вредны; не успокоюсь я вполне до того времени, пока не узнаю что-либо положительное о судьбе Чехова. Я рад был бы прожить с ним месяцы, — но в Вейдлингау ему делать нечего: два-три дня и довольно; но *быть* куда ему? Вот вопрос, который можно разрешить только тогда, как Вы будете постоянно извещать меня о Вашем пребывании; везде оставляйте адрес следующего места, куда отправляетесь, на почте; тогда есть еще какая-то возможность Чехову догнать Вас. Я уеду 1-го Августа нового стиля в Париж и остановлюсь по обыкновению: Rue du Helder, Hôtel du Tibre. Ради Бога запомните этот адрес и не затеряйте его. Простите мне мое маранье, спешу и к тому же две ночи не спал. [15]

Суворин в конце концов, очевидно, известил Григоровича о том, что Чехов не приедет. Григорович реагировал письмом от 30 июля, в котором, повторяя, что выезжает в Париж 1 августа и остановится в Hôtel du Tibre, писал по поводу Чехова:

Чехов поступил с нами всетаки не по-европейски: следовало бы обстоятельно написать или телеграфировать о своем намерении, а не заставлять Вас ждать, а меня двое суток тереться на станции ж.д. Что бы там ни было, — но он никогда более не вернет того, что потерял, променяв Ялту на путешествие с Вами: славянин распущенный без твердой внутренней опоры, помогающей управлять собою — вот и все! Насколько за него радовался — настолько теперь сержусь на него. [16]

Дал ли Чехов Григоровичу какое-нибудь объяснение того, что произошло, мы не знаем. Едва ли. Во всяком случае та-

---

[15] Там же, стр. 38-39.
[16] Там же, стр. 39-40.

кого письма не сохранилось. Но так как письма Суворина
Чехову неизвестны, мы не знаем также, рассказал ли ему
Суворин о всех треволнениях Григоровича в связи с этой
несостоявшейся поездкой. Самому Суворину Чехов счел
нужным дать некоторые запоздалые объяснения два с лишним месяца спустя. Имя Григоровича при этом даже не упоминается. Вот что писал Чехов Суворину 13 октября 1889 г.:

> Говорить ли, отчего я не поехал заграницу? Если не
> скучно, извольте. 1 июля я выехал заграницу в подлейшем
> настроении, оставив в таком же настроении всю семью.
> Настроение было безразличное: в Тироль ли ехать, в Бер-
> дичев, в Сибирь ли — все равно. Зная, что в Тироле Вы
> проживете целый месяц, я решил заехать по пути в Одессу,
> куда телеграммами приглашал меня Ленский. В Одессе я
> застал труппу Малого театра. Тут я, лениво философствуя
> и не зная, куда деваться от жары, размыслил, что на дорогу
> у меня не хватит денег, но все-таки решил ехать в Тироль.
> Но вот что ударило меня по ногам и сбило с толку: Ваши
> телеграммы я получал, а мои телеграммы не доходили до
> Вас, и я получал такой ответ: „Souvorin inconnu. Dépêche en
> dépôt-direction". А тут пошли всякие соблазны, финансовые
> соображения и проч., что все вместе взятое окончательно
> сбило меня, спутало, и я из Одессы, имея в кармане менее
> 400 руб., поехал в Ялту. Здесь застрял. Описывать свои
> крымские похождения не стану, ибо для этого у меня не
> хватает таланта английского юмориста Бернарда. [17]
>
> Я жалею, что не был заграницей, мне стыдно перед самим
> собой и Вами, которому я доставил столько хлопот, но
> в то же время я немножко рад этому. Ведь если бы я
> поехал, то я завяз бы по уши в долги, вернулся бы только
> теперь, ничего бы не сделал, а все это для такого труса, как
> я, пуще игоревой смерти (XIV 413).

В то время как начальные строки этого письма несомненно
указывают на то, что одной из причин странных метаний
Чехова в это время был шок, испытанный им и его семьей от
смерти Николая, есть в письме странное противоречие с
письмом от 2 июля. Тут Чехов пишет, что он выехал *1* июля

---

[17] Речь идет, видимо, о Бернанде (Sir Francis Cowley Burnand, 1836-
1917), английском юмористе, редакторе и главном сотруднике журнала
„Punch" с 1880 по 1906 год (ср. XIV, 535). У Чехова в одном более раннем
письме Суворину есть выражение „мысли бернардовского пошиба" (XIV
242). Очевидно, Чехов был знаком с писаниями Бернанда (может быть,
по юмористическим журналам?). Самым известным его произведением
были „Счастливые мысли" (*Happy Thoughts*).

и где-то по пути переменил маршрут и решил заехать в Одессу. Между тем в письме от *2* июля (из Сум или уже с пути?) Чехов писал, что поедет в Одессу, куда влечет его „неведомая сила”. В промежутке между двумя письмами Суворину имеется еще письмо Н. А. Лейкину от 13 августа (по возвращении из Ялты). Ему Чехов тоже пишет, что, прожив после смерти Николая дома, чтобы дать семье „попривыкнуть” к утрате, он уехал заграницу, направляясь в Вену, но

> со станции Жмеринка я взял несколько в сторону и поехал в Одессу; здесь прожил я 10-12 дней, купаясь в море и варясь в собственном соку, сиречь в поте. В Одессе, благодаря кое-каким обстоятельствам, было прожито денег немало; пришлось насчет заграницы отложить всякое попечение и ограничиться одной только поездкой в Ялту. В сем татарско-дамском граде прожил я недели три, предаваясь кейфу и сладостной лени. Все пущено в трубу, осталось только на обратный путь. В стране, где много хорошего вина и отличных коней, где на 20 женщин приходится один мужчина, трудно быть экономным. Наконец я дома, с 40 рублями . . . (XIV 388).

Как и всегда в письмах Чехова Лейкину (да и многим другим корреспондентам), тон письма шутливый. Вся экспедиция в Одессу изображена как плод внезапного решения уже на пути в Вену. Ни о зазывах Ленского ни о Малом театре в Одессе нет ни слова. Поездка же в Ялту приписана чисто финансовым соображениям.

6.

Интересна фраза, оброненная Чеховым в письме А. Н. Плещееву от 6 октября 1889 г.: „У меня ведь только два указчика: Вы и Суворин. Был когда-то еще Григорович, да сплыл” (XIV 409). Смысл этой фразы на первый взгляд не совсем ясен: ведь меньше чем за год до того Григорович еще писал Чехову, восторгаясь его *Припадком,* и давал ему советы. Письмо Чехова к Плещееву написано непосредственно перед эпизодом, который мог отразиться на отношении Чехова к Григоровичу: неофициальный театральный комитет в составе Григоровича, И. А. Всеволожского, А. Н. Потехина и Н. Ф. Сазонова, рассмотрев пьесу Чехова *Леший,* забраковал ее для постановки. Об этом сообщил Чехову артист П. М. Свободин, который читал пьесу перед Комитетом (Свободин

в это лето посетил Чехова в Сумах). О том же Свободин
писал редактору *Русской Мысли* В. М. Лаврову. Сам Чехов
коснулся этой истории в уже цитировавшемся письме Суворину от 13 октября. [18] Несмотря на шутливый тон письма,
чувствуется, что он был сильно задет. Упомянув о том, что,
едва кончив „повесть в 4½ листа" (*Скучную историю*), он
„разбежался и по инерции написал четырехактного *Лешего*
... уничтожив все, написанное весной", Чехов продолжал:

> Работал я с большим удовольствием, даже с наслаж-
> дением, хотя от писанья болел локоть и мерещилось в
> глазах чорт знает что. За пьесой приехал ко мне Свободин
> и взял ее для своего бенефиса (31 октября). Пьеса читалась
> Всеволожским, Григоровичем и Ко. О дальнейшей судьбе
> ее, коли охота, можете узнать от Свободина, лица заинте-
> ресованного, и от Григоровича, бывшего председателем
> того военно-полевого суда, который судил меня и моего
> *Лешего*. Пьеса забракована. Забракована ли она только
> для бенефиса Свободина (великие князья будут на бене-
> фисе), или же вообще для казенной сцены, мне неизвестно,
> а уведомить меня об этом не сочли нужным (XIV 412).

9 октября Свободин читал *Лешего* перед Комитетом, а на
следующий день получено было от цензуры разрешение на
постановку пьесы с небольшими купюрами. В тот же день
Свободин писал Чехову по поводу забракования пьесы:

„Замечания относительно живых лиц, характеров, талант-
ливости автора перемешивались с суждениям об отсутствии
действия, длиннотах и проч." Признаваемые достоинства, по
словам Свободина, „непонятным образом становились недо-
статками пьесы для представления". Свободин отказался
вообще от бенефиса. В письме редактору *Русской Мысли* В.

---

[18] В тот же день, когда Чехов писал Суворину, ему о забраковании
Лешего писал Плещеев, причем в письме его была такая фраза: „Двоедушный Григорович, впрочем, с похвалой отозвался о втором акте
Вашей пьесы" (XIV 582). Письма этого нет в сборнике *Слово* среди
напечатанных там писем Плещеева. Но там всего 18 писем из сохрани-
вшихся в архиве Чехова 54. Еще до всей истории с *Лешим,* 27 сентября
Плещеев писал Чехову о том, что видел Григоровича и что тот сказал
ему о последовавшем упразднении Литературно-Театрального Комитета. Вместо того в помощь дирекции должны были быть приглашены
два литератора, на жалованьи. Григорович предлагал Плещееву быть
одним из них, и Плещеев согласился, чтобы Григорович назвал его
директору Императорских театров, И. А. Всеволожскому. Но Чехову он
писал: „Признаюсь Вам, ничему этому я не верю. Зная двоедушие Григоровича, я вполне убежден, что одним из этих чтецов останется сам
Григорович, а другим будет вероятно Вейнберг" (*Слово,* II, 273).

М. Лаврову, признавая некоторые формальные недочеты пьесы, он говорил: „*Леший* не комедия по форме, но живые лица, живые речи и характеры таковы, что вся александринская дребедень не стоит и половины пьесы Чехова". Два других театральных знакомых Чехова были иного мнения о *Лешем*. А. П. Ленский писал Чехову: „Одно скажу: напишите повесть. Вы слишком презрительно относитесь к сцене и драматической форме. Слишком мало уважаете их, чтобы писать драму". В. И. Немирович-Данченко не шел так далеко: соглашаясь с Ленским, что Чехов чересчур игнорирует сценические условия, он не видел презрения к ним у Чехова. Дело было скорее в незнании их. Мы знаем, что позднее Немирович-Данченко был очень высокого мнения о пьесах Чехова, считая их высоко оригинальными. [19]

Из одного письма Чехова Суворину можно заключить, что Григорович сказал Суворину, будто бы он выведен Чеховым в *Лешем* в лице Серебрякова, ибо 17 октября Чехов писал Суворину:

Не радуйтесь, что Вы попали в мою пьесу. Рано пташечка запела. Ваша очередь еще впереди. Коли буду жив, опишу феодосийские ночи, которые мы вместе проводили в разговорах, и ту рыбную ловлю, когда Вы шагали по палям линтваревской мельницы, — больше мне от Вас пока ничего не нужно. В пьесе же Вас нет, да и не может быть, хотя Григорович со свойственною ему проницательностью и видит противное. В пьесе идет речь о человеке нудном, себялюбивом, деревянном, читавшем об искусстве 25 лет и ничего не понимавшем в нем; о человеке, наводящем на всех уныние и скуку, не допускающем смеха и музыки и проч. и проч., и при всем том необыкновенно счастливом. Не верьте Вы, Бога ради, всем этим господам, ищущим во всем прежде всего худа, меряющим всех на свой аршин и приписывающим другим свои личные лисьи и барсучьи черты. Ах, как рад этот Григорович! И как бы все они обрадовались, если бы я подсыпал Вам в чай мышьяку или оказался шпионом, служащим в III Отделении. Вы скажете, конечно, что все это пустяки. Нет, не пустяки. Если бы моя пьеса шла, то вся публика с легкой руки изолгавшихся шелопаев говорила бы, глядя на сцену: „Так вот какой

---

[19] Были у *Лешего* и защитники. К ним принадлежали Д. С. Мережковский и кн. А. И. Урусов. Последний позднее считал, что, переделав *Лешего*, Чехов испортил пьесу: „Вы его окромсали, свели к конспекту и обезличили" (*Слово*, II, 288). В восторге от пьесы был известный киевский актер и режиссер Н. Н. Соловцов (см. Гитович, стр. 246).

Суворин! Вот какая его жена! Гм ... Скажите, а мы и не знали" (XIV 416).

Если фраза о „проницательности" Григоровича звучит иронически, то в дальнейшей части письма — о господах с лисьими и барсучьими чертами — проскальзывают уже гневные нотки. Григоровича Чехов явно зачисляет в разряд „этих господ" („Ах, как рад этот Григорович!"), но трудно представить себе, чтобы он к нему применял выражение „изолгавшиеся шелопаи" — так оно не идет к почтенному, седовласому старцу.

Через два дня после этого письма, 19 октября, в *Петербургской Газете* появилась заметка о том, что драма Чехова „встретила некоторое колебание в ее постановке. Говорят, будто бы нашли, что это прекрасная драматизированная повесть, а не драматическое произведение" (XIV 582). Эта не совсем грамотно составленная заметка стала сразу же известна Чехову; он упоминает о ней в письме Плещееву от 21 октября, в котором опять жалуется, что он лично никакого извещения о пьесе еще не получил:

О моей пьесе ни слуху ни духу. Съели ли ее мыши, пожертвовала ли ее дирекция в Публичную библиотеку, сгорела ли она со стыда за ложь Григоровича, который любит меня как родного сына, — все может быть, но пока мне *ничего* неизвестно. Никаких извещений и мотивировок ни от кого я не получал, ничего не знаю, а запросов никаких не делаю из осторожности, чтобы запрос мой не был истолкован, как просьба или непременное желание венчать себя александринскими лаврами. Я самолюбив ведь как свинья.

Упорное молчание гг. членов того военно-полевого суда, который судил моего *Лешего,* я могу объяснить не чем иным, как только горячим сочувствием к моему таланту и желанием продлить то райски-сладострастное наслаждение, какое доставляет мне приятное неведение. Кто знает? Быть может, моя пьеса признана гениальной ... Разве не сладко гадать?

Петербургская Газета извещает, что моя пьеса признана „прекрасной драматизированной повестью". Значит, что-нибудь из двух: или я плохой драматург, в чем охотно расписываюсь, или же лицемеры все те господа, которые любят меня как родного сына и умоляют меня Бога ради быть в пьесах самим собою, избегать шаблона и давать сложную концепцию (XIV 419-20).

В этом письме тоже под шутливыми фразами и выражениями чувствуется глубокая задетость — у Чехова недаром вырвалась фраза о самолюбии. Чувствуется и обида на Григоровича лично, особенно сказывающаяся в конце письма в варианте фразы о господах, которые, мол, любят его как родного сына: первоначально такая же фраза отнесена прямо к Григоровичу, который вероятно не раз объяснялся Чехову в любви в таких приблизительно выражениях.

Фигурирует Григорович и в следующем письме на тему *Лешего* — Суворину от 28 октября 1889 г. Суворин, очевидно, просил Чехова дать ему прочесть пьесу. Чехов отвечает:

> *Лешего* я Вам не дам читать из страха, что Вы о нем будете говорить с Григоровичем. Месяц тому назад (или 20 дней — не помню) мне многих усилий стоило, чтобы не писать Вам о своей пьесе, теперь же я совершенно успокоился и со спокойным духом могу не писать о ней (XIV 423).

Как мы видели выше, Чехов писал Суворину о *Лешем* за одиннадцать и за пятнадцать дней до этого письма. А нежелание, чтобы Суворин разговаривал о пьесе с Григоровичем, едва ли свидетельствует об успокоении.

В ноябре того же года Плещеев упрашивал Чехова дать ему *Лешего* для *Северного Вестника,* причем опять упоминал о „двоедушном” Григоровиче: „Какое нам дело до того, что она не сценична. Сам двоедушный Григорович говорит, что в ней есть крупные литературные достоинства” (*Слово,* II, 275). Но когда позже Плещеев ознакомился с *Лешим,* он присоединился к отрицательному мнению о нем; в письме от 24 апреля 1890 г. он писал Чехову: „... это первая Ваша вещь, которая меня не удовлетворила и не оставила во мне никакого впечатления”. В том же письме он сообщал о таком же отрицательном впечатлении своего знакомого В. А. Фаусека, большого поклонника Чехова. При этом Плещеев подвергал пьесу детальной критике. О напечатании ее в *Северном Вестнике* уже не было речи, так как тут же Плещеев сообщал о закрытии журнала (там же, 279).

Возможно, что из писем Свободина, из которых редакторами чеховских писем и Н. И. Гитович опубликованы лишь отрывки, Чехов знал больше об отрицательных отзывах о *Лешем* лично Григоровича. [20] Как будто похоже, что

---

[20] В комментарии к письмам Чехова в ПССП говорится, что в архиве Чехова сохранилось большое количество писем Свободина и что в письмах, относящихся к *Лешему,* приводятся высказывания Григоровича о пьесе (XX 462-63). 12 ноября Свободин писал Чехову: „... подумайте,

именно на него он затаил обиду (на отношении Чехова к
Плещееву отрицательный отзыв о *Лешем* как будто не
сказался). Во всяком случае, повторяем, в письмах после 1889
года все чаще попадаются иронические или не совсем
доброжелательные отзывы о Григоровиче. В какой-то связи,
не совсем ясной, поскольку мы не знаем писем Суворина,
Чехов пишет последнему 17 декабря 1890 г.: „Григорович
никогда не был дворником на Песках, потому так дешево и
ценит царство небесное. Врет он" (XV 136). И вскоре после
этого (14 января 1891 г.) сестре Марии Павловне: „Вчера
приходил Григорович; долго целовал меня, врал и все просил
рассказать ему про японок" (XV 149). В том же 1891 году
Григорович очень рассердил Чехова одним своим замечанием.
Весной этого года Чехов, вернувшийся сравнительно незадолго до того с Сахалина, отправился вместе с Сувориным
в путешествие по Италии и Франции. Григорович, который
приехал в Париж через несколько дней после того как Чехов
и Суворин уехали оттуда, писал некоторое время спустя
Суворину:

> . . . я зашел к Плещееву и был крайне раздосадован, узнав,
> что Вы едва ли не накануне уехали вместе с милым Вашим
> спутником Чеховым. Воображаю, какое впечатленье после
> Сахалина — должны были сделать на Чехова Италия и
> Париж! Таких противуположностей вряд ли кому достается
> увидеть в течение одного и того же года. Италия, впрочем,
> вряд ли могла ему понравиться; там положительно не
> знаешь, куда преклонить голову без специальной подго-
> товки; Венеция, Флоренция и т.д. — больше ничего как
> скучные города для человека даже умного, — но который
> прежде не интересовался искусством настолько, чтобы
> произведения величайших мастеров и даже имена их — не
> встречались полнейшим равнодушием. Чехов тут непричем:
> русское образование вычеркнуло почему-то изучение древ-
> него искусства; кроме того, Чехов принадлежит к поколе-
> нию, которое заметно стало отклоняться от Запада и ближе
> присматриваться к своему. Так, может быть, и следует. [21]

Это письмо Григоровича Суворин, очевидно, переслал или
цитировал или показал Чехову. Последний в письме Суворину

нельзя ли что-нибудь сделать из *Лешего,* чтобы он сразу понравился не
только мне, Суворину и тем, кто читал его и советовал не бросать, а и
тем, кто советовал сжечь, как Вы пишете" (см. Гитович, стр. 247). Цитаты
из писем Свободина о *Лешем* см. у Гитович под соответствующими
датами.
[21] *Письма русских писателей. . .,* стр. 30-31.

от 27 мая 1891 г. советует показать это письмо жене, Анне Ивановне, которую называет (вероятно, полушутливо) своим врагом — „пусть у нее душа порадуется". Процитировав дальше несколько фраз из письма Григоровича, кончая тем местом, где он говорит, что даже для умного человека Венеция и Флоренция просто скучные города, Чехов возмущенно пишет:

Merci, но я не понимаю таких умных людей. Надо быть быком, чтобы, приехав первый раз в Венецию или во Флоренцию, стать „отклоняться от запада". В этом отклонении мало ума. Но желательно было бы знать, кто это старается, кто оповестил всю вселенную о том, что будто заграница мне не понравилась? Господи ты Боже мой, — никому я ни одним словом не заикнулся об этом. Мне даже Болонья понравилась. Что же я должен был делать? Реветь от восторга? Бить стекла? Обниматься с французами? Идей я не вывез, что ли? Но и идеи, кажется, вывез . . . (XV 173).

По тону письма следует заключить, что и это замечание Григоровича об отношении Чехова к Западу осталось не без влияния на возраставшее охлаждение Чехова к „старику", как он его часто называл. Из фразы Григоровича, с другой стороны, не видно чтобы он осуждал Чехова за „отклонение от Запада". Сам Григорович, получивший чисто французское воспитание и в молодости говоривший и писавший лучше по-французски, чем по-русски (мать его была француженка), был во многих отношениях западником (ср. его сердитые замечания о славянской распущенности в письмах Суворину 1889 года, цитировавшихся выше), но была в нем и сентиментально-народническая закваска. Из одного более позднего письма Чехова Суворину можно сделать вывод, что сам Суворин способствовал созданию у Григоровича (а, может быть, и у других) впечатления о том, что Чехов остался равнодушен к Италии. 23 марта 1895 г., когда Суворин уезжал заграницу, Чехов писал ему:

. . . Поклонитесь Италии. Я ее горячо люблю, хотя Вы и говорили Григоровичу, будто я лег на площади св. Марка и сказал: „Хорошо бы теперь у нас в Московской губернии на травке полежать!" Ломбардия меня поразила, так что, мне кажется, я помню каждое дерево, а Венецию я вижу закрывши глаза (XVI 229).

В начале 1892 года (если положиться на датировку — как мы видели, далеко ненадежную — *Писем русских писателей к А. С. Суворину* — см. стр. 33-34) Григорович запрашивал Суворина о Чехове:

> Что делает наш милейший Чехов? Я часто о нем думаю, — и думаю также, что пора и как еще пора! выступить ему с чем нибудь крупно-выдающимся. Он не должен забывать, что память у публики коротка и чтобы держаться в ней, — необходимо ее подстегивать...

В знаменитом письме Суворину от 25 ноября 1892 года, где он пишет о том, что у его поколения писателей нет алкоголя, что оно способно производить только литературный „лимонад", Чехов не щадит и Григоровича: „мы... умеем рождать только гуттаперчевых мальчиков" (XV 445).

7.

Личные отношения между Чеховым и Григоровичем не прекращались, но встречи их становились все реже и реже с годами. А в 1894 году Чехов даже сбежал от чествования в Москве Григоровича по случаю 50-летия его литературной деятельности. Не было Чехова и на более раннем чествовании в Петербурге, о котором И. Н. Потапенко писал, что это „было что-то необыкновенно торжественное, кажется, единственное и небывалое в летописях литературы". Чехов уже загодя в тоне некоторой тревоги запрашивал Суворина в письме от 16 июня 1892 г.: „Правда ли, что нас ожидает литературное торжество — 50 летний юбилей Григоровича?" (XV 392). Так как Григорович был сотрудником *Русской Мысли,* то редактор последней, В. М. Лавров, хотел, чтобы и Москва почтила юбиляра. Чествование это состоялось в январе 1894 г. [22] Конечно, это „филиальное чествование", как писал Потапенко, „не могло быть даже и тенью петербургского юбилея, но все же — Эрмитаж, несколько десятков приглашенных, заранее предусмотренные речи". Чехов был в то время в Москве, и устроители, разумеется, расчитывали не только на его участие, но и на выступление. По словам Потапенко, „с одной стороны хотелось показать петербургскому литератору лучшее, что есть в литературной Москве и чем

---

[22] Дату чествования Григоровича в Москве мне не удалось установить. В январе 1894 года Чехов был в Москве только 13-го и 14-го. 13-го он обедал с редакторами *Русской Мысли.* 14-го он уехал назад в Мелихово (см. Гитович, стр. 354-55). Из нижеприводимого рассказа Потапенко вытекает, что чествование должно было происходить 16-го.

она гордится, а с другой стороны, — имелись в виду особые отношения между Чеховым и Григоровичем. Ведь старый писатель первый, кажется, заметил талант Чехонте в его маленьких рассказах, печатавшихся в сатирических журналах, обратил на него внимание Суворина, написал ему трогательное отеческое письмо.'' Потапенко продолжает:

Антону Павловичу все это было поставлено на вид, и уж само собою разумелось, что он будет украшением „филиального чествования''.

Антон Павлович впал в мрачность. Целый день с ним ни о чем нельзя было говорить. Он, обыкновенно ко всему и ко всем относившийся с добродушной терпимостью, для всех находивший извиняющие объяснения, вдруг сделался строг ко всему и ко всем, просто огрызался, так что лучше было к нему не приставать.

К вечеру он стал мягче. К нему вернулся его обычный юмор, и он от времени до времени прерывал свое молчание отрывочными фразами из какой-то неведомой, повидимому, речи:

— Глубокоуважаемый и досточтимый писатель ... Мы собрались здесь тесной семьей ... — Потом, после молчания, опять: — Наша дружная писательская семья, в вашем лице, глубокочтимый ...

— Что это ты? — спросил я.

— А это я из твоей речи, которую ты скажешь на обеде в честь Григоровича.

— Почему же из моей? Ты бы лучше из своей что-нибудь.

— Так я же завтра уезжаю.

— Куда?

— В Мелихово.

Я возмутился:

— Как же так? Григорович, его письмо ... Такие отношения .. Наконец, разочарование Лаврова и всех прочих ... И тут он начал приводить свои доводы:

— Ведь это же понятно. Я был открыт Григоровичем и, следовательно, должен сказать речь. Не просто говорить что-нибудь, а именно речь. И при этом непременно о том, как он меня открыл. Иначе же будет нелюбезно. Голос мой должен дрожать и глаза наполниться слезами. Я, положим, этой речи не скажу, меня долго будут толкать в бок, я всетаки не скажу, потому что не умею. Но встанет Лавров и расскажет, как Григорович меня открыл. Тогда подымется сам Григорович, подойдет ко мне, протянет руки и заключит меня в объятия и будет плакать от умиления. Старые писатели любят поплакать. Ну, это его дело, но самое главное, что я должен буду плакать, а я этого не умею. Словом, я не оправдаю ничьих надежд. Ведь ты же на себе испытал, что значит не плакать от умиления...

[Здесь, как Потапенко объясняет, Чехов имел в виду эпизод с присуждением Потапенко половинной Пушкинской премии, когда Потапенко поехал благодарить Григоровича и тот не нашел в нем достаточно „умиления".]
Потапенко продолжает:

> ...все то, что говорил Чехов, совсем не казалось ему шуткой. Он действительно испытывал страдание, представляя себя героем нарисованной им сцены. И в сущности сцена была изображена вполне правдиво. Так именно и должно было произойти.
> И вот за два дня до юбилейного обеда, когда из Петербурга была получена телеграмма, что юбиляр приедет, А. П. уложил свои дорожные вещи и уехал в деревню, сделав мне на прощание такого рода ответственное поручение:
> — А ты там как-нибудь уж... уладь. Главное, успокой Лаврова.

Но уладить, говорит Потапенко, было трудно. Лавров чуть не заболел, когда узнал о бегстве Чехова (кстати, вспоминается бегство Чехова — при совершенно других, правда, обстоятельствах — после петербургского провала *Чайки*) — ведь это был „главный кирпич" в его „великой постройке". В конце концов обед все же состоялся, причем Потапенко, по его словам, оскандалился на всю жизнь. Вняв увещаниям Гольцева (соредактора Лаврова по *Русской Мысли*), он решил сказать речь о Чехове, о том, как он страстно желал быть на обеде, но болезнь де помешала ему и он уехал в деревню.

> И Господь наказал меня за ложь (писал в своих воспоминаниях об этом эпизоде Потапенко). С первых же слов я, никогда еще в жизни не выступавший с публичными речами, сбился. Я только и успел упомянуть о Чехове, который...
> А милый старик, видя, должно быть, мое затруднение, сейчас же и выручил меня и сам заговорил о Чехове, о том, как он открыл его талант, о его письмах, — словом, все то, что мы теперь так хорошо знаем. [23]

Чехов оказался хорошим провидцем.
Конечно, отношение Чехова нетрудно понять: сентиментальная умиленность всегда претила ему, и он не раз высмеи-

---

[23] *Чехов в воспоминаниях современников,* 1947, стр. 239-41.

вал ее в своих рассказах. Но всетаки, если бы все отношение Чехова к Григоровичу к этому времени не изменилось, он, вероятно, согласился бы из внимания к „старику", который как никак в самом деле сыграл в его жизни большую роль, пожертвовать собой и принять участие в банкете. А так он, повидимому, не счел даже нужным приветствовать Григоровича личным письмом. Через некоторое время после юбилея Чехов писал Суворину:

Московский Листок упал [...], и те, которые давали обед приезжавшему Григоровичу, говорят теперь: как много мы лгали на этом обеде и как много он лгал! (XVI 118).

На отношении Григоровича к Чехову этот эпизод нисколько не отразился: едва ли может быть сомнение, что „болезнь" Чехова он принял за чистую монету.

Единственная после этого личная встреча с Григоровичем, засвидетельствованная в переписке Чехова, произошла в Петербурге в 1896 году: о ней Чехов вскользь упомянул в письме Т. Л. Толстой (см. выше). Григорович поразил его тогда своим болезненным, мертвешным видом, но от выражения каких-нибудь чувств при этом Чехов воздержался и ни одному из своих постоянных корреспондентов об этой встрече не упомянул.

8.

В последние годы жизни Григоровича его имя совсем редко попадается в письмах Чехова, и почти все упоминания либо безразличны либо недоброжелательны. 8 ноября 1896 года, прочтя в Новостях Дня, что Григорович опасно заболел, Чехов запрашивает Суворина, правда ли это (XVI 386). В 1897 г. в Ницце Чехов часто встречается с художником Якоби и дважды совершенно равнодушно, без всякого возмущения, передает крайне резкие суждения его о Григоровиче. 1 октября он пишет Суворину: „Тут же и художник Якоби, который Григоровича называет мерзавцем и мошенником, Айвазовского — сукиным сыном, Стасова — идиотом и т.д." (XVII 140), а 24 октября редактору Русских Ведомостей В. М. Соболевскому:" [Якоби] вчера уверял всех нас, что Григорович — шпион" (XVII 157).

Тогда же из Ниццы, восхищаясь данью, которую своими статьями заплатили Альфонсу Додэ французские писатели после его смерти, Чехов пишет Суворину, что в России было бы не то: „... умри Лев Толстой, и написать статью некому. Напишут публицисты, а беллетристы, с Григоровичем и Боборыкиным во главе, только почешутся" (XVII 189).

В 1898 году, когда толстовец П. А. Сергеенко написал ему по поводу проектировавшейся по случаю 70-летия Л. Н. Толстого поездки в Ясную Поляну группы лиц, близких Толстому „по душе или по своей деятельности", предлагал ему самому принять участие и прибавлял, что из лиц, присутствие которых было бы приятно самому Толстому, не уведомлен Григорович, а потому было бы хорошо, если бы Чехов, если знает его адрес, ему написал, Чехов отвечал, что адрес Григоровича ему неизвестен, что он живет где-то около Вены, в имении своей жены. К этому времени и личные и эпистолярные отношения между Чеховым и Григоровичем фактически прекратились. Даже упоминания о Григоровиче в письмах другим лицам становятся все реже и реже. За весь 1899 год имя Григоровича упоминается только раз и то в безличном контексте. Упоминая о своих беседах с академиком Н. П. Кондаковым по поводу создания при Академии Наук разряда изящной словесности, Чехов пишет Суворину 6 февраля 1899 г.: „Оттого, что Случевский, Григорович, Голенищев-Кутузов и Потехин станут академиками, произведения русских писателей и вообще литературная деятельность в России не станут интереснее" (XVIII 67). В этих словах, конечно, не выражается никакого отношения к Григоровичу. Но чувствуется, что он для Чехова — только один из „заслуженных" писателей, кандидатов в академики. Отметим, кстати, что отношение Чехова к литературной Академии осталось последовательным до конца. Когда Чехов сам был выбран почетным академиком, он писал М. О. Меньшикову: „Званию академика рад, так как приятно сознавать, что мне теперь завидует Сигма. Но еще более буду рад, когда утеряю это звание после какого-нибудь недоразумения. А недоразумение произойдет непременно, так как ученые академики боятся, что мы будем их шокировать. Толстого выбрали скрепя сердце. Он, по-тамошнему, нигилист. Так, по крайней мере, назвала его одна дама, действительная тайная советница, — с чем от души его поздравляю" (XVIII 313-14). Два года спустя, в результате не совсем такого „недоразумения", какое ему предносилось — а именно, отмены избрания Горького — Чехов звание академика с себя сложил.

9.

Отношение Григоровича к Чехову на протяжении всех этих лет не изменилось. Мы видели, с каким волнением ждал он его под Веной в 1889 году, как, несмотря на свои 67 лет и хвори, два дня подряд вставал с петухами и ездил встречать его на вокзале, как волновался, что он потеряется и не разыщет Сувориных. Правда, рассердившись, он писал Суворину о „славянской распущенности" и „не-европейском" поведении Чехова. Но это было именно в сердцах. Прошло девять лет, и Григорович неожиданно обнаружил, как высоко он расценивал Чехова, как человека, в связи с одним обстоятельством, которое как-то не привлекло до сих пор внимания биографов Чехова. 29 октября 1898 года Григорович пишет письмо А. С. Суворину, повидимому, в ответ на уведомление его и его жены о том, что их дочери Насте сделал предложение журналист С. Н. Сыромятников (Сигма), сотрудник *Нового Времени,* бывший одно время редактором газеты *Русь.* Григорович писал Суворину: [24]

Вы и Анна Ивановна поразили меня предложением Сигмы! — Ни за что на свете! Он весь — одна неопределенность; он до сих пор не выяснился ни одной сколько-нибудь ясной чертой; его черные, быстрые, беспокойные глаза не предвещают ничего доброго. Относительно Вашей Настеньки я всегда мечтал о Чехове... Вот этот был бы другое дело; не считая сердечную нравственную связь между ним и Вами — вытекающую из взаимной оценки и служащую гарантией для счастья в будущем, — он сам по себе так мил и честен и талантлив, — что лучшего и желать нельзя. Но как Настенька? Вот вопрос. Как разгадать сердечные стремления молоденькой девушки? Их часто увлекает то, что сознательно противно другим, и тут уже не помогут никакие увещания. Они в жизни — как в котильоне — подводят кавалеров, спрашивают: розу или крапиву? Они чаще всего, наперекор всякому здравому смыслу, — выбирают крапиву... [25]

Всякому знакомому с биографией Чехова, а тем более с перепиской его, известно, что Суворин еще за десять лет до того сватал ему свою дочь, тогда маленькую девочку. 24 марта 1888 г. Чехов писал своему брату Александру: „Суворин пресерьезнейшим образом предложил мне жениться на его дщери, которая теперь ходит пешком под столом..." (XIV 57).

---

[24] *Письма русских писателей...,* стр. 34.
[25] *Письма русских писателей...,* стр. 42-43.

В одном из писем Суворину после этого Чехов шутя называет его жену своей тещей (XIV 70). Настя в эти первые годы часто фигурирует в письмах Чехова к Суворину. Однажды он называет ее „девочкой с толстыми губами" (XV 161). В другой раз пишет юмористически: „Вы пишете, что Настя переросла Анну Ивановну. Нужно расти не вверх, а в ширину. Высокий рост, когда плечи не широки, не в ладу со здоровьем. Надо гимнастику делать, а то я замуж не возьму. В гимнастику я верю сильно" (XIV 439). Позднее нет письма к Суворину, в котором бы Чехов не передавал привета членам семьи и особенно Анне Ивановне и Насте. 20 июня 1896 г. он пишет: „Все вы мне снились, и во сне я разговаривал с Анной Ивановной и с Настей" (XVI 336). В сентябре 1897 г. в Париже он вместе с Настей идет в Magasin du Louvre и покупает себе фуфайку, галстуки и другие предметы одежды (XVII 127). В декабре того же года он называет Настю „будущей великой артисткой" (XVII 186). Но нет ничего, что бы указывало на то, что Чехов имел серьезные „виды" на Настю Суворину. Едва ли и Суворин впоследствии относился серьезно к своему давнему „предложению". Один лишь Григорович, любивший искренно Чехова и явно хорошо относившийся к Насте и желавший ей счастливого брака, лелеял эту мечту, о которой, впрочем, до 1898 года не заикался даже Суворину.

Даже после расхождения с Сувориным и прекращения сотрудничества в *Новом Времени* Чехов писал Суворину: „К Вашей семье я привязан почти как к своей, и в искренность моего пожелания Вы можете верить..." (XVIII 414, письмо от 16 ноября 1900 г.).

Реакция Чехова на предложение Сыромятникова нам неизвестна. Неясно, к кому относятся слова Чехова в письме сестре от 6 октября 1898 г.: „Настя разошлась со своим женихом. Каждый год все новые женихи и новые собаки" (XVII 323). Письмо Григоровича помечено 29 октября без указания стиля; если дата дана по новому стилю (так часто делал Григорович в письмах из заграницы, хотя иногда ставил обе даты), то это выходит 17 октября по старому стилю. Чехов уже 6 октября знал о расхождении Насти с женихом: похоже, что тут речь идет о предшественнике Сыромятникова. Последнего Чехов недолюбливал, и если бы речь шла о нем, вероятно, как-то бы отозвался. В 1895 году по поводу обедов беллетристов он писал брату Александру: „...надо терпеть и Лейкина, и Сыромятникова с его калужским шиком" (XVI 281). В 1896 году ему же:" „Что

касается *Руси,* то работать в ней не буду. Я Сигме не то-
варищ" (XVI 397). В 1897 году Ф. Д. Батюшкову, который стал
на место Сыромятникова редактором русского отдела журнала *Cosmopolis* и просил у Чехова рассказа: „В руках Сигмы
русский отдел не имел бы никакого успеха ни у публики ни
у литераторов, у Вас же он пойдет..." (XVII 66). Позже, как
мы видели, когда его выбрали почетным академиком, он
одной из причин своей радости выставлял то, что ему
„теперь завидует Сигма" (XVIII 313). [26]

О том, как высоко ставил Григорович Чехова, как писателя,
есть свидетельство Вл. И. Немировича-Данченко. По словам
последнего, когда при Григоровиче стали сравнивать с Чеховым одного мало даровитого, но „идейного" писателя,
Григорович сказал: „Да он недостоин поцеловать след от
той блохи, которая укусит Чехова". А о рассказе Чехова
Холодная кровь Григорович отозвался так: „Поместите
этот рассказ на одну полку с Гоголем" и сам прибавил: „Вот
как далеко я иду". Свое сравнение с Гоголем Григорович,
говорит Немирович-Данченко, произнес „почти шопотом, как
что-то очень дерзкое". [27]

Григорович скончался 23 декабря 1899 года. Чехов был в
это время в Крыму. В опубликованных его письмах мы не
находим никакой реакции его на смерть человека, потеря которого за десять лет до того представлялась ему „незаменимой" и который до конца своих дней несомненно продолжал
любить и высоко ценить Чехова. О похоронах Григоровича
написал Чехову один из его бывших редакторов, С. Н.
Худеков. Упоминая о своей последней встрече с Григоровичем, он писал: „Долго и много вспоминал про Вас и как
душевно отзывался он о ,невольном изгнаннике', обреченном
жить вдали от друзей ... в прескучной Ялте". Отклика Чехова
на это письмо, если он был, мы не знаем. В письмах Суворину
Чехов тоже не отзывается на смерть Григоровича. Нет никаких упоминаний и вспоминаний о Григоровиче и в переписке
Чехова в годы после 1899-го. Один из мемуаристов, правда,
отмечает, что Чехов в разговоре с ним вспоминал о знаменитом письме Григоровича, как о просвете в трудный

---

[26] По словам редактора *Дневника* Суворина, дочь его вышла замуж за
моряка Мясоедова-Иванова, после революции оказалась в эмиграции и
выступала как актриса в Нью Йорке. См. *Дневник* А. С. Суворина.
Редакция, предисловие и примечания Мих. Кричевского. М.-П. 1923, стр.
398. Проверить эти сведения мне не удалось.

[27] См. В. И. Немирович-Данченко, *Из прошлого,* М. 1938, стр. 9-10.

период начала его литературной деятельности: „Бывали и отрадные случаи. Помню, получаю письмо [Григоровича]. Я тогда писал в *Петербургской Газете.* Письмо было с самыми лучшими пожеланиями, самое сердечное ... Становилось на время легче. . .” [28]

10.

Сдается, что прослеженная нами в деталях история личных отношений между Чеховым и Григоровичем подтверждает мнение тех, кто склонен считать, что Чехов в своем отношении к людям, с которыми его сталкивала судьба, был большей частью равнодушен и холоден, что он неспособен был к тесной дружбе, к горячим чувствам, что он сознательно создавал вокруг себя атмосферу известного холодка и тем оберегал себя от чужого вторжения в свою жизнь. Конечно, Чехов был „гуманистом”; конечно, он любил отвлеченно человечество и самоотверженно служил ближним — об этом свидетельствуют и его деятельность во время голода и холерной эпидемии, и его благотворительность, и многое другое. Но во всех его отношениях с отдельными людьми чувствуется холодок, отчужденность. Люди интересовали Чехова, как писателя, как предмет наблюдения и изучения, и он охотно расширял круг своих знакомств. Переписка его огромна. Но были ли у него настоящие друзья? Были ли у него с кем-нибудь теплые дружеские отношения? О людях, к которым он был привязан, которым во всяком случае изъяснялся в неизменной привязанности, он мог писать самые нехорошие вещи (см., например, письмо брату Михаилу от 22 февраля 1901 года о Суворине и его семье, XIX 43), как мог спокойно, „объективно”, без всякого протеста и возмущения передавать злостные измышления Якоби о Григоровиче. На примере отношений с Григоровичем это внутреннее равнодушие к людям иллюстрируется, мне кажется, очень хорошо. Возьмем письмо его к М. В. Киселевой в марте 1887 года, где он описывает сидение у постели больного Григоровича, когда с тем от радостного волнения приключился припадок грудной жабы. Никакого настоящего сочувствия больному, никакой теплоты в нем не чувствуется. И дело вовсе не только в целомудренной сдержанности Чехова: мы видели на примере

---

[28] Г и т о в и ч, стр. 747. А. И. Куприн вспоминал, что у Чехова в его ялтинском доме рядом с портретами Тургенева и Толстого висел портрет и Григоровича (*Чехов в воспоминаниях современников,* 1954, стр. 503).

переписки с тем же Григоровичем, что Чехов далеко не всегда
был сдержан в выражениях. Чехов почти не скрывает, что ему
было скучно и досадно сидеть у постели больного; он рад,
что приход Бертенсона дал ему возможность „бежать". Свои
впечатления он резюмирует едва ли уместной шуточкой:
„Каковы впечатления? Право, запить можно". Может быть,
иногда такого рода „шуточки" и маскируют у Чехова
настоящие чувства, но тут этого не ощущается. И как харак-
терна заключительная фраза: „Впрочем, говорят, для беллетриста все полезно". Несмотря на „говорят", создается
впечатление, что так именно смотрел и сам Чехов: писателю
все на потребу. И по-своему он, разумеется, был прав. Дело
вовсе не в том, чтобы уличить Чехова в отсутствии „маленькой доброты". Но надо смотреть правде в глаза, а не приук-
рашивать и идеализировать. [29] Для Чехова — и как писателя,
и как человека — было характерно сдержанно-бесстрастное,
скептическое и недоверчивое отношение к людям. И то, в чем
можно усмотреть человеческий недостаток Чехова, составляло
силу его как писателя. Неслучайно почти через все произведения Чехова проходит красной нитью мотив взаимной отчуж-
денности людей, их разгороженности непроницаемыми пере-

---

[29] Конечно, говоря об отношениях Чехова и Григоровича, не следует
„идеализировать" и Григоровича. И Суворин, и Плещеев, которые его
хорошо знали, говорят о нем много нелестного. См. особенно *Дневник*
Суворина за 1893 год, когда они вместе с Григоровичем были в Италии
(стр. 34-35), и письма Плещеева к Суворину за 1891 год (*Письма русских
писателей...*, стр. 131-32). Но хотя Григорович в Венеции очень „надоел"
Суворину, он отмечает, что, когда он заболел, Григорович как нянька
ухаживал за ним, и прибавляет: „В его улыбке всегда мне казался
добрый человек" (стр. 32). С безразличием, проявленным Псковым к
смерти Григоровича, контрастирует следующая запись в дневнике
Суворина, сделанная недели две спустя: „Очень жаль Д. В. Григоровича.
Лежит теперь, бедный, и никогда его не увидишь. Когда умирают люди,
самое грустное именно эта мысль, что никогда их не увидишь, никогда
не скажешь с ними ни одного слова, а затем жалеешь, отчего не всегда
был с ними предупредителен, любезен, ласков. Не следует огорчать кого
бы то ни было. А я вчера был такой вспыльчивый, такой нервный" (стр.
219). Тот же Суворин через три года после смерти Чехова записал:
„Прежде переписывался, особенно с Чеховым. А теперь не с кем" (стр.
334). Чехов едва ли бы что-нибудь такое сказал после смерти Суворина.
Что до Плещеева, то он в одном письме метко называет Григоровича
„замшевым или ваточным": „Григорович удивляется, что Вы его назвали
в письме ко мне ,железным человеком'. ,Железный' — действительно
эпитет для него неподходящий. Он скорей и сам замшевый или
ваточный, как его герои" (*Письма русских писателей...*, стр. 128). Эта
„замшевость" наверняка не нравилась Чехову. Не ему ли и принадлежит
это определение?

городками, их неспособности понять другого. Не потому ли все персонажи его пьес так странно разговаривают? Они как бы говорят мимо друг друга, слушая только себя, равнодушные к тому, что говорят собеседники.

О „доброте" Чехова недавно завел спор советский писатель Илья Эренбург. Ему не понравилось то, что написала на эту тему французская почитательница Чехова, г-жа Софи Лаффит, в книжке „Чехов, им самим рассказанный". [30] Эренбург вырывает из книги г-жи Лаффит отдельные фразы, разбросанные на протяжении десяти страниц, и так подносит их своему читателю:

> Любил ли он человека? Кажется, что все другие, незнакомые были для него прежде всего объектами эстетического восприятия. Если люди красивы или входят в красивый пейзаж, он к ним расположен. В противном случае его поспешное суждение остро и в общем неблагоприятно... Всюду морды, рыла, хари, рожи... Тот же холод в отношениях Чехова к знакомым. Если он всегда окружен роем поклонников, если в его доме неизменно гости, если столько людей называют себя его приятелями, то по существу у него нет друзей... Тот же холод, та же усталость в его отношении к больным. Величайшая скука, граничащая с отвращением... Все, в том числе он сам, сходятся на признании этого холода, этой затаенной враждебности к людям... Все в нем показывает страстную волю к доброте, но также равнодушие и не меньшее презрение к людям, к жалким погремушкам, которые их забавляют... [31]

Эренбург опускает при этом не только длинные цитаты и из писем Чехова и из воспоминаний современников, призванные иллюстрировать эти положения, но и пояснительные фразы самой г-жи Лаффит. При этом он говорит, что г-жа Лаффит ссылается преимущественно на письма Чехова и его в них „самокритику" — на то, что он сам говорил, например, что он „из породы злых". По словам Эренбурга, это самоосуждение, как и другие многочисленные примеры самоуничижения (Чехов часто говорил о своей лени, бездеятельности, без-

---

[30] Sophie Laffitte, *Tchekhov par lui-même*. „Ecrivains de toujours", Aux Editions du Seuil, Paris 1955, 192 pp. Статья Эренбурга, озаглавленная *Перечитывая Чехова,* напечатана в № № 5 и 6 *Нового Мира* за 1959 год. В ней есть небезынтересные мысли рядом с неизбежными клише.

[31] Эти цитаты взяты Эренбургом со страниц 160, 161, 162, 168 и 171. Я даю их в переводе самого Эренбурга, хотя в нем есть некоторые неточности.

дарности и т.п.), „было продиктовано удивительной скромностью”. Я не буду говорить о том, что пресловутая чеховская скромность производит иногда впечатление унижения паче гордости: Чехов хорошо знал себе цену. Как доказательство „необычайной доброты” Чехова Эренбург противопоставляет суждениям самого Чехова ряд свидетельств его друзей (Елпатьевского, Сергеенко, Лазарева-Грузинского). „Без этой органической, редкой доброты никогда Чехов не смог бы написать того, что он написал”, пишет Эренбург.

На самом деле г-жа Лаффит отнюдь не ограничивается ссылкой на „самоприговоры” Чехова, она в подкрепление тоже цитирует показания друзей Чехова и людей, его хорошо знавших (Куприна, Бунина, Сергеенко и др.). Мне кажется, что вся история отношений Чехова с Григоровичем (и то же самое относится к его отношениям с Сувориным и многими другими друзьями в разные периоды жизни) подтверждает многое из того, что говорит г-жа Лаффит. Эренбург, конечно, прав, говоря, что нельзя от проповеди художнического бесстрастия, „нейтральности”, воздержания от решения вопросов — а образчики такой проповеди разбросаны по всей переписке Чехова с его литературными друзьями и с начинающими или неопытными писателями — нельзя от нее заключать к характеру самого писателя. Но не правильнее ли было бы все-таки сказать, что Чехов никогда не смог бы написать того, что он написал, если бы он не был сам наделен тем бесстрастием, которое он считал обязательным „реквизитом” писателя?

II

1.

Можно ли говорить о влиянии Григоровича на творчество Чехова? На этот вопрос, мне кажется, следует ответить: и да, и нет. О прямом влиянии Григоровича, как писателя, едва ли может быть речь. В 80-ые годы Григорович, как писатель, автор *Деревни, Антона Горемыки, Рыбаков* и *Переселенцев,* был весь уже в прошлом. Он был один из стаи славных, на нем лежал отсвет славы Тургенева, Достоевского и Толстого, с которыми его когда-то связывали близкие личные отношения. Он представлял традицию, но его собственные произведения 80-х и 90-х годов прошли малозамеченными и сейчас забыты, не имея и того историко-литературного значения, которое имели его первые вещи. С завидной скромностью он сам видел в себе не столько творческую силу, сколько опытного ценителя и критика литературы (см. цитированное выше, на стр. 215 письмо его к Чехову от 30 декабря 1887 г.).

Но если нельзя говорить о прямом влиянии Григоровича, как писателя, на Чехова, то можно, думается, указать на некоторые случаи, когда Григорович как бы „подстегнул" Чехова к написанию рассказа. На один из таких случаев, как уже упомянуто, мимоходом указывал в уже цитированной работе П. М. Бицилли, отмечая, что сюжет рассказа *Володя* мог быть „подсказан" Чехову Григоровичем, который предложил ему написать роман о самоубийстве 17-летнего мальчика. Бицилли при этом не указал на то, что *Володя* представляет собой переделку более раннего рассказа *Его первая любовь,* напечатанного в *Петербургской Газете* 1 июня 1887 года (этот рассказ дан в примечаниях в ПССП VI). В этом раннем рассказе никакого самоубийства нет; рассказ был значительно переделан и „продолжен" Чеховым, и это подтверждает мысль Бицилли о том, что тема самоубийства могла быть подсказана Чехову Григоровичем: переделка была произведена Чеховым, по всей видимости, после получения письма от Григоровича. 9 апреля 1888 года Чехов писал Короленко: „Посылаю Вам, добрейший Владимир Галактионович, рассказ про самоубийцу. Я прочел его и не нашел в нем ничего такого, что могло бы показаться Вам интересным, — он плох, но все-таки посылаю, ибо обещал" (XIV 79). В примечании к этому письму сказано: „Остается невыясненным, о каком рассказе идет речь. Рассказ Чехова о самоубийце *Володя появился впервые в печати лишь в 1895 г.* [подчеркнуто мною — *Г. С.*]. Первая часть этого рассказа составляла самостоятельный рассказ, напечатанный в 1887 г. — *Его первая любовь,* но тема самоубийства здесь даже не затронута. Неизвестно, существовало ли уже тогда продолжение рассказа, или оно было написано лишь позднее, подобно тому, как рассказ Чехова *Учитель словесности,* гл. I-II, 1894 г., образовался из рассказа *Обыватели,* к которому была добавлена вторая часть" (XIV 487-88). Между тем в т. VI того же издания совершенно правильно указано, что рассказ *Володя* был в переработанном виде включен в сборник *1890 г.* (*Хмурые люди*) и что для него „вновь написаны были две сцены: ночное свидание Володи с Нютой и его самоубийство"

(VI 502). [32] Иными словами, *Володя* был, по всей вероятности, написан не позднее 1889 года. Нет оснований думать, что Чехов непременно имел в виду уже напечатанный рассказ — он мог бы послать Короленко и рукопись *Володи,* хотя слова „Я прочел его" (если только это не ошибка вместо „перечел") могут побудить усомниться в том, что речь идет о рассказе самого Чехова. Все же такая возможность существует, и тогда *Володю* следует датировать началом 1888 года, что подтверждало бы связь рассказа с письмом Григоровича. Бицилли отмечал, однако, что, тогда как Григорович, как видно из его письма, понимал предлагаемую им тему, как „социальную", дающую возможность высказать „общественную мысль" и „коснуться наболевшей общественной раны", в рассказе Чехова „ничего этого нет" и тема „обработана... по-мопассановски". [33] Вполне ли прав Бицилли? В рассказе Чехова, мопассановском по теме, а отчасти и по трактовке, социальная тема, конечно, не выпирает, но в скрытой, завуалированной форме он все же перекликается с тем, что Чехов писал Григоровичу по поводу „русских самоубийц". С той беспощадной характеристикой русской жизни, которую он дает в письме Григоровичу (см. выше, стр. 217-18) можно, например, сопоставить не только общую картину пошлости жизни в *Володе,* но и специфически следующее место:

> И чем тяжелее становилось у него на душе, тем сильнее он чувствовал, что где-то на этом свете, у каких-то людей есть жизнь чистая, благородная, теплая, изящная, полная любви, ласк, веселья, раздолья ...(VI 158).

2.

Другой случай, когда Григорович, мне кажется, сыграл роль возбудителя и навеял Чехову один из лучших его рассказов среднего периода, может показаться более сомнительным. Стимулирующая роль Григоровича тут во всяком случае была более косвенная.

В январской книге *Русской Мысли* за 1887 год был напечатан рассказ Григоровича *Сон Карелина,* носивший подзаголовок „Отрывок из романа *Петербург прошлого времени".*

---

[32] До включения в сборник *Володя,* повидимому, нигде не печатался. Между прочим, гораздо позднее некий Собольщиков-Самарин переделал *Володю* в пьесу под названием *Гадкий утенок.* Пьеса эта была в 1903 году запрещена к постановке цензурой (см. XV 754).

[33] Цит. соч., стр. 10.

Рассказ этот вошел потом в том X прижизненного собрания сочинений Григоровича (1890 г.). Ныне совершенно забытый, он заслуживал бы внимания уже потому, что он не только обратил на себя внимание Чехова, но и очень понравился ему. Главное же, он настолько заинтересовал его одной своей стороной, что побудил его написать по свежим следам (12 февраля 1887 года) длинное письмо Григоровичу, которое мы и приводим здесь полностью:

Сейчас я прочитал „Сон Карелина", и меня теперь сильно занимает вопрос: насколько изображенный Вами сон есть сон? И мне кажется, что мозговая работа и общее чувство спящего человека переданы Вами замечательно художественно и физиологически верно. Конечно, сон — явление субъективное и внутреннюю сторону его можно наблюдать только на самом себе, но так как процесс сновидения у всех людей одинаков, то, мне кажется, каждый читатель может мерить Карелина на свой собственный аршин, и каждый критик поневоле должен быть субъективен. Я сужу на основании своих снов, которые часто вижу.

Прежде всего, чувство холода передано Вами замечательно тонко. Когда ночью спадает с меня одеяло, я начинаю видеть во сне громадные склизкие камни, холодную осеннюю воду, голые берега — все это неясно, в тумане, без клочка голубого неба; в унынии и в тоске, точно заблудившийся или покинутый, я гляжу на камни и чувствую почему-то неизбежность перехода через глубокую реку; вижу я в это время буксирные пароходики, которые тащат громадные барки, плавающие бревна, плоты и проч. Все до бесконечности сурово, уныло и сыро. Когда же я бегу от реки, то встречаю на пути обвалившиеся ворота кладбища, похороны своих гимназических учителей... И в это время весь я проникнут тем своеобразным кошмарным холодом, какой немыслим наяву и ощущается только спящими. Он очень рельефно припоминается, когда читаешь первые страницы Карелина, а в особенности верхнюю половину 5-й страницы, где говорится о холоде и одиночестве могилы...

Мне кажется, что, родись и живи я постоянно в Петербурге, мне снились бы непременно берега Невы, Сенатская площадь, массивные фундаменты...

Ощущая во сне холод, я всякий раз вижу людей. Случайно я читал критика *Петерб[ургских] Ведомостей,* который сетует на Вас за то, что Вы вывели „почти-министра" и тем нарушили общий величавый тон рассказа. Я с ним не согласен. Нарушают тон не лица, а их характеристики, прерывающие в нескольких местах картину сна. Лица снятся, и обязательно несимпатичные. Мне, например, всегда при ощущении холода снится один благообразный и ученый протоиерей, оскорбивший мою мать, когда я был мальчиком, снятся злые, неумолимые, интригующие, злорадно улыбающиеся, пошлые, каких наяву и не увидишь. Смех в окнах вагона — характерный симптом карелинского кошмара. Когда во сне ощущаешь давление злой воли, неминуемую погибель от этой воли, то всегда приходится видеть что-нибудь вроде подобного смеха... Снятся и любимые люди, но они обыкновенно являются страдающими заодно со мною...

Когда же мое тело привыкает к холоду, или же кто-нибудь из домашних укрывает меня, ощущение холода, одиночества и давящей злой воли постепенно исчезает. Вместе с теплом я начинаю уже чувствовать, что как будто хожу по мягким коврам или по зелени, вижу солнце, женщин, детей... Картины меняются постепенно, но резче, чем наяву, так что, проснувшись, трудно припомнить переходы от одной картины к другой... Эта резкость у Вас хорошо чувствуется и усиливает впечатление сна.

Сильно бросается в глаза также и одна подмеченная Вами естественность: видящие сон выражают свои душевные движения именно порывами, в резкой форме, по-детски. Это так верно! Сонные плачут и вскрикивают гораздо чаще, чем бодрствующие.

Простите, Дмитрий Васильевич, мне так понравился Ваш рассказ, что я готов исписать Вам дюжину листов, хотя отлично знаю, что не могу сказать Вам ничего нового, хорошего и дельного. Боясь надоесть и сказать несообразность, я обуздываю себя и умолкаю. Скажу только, что Ваш рассказ кажется мне великолепным. Публика находит его „туманным", но для пишущего, смакующего каждую строчку, подобные туманы прозрачнее крещенской воды. При всем моем старании в рассказе я мог уловить только два неважных пятнышка, да и то с натяжкой: 1) характеристики лиц прерывают картину сна и дают впечатление объяснительных надписей, которые в садах прибиваются к деревьям учеными садовниками и портят пейзажи, 2) в начале рассказа чувство холода несколько притупляется в читателе и входит в привычку от частого повторения слова „холод".

Больше я ничего не мог найти и сознаю, что в моем литераторском существовании, когда чувствуется постоянная потребность в освежающих образчиках, *Сон Карелина* составляет явление блестящее. Потому-то вот я и не воздержался и дерзнул передать Вам частицу моих впечатлений и мыслей.

Простите за длинноту письма и примите искренние пожелания всего хорошего от преданного

А. Чехова

(XIII 279-81).

Григорович, как мы видели (см. выше, стр. 213), по болезни долго не отвечал Чехову, а когда наконец ответил, то выразил удивление той оценкой, которую Чехов дал рассказу. Он писал:

> ...Переходя к литературе, скажу Вам искренно: меня крайне обрадовала, но вместе с тем и удивила оценка Ваша моего рассказа; Вы хвалите то именно, о чем я менее всего думал, когда писал. Верная передача впечатлений процесса сна собственно занимала меня несравненно менее, чем мысль изобразить внешнюю и общественную картину известной среды в Петербурге — выразить недовольство, тоску от окружающей лжи и пустоты — и кончить этот кошмар примиряющим светлым впечатлением. Вводные лица и описания их вредят, быть может, строю и целости рассказа, — но без них не была бы достигнута цель тягостного впечатления — о чем я преимущественно заботился. В нашем деле не часто ли впрочем так бывает, что то, над чем хлопочешь, — выходит всего слабее, а то, что пропето бессознательно как птица поет, — выходит всего удачнее! Вы вероятно сами на себе не раз это испытали. Во всяком случае спасибо Вам от всего сердца за Ваш сочувственный отзыв; я мало этим избалован (204-05).

Этот обмен письмами интересен в разных отношениях. Чехов прошел мимо того социально-сатирического элемента в рассказе Григоровича, который для самого автора был центральным, и обратил внимание на то, что автору казалось второстепенной и подсобной деталью — на художественное изображение сонных переживаний. Григорович высказывает предположение, что Чехов сам наверное не раз испытал на себе нечто подобное. Бывало ли так с Чеховым в этот ранний период его творчества, мы не знаем, но впоследствии ему не раз приходилось жаловаться на нечувствительность и слепоту критиков. И не далее как в 1889 году, мы видели, Чехов от себя как бы выдал диплом Григоровичу, отметив, что Григорович один заметил как „подан" первый снег в рассказе *Припадок*. Ситуация, впрочем, здесь была несколько иная, ибо в данном случае для самого автора существенна была маленькая художественная деталь, и его обрадовало то, что другой писатель своим глазом художника заметил ее. Это, конечно, характерно для всего отношения Чехова к литературе и к писательскому мастерству, и в этом смысле можно привести много его высказываний и в художественных произведениях и в письмах. Но нас здесь сейчас интересует другая сторона чеховского письма к Григоровичу. В этом письме проявился интерес Чехова к снам и изображению их в литературе.

Покойный А. М. Ремизов, этот самый неуемный сновидец в русской литературе, сказавший много интересного о снах у Гоголя, Тургенева, Толстого, Достоевского и других русских писателей, считал, что Чехову сны не снились и он их не изображал. Так ли это на самом деле?

О том, что Чехов видел сны — и даже часто — мы имеем его собственное свидетельство в письме к Григоровичу. Принимая во внимание интерес, проявленный Чеховым в этом письме к передаче сна в рассказе Григоровича, трудно представить себе, чтобы сам Чехов не попробовал ввести сновидения в ткань какого-нибудь своего рассказа. И действительно, почти ровно через год после прочтения им *Сна Карелина,* Чехов пишет небольшой рассказ, в котором сон играет большую роль. Рассказ этот — *Спать хочется,* одна из ранних Чеховских жемчужин. [34] Рассказ написан Чеховым, так сказать, между делом, в период интенсивной работы над первой большой вещью — *Степью* — для журнала *Северный Вестник,* с которым свел его Плещеев. 19 января 1888 года Чехов писал Плещееву:

> Весь январь я работаю над степью, ничего больше не пишу а потому разорился в пух и прах. Если *Степь* будет напечатана позже марта, то я взвою волком. Вышлю я ее Вам к 1 февраля. Если Вы предвидите, что в мартовской книжке места не будет, то, дорогой мой, дайте мне знать; я не буду спешить со *Степью* и нацарапаю ради гонорара что-нибудь в *Новое Время* и *Пет[ербургскую] Газету.* Писать большое очень скучно и гораздо труднее, чем писать мелочь (XIV 21).

Именно „ради гонорара", для *Петербургской Газеты* Чехов и „нацарапал" *Спать хочется.* Рассказ был уже написан, когда

---

[34] *Спать хочется,* как и *Володя,* вошло в сборник *Хмурые люди.* За одним существенным исключением, о котором речь будет ниже, Чехов почти не внес изменений в рассказ. Все небольшие изменения свелись к сокращениям, к устранению того, что все еще казалось Чехову лишним (ср. VII 517).

Чехов получил письмо от Плещеева в ответ на свое от 19 января. Плещеев предлагал ему печатать мелкие рассказы также в *Северном Вестнике* и писал:

> ... было бы в высшей степени грустно, если бы Вы отложили *Степь* и принялись за маленькие вещицы *ради гонорара* для какой-нибудь петербургской газеты. Не разбрасывайтесь вы так, голубчик! Разве вы не можете давать и ваши маленькие вещицы в журнал? По три, даже по два рассказца в книжке можно печатать, как делал Тургенев с своими *Записками охотника*. Деньги всегда можно будет вам выслать вперед. Ведь дают же уйму денег Успенскому, который из долгов не выходит во всех редакциях. Мне больно, что вы написали столько прелестных, истинно художественных вещей — и пользуетесь меньшей известностью, чем писатели недостойные развязать ремня у ваших ног. И все это благодаря каким-нибудь паршивым газеткам, которые сегодня прочтут и завтра употребят на обертку, да и читает-то какая публика ...[35]

23 января Чехов отвечал Плещееву:

> Милый и дорогой Алексей Николаевич, большое Вам спасибо за Ваше доброе, ласковое письмецо. Как жаль, что оно не пришло тремя часами раньше! Представьте, оно застало меня за царапаньем плохонького рассказца для *Пет [ербургской] Газеты* ... Ввиду предстоящего первого числа с его платежами я смалодушествовал и сел за срочную работу. Но это не беда. На рассказ потребовалось не больше полудня, теперь же я могу продолжать свою *Степь* ... (XIV 23).

Итак, рассказ *Спать хочется* был написан Чеховым меньше, чем в один день, между 21 и 23 января 1888 года. Сам Чехов — может быть, не без ложной скромности — назвал его „плохоньким рассказцем". На самом деле это один из лучших рассказов Чехова не только в средний период его творчества, но и вообще — прекрасный образец предельно скупого использования художественных средств и один из первых образчиков его импрессионистической манеры, по поводу которой Толстой так метко сказал:

> Чехова, как художника, нельзя даже и сравнивать с прежними русскими писателями — с Тургеневым, с Достоевским или со мной. У Чехова своя особенная манера, как у импрессионистов. Смотришь, как человек будто без всякого разбора мажет красками, какие попадаются ему под руку, и никакого как будто отношения эти мазки

---

[35] *Слово*, II, стр. 235-36.

между собою не имеют. Но отойдешь на некоторое расстоя-
ние, посмотришь, и в общем получается цельное впечатление. Перед вами яркая, неотразимая картина природы. [36]

3.

Не надо заблуждаться: между *Сном Карелина* Григоровича
и *Спать хочется* Чехова нет ничего общего кроме того, что
в обоих рассказах большую роль играют сонные переживания. Присмотримся ближе к обоим этим рассказам, ибо на
их различиях можно иллюстрировать своеобразные и нова-
торские черты индивидуальной манеры Чехова. Мягко упрек-
нув Григоровича за то, что он ненужными отступлениями и
длиннотами нарушил и испортил то, что ему, Чехову, показалось самым интересным и ценным в рассказе, Чехов через год
как бы преподал наглядный урок Григоровичу — как надо
изображать сон в рассказе.

Рассказ Григоровича занимает 30 страниц в т. Х его
Собрания сочинений. Рассказ ведется от имени Карелина,
который очевидно должен был быть героем задуманного
романа (так и не написанного Григоровичем). Начиная
описание своего сна, он говорит: „Ни накануне, ни даже за
несколько дней перед тем я вовсе не думал о Петербурге.
Между тем, едва начинаю припоминать вчерашний сон, все
мои представления ближайшим образом связываются с этим
городом”. Карелин видит себя на Сенатской площади. Все
описание пронизывает мотив „нестерпимого холода”. Ему
видятся рыбный садок, „бледно-розовое длинное пятно
здания Первого Кадетского корпуса”, арки Николаевского
моста. Потом он „мысленно” переносится дальше, перед ним
мелькает Кронштадт, снежная пустыня, затем вдруг открывается море „с настоящими холодными волнами”. Карелиным
овладевает „до слез радостное чувство”, ему хочется как
птице „взмахнуть крыльями и с криком броситься вперед”.
Но вдруг он опять оказывается на Сенатской площади и
снова ощущает нестерпимый холод. Внимание его привлекает
памятник Петру Великому. [37] Затем он видит странную
похоронную процессию, которую описывает в чуть-чуть гро-
тескных тонах:

---

[36] Цитировано в книге Ю. Соболев, *Чехов,* М., изд-во „Федерация”,
1930, стр. 59. Сборник о Толстом (1904 г.), на который ссылается
Соболев, остался мне недоступен.

[37] Обращаю внимание тех, кого интересует тема Петербурга и Мед-
ного Всадника в русской литературе, на это описание.

Сначала шли все мальчики, расставленные попарно, таким образом, что задняя пара постепенно была выше передней; головы их, без шапок, туго были перевязаны платками; они, повидимому, ежились в плохих шубенках и неровно передвигали ногами, стараясь при каждом шаге шевелить пальцами ног в глубине неуклюжих сапогов. Далее, также попарно и также с перевязанными головами, шли совершенно уже зрелые люди, иные — с резкими, угловатыми чертами лица, другие — с опухшими багровыми и крайне нахмуренными лицами. За ними выступала группа священников и дьяконов, большей частью плотных, хорошо выкормленных, закутанных в лисьи шубы с приподнятыми воротниками; двое были в камилавках, и один из них, согбенный старичок, шел дробным шажком, скрестив руки, глубоко запрятанные в лиловую муфту.

Помню, — очень хорошо помню, — мне особенно стало жалко лиц, следовавших за духовенством; их было шесть или семь; они шли один за другим, как утки ходят на воду; хотя головы их и были покрыты, но они, видимо, коченели от холода. На руках каждого красовалась подушка, туго набитая сеном, обтянутая красным трипом и обшитая позументом, точно жеваным; иней, покрывавший подушки, обивался только посередине, там, где вздрагивали крест или медаль, пришпиленные булавкой ...

Далее следует описание катафалка с открытым гробом, причем подчеркивается опять мотив холода. Покойник оказывается штатским генералом, которого Карелин немного знал и которому как раз сулили назначение в какую-то комиссию, „где обходительность и мягкость нрава составляли главное условие". По этому поводу Карелину приходят в голову мысли о тщете всего земного. Потом идет описание того, что происходит на улицах, разукрашенных флагами по случаю какого-то праздника. Карелину попадается какой-то „общественный экипаж", и в описании его и его пассажиров опять звучит нота гротеска. Появляется также тема контраста роскоши и нищеты („... посмотреть в одну сторону: перспектива великолепных домов, блестящие экипажи, уносимые стремглав дорогими рысаками, зеркальные окна магазинов, ряды газовых фонарей; посмотреть в другую: в непроглядную глубокую даль рассыпаны повсюду косые бревенчатые избы, бросаются в глаза тощие кривые столбики, обдерганные рогожи, веревочки, перевязанные узлами, щепочки, мочалки, линялый ситец, общипанная овчина и проткнутые лукошки...").

Карелин встречает знакомого, некоего Пузырева, человека,

пробившегося из низов в „общество", и целую главку (пол-
торы страницы) Григорович посвящает биографии и харак-
теристике Пузырева. Последний напоминает Карелину, что
вечером они должны встретиться на приеме у княгини Астра-
ханской. Следующая — длинная — глава посвящена описа-
нию, выдержанному в сатирических тонах, вечера у
Астраханских и собравшихся там людей. Это тоже часть сна
Карелина, но читатель как-то уже забывает об этом: внимание сосредоточивается на сатирическом изображении
„большого света". Среди гостей на вечере внимание Карелина
привлекает сидящая поодаль красивая дама. Он узнает в ней
некую Мери, которую знавал девушкой и которая к его
удивлению вышла замуж за очень к ней неподходящего и
весьма неприятного господина, некоего Пыщина, описанного
перед тем.

Затем сон снова принимает очертания кошмара: Карелин
видит себя сидящим в каком-то тесном возке, где еще холод-
нее, чем было на улице. По обе стороны его сидят два человека с лицами, запрятанными в меховые воротники. Они хранят
упорное молчание. Возок едет по Неве. Карелина мучат
предчувствия, какое то тоскливое ожидание. Все нарастаю-
щий ужас овладевает им, и он кричит отчаянным голосом,
что он ничего не сделал дурного ни людям, ни против собственной совести, что он лишь высказывал свои личные
впечатления о том, что ему казалось ложью, неправдой, лице-
мерием. „Вы могли это думать сколько вам было угодно",
неожиданно произносит один из его до сих пор молчавших
спутников учтиво-ровным голосом, от которого у Карелина
„похолодел мозг костей". Карелин пробует возразить, но его
перебивает другой спутник. Возок едет через поле, пересечен-
ное рельсами железной дороги. Надвигается паровая машина.
Карелин видит ползущего к рельсам муравья, хочет его
спасти, отбросить от надвигающегося поезда, но муравей
забирается на рельсы. В кошмар вдруг вступают описанные
ранее персонажи:

Где муравей? . . . Я поднял голову: за локомотивом не-
скончаемо бежал ряд вагонов; в открытых окнах сидели
князь Астраханский, величественная особа, все еще дер-
жавшая чайную чашку в руке, Пузырев, Пыщин, Филомо-
фенский, „человек анекдота", Годунов, — словом, все, с
кем я виделся сегодня на вечере. Веселость была на всех
лицах, они говорили и смеялись.
„Чему вы смеетесь?" спрашивает Карелин. „Оттого, что мы

— сила, а вы... вы — муравей", отвечают ему. Карелин в ответ разражается немного странным монологом о карте Европы, на которой небольшой клочок земли представляет Великобританию, а в нижней части ее точка с булавочную головку — Лондон. Эта булавочная головка непропорционально велика. В ней живет четыре миллиона человек. Это доказывает, какой человек маленький, какие все люди маленькие: „Ничего больше как пыль, да, живая пыль, рассыпанная кое-где по земле". Какие-нибудь льды Северного Океана или тайфун, говорит Карелин, сметут и снесут эту человеческую пыль как прах. Стоит ли перед лицом этого утверждать свою силу? „Настоящая сила не в нас, а в чем-то другом, где-то выше над нами. У нас существенно и драгоценно только одно: сознание жизни и чувство свободы..." В заключение монолога Карелин просит отпустить его на свободу. Возок между тем продолжает скользить по снегу в кромешной тьме, потом въезжает под какие-то нескончаемые своды. Карелин, обессиленный, закрывает глаза. Затем сцена меняется, он видит себя в березовой роще и там встречает очаровательную Мери. Ему кажется, что эта встреча была целью его жизни. Она протягивает к нему руки, он с криком бросается к ее ногам и — просыпается. Со двора доносится до него „унылый, однообразный голос: Халаты... халаты хорошие... халаты..." „Господи, зачем я проснулся?" думает Карелин. Так кончается григоровичевский рассказ.

4.

Чехов правильно отметил недостатки рассказа Григоровича. Изображение сна (а рассказ как никак называется „Сон Карелина", и не забудем, какое значение Чехов придавал заглавиям) в нем не выдержано; оно нарушается и разрушается длинными отступлениями с социально-сатирической и философской направленностью.

В рассказе Чехова нет и шести страниц. Он не претендует быть изображением сна, но сонные переживания и состояние на грани яви и сна составляют не менее половины рассказа, и весь рассказ представляет собой сложное переплетение яви и сна: явь переходит в сон, и сон вдруг оборачивается явью. При этом сон не только сам по себе подан „реалистически", но и с тем максимальным лаконизмом, к которому стремился Чехов, использован для того, чтобы придать пространственную и временную глубину рассказу, раздвинуть его рамки и, хотя самое действие рассказа охватывает всего сутки, показать читателю чуть ли не всю предыдущую жизнь Варьки: смерть отца от грыжи в земской больнице, их с матерью нищету и побирание после того. В своем письме Григоровичу Чехов настаивает на тесной связи между своими снами и внешними обстоятельствами и ощущениями действительности, например холодом. Эту свою мысль он иллюстрирует в рассказе. Начиная засыпать, Варька „видит темные облака, *которые гоняются друг за другом по небу и кричат как ребенок"*. Потом дует ветер, облака пропадают,

и Варька видит широкое шоссе, покрытое жидкой грязью; по шоссе тянутся обозы, плетутся люди с котомками на спинах, носятся взад и вперед какие-то тени; по обе стороны сквозь холодный, суровый туман видны леса. Вдруг люди с котомками и тенями падают на землю в жидкую грязь. „Зачем это?" — спрашивает Варька. — „*Спать, спать!" отвечают ей. И они засыпают крепко, спят сладко,* а на телеграфных проволоках сидят вороны и сороки, *кричат как ребенок и стараются разбудить их.*
— Баю-баюшки-баю, а я песенку спою... — мурлычет Варька и уже *видит себя в темной, душной избе.*

Затем ей снится болезнь отца, визит доктора, увоз отца в больницу и возвращение матери с известием, что отец „к утру Богу душу отдал" —

Варька идет в лес и плачет там, но вдруг *кто-то бьет ее по затылку с такой силой, что она стукается лбом о березу.* Она поднимает глаза и видит перед собой хозяина-сапожника.

Когда она снова засыпает, ей опять снится шоссе, покрытое жидкой грязью:

Люди с котомками на спинах и тени разлеглись и крепко спят. *Глядя на них, Варьке страстно хочется спать; она легла бы с наслаждением,* но мать Пелагея идет рядом и торопит ее. Обе оне спешат в город наниматься.
— *Подайте милостыньки Христа-ради!* — просит мать у встречных. — Явите божескую милость, господа милосердные!
— *Подай сюда ребенка!* — отвечает ей чей-то знакомый голос. — *Подай сюда ребенка!* — повторяет тот же голос, но уже сердито и резко. — Спишь, подлая?
Варька вскакивает и, оглядевшись, понимает, в чем дело: нет ни шоссе, ни Пелагеи, ни встречных, а стоит посреди комнатки одна только хозяйка, которая пришла накормить своего ребенка.

Просьба матери о милостыньке, составляющая часть сна Варьки, и требование хозяйки подать ребенка, врывающееся из яви, не только как бы перебрасывают мост от сна к яви, но и, благодаря употреблению глагола „подать", являют пример использования Чеховым поэтического приема „словесных внушений", о котором есть интересные замечания в работе Бицилли. [38]

Когда днем Варьке приказывают почистить хозяйские калоши,

> Она садится на пол, чистит калоши и думает, что хорошо было бы сунуть голову в большую глубокую калошу и подремать в ней немножко... *И вдруг калоша растет и пухнет, наполняет всю комнату.* Варька роняет щетку, но тотчас же встряхивает головой, пучит глаза и старается глядеть так, чтобы предметы не росли и не двигались в ее глазах...

Незадолго до того, как им был написан этот рассказ, Чехов в письме к Короленко очень лестно отзывался о его рассказе *Соколинец* (о побеге каторжан с Сахалина). Говоря, что этот рассказ кажется ему „самым выдающимся произведением последнего времени", Чехов прибавлял: „Он написан как хорошая музыкальная композиция, по всем тем правилам, которые подсказываются художнику его инстинктом" (XIV 12). В устах Чехова это, очевидно, была высшая похвала. Но эта характеристика еще больше подходит к лучшим рассказам самого Чехова и, в частности, к *Спать хочется.* Трудно найти даже у Чехова рассказ более экономный по средствам и более совершенный по композиции. Разбирая его, можно легко разложить его на „музыкальные фразы". Большую роль играют в нем повторы — и образные, и словесные — как бы возвращающиеся мотивы. Рассказ начинается с незабываемого описания, в котором реалистические черточки, подчеркнутые нарочито короткими, иногда однословными или двухсловными, предложениями, перемежаются с импрессионистическими „мазками", о которых говорил Толстой: [39]

---

[38] Цит. соч., стр. 37-40.

[39] Толстой, кстати, был высокого мнения о рассказе *Спать хочется.* Согласно письму его сына, Ильи Львовича, к Чехову от 25 мая 1903 года, он делил все рассказы Чехова, которые ему нравились, на два „сорта" — первый и второй. Рассказ *Спать хочется* был отнесен им к первосортным (см. XV 464). И Горбунов-Посадов, и Чертков просили Чехова разрешить включить рассказ в сборники *Посредника* (см. XVI 66, 431 и 443).

Ночь. Нянька Варька, девочка лет тринадцати, качает колыбель, в которой лежит ребенок, и чуть слышно мурлычет:

Баю-баюшки-баю,
А я песенку спою...

Перед образом горит зеленая лампадка; через всю комнату от угла до угла тянется веревка, на которой висят пеленки и большие черные панталоны. От лампадки ложится на потолок большое зеленое пятно, а пеленки и панталоны бросают длинные тени на печку, колыбель и Варьку... Когда лампадка начинает мигать, пятно и тени оживают и приходят в движение, как от ветра. Душно. Пахнет щами и сапожным товаром.
Ребенок плачет...

Отметим здесь намек на оживотворение зеленого пятна и теней. Позднее Чехов сильно упрекал Горького за его склонность к антропоморфизму, за его пресловутое „Море смеется”. Но у самого Чехова — в вещах разных периодов — немало примеров оживотворения неживых предметов (см. на эту тему интересные замечания в работе Бицилли, стр. 47). Дело, однако, в том, что Чехов протестовал против *бесцельного* антропоморфизма у Горького. У самого Чехова подобные „оживотворения” несут композиционную и стилистическую функцию, а в данном случае, как мы увидим, зеленому пятну и теням от пеленок и панталон принадлежит и более существенная роль.
В дальнейшем зеленое пятно от лампадки и тени от пеленок несколько раз возвращаются как музыкальные рефрены, составляя вместе с тем часть сонного навождения Варьки:

Лампадка мигает. Зеленое пятно и тени приходят в движение, лезут в полуоткрытые, неподвижные глаза Варьки и в наполовину уснувшем мозгу складываются в туманные грезы...
Когда хозяин бьет ее, потому что она задремала, Варька
встряхивает головой, качает колыбель и мурлычет свою песню. Зеленое пятно и тени от панталон и пеленок колеблются, мигают ей и скоро опять овладевают ее мозгом...

Другой повторяющийся образ — сверчок, который кричит в печке. Перед самой концовкой рассказа эти образы возвращаются вместе:

В печке кричит сверчок: зеленое пятно на потолке и тени

от панталон и пеленок опять лезут в полуоткрытые глаза Варьки, мигают и туманят ей голову.

Описание дневного времяпровождения Варьки на побегушках у хозяев между утренним кормлением ребенка и вечерним возвращением к качанию колыбели тоже музыкально организовано при помощи хозяйских приказаний, которые как стаккато — и притом идя crescendo — разбивают рассказ на короткие отрезки реалистических описаний: „Варька, затопи печку!”, „Варька, поставь самовар!” „Варька, почисть хозяину калоши!”, „Варька, помой снаружи лестницу...”, „Варька, ставь самовар!”, „Варька, сбегай купи три бутылки пива!”, „Варька, сбегай за водкой! Варька, где штопор? Варька, почисть селедку!” и наконец „Варька, покачай ребенка!” Рассказ, описав полный круг, возвращается к начальной точке: этот последний приказ читатель легко может представить себе предшествующим зачину рассказа. Круг завершен, и начинается повторение его:

В печке кричит сверчок; зеленое пятно на потолке и тени от панталон и пеленок опять лезут в полуоткрытые глаза Варьки, мигают и туманят ей голову.
— Баю-баюшки-баю, — мурлычет она, — а я песенку спою.
А ребенок кричит и изнемогает от крика. Варька видит опять грязное шоссе, людей с котомками, Пелагею, отца Ефима...

Но на этот раз порочный круг разрывается: Чехов готовит одну из своих наиболее удачных, неожиданных, драматических развязок. Подготовке и мотивировке развязки уделен какой-нибудь десяток строк:

...Она все понимает, всех узнает, но сквозь полусон она не может только никак понять той силы, которая сковывает ее по рукам и по ногам, давит ее и мешает ей жить. Она оглядывается, ищет эту силу, чтобы избавиться от нее, но не находит. Наконец, измучившись, она напрягает все свои силы и зрение, глядит вверх на мигающее зеленое пятно и, прислушавшись к крику, находит врага, мешающего ей жить. Этот враг — ребенок.
Она смеется. Ей удивительно: как это раньше она не могла понять такого пустяка? *Зеленое пятно, тени и сверчок тоже, кажется, смеются и удивляются.*
Ложное представление овладевает Варькой. Она встает с табурета и, широко улыбаясь, не мигая глазами, прохаживается по комнате. Ей приятно и щекотно от мысли, что

она сейчас избавится от ребенка, сковывающего ее по рукам
и ногам... Убить ребенка, а потом спать, слать, спать...

Здесь только одна, пожалуй, фальшивая нота — фраза
относительно „ложного представления” кажется как будто
лишней.

Самая развязка дана еще короче — как неожиданный
заключительный аккорд. Ее бесстрастную лапидарность интересно сравнить с концовками некоторых более ранних рассказов, в которых еще чувствуется надуманная рассудочность
(например, в концовке такого в общем удачного рассказа как
Враги, 1887 г.). Настоящая находка во всей этой заключи-
тельной странице — использование по-новому образов зеленого пятна и теней, которые таким образом приобретают
особую значительность (см. выше и ниже подчеркнутые мною
места). Вот эта замечательная чеховская концовка:

Смеясь, подмигивая и грозя зеленому пятну пальцами,
Варька подкрадывается к колыбели и наклоняется к ребен-
ку. Задушив его, она быстро ложится на пол, смеется от
радости, что ей можно спать, и через минуту спит уже
крепко, как мертвая...

Дальше в бесстрастном лаконизме идти нельзя. Сейчас нам
трудно и странно представить, что в первой, газетной, версии
рассказа последней фразы (от слова „Задушив”) вообще не
было (VII 517). Написал ли Чехов первоначально рассказ без
этой фразы, или же редактор решил пощадить чувства
читателей *Петербургской Газеты,* остается неизвестным. Но
какой контраст между этим предельно сжатым, до отказа
насыщенным рассказом и растянутым, написанным большей
частью „по старинке” *Сном Карелина* с его потугами на фило-
софствование! И все же весьма вероятно, что Григорович был
косвенным „виновником” этого рассказа. В целом ряде пунк-
тов в рассказе отразился интерес и к физиологии, и к психо-
логии сна, проявленный Чеховым в письме к Григоровичу.

5.

Мне известен только один более или менее детальный
разбор рассказа *Спать хочется,* принадлежащий советской
исследовательнице Л. И. Мышковской. [40] Она подчеркивает

---

[40] Л. Мышковская, *Чехов — мастер малого рассказа. Литературная
Учеба,* 1933 № 9.

глубоко социальное содержание рассказа, который, по ее словам, посвящен теме жестокой эксплоатации ребенка — „теме, взволновавшей Чехова, к которой он возвращался несколько раз (рассказ *Ванька* и статья его о приказчиках и служащих-подростках)". Чеховым, по словам Мышковской, в первый период творчества „владела одна тема — тема мелкого человека, его убогого, затхлого быта, насквозь пропитанного азиатчиной старой России". Но Мышковская останавливается и на приемах Чехова; подчеркивая сжатость и экономность рассказа и отмечая перекрещивание сна и яви в нем, она пишет: „Эта тонкая нить сна и действительности, их постоянное сплетение ведется Чеховым с поразительным реализмом, реалистическими мотивировками каждого движения. Сама развязка, убийство ребенка — тоже совершается в сплетении тех же двух линий — сна, грез и реальности". Общей проблемы изображения сна в литературе Мышковская не касается и о *Сне Карелина* не упоминает.

П. М. Бицилли в своей работе о Чехове лишь мимоходом упоминает *Спать хочется* — правда, заодно с *Володей*, но без всякой связи с Григоровичем, хотя в другом месте он отмечает роль Григоровича в литературном развитии Чехова. [41] По мнению Бицилли, *Володя* и *Спать хочется* — две вещи, стоящие „сюжетно особняком" у Чехова, в них „есть что-то от Гаршина, трагически-трогательное", и вместе с тем в них Чехов „сближается, как кажется, еще более с Мопассаном, которого он очень полюбил еще в раннюю пору". Бицилли считает, что впоследствии „мопассановское влияние слабеет" и „мопассановский *сарказм* преодолевается *юмором*". [42] Вопрос о влиянии Мопассана на Чехова до сих пор еще по-настоящему не изучен. Высокое мнение Чехова о Мопассане и его „революционной" роли в литературе засвидетельствовано его друзьями и младшими литературными современниками, А. И. Куприным и И. А. Буниным. [43] Оно нашло себе выра-

---

[41] Бицилли подчеркивает, что между Чеховым и Григоровичем „установилась тесная связь, причем в первую пору их знакомства Григорович был до некоторой степени его руководителем на творческом пути — правда, только как советчик: никакого влияния своими беллетристическими произведениями, весьма слабыми, на Чехова он не оказал". Цит. соч., стр. 40-41. О впечатлении, произведенном на Чехова *Сном Карелина,* Бицилли не упоминает.

[42] Цит. соч., стр. 10.

[43] См. И. Бунин, *Полное собрание сочинений,* 1915, VI 298 и А. Куприн, *Полное собрание сочинений,* 1912, VII 129. И. то и другое раньше в сборнике *Знание* за 1904 г., кн. 3-ья (СПб. 1905).

жение и в его переписке, и в его рассказах (*Бабье царство*).
В России когда-то вышла довольно бессодержательная книж-
ка, в которой проводится поверхностная параллель между
обоими писателями. [44] Более обстоятельно отношение Чехова
к Мопассану разобрано в одном немецком сравнительно-
литературном исследовании, автор которого сравнивает Чехова с Э. А. По и Мопассаном, как авторами коротких рассказов,
называя По „лириком", Мопассана „эпиком", а Чехова
„мелодраматиком". [45] Он проводит много параллелей между
Чеховым и Мопассаном, но и противополагает их, видя в
Чехове новую стадию в развитии короткого рассказа, как
литературной формы. Он дает также список десяти рассказов,
написанных Чеховым между 1884 и 1895 гг., в которых видит
прямое влияние Мопассана. Ни *Володи* ни *Спать хочется*
среди этих рассказов нет. [46] С другой стороны, Илья Эренбург
в уже упоминавшейся статье утверждает, что Чехов в сущест-
венном не похож на Мопассана, и называет сопоставление
между ними „ненужным и неудачным". [47]

6.

Тема снов в творчестве Чехова выходит за пределы настоя-
щей статьи. Укажем только, что Чехов так и не написал
рассказа, который был бы сплошным изображением сна, хотя
эта мысль и заинтересовала его после прочтения *Сна Карелина*. Но в ряде его вещей сны играют эпизодическую роль.
Интересный небольшой отрывок сна дан в рассказе *Жена*.
Несколько снов   в повести *Три года*, причем в сне Юлии
мы находим мотив вторжения яви в сон. Ей снятся

> ... какие-то портреты и похоронная процессия... открытый
> гроб с мертвецом внесли во двор и остановились у двери,
> потом долго раскачивали гроб на полотенцах и со всего
> размаха ударили им в дверь. Юлия проснулась и вскочила
> в ужасе. В самом деле, внизу стучали в дверь и проволока
> от звонка шуршала по стене, но звонка не было слышно ...
> В самом сне Юлии (похоронная процессия, открытый гроб),

[44] А. Д. Альман, *Антон Чехов и Гюи де Мопассан. Критический очерк,*
Саратов 1908, 39 стр.

[45] Hans Halm, *Anton Tschechows Kurzgeschichte und deren Vorläufer.*
Forschungen zur neueren Literaturgeschichte... LXVII, Weimar, Drucker, 1933,
181 SS.

[46] Цит. соч., стр. 50.

[47] И. Эренбург, *Перечитывая Чехова, Новый Мир* 1959, VI, стр. 191.

может быть, слышится отдаленный отголосок сна Карелина у Григоровича.

В той же повести Ярцев видит сон о половцах, а Федору одно время каждую ночь снится его сестра Нина.

В рассказе *Черный монах* — неудачной попытке выйти за пределы реализма и потому одной из самых слабых его вещей — Чехов, по его собственным словам, использовал приснившийся ему самому сон.

P.S. Настоящая статья была уже написана и сдана в набор, когда мне довелось прочесть статью Н. К у ч е р о в с к о г о, представляющую подробный анализ рассказа *Спать хочется* (N. K u č e r o v s k i j, *Bemerkungen zur künstlerischen Meisterschaft A. P. Čechovs* [Analyse einer Erzählung], *Zeitschrift für Slawistik*, Bd. IV, Heft 4, 1959, SS. 518-533; автор статьи — доцент Педагогического Института в Калуге, в прошлом году препо-дававший в Университете им. Карла Маркса в Лейпциге). Подобно Мышковской, Кучеровский подчеркивает значение социальной темы рассказа, но в то же время уделяет много внимания и его композиции. Отмечая переплетение в нем сна и яви, он упоминает об интересе Чехова к физиологии сна, проявившемся в его письме к Григоровичу, но рассказа Чехо-ва с рассказом Григоровича не сопоставляет. С другой стороны, указывая на то, что Чехов написал *Спать хочется* во время работы над *Степью*, он проводит сближение между *Спать хочется* и некоторыми местами в главах III и IV *Степи*, где действительность отчасти дается через полусонные вос-приятия Егорушки, тоже ребенка. Указание это заслуживает внимания, хотя особенной близости я тут не вижу. В статье Кучеровского есть отдельные интересные замечания, относя-щиеся к композиции рассказа, но есть и весьма спорные домыслы.

ILJA SVATOŇOVÁ

О ЛИРИЗМЕ ЧЕХОВА
Несколько заметок

Из всего богатого творчества Чехова нам хотелось бы остановиться только на цикле его рассказов, которые своим характером особенно производят впечатление „интимной миниатюры". Мы имеем в виду такие, как *Дом с мезонином, Дама с собачкой, Черный монах, О любви,* которые мы считаем типичными образцами такого рода рассказов. Конечно, они не представляют собой чего-то самостоятельного, обособленного от всего творчества, что вполне естественно, но нам кажется, что эти рассказы особенно выразительно представляют новые черты чеховского реализма: Чехов в них менее всего зависит от своих предшественников в русской литературе, и его видение мира нашло в них и в драмах свое самое адекватное выражение.

По сравнению с могучими драматическо-эпическими концепциями повествовательной прозы великих реалистов XIX века (в русской литературе на фоне произведений Толстого и Достоевского), чеховская проза производит впечатление интимности, лирической рефлексии.

Отличие чеховского творчества от классического реализма чувствовали уже современники Чехова. Если мы оставим в стороне узко утилитаристическую часть критики, то те рецензенты Чехова, которые не выделяли из чеховского творчества отдельных мыслей, а старались определить его общую тенденцию, останавливались перед его прозой в смущении, потому что — измеряемая классическими образцами — она представлялась им как обломки деталей, лишенных ясных связей. (Очень выразительным примером являются рецензии Н. К. Михайловского). В чешской среде того периода Чехова ценили сначала скорее за отдельные черты, которыми он напоминал некоторых своих предшественников, чаще всего Толстого или Тургенева. Только рассказ *Мужики* (переведенный на чешский язык в 1898 году) обратил внимание на чеховское своеобразие. С этого времени стали писать о том, что Чехов ближе к французским реалистам типа Флобера и Мопассана, чем к русской традиции.

С новым взглядом на отношение чеховской прозы к классикам русской литературы пришли некоторые представители

литературного поколения начала столетия (например, Андрей
Белый, молодой Мейерхольд, из чешских — Иржи Маген).
Они понимали чеховское творчество как творчество новей-
шей чеканки, которое занимает место на рубеже между так
называемой литературой модернистской и классическим
реализмом без того, чтобы выходило из рамок реалистиче-
ского искусства. Резко отделяют Чехова от своих современников, эпигонов реализма. В чем видели новизну чеховского
искусства и свое родство с ним, хотя сами чувствовали огра-
ниченность возможностей флоберовско-мопассановского направления для выражения жизни современного человека? На
их взгляд, Чехов был близок своему и их времени в сфере
лирического восприятия. Они считали, что единственно через
лирическое выражение было возможно в данную эпоху
приблизиться в художественном произведении к „правде
жизни", то есть, коснуться запутанности и сложности общественных отношений хотя бы так, как они воздействуют на
индивида, как отражаются в его душе, когда их связь и
закономерность остаются для него закрытыми. Поэт и драматург Иржи Маген, типичный представитель поколения, которое подверглось влиянию русского романа и одновременно
переживало очарование современной французской литературы, приводит Чехова среди духовных близнецов своего
поколения. Он считал Чехова творцом, который вел к
преодолению субъективизма, так как его творчество учило
искать „лирику вне себя". [1]

И у самого Чехова мы находим неоднократно прямые
доказательства того, что он сам считал произведения своих
предшественников органически не способными для выражения современности: „Теперь уже Гаршина нельзя читать, а
про Потапенку и говорить не стоит. Мопассан сделал
огромный переворот в беллетристике. После него все это так
старо, что кажется чем-то отжившим их манера писания." [2]
Он чувствовал свое родство с Мопассаном, Гауптманом, автором „Одиноких", Метерлинком, между тем как в родной
литературе, несмотря на личные симпатии к Гаршину и глубо-
кое уважение к Толстому, не находит прямых союзников и
много раз подчеркивает, что перед ним и всем последующим

---

[1] „Lyrika, která do té doby byla hodně osobní, hledala nový výraz v člověku"
(Jiří Mahen, *Kapitola o předválečné generaci,* Praha 1934, str. 23).
[2] Н. И. Гитович, *Летопись жизни и творчества А. П. Чехова,* Москва
1955, стр. 744.

литературным поколением стоят новые задачи, которые можно решить только усилием целого поколения, хотя бы и ценой того, что когда-нибудь о них будут писать, не называя имен, как о „поколении девяностых годов". Чеховские слова, в которых он задумывается над новым предназначением писателей, выливаются чаще всего в девизы: „Мне кажется, что не беллетристы должны решать такие вопросы, как бог, пессимизм и т.п. Дело беллетриста изобразить только, кто, как и при каких обстоятельствах говорит или думает о боге или пессимизме. Художник должен быть не судьею своих персонажей и того, что говорят они, а только беспристрастным свидетелем." [3]

Это стремление к максимально объективному выражению, которое можно подтвердить многими высказываниями и отдельными мыслями Чехова, вложенными в уста героев его рассказов 1888-1894 годов, часто приводится в истории литературы как рубеж между ним и предшествующей русской реалистической прозой. Эти высказывания, однако, постигают только часть истины. С одной стороны, потому что „объективизированное" изображение действительности свойственно и произведениям классиков реализма XIX столетия до Чехова, а в реалистическом флоберовско-мопассановском направлении достигает только крайнего выражения; с другой стороны, потому что и в произведениях поздних реалистов можно проследить личную концепцию индивида и общества, которая придает, несмотря на общие признаки, ярко индивидуальный характер стилю творчества каждого из них. Их программное стремление подавить факторы, которые бы нарушали идеал искусства как „иллюзию действительности", сопровождается щепетильной заботой о совершенности стиля (чем прежде всего прославился Флобер и что иногда приписывается его личным качествам). Эта забота о совершенности стиля, однако, не является, на наш взгляд, проявлением артистической исключительности и вообще свойств характера, но логическим дополнением того же „объективизма" — то есть, стремлением при максимально объективном изображении действительности наложить на нее точно и выразительно печать своего индивидуального восприятия. Вспомним слова Мопассана: „*Voir*: tout est là, et voir juste. J'entends par voir juste, voir avec ses propres yeux et non avec ceux des maîtres. L'originalité d'un artiste s'indique

---

[3] Письмо А. С. Суворину, 30 мая 1888. XIV 118.

d'abord dans les petites choses et non dans les grandes. Des chefs-d'oeuvre ont été faits sur d'insignifiants détails, sur des objets vulgaires. Il faut trouver aux choses une signification qui n'a pas encore été découverte et tâcher de l'exprimer d'une façon personelle." [4]

Характеризовать прозу Чехова последнего десятилетия только и прежде всего этой объективностью было бы слишком общим. Вместе с общим необходимо искать и то специфически чеховское: это общее частично обнаружили уже старшие современники Чехова из рядов литературных критиков, несмотря на то, что тенденцию отказа от какой-либо прямой оценки они квалифицировали отрицательно. Однако только отдельные представители поколения на две-три генерации моложе, тем, что обратили внимание на цельность впечатления в рассказах Чехова, дали повод к тому, чтобы мы занялись новизной общего характера чеховского творчества, под которой скрывается новый взгляд на личность в отношении к русским общественным условиям, небывалый в русской литературе.

Чеховскую прозу последнего десятилетия можно характеризовать как лирические, интимные миниатюры. Такие рассказы, как *Черный монах, Дом с мезонином, О любви, Дама с собачкой,* из более ранних, напр., *Тапер, Горе, Припадок, Скучна история,* это как бы свободно набросанные этюды, обломки мгновений, в которых одинокая личность продирается к пониманию своего положения в общественной деятельности. Это лирические рефлексии автора, хотя внешне они сохраняют характер объективных „картин быта" и касаются тех фактов действительности, которыми занималась русская литература 70-х и 80-х годов.

В истории литературы закрепилось определение „лирические" за чеховскими драмами. В связи с ними говорится, прежде всего, о лиризме, об эмоциональности, музыкальности, театре настроения и т.п. Большое внимание лиризму чеховских драм уделял С. Д. Балухатый. Однако, в его работах этот вопрос продолжается трактоваться в плоскости чисто художественных приемов. С новой точки зрения к этой проблеме подошел А. Скафтымов в статьях *К вопросу о принципах построения пьес Чехова* и *О единстве формы и содержания в Вишневом саде А. П. Чехова,* [5] так как проблему

[4] À M. Maurice Vaucaire. Guy de Maupassant, *Oeuvres complètes. Boule de Suif — Correspondence,* Paris 1926.
[5] А. Скафтымов, *Статьи о русской литературе,* Саратов 1958.

„лиризма" чеховских пьес решает в области отношения
содержания и формы на фоне развития жанра русской бытовой пьесы. В работах о чеховской прозе, однако, не прини-
мается во внимание специфичность её лиризма. Лиризм
понимается просто как прием, достойный восхищения; однако, этот лиризм понимается внешне, вне отношения к смыслу
произведения, только как „повествовательный тон". Нам
кажется, что в этом интимном „лирическом тоне" заключено
специфически чеховское понимание человека и жизненных
обстоятельств. Уже сам факт, что тип интимной прозы, который начинает появляться в творчестве Чехова в переходный
период (приблизительно в 1888-1894 годах) и постепенно, по
мере того, как Чехов глубже овладевает действительностью
согласно своим представлениям о литературе, получает в его
творчестве перевес и высокую культивированность, вызывает
к тому, чтобы не пройти мимо него только как мимо случай-
ного признака творчества. Спрашивается, о чем новом в отношении героев к русской жизни он свидетельствует. Ведь это в
своем большинстве рассказы, которые относятся к традиции
так называемых проблемных сюжетов в русской литературе
70-х и 80-х годов, обильно встречающихся в народнической
литературе, об общем направлении которой Короленко заявил:
„Для Гаршина и его поколения вся психология „проклятых
вопросов" сводилась к вопросу о правде в конечной области
людских отношений." [6] Однако, на том же цикле проблем, с
теми же фактами жизни и оставаясь также „в конечной
области людских отношений", Чехов создал прозу совсем
другого характера.

Впечатление „лиризма" его рассказов вызвано, прежде
всего, характером конфликта, который всегда заключен в
душе персонажа, а из душевного состояния своего героя
автор бросает обратный свет на бытовой материал, которым
герой окружен и вместе с которым он представляет неделимое
мое целое. Правда, этот прием не представляет собой после
Достоевского ничего нового, также в нем не было бы ничего
специфически лирического, а поэтому мы должны обратить
внимание на то, какого рода этот психологический конфликт.

Большинство чеховских интимных рассказов концентри-
руется своим сюжетом вокруг жизненных моментов, в которых герой осознает цинизм своей протекшей жизни (которая, однако, ничем не отличается от того, „как все живут")

---

[6] В. Г. Короленко, *Собрание сочинений,* т. 8, Москва 1955, стр. 222.

и одновременно окружающего мира. Через этот кризис Чехов проводит людей различнейших привычек, чувств, интеллектуального направления и социального положения (сравним, напр., рассказы *Горе, Дама с собачкой, Скучная история*). Иногда фабула начинает развиваться именно после этого момента, но и тогда автор возвращается к нему в процессе повествования как к исходной точке. Композиционно в таком случае этот момент всегда является центром фабулы, к которому автор направляет выбор жизненных фактов. Вокруг подобных моментов и в тесной, хотя лишь очень редко прямолинейной связи с ними, он группирует биографические детали героев и избранные синтетические черты быта. Эти детали образуют потом совокупность фактов окружающего мира, заостренную в определенном направлении. Черты быта определют, какие именно симптомы окружающей действительности вызывают в герое кризис. Они несут на себе печать именно авторского восприятия и отнюдь не индивидуальных психологических свойств героев. В связи с литературой 80-х годов важно заметить, что Чехов вкладывает в эти моменты в уста своих героев мысли, ставящие под сомнение истины, провозглашенные этой литературой, еретические по отношению к ней, как напр.: „Что же мне делать?" „Что ответить ей? Легко сказать: ,трудись', или ,раздай свое имущество бедным', или ,познай самого себя', и потому, что это легко сказать, я не знаю, что ответить." (*Скучная история*) — „Что ты разумеешь под вечной правдой?" Монах не ответил. (*Черный монах*) — „Ни один из житейских вопросов не имеет специального решения." (Из первой редакции рассказа *Соседи.*) Или состояния очистительных кризисов выливаются в стремление „начать новую жизнь", к которому примыкает безответное или проблематическое „как" („как начать", „с чего начать"). Если Чехов провожает своего героя за этот, в понимании автора наиболее значительный жизненный перекресток, и дает ему решать его личное положение каким-нибудь поступком, от которого герой ожидает изменений в своей жизни, автор сразу же покажет тщетность его надежд.

Чехов находит на своих героях очень глубокие следы общественных форм, выращенных настоящим временем. Все находятся под их влиянием и затронуты ими, независимо от того, если они это сознают или нет, и не могут освободиться от них. Мир будто бы катился, как стихия, через них. Поступки даже наиболее активных героев („талантов" — сказано словами Чехова — наделенных „смелостью, свободной голо-

вой, широким размахом"), которые будто бы наиболее
освободились от конвенции быта, имеют в трактовке Чехова
необходимо лишь весьма узкое воздействие. Все остаются
волей неволей — частными лицами. В этом заключается
чеховская трагедия современной жизни.

Впечатление миниатюрности и интимности рассказов Чехова связано именно с этим пониманием личности и ее места в
современных условиях. Конфликт, происходящий в душе
героя, однако, перенесенный автором в указанные связи,
приобретает потом значение утаенного, вездесущего и, значит,
наиболее специфического признака русской жизни данной
эпохи. Во всех рассказах рассматриваемого нами типа он в
различных вариациях, но в неизменной сущности, постоянно
возвращается и повторяется.

Герой Чехова, несмотря на то, что не желает отказаться от
своих мечт (хотя и не видит возможности их реализации или
плодотворных результатов этой реализации), вынужден
оставаться, таким образом, замкнутым в кругу интимной
жизни. Эта необходимость, замечательно выражена как *пере-
ходное* свойство *настоящего* времени, с чем так великолепно
гармонирует стиль чеховской прозы последнего десятилетия.

Чем было достигнуто часто почти суггестивного впечатления настоящего? Настоящего, которое создает иллюзию
только что проживаемой действительности конкретного
данного времени? (В отличие, напр., от нейтральной по
времени плоскости романов Флобера).

Автор помещает основной конфликт во времени так, что
это получает свой особый смысл. В прозе Чехова создана
особая связь между прошлым, настоящим и будущим. Главный конфликт в интимной прозе Чехова происходит всегда
в настоящем, а именно, в подчеркнутом настоящем. Он не
разложен в цепь событий или внутренних реакций героев по
примеру эпики или драматического жанра, а дается как душевное действие, происходящее в данный момент и концен-
трированное в наиболее напряженные мгновения, освещенные
автором всегда с одной точки. Это прием весьма близкий
лирическому жанру. [7]

---

[7] Напоминает нам признание Блока: „Я привык сопоставлять факты
из всех областей жизни, доступных моему зрению в данное время, и
уверен, что все они вместе всегда создают единый музыкальный напор"
(А. Блок, *Собрание сочинений,* т. 5, Ленинград 1933, стр, 29, Предисловие
к *Возмездию*.)

Критический момент в жизни героя изображается так, что окружающий мир в данное мгновение и его прежняя жизнь ему кажутся „призрачными", „несуществующими", „фантастическими", перенесенными в прошлое и, напротив, его собственный душевный мир ему кажется единственной реальностью. [8] Классическим примером может служить рассказ *Дама с собачкой*, где аналогичное душевное состояние героя описывается автором следующими словами: „У него были две жизни: одна явная, которую видели и знали все, кому это нужно было, полная условной правды и условного обмана, похожая совершенно на жизнь его знакомых и друзей, и другая — протекавшая тайно. И по какому-то странному стечению обстоятельств, быть может случайному, все, что было для него важно, интересно, необходимо, в чем он был искренен и не обманывал себя, что составляло зерно его жизни, происходило тайно от других, все же, что было его ложью, его оболочкой, в которую он спрятался, чтобы скрыть правду, как, например, его служба в банке, споры в клубе, его „низшая раса", хождение с женой на юбилеи, — все это было явно. И по себе он судил о других, не верил тому, что видел, и всегда предполагал, что у каждого человека под покровом тайны, как покровом ночи, проходит его настоящая, самая интересная жизнь. Каждое личное существование держится на тайне, и, быть может, отчасти поэтому культурный человек так нервно хлопочет о том, чтобы уважалась личная тайна." Подобных мотивов можно обнаружить в творчестве Чехова позднего периода гораздо больше (напр., в *Трех сестрах*: „Может быть, нам только кажется, что мы существуем, а на самом деле нас нет").

Однако, нас не интересует этот факт только тогда, когда автор дал ему прямое выражение. Дело в том, что подобное понимание настоящего пронизывает рассматриваемый тип чеховских рассказов постоянно. Возьмем, например, другой вариант того же — в *Доме с мезонином*. Фабула рассказа развивается во времени реалистически эпическом: начало лета, его разгар, ранняя осень, утра, дни и ночи. Это время „картины деревенского быта", воспринимаемой художником-пейзажистом. Но над этим временным определением наслаивается другой смысл: учительница Лидия со своими заботами о том, кто дает направление социальным преобразованиям в

---

[8] О чеховском мотиве „нормальное ненормально" см. Г. А. Бялый, *К вопросу о русском реализме конца XIX века. Труды юбилейной научной сессии, секция Филолог. наук*. Ленинград, 1946.

уезде — вот это настоящее, русская действительность данной
эпохи (то, что в *Дяде Ване* Астровым названо „наша жизнь,
уездная, русская, обывательская"): однако для художника, от
имени которого ведется повествование, это лишь ограничен-
ное настоящее, духовное прошлое. Он сам проникнут полным
отрицанием всего, с чем он встречается в деревне, как в бедных
условиях жизни мужиков, так у людей, которые им хотят
помочь, и он удаляется из настоящего Лидии в будущее во
имя идеала. В эпилоге автор подводит итоги обеим линиям
рассказа. В личной жизни художника ничего не изменилось,
его мечта об основных преобразованиях осталась утопией
и заключительным „Мисюсь, где ты?" автор отодвинул ее
исполнение еще дальше в будущее, в бесконечность. Напротив, жизнь Лидии изменилась, она добилась своей цели,
вместе со своими друзьями свергла противника на выборах
и получила, благодаря этому, больше возможностей действо-
вать, тем не менее этим в русских условиях ничего не изменилось. Двойное определение времени, созданное автором, спо-
собствовало повышению рассказа художника о любви на
уровень проблем, в какой мере современный человек может
или не может найти круг деятельности в рамках, данных
определенными общественными условиями, такой деятельности, которая бы отвечала его идеалам и одновременно при-
носила общеполезные результаты в случае, если бы она могла
быть осуществлена. Двойным определением времени были
расширены узкие рамки реалистической „картины быта".
Прошлое в рассказах Чехова характеризуется верой в возможности разрешения личных и общественных проблем, настоящее — потерей этой веры, разрывом с иллюзиями. Или то
же самое мотивировано по-другому: прошлое — это автома-
тическое условное существование, настоящее — мечта о новой, другой жизни. Будущее появляется в произведениях
Чехова как сон, содержанием которого является вера в вос-
становление гармонии гуманных отношений „культурного"
человека в „культурном" мире. Мотив будущего обычно встречается как заключительная концовка рассказа, высказанная
рассказчиком или самим автором. Она звучит как подытожи-
вающая отрицательная оценка конкретной действительности,
в которой живут герои Чехова и в которой разобраться им
невозможно, и поэтому их духовная борьба и поиски смысла
собственного существования остаются для них трагическим
процессом без конца. Читателю же они представляются имен-

но тем, как эти проблемы автор определяет во времени, преходящим, временным признаком данной эпохи.

Таким образом осмысленное взаимоотношение между отвергнутым прошлым в жизни героев и между настоящим, которое будто бы могло произойти только в душе героя и не имело реального выхода, а часто даже сочувствия у других людей, обусловливает языковую структуру интимной прозы Чехова (диалоги, которые бывают независящими друг от друга монологами; свободно разбросанные реплики, которые первые чешские переводчики Чехова в начале 90-х годов иногда пропускали, стремясь сделать предложение Чехова более сжатым в смысле классической новеллы; эмоционально окрашенные детали против деталей, видимых извне, будто бы глазами живописца, которыми окружает своих героев Мопассан и т.д.) и вызывает в нас впечатление музыкальной композиции.

Итак, не так называемая объективность Чехова, воспринимаемая сама по себе, а по-новому освещенная зависимость личности и быта, заключенная в лирической структуре рассказов Чехова, является тем решающим признаком, который отличает прозу Чехова от его предшественников в русской литературе.

CHARLES B. TIMMER

THE BIZARRE ELEMENT IN ČECHOV'S ART

I

A study in literature, whether on Gogol', Dostoevskij or Čechov is bound to involve a study in anti-reason: it cannot limit itself to a study of aesthetic laws only, unless we are prepared to assume that the grotesque, the bizarre, the absurd elements in the works of these authors are unexplainable phenomena.

The grotesque, the bizarre, the absurd, — by using these words I realize that I am bringing to the foreground certain aspects of Čechov's art, which to my knowledge did not thus far have the attention they undoubtedly deserve. It is certainly not my ambition to exhaust the subject in these notes; my purpose is merely to outline it and to make an attempt to trace the difference between the technique of the bizarre in Čechov's last works and his use of the bizarre element in his early stories; for example, between a little scene like this in "The Cherry Orchard" (1903-04):

Varja: The estate will be up for sale in August.
Anja: Oh dear!
Lopachin: (*puts his head through the door and bleats*) M-e-e-e... (*Disappears*)" [1]

and 'bizarre' stories like "On Christmas Eve" (1883), "At Sea" (1883), "Oysters" (1884), "The Mistress" (1882), "In the Home for Incurables and the Aged" (1884) and many others from Čechov's early period, stories that are bizarre either in style or theme, or both. When we consider Čechov's literary output as a whole, we cannot fail to notice one remarkable fact, namely, that the bizarre element is abundantly represented in the early, the 'Čechonte' stories, that it gradually disappears in his later and riper work, but reappears, more profusely than ever, in his plays.

But what really is the meaning of the bizarre in art and what is its function? When do we call a certain phenomenon, a situation, a statement *bizarre*?

The word defies precise definition. However, it is possible to mention one inherent quality: — its irrelevancy, and one typical effect: — its capability of producing bewilderment. In this it differs from the

---

[1] Anton Chehov, *Three plays,* transl. by Elisaveta Fen, London 1953, p. 30.

grotesque, which really is nothing but comical exaggeration, showing us the ludicrous side of 'extreme situations'; it likewise differs from the absurd, which lies already wholly in the realm of the irrational. The *bizarre* is not necessarily absurd: it is, as it were, a statement, or a situation, which has no logical place in the context or in the sequence of events, the resulting effect being one of sudden bewilderment; the bizarre brings about a kind of mental 'airpocket': one gasps for breath, until the tension is relieved by laughter. The *absurd* is contrary to reason and does not necessarily contain this element of playful, whimsical strangeness, which is so characteristic for Čechov in the youthful wantonness of his art, a strangeness, which comes so strikingly to light again in many characters and situations in his plays. It is difficult, if not impossible to draw a distinct line between such conceptions as 'the absurd', 'the bizarre', 'the grotesque'; they often overlap and flow together. And besides, in all these matters the factor of personal appreciation by the reader or spectator and therefore of subjective interpretation influences the definition. A few examples by way of illustration, taken from Čechov's Notebooks — this rich fund of grotesque, bizarre and absurd fancies and observations —, may throw some more light on the matter. Thus the following situation might be called simply 'grotesque': "A shy young man came on a visit for the night; suddenly a deaf old woman of eighty came into his room, carrying a clyster-pipe and administered a clyster to him; he thought that this must be the usual thing and so did not protest; in the morning it turned out that the old woman had made a mistake." [2] Here my contention that the characteristic quality of the grotesque lies in the exaggeration, in the hyperbolism of a *possible* situation, is clearly demonstrated by the English translation of this passage, [3] in which, possibly for reasons of modesty, the clyster-pipe is replaced by a cupping glass and the victim is bled. Suppose another translator would go one step further and change the syringe for a cup of tea — then the grotesque element would have disappeared altogether. The bizarre element can be found in a statement like this: "When I become rich, I shall have a harem in which I shall keep fat naked women, with their buttocks painted green." This is a good example of that particular kind of 'mental leap', so typical of the bizarre, with

---

[2] *The Personal Papers of Anton Chekhov,* New York 1948, p. 104. The translation of the Notebook is by S. S. Koteliansky and Leonard Woolf and quoted here with some corrections.

[3] The passage referred to reads in the English translation: "Suddenly a deaf old woman came into the room, carrying a cupping-glass, and bled him". Cf. A. P. Čechov, PSSP XII 284: "Vdrug vošla starucha let 80, gluchaja, s klistirnoj kružkoj i postavila emu klistir."

the clear-cut caesura in the logical sequence after the third section of this statement. Finally, the absurd is demonstrated in a note of the following kind: "N., a singer; speaks to nobody, his throat muffed up — he takes care of his voice, but no one has ever heard him sing." Which, in my opinion, is a good exampe of irrational behaviour.

In the beginning of his career as a writer the bizarre element in Čechov's work comes very close to the grotesque; wherever it appears in his later prose-writings and in his plays, it has more in common with the absurd. This is important and fully in harmony with the wellknown fact that the laughter in Čechov's stories gradually dies down. In his early period it seems hardly likely that Čechov used the bizarre deliberately as a consciously worked out technique: it rather appears that bizarre thoughts, statements, situations found their way in his work quite naturally, as the fruit of unbridled inspiration; they arose understandably from a youthful *brio*, playfulness and boldness in the author himself; they are, if I may quote Dylan Thomas, "A portrait of the artist as a young dog". More often than not the stories, in which the bizarre element is very evident, can be found in that group of narratives, which Čechov himself did not include in his collected works and which form a part of his literary inheritance. The genuinely grotesque-bizarre stories are published under the penname 'Čechonte', a pseudonym rather bizarre in itself, at least for Russian ears.

Quite frequently the stories, containing bizarre elements, are written in the first person singular or plural, e.g. "The Crooked Mirror", "At Sea", "The Confession", "The Only Remedy", "At a Spiritualist Seance", "The Ninny", "A Charitable Publican", "The Guardian", "From the Reminiscences of an Idealist", "The Dream", etc. They are often provided with a sub-title in the way of "A Christmas Story", or "A Psychological Etude", or "Lament of a Ruined Man". In all these cases the bizarre character of the story is evoked by a peculiar blend of mystification, exaggeration and the deadly serious tone of the story-teller. A story like "At Sea" for instance, bearing the sub-title "A Sailor's Story", deals with anything but life at sea; this tale gives a perfect demonstration of the method of disguise and it leaves a peculiar impression of bewilderment and oppression with the reader, who at the same time feels inclined to laugh the whole thing off. The bizarre in stories of this kind, as also in "On Christmas Eve", an early story, written in a pseudo-romantic vein, and in quite a few others is realized by way of a subtle mockery of the 'terrible'; the element of horror is played with, rather flippantly sometimes, with the effect that horror becomes funny. Most of these stories have a definite point, with a surprising denouement, which does not however solve a problem or a mystery, but intensifies the comical effect of the narrative. Upon

finishing his play "Ivanov", Čechov wrote in a letter to his brother
Aleksandr: "This is the first play I wrote, ergo — I was bound to
make mistakes. The subject is complicated and not stupid. Every act
I end just like my stories: throughout the whole act everything goes
on peacefully and smoothly, but towards the end I give the spectator
a punch on the nose." [4] It is in this "punch on the nose", in this sudden
uncovering of "green-painted buttocks", that the typical bizarre element
in Čechov's early work is revealed and it is not without reason that his
second collection of stories, which Čechov published in 1886, bore the
title "Motley Stories". Nor is it fortuitous that Čechov did not include
in this collection any work of his hand that had appeared under his
own name in the literary magazine "New Times", work that he wanted
to save for 'a more important publication'. Seen against the background
of Čechov's later, much more complicated and serious output, we can
understand that the author at the height of his creative powers felt
rather reluctant to include certain of his bizarre 'trifles' (as he calls
them) in his collected works, although Čechov's harsh judgment seems
to us unwarranted: in their class these stories are priceless.

As I pointed out, the bizarre gradually disappears in Čechov's later
work, or rather, it loses its grotesque aspect and approaches more and
more that particular attitude towards things, which we call the absurd.
Here it must be stated at once, however, that the absurd as such in
Čechov's art is always treated merely incidentally, never programmatical-
ly, dogmatically or from the platform of a certain philosophy. For Čechov
life as such (existence) is neither absurd nor intelligible. The absurd
elements in his stories should therefore not be confused with the absurd
as idea. The absurd is the confrontation with the irrational; it is, what
in relation to human judgment is considered as unreasonable. If we
think of a scientist, whose knowledge in a certain field of science is
unique and of immeasurable value to mankind, who suddenly dies in a
car-accident, we may speak of an absurd occurrence, the absurd in this
case consisting in the fact that such a tremendous wealth of knowledge
and experience can be destroyed within a fraction of a second. Death
in its finality is bizarre in so far as it causes bewilderment, it is absurd
in so far as we consider it unreasonable. Čechov had a wonderful
feeling for the whole scale of subtle shades between the bizarre and the
absurd in life and death. The long standing controversy, whether
Čechov was an optimist or a pessimist, with ardent partisans on both
sides, loses its meaning, when we realize that Čechov, like every
sensitive artist, was torn between two contrary insights: that the world,
or life as such, is unreasonable and at the same time, that man cannot

---

[4] PSSP XIII 372.

leave off trying to find a reasonable explanation for this world, or, in the words of Albert Camus, this philosopher of the absurd (whose own death can stand as an example of absurdity): "Ce monde en lui-même n'est pas raisonnable... Mais ce qui est absurde, c'est la confrontation de cet irrationnel et de ce désir éperdu de clarté dont l'appel résonne au plus profond de l'homme." [5] Čechov's dithyrambic dreams of a better life in the future, expressed in his last plays and in some of his stories, are no proof of his „optimism", but only of his desperate desire to find a solution to the problem of the antagonism, existing between absurd reality and rational ideality, his desire to bring about a peace between life as it is lived: — an apparently bizarre and senseless undertaking, — and life as it could be projected in the mind: — beauty, justice and harmony. On the other hand, if Čechov were convinced that such a peace would a priori be impossible, that the search for a reasonable explanation of the world is an enterprise, foredoomed to failure, then we might be justified in calling him a pessimist; but he never made such a statement, on the contrary: somewhere, at some time in the future the solution will be found, he says. This is not optimism, but the firm conviction that life itself generates hope. Converted to secular values, we may compare Čechov's faith with the 'Credo quia absurdum' of Tertullian, philosophically speaking the most optimistic statement ever made, if we put the stress on the 'credo', but at the same time the most pessimistic one, if we realize that we can never overcome the absurd, that we, as long as there is life, shall never be able to say: we believe in it, because it is reasonable. In other words: that faith can never be replaced by knowledge, Čechov's dream of happiness 'after two hundred years' is nothing else than this *désir éperdu de clarté*, of which Camus speaks. In fact, hope and expectation are blended so masterfully in Čechov's art with hopelessness and despair, the technique of evoking bizarre effects by letting hope clash on despondency is handled so skilfully, that we can say without hesitation that here we find the clue to that unique fascination, which emanates from his work and the spell it exercises on the reader. A perfect demonstration of this we find in stories like "Dreams" (1886), or "Happiness" (1887), in "Peasants" (1897), "In the Ravine" (1900) and many others. In the story "Happiness" an old shepherd is telling about the treasures, hidden, according to legend, somewhere in the vast Russian steppe. A young shepherd listens attentively to the old man's stories. "But, if you find the treasure, what are you going to do with it?", he asks in the end. The old man does not know; all through his long life he has dreamed of finding one of these legendary treasures, but the thought, what to

---

[5] Albert Camus, *Le mythe de Sisyphe*, Paris 1942, p. 37.

do with it, has never occurred to him: that was not important. The young man also starts to wonder at the curious fact that only old men and women were so interested in these treasures, only the old kept constantly talking about them. At last the young shepherd falls silent and thinks about all the things he has heard in the course of the summernight. "He was not interested so much in happiness in itself, which he did not need, and which he could not comprehend, as in the fantastic, the fairytale side of human happiness...", concludes Čechov.

One of Čechov's notions of the bizarre, — and probably one of the most important ones, — is that in an apparently hopeless life there is still hope, that, as I said before, life itself generates hope. That, if there is seemingly no way out, — there *is* nevertheless a way out: by being interested, fully, humanly interested in "the fantastic, fairytale side" of every situation. To the question of what life *means*, Čechov had no other answer than: it is what it is, as in "Three Sisters", when Maša asks: "Isn't there some meaning?" and Tuzenbach answers: "Meaning?.. Look out there, it's snowing. What's the meaning of that?" 6 In the same play the final conclusion of Andrej, when Čebutykin asks him: "What about your wife?" is: "My wife is my wife". 7 But even if every life is condemned to end in failure, even if it has many terrible aspects, it still is hopeful, because it is life, because it can be seen and felt and tasted and experienced, because it can be told. In the story "Peasants" this hope, this life, this Čechovian conception of indestructible continuation is impersonated in the little girl Saša, who as an innocent witness of poverty and misery wanders through the whole story with eyes to see and to bear witness. The little girl is not a judge, she just observes and sees. The fact that in life there are eyes to see the injustice, the absurdity, is enough: this is all the hope there is. Well, and this is precisely the case with Čechov himself: *he just sees*. And to see, really to see, with inquisitive, childlike eyes, means to discover the hidden relationships in life, to reveal its fairytale side. In many of Čechov's stories it is the child, or the grown-up with the childlike mind that sees in this manner: it is the child and the artist, who possess this talent for discovering. And again, it is children and artists who have the genuine taste for the bizarre, the feeling for the absurd; it is they also, who can recreate it, because playfulness is an intrinsic part of their being, they represent the *homo ludens* with his taste for freedom. In Čechov's first long story "The Steppe" (1888) it is through the eyes of the little boy Egoruška that the steppe and life in it are recreated. In the story "In Exile" (1892)

---

6 Anton Chehov, *Three Plays,* transl. by Elisaveta Fen, London 1953, p. 126.
7 Id. p. 162.

it is the poor, illiterate Tartar with the mind of a child, who understands and grasps the 'hidden relationships' and stammers the truth in his broken Russian: "The gentleman is a good soul, very good, and you are a beast, you are bad! The gentleman is alive and you are dead... God made man that he should be alive, that he should have happiness, sorrow, grief, and you want nothing, so you are not alive, but a stone! A stone wants nothing and so do you...". [8]

When comparing the bizarre in Čechov's work with the bizarre in Dostoevskij, we find some striking differences in their approach, both in technique and its application. In the great novels of Dostoevskij the bizarre element is mainly demonstrated in some of the secondary characters and they are always slices of enlarged humanity. Mentally, intellectually, the reader believes in a captain Lebjadkin ("Evil Spirits"), in a Lebedev ("The Idiot") and queer characters like these, although they possess a reality, built up out of isolated psychological components and the bizarre in them lies in their psychological hyperbolism. Lebedev in "The Idiot" is a vulgar scoundrel and a drunk, but at the same time a man, who prays at night for the salvation of the unfortunate comtesse Du Barry; he is a specialist in the exegesis of the Apocalypse, and in some casual, enigmatic remarks he gives a clue to the main theme of the whole novel. In the hundreds of characters in Čechov's stories not one is in this sense 'enlarged' and hyperbolic; they always stay human in every respect; the bizarre with them, — even with the queerest characters we meet in his plays, — does not appear so much in what they are, as well in what they do. Looking for the bizarre in Čechov's work, we do not find it in the characters, but in their situation, in their mutual relationships. The reason for this may be found in the fact that Čechov's characters nearly all are 'whole', while Dostoevskij's characters are practically all 'split personalities', or combined doubles; they are dramas, tragedies *in themselves,* while Čechov's people through their interrelationship create tragedies and dramas *amongst themselves.* Čechov's characters long for things they do not possess (Moscow, talent, love, gooseberries), or for what they are not and cannot be (famous, active, energetic) and the author knows how to uncover the bizarre element in such hopeless longing: in this respect the epithet of "a cruel talent" could be given to Čechov also! But Dostoevskij's heroes are both mean and noble, both evil and good, both vulgar and highminded; alternatively the one or the other quality breaks out and suppresses the opposite impulse. Therefore the bizarre with Dostoevskij is one of inner conflict and of being; with Čechov of outer conflict and of situation. In 1886 Čechov wrote in a letter to

[8] The Stories of Anton Tchekov, ed. by Robert N. Linscott, N.Y. 1932, p. 180.

his brother Aleksandr: "Heaven forbid that we indulge in the use of commonplaces! The best would be to avoid in your stories the description of the mental state of your heroes altogether. You must try to develop this state out of the actions of your heroes." [9] This is exactly the opposite of Dostoevskij's method, where the action is rather a result, the outcome of the mental state of the hero, of what I call his 'inner conflict'. Nikolaj Čikildeev in the story "Peasants" had to give up his job as a waiter in a Moscow hotel because of ill health and returned with wife and child to his native village, where he slowly withers away. In the famous description of a night at the peasant-cottage Čechov relates, how "Nikolaj, who had not slept all night, got down from the stove. He took his dress-coat out of a green chest, put it on, and going to the window, stroked the sleeves, fingered the coat-tails — and smiled. Then he carefully removed the coat, put it away in the chest, and lay down again." [10] There is no question in Nikolaj's bizarre behaviour in the middle of the night of a description of inner conflict: Nikolaj is quite an ordinary man, but he is placed in an extraordinary situation, a man beyond hope and help, who attires himself at night with the only remaining attributes of his former happiness and dignity. In the given situation the bizarre lies in the fact that the ex-waiter, placed in the position of a parasite on the village-life, caresses as a symbol of liberty and human dignity an object, a waiter's dress-coat, which in fact should stand as a symbol for human servitude and humiliation. [11] It will be clear, from an example like this, that the technique of the bizarre, as used by Čechov in this passage, is quite a far cry from the overt and wanton caprices in his 'Čechonte'-period; now the bizarre comes to us as a technique, subtly handled by a masterhand and only recognizable as bizarre through the intellectual cooperation of the reader.

II

In the confrontation with the bizarre man is conscious of his existence as an enigma. Although Čechov, being through education a man of science himself, believed in the civilizing and beneficent powers of knowledge and enlightenment, his faith was not a blind faith in nineteenth century positivism and progress. Nobody saw clearer than Čechov the danger of the so-called 'intellectualism', nobody realized better the limits of pure rationalist thinking. Stories like e.g. "A Dreary Story" (1889), "Ward No. 6" (1892), or "The Black Monk" (1894) provide ample substance for this contention. Čechov himself was a

---

[9] PSSP XIII 215.
[10] *The Portable Chekhov,* ed. by Avrahm Yarmolinsky, N.Y. 1947, p. 339.
[11] Cf. A. Derman, *O masterstve Čechova,* Moskva 1959, p. 42.

highly intelligent man, a keen observer, capable of putting two and two together in all the phenomena of life. But here he added one element to his intelligence — and in this we recognize his genius, — namely, his readiness to accept, to admit and to tolerate the statement that two and two can be five, at least to grant the possibility of such a statement, were it only as a form of protest. Protest against what? My answer would be: a protest against the *law*.

Amongst the few types of wholly negative characters in the work of Čechov, a prominent place is given to the "man in a shell", of whom it is said that "the only things that were clear to him were Government regulations and newspaper notices in which something was forbidden." [12] This man-in-a-shell type of the intelligentsia, this Belikov, has a close relative in a slightly different hero, one somewhat more sociable and congenial, but likewise inclined to terrorize his neighbourhood: the type of the Von Koren in the story "The Duel" (1891), or his pendant L'vov in the play "Ivanov" (1887-89). They are the personifications of what we may call the 'guardians of duty', 'the pillars of law and order', — men, who are honest, correct, intelligent, but absolutely devoid of imagination, men with no feeling, no taste and no understanding at all for the *bizarre*. Both the story "The Duel" and the play "Ivanov" are built up around three heroes: in "The Duel" this trio is formed by Laevskij, Von Koren, and Samojlenko. In the play "Ivanov" we meet the same trio in the persons of Ivanov, L'vov and Lebedev. The positions of these three types are clear: Laevskij/Ivanov is the man fighting with, and eventually becoming the victim of the bizarre; Von Koren/L'vov is the man who does not admit the existence of the bizarre, while Samojlenko/Lebedev accepts the bizarre as an intrinsic part of life. In the last act of "Ivanov", when Ivanov, a prey to despair and harassed by self-accusations, informs his bride Saša that he cannot marry her, when L'vov walks around as a Nemesis, firmly decided to unmask Ivanov once and for all, then the 'fool' Lebedev, this apparent good-for-nothing, utters some words of plain common sense. In a conversation with his future son-in-law and friend Ivanov it is he, who exclaims: "Look at things simply, as everybody else does! In this world everything is simple. The ceiling is white, the boots are black, sugar is sweet. You love Saša, she loves you. If you love her — stay with her, if you don't love her — go, we won't bear you any malice. It's really as simple as that!" [13]

With Čechov, just as with Shakespeare, we must above all things be attentive to what the 'fool' has to say. The Lebedev-element, this third

---

[12] *The Portable Chekhov,* ed. by Avrahm Yarmolinsky, .NY. 1947, p. 356.
[13] Anton Chehov, *Three Plays,* transl. by Elisaveta Fen, London 1953, p. 251.

aspect of human intelligence, is innocence, presented — as is so often
the case — in the disguise of foolishness. It is the voice of life itself
as it is lived, when we are told: "In this world everything is simple!",
an observation which must sound as the height of absurdity in the ears
of pathetic Ivanovs, caught in a mess of guilt-complexes, or of the
stern L'vovs who want to reduce life to a complicated system of regulations. But what we hear in Lebedev and Samojlenko, apart from a
certain amount of *naïveté,* is the voice of confidence, this utter and
stable confidence that cannot be shaken by all the horrors in the world.
It is Čechov's confidence in the regenerating powers of life. It is the
voice of unassailable innocence in human intellect, of its inviolable
virginity. It is the voice that will be heard "two hundred years from
now..." The Lebedevs and Samojlenko's together with the little girl
in "Peasants", with Lipa in "In the Ravine", with Gusev in the story
of that name, with father Anastasij in "The Letter", with the Tartar in
"In Exile", — these are the ones, of whom I said that they are the
children and artists, who see and accept the bizarre, who are free and
possess the talent for discovering the hidden relationships.

However, it is not Čechov's philosophy or outlook on life, that I am
concerned with here. The problem of the grotesque-bizarre-absurd in
his art is not a philosophical problem, but one of style and technique. I
already pointed out that in the 'Čechonte'- stories the bizarre element
appears to be used as a series of outbursts of youthful spontaneity
rather than a consciously applied literary technique. It was found that
this element gradually disappears in his stories of a later date; whenever we find traces of it, it is used with much restraint and *con
sordino,* the technique is usually applied in the form of a quick, unexpected shifting of various moods. We only need to compare a story
like "At Christmas Time" (1900) with one of the 'Čechonte'-stories to
see the difference in function of the bizarre. At first glance this element
seems to be present in this story as well with the same nonchalant brio
as for instance in "For Stealing Apples" (1880), but soon it becomes
clear that it is used in quite a different technique; while in the early
story the bizarre was nothing but ornament, here it is the canvas, on
which the story is embroidered.

But it is especially in the plays, and most of all in "Uncle Vanja",
"Three Sisters" and "The Cherry Orchard", that we find the technique
of the bizarre applied consciously and deliberately with an eye on the
effect it will produce. The functions of the bizarre as consciously
applied technique are manifold. In the first place there is the function
of *retardation* of the action. A good example can be found in the last
act of "Uncle Vanja". In the stage-directions at the beginning of this
act it says: *On the wall a map of Africa, obviously serving no useful*

purpose here. [14] The 'purpose' of this map, indeed a rather bizarre object in the study of an estate somewhere in the Russian province, becomes clear when Astrov takes his final leave. Astrov is firmly resolved to take his departure and to stay away for a long time to come, but he does not want to go at all. There really is nothing more to be said, but everybody feels the necessity of some remark being made, never mind what, only so that the final moment may be put off. It is then that Astrov walks up to the map of Africa and says: "I suppose down there in Africa the heat must be terrific now!" On this bizarre and quite irrelevant remark of the doctor in the prevailing situation Vanja reacts laconically with the words: "Yes, very likely." [15]

Apart from retardation the above example reveals another function of the bizarre and a very important one too, namely, to give a suggestion of indifference. It is well known, what importance Čechov attached to 'coldness', 'non-attachment' in the creative process. The impact of emotions, of distress, delight, of grief and joy is felt much stronger, when they are suggested and not described. If, in the given situation, Astrov would have said: "How awful to have to leave your people; I don't want to go, but have to, you know!" or something of the kind, the impression on the spectator would be nil, because that would be exactly the thing he had expected. Instead, Astrov says: "I suppose down there in Africa the heat must be terrific now!" and this element of restraint, applied in a scene that is charged with emotions, greatly intensifies the impression on the spectator. The element of the bizarre as a technique to retard the action and restrain the emotions is used frequently by Čechov in his plays.

A third function of the bizarre is the communication of a hidden meaning. This end is often attained by way of an understatement. It may happen that one of the characters makes an apparently nonsensical remark, which stupefies the reader or spectator. In "Three Sisters" the old and doting doctor Čebutykin has the habit of reading aloud from some old newspaper he always carries around with him. In act II, in the midst of a lively conversation on the meaning of happiness, he suddenly, reading from his newspaper, remarks: "Balzac was married at Berdičev". [16] This in the given context seemingly quite senseless remark is repeated twice, showing that the author did not regard it as just a casual interjection by a drunk, but that these words were meant to communicate some hidden message, an allusion to something, which,

---

[14] Anton Chehov, *The Seagull and Other Plays,* transl. by Elisaveta Fen, London 1954, p. 140.

[15] Id., p. 150.

[16] *The Plays of Anton Tchekov,* transl. by Constance Garnett, N.Y. n.d. p. 146.

however, is nowhere explained in the further development of the conversation. But what possible meaning could be concealed in the bizarre observation of an old, dilapidated country-physician, in a play, the action of which takes place around 1900, while the words "Balzac was married at Berdičev", read from a newspaper, point to an event that surely happened before Balzac's death in 1850? The theme of the play is the expectation of happiness: Veršinin projects the 'coming happy life' in the future; the sisters believe that they will find happiness and fulfilment as soon as they will be in Moscow. When we remember that Berdičev is an ugly little bordertown in Western Russia, the remark of Čebutykin becomes meaningful, without losing its bizarre character: it means to say that, if Balzac could find his happiness in such a doghole as Berdičev, it is quite unnecessary to go to Moscow to look for happiness, because it can be found anywhere, and further: why project your dreams of happiness in the future, when we only need to open some old newspaper in order to find ample proof of happiness and fulfilment in the past? The function of the bizarre in this instance is first to stupefy and to shock, to disrupt the logical sequence of thoughts by some eccentric observation, secondly to provide this observation with an undercurrent of deeper meaning. Another example of this technique we find in the long story "The Duel" (the scene, when doctor Samojlenko and Von Koren carry on an animated conversation about the 'superfluous man' Laevskij). In the course of the conversation both get more and more excited. There is a third person in the room, a young deacon, a rather silly man who chuckles and giggles all the time, a man in whom we recognize once more one of these typical Čechovian fools, who are not directly involved in the conflict, but who at unexpected moments come forward with their comments and who, in this respect, have a rather similar function to that of the 'chorus' in the Greek tragedy. When the conversation between Samojlenko and Von Koren reaches its climax and both are about ready to cut each others throat, this little, insignificant deacon suddenly makes the casual observation: "Our Eminence does not travel by coach through his diocese, he always goes on horseback..." and then he compares the bishop in his humility and simplicity with a Biblical character. The interruption had nothing whatsoever to do with the conversation, there was no talk at all about bishops, coaches or horses and to all appearance the deacon's words are out of place and sheer nonsense. Yet it brings the conversation to a sudden stop, the heat of the quarrel has abated and the observation carried a hidden meaning as well: the hint to both hotheaded antagonists to follow the bishop's example and to be more humble.

In "Gooseberries" (1898) Čechov makes the following observation:

"What is terrible in life goes on somewhere behind the scenes..." [17] The bizarre is indeed quite frequently an eruption of the terrible on the smooth surface of common everyday life. Such an eruption takes place in the story "The Murder" (1895), in which the bizarre is an intrinsic part of the whole intrigue and a man is murdered, because during Lent he wanted to help himself at dinner to some oil; the instrument he is killed with is the oil-bottle.

Sometimes Čechov does not leave the bizarre unexplained, but reveals the meaning of it in an exposé, for instance, in "The Lady with the Pet Dog" (1899), in the following fragment: "One evening, coming out of the physicians' club with an official with whom he (the hero) had been playing cards, he could not resist saying: 'If you only knew what a fascinating woman I became acquainted with at Jalta.'" The official has no better reply to this beginning of a lover's confidential confession than the sordid and bizarre words: "Dmitrij Dmitrič! ...You were right this evening: the sturgeon was a bit high!" [18] Whereupon Čechov enters into a long explanation of why the hero was so infuriated by the vulgarity of the official's words.

A further function of the bizarre, — and this mainly in the plays again, — is to emphasize the salient features of certain characters, in other words, to show them in their absurdity. One of the most bizarre characters in Čechov's plays is Solenyj in "Three Sisters", a sinister man, belonging to the family of the 'men-in-a-shell', in so far as meanness and limitations are not only the result of social maladjustment, but also caused by his private inhibitions. He has a very important function in the drama and is, as his name indicates, the salt in the play. His condition of being a potential murderer Solenyj can only cover up by spraying his hands frequently with perfume. Everything he says or does is absurd.

In order to give a note of the bizarre to his characters Čechov often makes use of the attribute of gluttony. Quite a few of his early comical stories are based on this human weakness. But this element also appears in his later stories and in the plays. The official in "The Lady with the Pet Dog" could only think of sturgeon when his partner wanted to talk about his beloved; Piščik, another bizarre character in "The Cherry Orchard" pours all the pills from a pill-box, brought by the valet to madame Ranevskaja, into his hand and eats them... We also hear that during Easter week he had consumed a gallon and a half of cucumbers. [19] Solenyj, in "Three Sisters", referring to Bobik, Nataša's baby, remarks: "If that child were mine, I'd fry him in a frying pan and eat

---

[17] *The Portable Chekhov*, ed. by Avrahm Yarmolinsky, N.Y. 1947, p. 381.
[18] Id., p. 424.
[19] *The Plays of Anton Tchekov*, transl. by Constance Garnett, N.Y. n.d. p. 72.

him," [20] in which words he certainly betrays his radicalism. A little later it appears that he has eaten all the chocolates from a box of sweets on the table. Gaev, in "The Cherry Orchard", frequently takes a box of caramels out of his pocket and sucks one.

Bizarre attributes are often used in drawing a character. Thus one notices Gaev's passion for billiards in "The Cherry Orchard" and his use of technical terms of the game, mostly in situations when he is confused and bewildered. Bizarre attributes, used in drawing Maša's character in "The Sea-gull", are the black dress she wears and her opening-line in the play: "I am in mourning for my life"; [21] in the case of Sorin, in the same play, it is his habit to use stock-expressions like: "and all that", "and all the rest of it", "and so on, and so forth", [22] which are all that is left of *l'homme qui a voulu*, the man, who in his youth had dreamt of becoming a literary man — and didn't... The pathos of an utterly lonely woman, the governess Šarlotta Ivanovna in "The Cherry Orchard", is accentuated by her bizarre talent to amuse the company with card tricks; equally bizarre is the way she makes her appearance in the first act with a little dog on a line and introduces herself with the words: "My dog eats nuts too". [23]

All this shows that in Čechov's plays the element of the bizarre both helps to build up a character and aids in preparing the surprise moment in the development of the action. Once they are firmly established as "queer characters", their quasi irrelevant observations cause a break in the dialogue. And here we touch upon one of the principal aspects of the bizarre, lying in the fact that, while all these observations and odd demeanours should normally bring about a certain bewilderment or at least some response in the others, this is not the case: more often than not there is no reaction at all, as if the others did not exist, as if the words were spoken in a void, as if all those persons were living in a vacuum, in other words: the bizarre is accepted, or rather tolerated, but not reacted upon. When in "The Cherry Orchard" the servantgirl Dunjaša, anxious to pour out her heart to her young mistress, says to Anja: "Epichodov, the clerk, made me a proposal just after Easter", [24] the answer is: "I've lost all my hairpins." When in the second act of this play Šarlotta Ivanovna all of a sudden starts to complain about her fate and says: "Always alone, alone, nobody belonging to me... and who I am, and why I'm on earth, I don't know", [25] there is no

---

[20] Id., p. 147.
[21] Id., p. 3.
[22] Id., p. 46.
[23] Id., p. 64.
[24] Ibidem.
[25] Id., p. 80.

response from the others. When in the third act of "Three Sisters" Čebutykin has broken the clock and Irina says: "That was mother's clock", the old doctor declares in drunkenness: "Perhaps... Well, if it was hers, it was..." — and then continues: "What are you staring at? Nataša has got a little affair on with Protopopov, and you don't see it... You sit here and see nothing, while Nataša has a little affair on with Protopopov..."[26] The only reaction to this grave accusation comes from Veršinin, who says: "Yes" and then immediately resumes his conversation about his own affairs. Time and again we hear in Čechov's stories and plays the desperate complaint: "To whom shall I tell my grief?", which is used as motto in the story "Misery" (1886), — but there is no response and by this frequently used technique Čechov succeeds in producing that oppressive atmosphere of human loneliness which is so typical for his art; the inability of people to understand each other, their complete lack of interest and attention is the core of all tragedy. Human coldness, indifference and careless cruelty — these form the main subject and the leading theme of many of Čechov's stories and plays.

Finally, in some of the plays, especially in "Three Sisters", Čechov succeeds in attaining a bizarre effect by frequently putting quotations from other writers in the mouth of his characters. In many cases these quotations have a definite function in the play, both to reveal a character and to create a certain "mood", to evoke an atmosphere. Two of the best known of these functional quotations in "Three Sisters" are: "A green oak grows by a curving shore, and round that oak hangs a golden chain..."[27] which are the opening-lines of Puškin's poem "Ruslan and Ljudmila", and: "He had no time to say 'Oh, oh!', before that bear had struck him low...",[28] two lines from Krylov's fable "The Peasant and the Farmhand", the first quotation being used by Maša, the second one by Solenyj, and not just once, but several times on appropriate occasions, thus becoming something like motives, played by solo-instruments in a symphonic work. Apart from literary quotations Čechov uses quotations, taken from actual life. An example of a quotation from life can be found in a letter by Ol'ga Knipper to Anton Pavlovič, written in 1900, in reply to a complaint of the author that he was becoming bald. In this letter Ol'ga Knipper writes: "I shall give you a fine recipe for falling hair. Take half a bottle of methylated spirit and dissolve in it two ounces of naphtaline, then rub the skin with this lotion..." Ol'ga Knipper took her recipe so seriously that she hastened to write to Čechov a few days later that she had made a

---

[26] Id., p. 161.
[27] Anton Chehov, *Three Plays*, transl. by Elisaveta Fen, London 1953, p. 98.
[28] Id., p. 99.

mistake in it: it should not be two ounces of naphtaline, but only half an ounce. But Čechov had already used the original passage in "Three Sisters", first act, where he lets the '*fool*' Čebutykin read the recipe from his newspaper. [29] The motive for the wellknown Tra-ta-ta conversation, — possibly the most mysterious and original 'love-talk' in literature, — between Maša and Veršinin at the end of the third act of "Three Sisters" is likewise taken from real life and based on an actual experience Čechov had in a restaurant. These examples, — and the notes in Čechov's notebooks could easily provide further ample material, — show, how keen an eye Čechov had for the bizarre, how much value he attached to such phenomena and how anxious he was to apply this material in his art. I wonder, whether it is only a matter of coincidence that Čechov's biographers managed to dig up such a remarkable variety of bizarre incidents in the life of the author. If we may believe one of his biographers, N. Telešov, the bizarre did not even leave Čechov on his deathbed: in the evening of July 15th 1904 in Badenweiler the doctor had ordered the sick man to drink a glass of champagne. Anton Pavlovič took the glass, remarked to his wife: "I have not tasted champagne in a long time", drank the glass to the bottom, lay down on his left side and died. "The oppressive silence of the night, — Telešov tells us, — was only disturbed by a large nightmoth that had flown in through the open window... After the doctor had gone, in the complete silence and stuffiness of the summernight, suddenly, with a terrific blow, the cork shot out of the half finished champagne bottle..." [30]

---

[29] Id., p. 96. Cf. *Teatr,* ežemesjačnyj žurnal dramaturgii i teatra, Moskva 1960, I: A. Vladimirskaja, *Zametki na poljach.*

[30] N. Telešov, *Zapiski pisatelja,* Moskva 1950, pp. 86-87.

DMITRIJ TSCHIŽEWSKIJ

ÜBER DIE STELLUNG ČECHOVS INNERHALB DER
RUSSISCHEN LITERATURENTWICKLUNG

I.

Čechov hat noch keinen festen Platz in der russischen Literaturgeschichte. Natürlich rechnet man ihn oft zu den „Realisten" wobei man
dann aus chronologischen Gründen gezwungen ist, ihn neben solche
Epigonen des Realismus wie V. Korolenko und D. Mamin-Sibirjak zu
stellen. Oder soll man ihn zusammen mit solchen Vertretern der neuen
realistischen Strömungen wie Maksim Gor'kij nennen? Oder ihn gar
in der Reihe der Vor- und Frühsymbolisten unterbringen? Eine solche
Einreihung eines Dichters in eine bestimmte literarische Gruppe ist
natürlich nicht die wichtigste Aufgabe der Literaturgeschichte und
ist auch nicht unbedingt notwendig. Es ist aber keinesfalls belanglos zu
erfahren, ob sich Čechov in einer näheren Beziehung zu einer literarischen Strömung seiner Zeit befand, oder ob er als Alleingänger seinen
dichterischen Weg durchschritt.

Čechov hat bekanntlich den jungen und kleinen Dichtern vielfach ge-
holfen und über sie günstige und freundliche Urteile abgegeben;
manche von diesen Urteilen erwecken jetzt unsere Verwunderung und
lassen uns entweder an der Sicherheit des literarischen Urteils Čechovs
oder an seiner Aufrichtigkeit zweifeln. In manchen Fällen aber gab
Čechov den werdenden Dichtern in der Form eines anerkennenden Urteils doch ziemlich scharf formulierte Verbesserungsvorschläge. Und
nicht selten begegnen wir in seinem Briefwechsel einer sehr scharfen
und pessimistischen Beurteilung der ganzen zeitgenössischen Literatur.
So z.B.: „In unseren Werken gibt es keinen Alkohol, der hätte trunken
machen und mitreißen können [...]. Wer von meinen Altersgenossen,
d.h. Menschen im Alter von 30-45 Jahren gab der Welt auch nur einen
einzigen Tropfen Alkohol? Sind denn Korolenko, Nadson und alle
heutigen Bühnendichter nicht bloß Limonade? [...]. Für unsereiner
ist diese Zeit mürbe, sauer und langweilig, und wir selbst sind sauer
und langweilig [...]. Erinnern Sie sich daran, daß alle Dichter, die wir
als groß oder einfach als gut bezeichnen und die uns trunken machen,
einen gemeinsamen und sehr wesentlichen Zug haben: sie gehen in
eine bestimmte Richtung und rufen uns auf, ebenfalls dorthin zu
gehen [...]. Wir haben aber weder nähere noch weitere Ziele, und
unsere Seelen sind flach und leer (darin „chot' šarom pokati"). Politik
haben wir nicht, an eine Revolution glauben wir nicht, es gibt [für uns]
keinen Gott, wir haben keine Angst vor Gespenstern [...], wer aber

nichts will, auf nichts hofft, keine Angst hat, kann kein Künstler sein".
Dieser Brief aus dem Jahre 1892 (an Suvorin vom 25. Nov. 1892)
enthält noch mehr: er enthält eine mehr oder weniger durchsichtige
Anspielung darauf, daß auch V. Garšin, daß ebenso die Dichter, die
„ihre Leere mit den alten Fetzen, etwa mit den Ideen der sechziger
Jahre, vollstopfen wollen", und auch die noch lebenden Vertreter der
älteren Generation, wie D. Grigorovič (geb. 1822), die Leser nicht
„trunken machen können"...

Diese vernichtende Beurteilung der damaligen russischen Literatur
ist viel schärfer als die D. S. Merežkovskijs in seinen programmatischen
Aufsätzen, die als Broschüre im nächsten Jahre erschienen („Über die
Ursachen des Verfalls und die neuen Strömungen der russischen Literatur") : da Merežkovskij alle in der Broschüre erwähnten Dichter mit
lobenden Prädikaten bedenkt, kann man jetzt kaum verstehen, was
die damaligen literarischen Kreise — außer dem kühnen Titel — an
dieser inhaltlich so bescheidenen Schrift beunruhigen konnte. Čechov
stellt allerdings keine Prognose und bietet keine Programme. Er verstand wohl zu gut, daß der Wunsch, trunken zu werden oder andere
trunken zu machen, noch keinen Tropfen „Alkohol" hervorbringen
kann...

Der Broschüre Merežkovskijs folgten im nächsten Jahr (1894) die
kleinen Gedichtsammlungen *Russkie simvolisty,* die erst die Empörung
der Leser und Kritiker (gar eines solchen wie Vladimir Solov'jev, der
ja selbst zur Entstehung der symbolistischen Dichtkunst beigetragen
hat) verständlich machte. Aber bereits seit einem Jahrzehnt stand
Čechov als Neuerer und somit als gefährlicher Zerstörer des damals
gültigen Kanons der Poetik im Zentrum der Angriffe fast aller an-
erkannten und maßgeblichen Kritiker. Denn fast bis 1900 sah man in
seinen Werken einen völligen Bruch mit dem allein seligmachenden
Realismus. So dachten nicht nur die Gegner Čechovs, sondern auch
seine Freunde, so z.B. Gor'kij, der sich damals keinesfalls als „Realist"
fühlte. Er schrieb an Čechov: „Wissen Sie, was Sie tun? Sie töten den
Realismus und Sie werden ihn bald erledigen — endgültig und für
lange Zeit. Diese Form hat ihre Zeit überlebt — das ist Tatsache!...
Sie werden den Realismus abmurksen (*ukokošite*). Ich freue mich
außerordentlich darüber. Genug! Soll er sich zum Teufel scheren! Für
die Zeit, die gekommen ist, ist das Heldenhafte nötig: alle wollen etwas
Anregendes, Grelles, etwas, das dem Leben nicht ähnlich, sondern
besser und schöner als das Leben wäre. Jetzt ist es unbedingt erforder-
lich, daß die heutige Literatur das Leben etwas verschönere, und wenn
sie das zu tun beginnt — wird auch das Leben schöner sein, das
heißt, die Menschen werden flotter, lichter leben" (1900).
Die letzteren Worte deutet allerdings das damalige dichterische Pro-

gramm von Gor'kij selbst. Mit dem Schaffen Čechovs hat aber dieses
Programm nichts zu tun. Vom Verfasser einer „Langweiligen Geschichte", der schon vor zehn Jahren zwei Reihen seiner Erzählungen
unter den Titeln „In der Abenddämmerung" (*V sumerkach,* 1887) und
„Finstere Menschen" (*Chmurye ljudi,* 1890 — kann wohl auch als
„Mürrische Menschen" übersetzt werden) publiziert hatte, konnte man
kaum erwarten, daß er das Leben „schöner", in helleren Farben malen
werde... Gor'kij, damals erfolgreicher literarischer Draufgänger,
konnte sich wohl kaum vorstellen, daß die Zukunft anderen als seinen
eigenen literarischen Idealen gehören werde. Er hat aber mindestens
richtig gespürt, daß sich Čechov von den realistischen Schilderern der
„Wirklichkeit" grundsätzlich unterschied. Worin? — diese Frage
konnte Gor'kij mit der ihm eigenen geradlinigen Primitivität des Den-
kens kaum richtig formulieren, — vielleicht auch nicht verstehen...

2.

War Čechov selbst sich im Klaren, daß er die alten Wege nicht gehen
konnte und nicht gehen durfte, war es auch Gor'kij klar, daß Čechov
in der russischen Literatur etwas Neues begann und etwas altes
„tötete", so war das auch denjenigen Kritikern klar, die die dichterischen Ideale des Realismus vertraten. Wie bereits gesagt, griffen
sie Čechov als einen gefährlichen Neuerer an, der ihre Weltanschauung
nicht teilte, und durch seine Werke der Literatur neue Wege — die für
Anhänger des Realismus nur Irrwege sind — wies. Das haben die
damaligen Kritiker auch mit derselben groben Offenheit gesagt, mit
der sie gewohnheitsgemäß und ergebnislos auch Dostoevskij, L. Tolstoj,
Leskov und Fet Jahrzehnte lang bekämpft hatten.

An erster Stelle ist der einflußreichste Kritiker jener Zeit, der auch
Literaturhistorische Arbeiten schrieb, A. M. Skabičevskij zu nennen.
Die „Bunten Erzählungen" Čechovs empfing er in *Severnyj Vestnik*
(1886 Nr. 6) mit einer Besprechung, die Čechov lange nicht verschmer-
zen konnte. Der Kritiker beurteilt die kleinen Erzählungen Čechovs
als „Clowniaden", als „Kinderklapper" (*pobrjakuški*), als „Bagatellen", die der Verfasser schrieb, „ohne über den Inhalt seiner
Erzählungen nachzudenken", und vor allem zählte Skabičevskij den
jungen Novellisten zu solchen „Zeitungsschriftstellern", die damit
enden, daß sie „völlig vergessen irgendwo unter einem Zaun sterben"... In der Zeitschrift *Nov'* nannte man im selben Jahr diese Erzählungen „Delirium eines Wahnsinnigen". Skabičevskij und andere
Kritiker hatten damals allerdings die Jugendwerke Čechovs vor sich.
Aber nicht anders wurden damals und später solche Werke wie „Die
Steppe", „Duell", „Bauern" empfangen, und selbst in den letzten Le-
bensjahren Čechovs lehnten die „berufenen" Stellen nicht nur seine

Dramen ab, sondern erteilten dem Verfasser ungebetene Ratschläge, wie er solche Bühnenwerke wie „Die Möwe" und „Onkel Vanja" „verbessern" solle. Einige Blicke in diese Urteile sind vielleicht doch lohnend.

Nach Erscheinen der „Steppe" warf der populärste Publizist N. K. Michajlovskij Čechov in einem Brief vor, daß er sich daran gewöhne „fragmentarisch" zu schreiben, „Sie gehen spazieren, unbekannt wohin und unbekannt wozu" (Februar 1888); die Zeitschrift *Russkaja Mysl'* bezeichnete dieselbe schöne Novelle als „inhaltslos" und „unfruchtbar", „man weiß nicht einmal, wozu dieses Stück geschrieben ist", der Stil sei „eintönig und langweilig", die Erzählung enthalte „weder Gedanken noch klare Bilder, weder Psychologie noch Handlung (*fabula*), nicht einmal ethnographisches Interesse — allein Plastik" (? was der Rezensent unter diesem Wort versteht, bleibt allerdings sein Geheimnis). Eine eingehende Kritik von E. Obolenskij (*Russkoe Bogatstvo* 1888) konkretisiert die Vorwürfe der Leser: sie möchten „Beschreibungen" lesen und finden nur Bilder, — das Bild der Steppe „ermangelt im großen Ganzen der Farben, als ob es nur mit dem Bleistift und in bloß zwei Farben entworfen wäre". Die Schilderung des Sonnenaufgangs bestehe nur aus einzelnen Strichen: die „violette Ferne" und die „gelb-goldenen Streifen", die durch die Steppe liefen, sei alles, was dem Leser statt der Beschreibung (die man etwa bei Turgenev finden könnte) Čechov bietet. Das Bild wird noch durch einzelne Züge bereichert, wie die Erwähnung der „braun-gelben Hügel" und der „geröteten" Steppenpflanzen. Der Kritiker bemängelt die Schilderung des Hintergrundes dieser einzelnen Farbflecken... Der Maler I. Repin erinnert sich (*Dalekoe blizkoe*, 1953), daß er selbst und mehrere andere Hörer der damals in einem kleinen Kreise vorgelesenen Novelle „Die Steppe" diese „sujetlos" und „inhaltsleer" fanden, — „keine Einheit, keine Idee".

Ende 1889 erscheinen einige nicht nur negative, sondern direkt verächtliche Urteile über die „Langweilige Geschichte".

1891 veröffentlicht Čechov die für seine Entwicklung so wichtigen Novellen, wie „Duell" und „Die Ehefrau" (*Žena*). Beide werden von den negativen Urteilen der Kritiker überschüttet: zu diesen Kritikern gehört wiederum Skabičevskij, aber auch der Moskauer Prof. I. I. Ivanov und der Romanschriftsteller J. Jasinskij (= Maksim Belinskij).

Eine rein negative Beurteilung der „Bauern" (*Mužiki*) gab später N. Michajlovskij (*Russkoe Bogatstvo* 1897, 6); allerdings konnten auch nicht sehr verständnisvolle Leser leicht merken, daß die Feder des Kritikers von seinen sozial-politischen Ansichten geführt wurde: die pessimistische Schilderung des russischen Dorfes und seiner Bewohner konnte dem führenden Ideologen der *narodniki* kaum gefallen. Daß die Sozial-Demokraten in der Novelle eine Bestätigung ihrer Ansichten über die Psychologie des Bauerntums fanden, konnte den Verfasser kaum trösten.

Auch noch 1901 begegnen uns negative Urteile über die jetzt über-arbeitete alte Novelle „Nachts" (zunächst erschien sie unter dem Titel *V more* bereits 1883), freilich vielleicht nur deshalb, weil Čechov sie in der Sammelschrift der Symbolisten *Severnye Cvety* veröffent-lichte.

Vielleicht noch trauriger ist die Geschichte der Bühnenwerke Čechovs. Daß „Ivanov" 1887 fast durchfiel, ist bekannt; einzelne negative Rezensionen waren weniger kennzeichnend als der Besuch des bekannten Bühnendichters Viktor Krylov, der Čechov vorschlug, das Stück zu verbessern unter der Bedingung, daß Krylov als Mitverfasser gelten solle.

„Die Möwe" wurde 1896 von einem Petersburger Theater-Ausschuß abgelehnt. Zu dem Ausschuß gehörten der erfolgreiche Bühnendichter A. A. Potechin (1829-1908), der bekannte Übersetzer und frühere Professor der europäischen Literaturgeschichte P. I. Vejnberg, und der Prof. der russischen Literaturgeschichte an der Petersburger Uni-versität I. A. Šljapkin. Ihr ablehnendes Urteil ist erhalten. Das Theaterstück leide „an wesentlichen Mängeln". Dazu gehörten zunächst der „Symbolismus" oder „Ibsenismus", die durch das ganze Werk hindurchgehen und die man „gar nicht brauchte". Die „Möwe" Čechovs erinnert den Rezensenten an „Die Wildente" Ibsens. Die Charakteristik Treplevs ist „unsinnig" (*nelepa*), die Charakteristiken Arkadinas und Trigorins „ärmlich". Man merke die unaufmerksame Arbeit des Ver-fassers, „einige Szenen sind aufs Papier zufällig geworfen ohne eine strenge Verbindung mit dem Ganzen und ohne dramatische Notwendig-keit". Auch nach den Aufführungen in Petersburg und Moskau er-schienen einige noch schärfere Urteile: J. Jasinskij bezeichnete das Stück als „chaotisch und wild" und „einfach Unsinn" (*dič*); man hielt das Stück auch für unmoralisch, schlecht aufgebaut, inhaltslos und lang-weilig… Allerdings versuchten manche Verehrer Čechovs „Die Möwe" in der Presse zu verteidigen. Die meisten beschränkten sich aber dar-auf, ihre positive Meinung dem Verfasser brieflich mitzuteilen…

Aber auch die späteren Theaterwerke Čechovs fanden geteilte Auf-nahme. „Onkel Vanja" wurde 1899 von dem Theater-Ausschuß, des-sen Mitglieder die einflußreichsten Moskauer Professoren der Literatur-geschichte, N. Storoženko, Aleksej Veselovskij und I. I. Ivanov waren (ihre negative Charakteristik in den Erinnerungen Andrej Belyjs entspricht keinesfalls ihre damaligen Stellung im russischen Leben), begutachtet. Der Ausschuß lehnte die Aufführung an der Moskauer

Bühne (*Malyj teatr*) entschieden ab. Das Stück durfte nur „nach Änderungen zum zweiten Male dem Ausschuß eingereicht werden", denn literarisch wäre das Stück voll von „Mängeln". „Unverständlich" oder „unmotiviert" seien verschiedene Worte und Handlungen der Helden, besonders des „Onkel Vanja" selbst, der Charakter der Heldin (Elena Andreevna) solle „mehr geklärt" werden, denn ihre Gestalt werde „kein Interesse bei den Zuschauer hervorrufen können", vor allem aber sollten die „Längen" beseitigt werden.

Auch die Besprechungen des letzten Bühnenwerkes Čechovs waren geteilt und zum Teil voll von Missverständnissen. Waren seine ersten Theaterwerke unverständlich, weil sie stilistisch zu neu waren, so fand man das Thema des „Kirschgartens" „zu alt". Man verstand das Stück als „Tragoedie des Adels, der das Opfer des Großbauertums (*kulačestvo*) wird", — dieses Thema, „die Verarmung" (*oskudenie*) des russischen Adels, fand wirklich schon früher einige Darsteller, z.B. S. Terpigorev-Atava (1841-1895), — die Kritiker merkten aber nicht, daß das Theaterwerk Čechovs vor allem *dichterisch* bedeutend und originell ist!

Diese Geschichte des mißverstandenen Dichters könnte man fortsetzen. Für uns ist aber hier von Bedeutung, daß die Kritiker und gerade die Verfasser der ablehnenden Beurteilungen doch manche wesentliche Züge des Čechovschen Stils bemerkt und, wenn auch unbeholfen, hervorgehoben haben.

3.

Čechov kam bereits in den 80-er Jahren zum Bewußtsein, daß er in der Literatur „neue Wege" bahnte. „Alles, was ich geschrieben habe, wird in 5-10 Jahren vergessen sein; aber die Wege, die ich bahne, werden unverändert erhalten (*cely i nevredimy*) bleiben — darin liegt mein einziges Verdienst" (an Lazarev-Gruzinskij, am 20. Okt. 1888). Von den früheren Gönnern und Verehrern Čechovs hat aber, wie es scheint, keiner die Eigenart seiner Dichtung bemerkt, jedenfalls keiner davon in seinen brieflichen oder gedruckten Äußerungen gesprochen. Am kennzeichnendsten sind die Bemerkungen L. Tolstojs, der 1889 die Erzählungen Čechovs in seinem Tagebuch als „hübsche Bagatellen" bezeichnet (*chorošen'kie veščicy*; am 15. März) und nach zwei Tagen bei der weiteren Lektüre sie nur als „schlecht, unbedeutend" (*nechorošo, ničtožno*; am 17. März) bezeichnen zu können glaubt. Aber bereits 1890 nennt Tolstoj Čechov „eine große Begabung" (*krupnyj talant*) und zwar neben Maupassant... Wie man aus späteren uns bekannten Äußerungen Tolstojs ersehen kann, hat er Čechov, wie auch die meisten Dichter, vor allem nach dem ideologischen Gehalt ihrer Werke zu beurteilen vermocht... „Čechov weiß nicht immer, was er will". „Čechov hat oft keine Idee, keine Ganzheit, man weiß nicht, wofür das geschrieben ist"... Vor allem Čechovs Theaterwerke lehnt Tolstoj ab: „Die Möwe" sei nur „wertloser Unsinn" (*vzdor, ničego ne stojaščij*); über den „Onkel Vanja" ist Tolstoj „empört", wie es scheint, vor allem deshalb, weil die Helden des Stückes „Nichtstuer" und unmoralische Menschen sind. Auch neben den vielen Erzählungen Čechovs, die Tolstoj schätzt, gibt es solche wie „Die Bauern", — diese Erzählung bezeichnet Tolstoj als „eine Sünde gegen das Volk..."

Nur der alte und literarisch damals nicht mehr sehr aktive literarische Feinschmecker D. Grigorovič (1822-1899) ist früh auf Čechov aufmerksam geworden, aber er lobte seine Werke nicht nur in unbestimmten Ausdrücken, sondern betonte auch vielfach, was er an diesen Werken bemerkenswert finde: die ausgezeichnete Bearbeitung der Einzelheiten und die Schilderungen der Personen und Landschaften eben durch diese Einzelheiten und Kleinigkeiten. Grigorovič bemerkte eine Erzählung Čechovs im Sommer 1885 („*Eger'* ") in der sonst völlig uninteressanten „Petersburger Zeitung" und machte sofort den Redakteur der *Novoe Vremja* A. Suvorin auf den jungen Dichter aufmerksam. Und in einem Brief vom März 1886 warnt Grigorovič den jungen Dichter vor weitere Gelegenheitsarbeit in der Tagespresse und hebt hervor „ihre Meisterschaft in den Beschreibungen", „in einigen Zeilen erscheint ein vollständiges Bild: die kleinen Wolken vor dem Hintergrund der ausgehenden Abenddämmerung — wie Asche auf den erlöschenden Kohlen —". Grigorovič wiederholt seine Warnungen auch in einem Brief aus Nizza 1888. Nicht ohne Einfluß Grigorovičs erteilte die Petersburger Akademie schon 1888 Čechov einen Teil des Puškin-Preises. Grigorovič drückt seine Verwunderung darüber aus, daß bei einer Vorlesung von Čechovs Erzählung „Der Anfall" (*Pripadok*) in Anwesenheit von einigen Dichtern niemand auf den Satz aufmerksam geworden war: „und wie schämt sich der Schnee nicht, wenn er in diese Gasse fällt" (die Gasse, in welcher sich die Freudenhäuser befinden; das Zitat ist ungenau, der Brief Grigorovičs vom 27. Dez.); ein paar Tage später sendet der alte Dichter Čechov wiederum einen Brief mit den Bemerkungen über die Erzählungen „Träume" (*Mečty*) und „Agafja": die Gestalten in diesen Erzählungen seien „kaum berührt [mit der Pinsel — meint Grigorovič, D. T. —] und trotzdem kann man nichts mehr hinzufügen, damit sie noch lebendiger werden", „dasselbe bei der Beschreibung der Naturbilder und der Eindrücke von ihnen: kaum berührt und [das Bild] steht direkt vor den Augen; solche Meisterschaft in der Wiedergabe der Eindrücke begegnet uns nur bei Turgenev und Tolstoj (solche Beschreibungen in „Anna Karenina")".

Die Bedeutung der „Einzelheiten" bei Čechov konnte auch Tolstoj merken, — an den Erzählungen, die ihm inhaltlich zusprachen. Leider kennen wir solche Äußerungen Tolstojs (1900-1) nur aus den Notizen

seines Freundes A. B. Gol'denvejzer: Čechov sei „ein seltsamer Dichter: er wirft Worte wie es scheint unpassend (*nekstati*) hin, und trotzdem lebt bei ihm alles. Und wie klug! Er hat niemals überflüssige Einzelheiten, sondern eine jede ist entweder nötig oder schön". Und ein
anderes Mal: Čechov habe „die Meisterschaft von einem höheren Rang
[...]. Trotzdem ist das alles nur Mosaik ohne die wirklich leitende
Idee [...]. Er wirft die Wörter scheinbar ohne Ordnung hin, erreicht
aber wie ein Maler-Impressionist mit seinen Pinselstrichen eine erstaun-
liche Wirkung".

Hier fällt auch bereits das richtige Wort: *Impressionist,* leider kann
man nicht sicher sein, ob das Wort von Tolstoj gebraucht oder nur ein
Kommentar Gol'denvejzers zu den Äußerungen Tolstojs war.

Die impressionistische Malerei Čechovs ist nicht nur die äußere
Form. Wie wir sehen werden, ist sie auch mit den tieferen Motiven
seiner Weltanschauung verbunden. Man soll aber auch betonen, daß
Čechov in dieser Beziehung nicht ganz ausserhalb der russischen Lite-
raturtradition steht. Wenn man auch von solchen Zeitgenossen Čechovs
absieht, die impressionistische Versdichter waren, wie A. A. Fet (1820-
1892) und K. Fofanov (1862-1911) (I. F. Annenskij (1865-1909)
war als Dichter damals noch kaum bekannt), so ist zweifelsohne L.
Tolstoj derjenige russische Dichter, der den impressionistischen Stil
als erster zur Geltung gebracht hat. I. S. Turgenev hat das schon früh
bemerkt und seine kritischen Äußerungen über die Romane Tolstojs
sind in diesem Sinne sehr bezeichnend. Turgenevs Bemerkungen über
die großen Romane L. Tolstojs befinden sich in seinen Briefen (wobei
Turgenev allerdings die künstlerische Höhe dieser Romane keinesfalls
leugnet): „Alle diese kleinen Stückchen, geschickt bemerkt und geziert
ausgesprochen, die kleinen psychologischen Bemerkungen [...], wie ist
das alles kleinlich vor dem weiten Hintergrund des historischen Romans" (an P. Borisov 16.III.65); Tolstoj sei bestrebt „die Schwan-
kungen, Vibrationen desselben Gefühls und derselben Lage wieder-
zugeben" (an Annenkov, 26.II.68). Die historischen Schilderungen
Tolstojs „schlagen mit ihren feinen Kleinigkeiten auf die Augen",
seine psychologische Kunst sei nur „launenhafte eintönige Beschäftigug
mit immer denselben Empfindungen" (an Polonskij, 6.III.68, vgl. noch
an Borisov vom 10.III.68, später an Baronin Vrevskaja 22.III.76).
Diese Bemerkungen bedeuten nichts anderes, als Angriffe auf den
impressionistischen Stil Tolstojs! Auch den impressionistischen Stil
der Dichtungen seines Freundes A. Fet lehnte Turgenev mit dem iro-
nischen Lächeln ab (vgl. seine Parodien auf die Gedichte Fets). Selt-
samerweise verteidigt derselbe Turgenev die französische impressionistische *Malerei* in einem Brief an Polonskij (1882). Ähnlich ist die
glänzende Charakteristik des Stils Tolstojs in dem damals kaum

beachteten und jetzt fast völlig vergessenem Buche K. Leont'evs über die Romane Tolstojs (bezeichnenderweise wird dieses Buch in den Wichtigsten Arbeiten über Leont'ev — von Berdjaev, Kologriviv und V. Zen'kovskij — nicht erwähnt!). Das Wort „Impressionismus" gebraucht Leont'ev natürlich nicht.

4.

Wollen wir aber die Novellen Čechovs stilistisch analysieren, wird uns nicht nur der sporadische Gebrauch der impressionistischen Stilmittel, wie das in den oben zitierten Bemerkungen der unbarmherzigen Kritiker oder der den Stil Čechovs anerkannenden Beurteiler (Grigorovič und L. Tolstoj) hervorgehoben wurde, auffallen. Nein! Die kleinen Erzählungen Čechovs, wie auch seine größeren Novellen und vor allem seine Bühnenwerke tragen *durchwegs* die Züge des literarischen Impressionismus.

Die Hauptzüge des literarischen Impressionismus kann man kurz etwa so formulieren — in der äußeren Form: 1. Unklarheit des Gesamtbildes, 2. dagegen Hervortreten der Einzelheiten und Kleinigkeiten. Diese beiden Züge entsprechen etwa der Malerei mit einzelnen Pinselstrichen. Den Inhalt der impressionistischen dichterischen Werke kennzeichnen weitere Züge: 3. Verzicht auf Formulierungen der Gedanken, vor allem Verzicht auf solche Elemente der „didaktischen" Dichtung wie der Gebrauch der Sentenzen und Gnomen, die dem Leser die Absicht, die „Tendenz" des Werkes übermitteln sollen, 4. dagegen die Schaffung einer „allgemeinen Stimmung", durch die gegebenenfalls gewisse „Ergebnisse" der dichterischen Darstellung wenn nicht dem Verstand, so doch dem Gefühl, dem Einfühlungsvermögen des Lesers suggeriert werden. 5. Zu dem Gefühl des Lesers sprechen aber bestimmte kleine Züge, Striche, Einzelheiten, Details, die Träger der leisen und leichten Schattierungen, „Differentialen der Stimmung" sind. Alle diese Kunstgriffe des dichterischen Impressionismus verwendet Čechov systematisch, absichtlich und meisterhaft.

Es ist für die Charakteristik des Dichters eigentlich von keinem großen Belang, ob, wie Michajlovskij es meint, die Eigenart des Čechovschen Stils wirklich unter dem Einfluß seiner Arbeit an den humoristischen Zeitschriften und an der Tagespresse entstanden sei. Čechov behielt diese Eigenart auch in den Werken (größere Novellen und Bühnenwerke) bei, an denen er längere Zeit arbeitete, die er umarbeiten und deren Stil er feilen konnte; übrigens können wir aus den Briefen Čechovs sehen, daß er auch gegenüber der Form der „Bagatellen" seiner *Jugend*jahre keinesfalls gleichgültig war, wenn er zunächst auch die glückliche Erfindung des Sujets vielleicht vor allem geschätzt hat.

Wir wollen unsere Aufmerksamkeit vor allem auf solche Werke wie „Die Steppe", „Langweilige Geschichte", „Mein Leben", „Drei Jahre" und auf die Bühnenwerke Čechovs richten. Čechov gilt noch jetzt für den europäischen Leser vielfach als „Humorist", und diese Vorstellung hat sich — auch unter den russischen Lesern — noch verstärkt, seitdem man solche Ausgaben seiner Werke hat, in die auch die vom Verfasser selbst aus der Gesamtausgabe ausgeschlossenen Jugenderzählungen in großer Anzahl aufgenommen sind. In solchen neuen Ausgaben füllen die kleinen humoristischen Erzählungen vielfach die gute Hälfte der der dichterischen Prosa Čechovs gewidmeten Bände. Hier soll über den dichterischen Wert dieser „Bagatellen" kein Urteil abgegeben werden. Man soll aber sagen, daß die Lektüre dieser „Humoresken" eher geeignet ist, statt der lustigen Stimmung eine tiefe Melancholie hervorzurufen. Man sieht in ihnen einerseits das äußerst niedrige geistige und sittliche Niveau der angeblich „höheren" Schichten, vor allem die Stumpfheit, Grobheit und Unmenschlichkeit dieser Reichen und Satten den Armen und Hungernden gegenüber. Aber auch die „Kleinen" und „Erniedrigten" sind vielfach so geschildert, daß man in ihnen kaum noch menschliche Züge entdecken kann.

In diesem Sinne ist die Charakteristik der „humoristischen" Erzählungen Čechovs in den meisten Arbeiten der Sowjet-Russischen Gelehrten durchaus zutreffend: die Unmenschlichkeit der Reichen und Satten ist ein durchgehendes Thema dieser Erzählungen. Erinnern wir uns nur an die Gelegenheitsarbeiten der Frühzeit Čechovs. Hier gibt es die grausamen Gutbesitzer, die bereits befreiten Bauern physisch und seelisch quälen (*Za jabločki* und *Barynja,* 1882). Mehr Interesse widmet der junge Dichter jedenfalls dem städtischen Leben, das er auch besser kennt: die Verachtung der in russischem Milieu lebenden Ausländer, die man beinahe nicht für Menschen hält (*Doč' Al'biona,* 1883, *Na čužbine,* 1885), die Behandlung der Gebildeten als grundsätzlich unehrlicher und käuflicher Menschen: man versucht einen Gymnasiallehrer zu bestechen (*Papaša,* 1880), man behandelt bei der Anstellung eines intelligenten Menschen als Verwalter diesen schon als einen zukünftigen Dieb (*Stena,* 1885). Ein Zeitungsarbeiter (*Korrespondent,* 1882), ein Musiker (*Taper,* 1885), ein Aushilfsstunden erteilender Gymnasiast (*Repetitor,* 1884), eine Hebamme (*Neobyknovennyj,* 1886), eine Gouvernante (*Perepoloch,* 1886) mögen sie auch keinen besonders hohen menschlichen Typus vertreten (wie etwa *Pisatel',* 1885), werden von den Menschen, die keinesfalls höher als sie stehen, verachtet, unbarmherzig ausgebeutet, beleidigt und auch ohne irgendein Ziel gekränkt und gequält. Natürlich wird die Lage der „Erniedrigten und Beleidigten" noch hoffnungsloser, wenn der „Reiche und Satte" ein Recht hat, über diese zu verfügen: Čechovs Erzählungen sind die

letzten Vertreter in der langen Kette der „Novellen über den armen
Beamten" (vgl. *Narvalsja*, 1882, *Reč' i remešok*, 1884). Man braucht
auch nicht besonders auf die Fälle grausamer Behandlung von Frau
und Kinder durch einen „pater familias" hinzuweisen. Bezeichnenderweise treten bei Čechov auch solche Menschen auf, die ohne jeden
Grund, allein aus der Lust am Unfug, die anderen beleidigen und
schädigen. Eine Szene direkt aus einer Komödie von A. N. Ostrovskij
glaubt man in der Erzählung *Maska* (1884) vor sich zu haben: ein
reicher „Wohltäter" treibt den gröbsten Unfug in einem Klub, und
niemand wagt es, sich ihm zu widersetzen. Und noch kennzeichnender
ist eine frühe Erzählung, in welcher ein müßiger Mensch mit dem
„satten, vom Fett glänzenden Gesicht", um die Zeit zu vertreiben ein
armes Mädchen Stundenlang mit unnötigen Gesprächen aufhält, um
ihr nachher mitzuteilen, daß sie in die falsche Wohnung geraten ist —
in der richtigen Wohnung angekommen, erfährt die Bittstellerin, daß
der Beamte, der ihre Bitte hätte erfüllen können (es handelte sich um
eine Freifahrkarte zu ihrer erkrankten Mutter), vor einer halben
Stunde verreist ist (*Baran i baryšnja*, 1883, bezeichnenderweise befanden sich in dem Tagebuch Čechovs Notizen über zwei weitere ähnliche
Sujets). Und die „Satten" glaubten vielfach im Recht zu sein, wenn
sie die Menschenwürde der Armen und Hungrigen nicht beachteten
(vgl. *Iz ognja da v polymja*, 1884, *Intelligentnoe brevno*, 1885)...

Das, was aber von der Čechov-Forschung wenig beachtet wird, ist
der Umstand, daß seine „humoristischen" Novellen ein im Wesen
noch viel finstereres Bild der Wirklichkeit zeichnen, als das soeben
andeutungsweise geschilderte. Seien doch die Ausgebeuteten, Unterdrückten und Erniedrigten kaum besser als die Ausbeuter und Unterdrücker! Der „Dünne" ist, als er von dem hohen Rang seines früheren
Schulkameraden, des „Dicken", erfährt, ekelerregend unterwürfig
(*Tolstyj i tonkij*, 1883), und falls der Niedrigstehende doch weitere
Menschen unter sich hat, behandelt er sie genau so, wie er von den
Höherstehenden selbst behandelt wird (*Dvoe v odnom*, 1883). Vor den
Höherstehenden verlieren die Helden Čechovs jedenfalls das Bewußtsein ihrer Rechte und ihrer Menschenwürde: eine Lehrerin wagt es
nicht, ihre Interesse zu verteidigen (*Razmaznja*, 1883), der Beamte, der
glaubt, in Namen seiner Kollegen den Amtsvorsteher um etwas bitten
zu dürfen, versagt von Angst überwältigt im Gespräch mit diesem
völlig (*Deputat*, 1883), ein Beamter stirbt, weil er einen höheren
Beamten im Theater durch sein Niesen gestört zu haben glaubt (*Smert'
činovnika*, 1883), selbst „Der Graf von Monte-Cristo" ist für einen
kleinen Beamten eine zu ernste und zu schwere Lektüre (*Čtenie*, 1884),
der kleine Beamte tritt zurück, wenn sein Vorgesetzter seine Frau zu
verführen geruht (*Na gvozde*, 1883). Aber auch die Vertreter der

unteren Klassen sind nicht besser: der Kunde kann einem Schneider nur imponieren, wenn er ihn ins Gesicht schlägt, der Schneider empfindet das sogar als beseligendes Zeugnis dafür, daß es noch „echte Herren" gäbe (*Kapitanskij mundir*, 1885), der „verabschiedete Sklave" findet es eine wunderbare Laufbahn, wenn ein Mädchen sich günstig verkauft (*Otstavnoj rab*, 1883), es erscheinen bei Čechov bereits damals Bauern, die an nichts anderes als an gerechte oder ungerechte Bereicherung denken (*Osen'ju*, 1883), und in einem Dorfgericht behandeln die Bauern einander nicht besser, als sie von der höheren Obrigkeit behandelt werden (*Sud*, 1882). Auch die Vertreter der Intelligenz: Ärzte (*Filantrop*, 1883), Juristen (*Perpetuum mobile*, 1884), Lehrer (*Orden*, 1884), Schauspieler (*Mest'*, 1882) usf. sind um nichts besser... Reichtum und Sattheit ergießen ihre Strahlen auch auf die ganze Umgebung, so daß nicht nur die Konkubine eines „Generals" (*Ženskoe sčast'e*, 1885), sondern auch Hunde und Katzen der Vorgesetzen (*Chameleon*, 1884, *Kot*, 1883) in den Augen der Untenstehenden von einer Aureole umgeben sind.

Mit einem Wort: die Welt des „Humoristen" Čechov ist eine traurige, finstere und unheimliche Welt. Und man kann kaum davon sprechen, daß der „fröhliche junge Dichter" sich später in einen melancholischen Pessimisten verwandelte. Vielmehr ist der Pessimismus der letzten Jahren Čechovs doch viel lichter und weltbejahender als die „Humoristik" seiner Jugendjahre. Uns begegnet bei dem späten Čechov keinesfalls die unversöhnliche Verurteilung der „Schlechten" oder „Andersdenkenden", die wir in der russischen Literatur sonst so oft finden: es genügt nur, an die Unbarmherzigkeit zu denken, mit der etwa L. Tolstoj in den „Volkserzählungen" oder in der „Auferstehung" ganz harmlose, oder gar gute, aber seinem Menschenideal nicht entsprechende Menschen schildert. Ein Vergleich Čechovs mit Tolstoj in diesem Sinne wäre sicherlich eine lohnende Aufgabe.

5.

Die versöhnliche, tolerante Einstellung des späteren Čechovs den Menschen gegenüber, erklärt sich mindestens zum Teil aus den Gedanken, die ihm in Verbindung mit der Entwicklung seines impressionistischen Stils gekommen sind. Wir wollen nun zum Schluß auf diesen Stil etwas näher eingehen. Viel Wichtiges über Čechovs Stil wurde bereits in dem wenig beachteten Aufsatz von N. Šapir „Čechov als Realist-Neuerer" (*Čechov kak realist-novator* in der Zeitschrift *Voprosy filosofii i psichologii*, Bde 79-80, 1904-5) und über Čechovs Dramen von Baluchatyj gesagt. Die ganze Problematik soll aber erst eingehend behandelt werden.

Čechov verzichtet weitgehend auf die für den Realismus so charakteristische eingehende *Motivierung* der Reden und Handlungen der handelnden Personen seiner Werke. So vieles geschieht in seinen größeren Novellen „ohne jeden Grund", daß wir bei ihm von einer Vorwegnahme der Grundtendenz der symbolistischen Dichtung denken dürfen, an die Tendenz, die Erscheinungen durch blinden Zufall zu erklären. Vielleicht hat eben dieser Zug Čechov an die Dramen Maeterlincks herangezogen, die er allerdings erst 1897 mit Begeisterung las (Brief an Suvorin vom 12.VII.1897). Er las gerade *die* Theaterstücke Maeterlincks, die den Einbruch der blinden unbarmherzigen Kräfte ins menschliche Leben schildern (*Les aveugles, L'intruse*), und nach dem Zeugnis Stanislavskijs interessierte sich Čechov später lebhaft für die Aufführung der beiden Stücke, die im Frühjahr 1904 vom Moskauer Künstlertheater vorbereitet wurde.

Während die realistische Tradition eine feste Verbindung zwischen den Erlebnissen und Handlungen des Menschen und den Ereignissen ihres Lebens suchte und darstellte, klafft bei Čechov zwischen den Ereignissen und Erlebnissen der Helden sowie zwischen ihren Erlebnissen und Handlungen fast immer ein Abgrund... Čechov hat, wie die Realisten, die Neigung, sich in den Daten, Ortsangaben und sonstigen „realia" seiner Werke an Wirklichkeit zu halten. Aber diese Wirklichkeit erscheint und wirkt in den Erlebnissen der Helden *nur* in einer unmotiviert verzerrten, unadaequaten Gestalt: zwischen den „äußeren Ursachen" und Erlebnissen besteht ein seltsames Mißverhältnis.

Die entscheidenden Veränderungen des menschlichen Lebens und der Schicksale sind nicht motiviert oder hängen von kleinen Ursachen ab. Noch mehr: die Wandlungen des Lebens entsprechen vielfach nicht den Ereignissen, die eigentlich zu den ganz anderen Folgen führen sollten. So erlebt der schwache, charakterlose Nichtstuer Laevskij eine Art sittliche „Wiedergeburt" gerade im Augenblick seines tiefsten Absinkens, und die Untreue seiner Freundin— unter häßlichsten Umständen — führt ihn nicht zum Bruch mit ihr, sondern befestigt umgekehrt unerwartet ihre Beziehungen. Diese „Wiedergeburt", die Wandlung Laevskijs, ist sein Sieg über den charakterfesten, von seinen weltanschaulichen und moralischen Grundsätzen fest überzeugten Darwinisten von Koren („Duell"). Der Prozeß der Wandlung wird nicht gezeigt, sicherlich absichtlich. — Das ganze Leben des Helden von „Mein Leben" verlief als eine Reihe solcher seltsamen unmotivierten Wendungen. — Und auch völlig unmotiviert werden oft die sinnvollen Handlungen „zufällig" nicht ausgeführt. Sehr gerne schildert Čechov die Liebenden, die sich ohne Grund oder fast ohne Grund zu keiner Erklärung entschließen: von *Veročka* (1887) bis zu „Kirschgarten" (1904) zieht sich eine Reihe solcher Szenen. Auch einfache menschliche Verhältnisse, wie Freundschaft, gute Bekanntschaft oder einfach fried-

Anton Čechov

liche Nachbarschaft können oft ohne jeden sichtlichen Grund nicht entstehen, als ob auch hier der blinde Zufall die Beziehungen der Menschen zueinander trübe (*Slučaj iz praktiki,* 1898). Manchmal bestimmen die kleinen Ursachen das ganze Leben der Menschen: ein Bauer
wollte zu Ostern kein Stück Osterbrot einem Kranken geben — „damit
begann die Zerrüttung" (*rasstrojstvo*) — stellt Čechov fest — des
seelischen Gleichgewichts dieses Bauern und dann auch der Ruin
seiner Wirtschaft und des ganzen Lebens (*Kazak,* 1887). Manchmal
zeigt Čechov den Grund einer Handlung in einer bestimmten Stimmung, aber die *unmittelbare* Veranlassung ist nichtig — so geschieht
der Brudermord in der Erzählung *Ubijstvo* (1895), weil der Ermor-
dete an einem Fastentage Pflanzenoel essen wollte. Auch Liebe, Ehe,
Freundschaft können „zufällig" entstehen (*Rasskaz neizvestnogo čelo-
veka, Tri goda, V rodnom uglu, Dama s sobačkoj* usf.).

Ohne die lange Reihe der Novellen Čechovs zu analysieren, genügt
es, auf einige weitere stilistische Züge hinzuweisen, die uns seit etwa
1890 fast in allen Werken Čechovs begegnen.

Die Wirklichkeit, die „Ereignisse", können schon deshalb nicht
irgendwie „objektiv" gemessen und beurteilt werden, weil sie dem Menschen nicht unmittelbar erscheinen, sondern in Form der Spiegelung
in der Seele des jeweiligen Individuums. Wie es scheint, sind die ersten
Novellen Čechovs, wo diese Tatsache betont wird, „psychopathologi-
sche" Schilderungen der einen oder anderen Art. Die Schwangerschaft
bei der Heldin von *Imeniny* (1887), überspitzte moralische Bewußtsein eines Studenten (*Pripadok,* 1887), der Prozeß des Alterns bei dem
alten Professor der *Skučnaja istorija* (1889) lassen die Menschen und
Ereignisse unmotiviert, oft sichtlich falsch (was der Dichter betont)
und mißverständlich, beurteilen. Seit jener Zeit führt Čechov die
Gedanken, Erlebnisse und (meist nicht ausgeführte) Entschlüsse auch
der völlig „normalen" Helden, ebenso wie der „kranken" durch
ständig wiederkehrende Formeln ein, wie „ihr schien", „sie sah in
einem jeden nur das Falsche" („während das alles gewöhnliche und
nicht schlechte Menschen waren"), „alle schienen ihr unbegabt, blaß,
einfältig, eng, falsch, herzlos zu sein", „ihm schien, daß", oder (mit
den Worten des Helden) „mit mir geschieht etwas *seltsames*", kleine
Ursachen (Klänge) „genügen, damit ein Glücksgefühl mich erfüllt",
usf. Der Gebrauch dieser Formel erreicht seinen Höhepunkt in den
Jahren 1893 ff., etwa in *Bab'e Carstvo* (1894), wo wir auf Schritt und
Tritt lesen: „sie wurde fröhlich" (ohne Grund), „ihr schien, daß",
„ihr schien, als ob", „sie möchte" (*„ej zachotelos'* "), „sie stellte sich
vor", „sie träumte" (*„ej mereščilos'* "), „sie war schon überzeugt" (ohne
Grund), „diese Erinnerung — unbekannt warum — rührte sie"; die
Heldin erlebt „die Sehnsucht der Erwartung", „sie wollte leidenschaft-

lich, daß die Änderung ihres Lebens sofort, gleich geschehe" (und nach kurzer Zeit verschwindet dieser Wunsch spurlos). Dasselbe begegnet uns in der Erzählung *Učitel' slovesnosti* (1894) : „es schien", „er empfand in der Seele einen unangenehmen Niederschlag" (*osadok*), „und er konnte auf keinerlei Weise verstehen, wesshalb", „trotzdem war es unangenehm", „er begann gegenüber dem weißen Kater aufgebracht zu sein". Und in gleicher Weise der Held der „Drei Jahre" (1895) : „ärgerte sich über sich selbst und über diesen schwarzen Hund" und auch „seine Stimmung änderte sich gleich [...]. Es schien ihm, daß alles, was er sagte, dumm war bis zum Ekel", und ebenso verlaufen die Erlebnisse der Heldin. Der Held der „Drei Jahre" hat die Empfindung, daß nicht er selbst, sondern „sein Doppelgänger" denke und handle, und dem Mörder in *Ubijstvo* (1895) „schien, daß nicht er selbst, sondern irgendein Tier, ein ungeheures und schreckliches Tier herumgehe", — und das, als er an den später geschehenen Mord ja noch gar nicht dachte.

Die Helden der impressionistischen Novellen Čechovs schwanken zwischen verschiedenen Stimmungen, Gedanken und Entschlüssen (s. oben) und manchmal erleben sie die entgegengesetzten Gefühle zugleich, ohne ihren Widerspruch zu empfinden. Čechov hebt besonders hervor, daß die Empfindungen, Erlebnisse in ewigem Fluß, in einem Prozeß der Veränderung sind. Er versucht vor allem das Schwinden der Erlebnisse (und Ereignisse) immer zu vermerken: „alles verging bei mir, wie bei allen, schnell, spurlos, wurde nicht geschätzt und schwand, wie Nebel ...Wo ist das alles?" (*Rasskaz gospoži N. N.*, 1887), „wie schön hätte das Leben sein können" (*Žena*, 1891), und es erhebt sich das Bewußtsein „ich habe es versäumt, versäumt" (*Prozevala*, 1892), „es ist schon zu spät zu träumen" (*Bab'e Carstvo*, 1894). Und vielleicht am stärksten wirkt dieses Motiv am Ende der letzten Erzählung Čechovs, *Archierej* (1902): nicht nur die Erlebnisse des verstorbenen Bischofs sind alle vergangen, verflogen, sondern sogar seine Existenz scheint jetzt nicht mehr real gewesen zu sein, — wenn seine Mutter von ihm erzählte „glaubten ihr nicht alle" ... — Auf diese Weise tritt die „Wirklichkeit" in den Hintergrund zurück, und die Ereignisse, die scheinbar Ursachen oder Veranlassungen der Erlebnisse bilden, wirken nur in der Gestalt, die sie annahmen, als sie in der Psyche der Menschen gebrochen und umgeprägt wurden.

Durch die Einbeziehung der so umgestalteten „Wirklichkeit" (die es als eine „objektive" Wirklichkeit eigentlich für Čechov gar nicht gibt) in den Fluß des individuellen Seelenlebens wird die Darstellung des Seelenlebens zu der zentralen, wichtigsten Aufgabe der Dichtung. Und da das Seelenleben eines Menschen nur einzelne Gipfel, Höhepunkte kennt und meist in den „Niederungen" der Alltäglichkeit verläuft, muß diese Darstellung mit zahlreichen „leeren Stellen" rechnen. Diese „leere Stellen", diese bedeutungslosen Augenblicke — oder gar Perioden — des menschlichen Lebens brauchen in der dichterischen Prosa nur flüchtig gestreift zu werden, können aber in den dramatischen Werken, die doch gewisse Zeitabschnitte vollständig darstellen sollen, nicht unbeachtet bleiben. Dadurch ist die Komposition der Čechovschen Theaterstücke weitgehend bestimmt: zwischen den Gipfeln der seelischen Erlebnisse und den Wendepunkten der Sujetentwicklung werden die Elemente der „Füllung" eingeschoben, die aus witzigen Episoden (Epichodov oder Simeonov-Piščik im „Kirschgarten"), nichtssagenden „alltäglichen" Gesprächen (lange Abschnitte des 2-ten Aktes derselben Komödie) oder sogar aus Schweigen bestehen. In den Erzählungen kann der Verfasser etwas freier über die „leeren Zeiten" der Handlung verfügen — und so kommen dort in der Funktion der Raumfüllung auch die Naturschilderungen und theoretischen Betrachtungen des Verfassers vor. Dadurch entsteht die impressionistische Komposition, die die Charakteristik der Helden und die Schilderung der Ereignisse (wie gesagt, mit den Augen der Helden gesehen) aus einzelnen Strichen und Farbflecken aufbaut...

Nicht ohne Bedeutung ist der Umstand, daß in den Novellen Čechovs die handelnden Personen sich meist am Ort der Handlung nur vorübergehend, oft nur zufällig aufhalten: Ärzte, die ihre Patienten besuchen, Feldmesser, Untersuchungsrichter, Gäste und zufällige Vorbeireisende sind Menschen, durch dessen Augen der Leser die Ereignisse sehen soll. Oder befinden sich die Helden der Erzählung zu Hause, so sind andere Personen der Handlung nur Gäste, die oft zum ersten Mal erscheinen. Man sieht die Welt gewissermaßen aus dem Fenster eines Eisenbahnwagens. Die Eisenbahn spielt überhaupt in den Werken Čechovs eine ungewöhnlich große Rolle! Wie viele seiner Helden wohnen auf den Bahnhöfen oder in der Nähe der Eisenbahn!... Vor ihnen huschen die Menschen vorbei „wie die Sternschnuppen". Solche Stellung ist eben die eines das Leben beobachtenden Impressionisten. Vielleicht am kennzeichnendsten ist die Erzählung *Na podvode* (1897): eine Volksschullehrerin fährt auf einem ärmlichen Bauernwagen eine elende Landstraße entlang in ihr Dorf zurück. „Der Schlagbaum auf dem Eisenbahnübergang war heruntergelassen: vom Bahnhof ging ein Schnellzug ab [...]. Da ist der Zug — die Fenster glänzen mit grellem Licht [...], so daß es schmerzlich war zuzusehen. Im Vorraum eines Wagens erster Klasse stand eine Dame..". Der Lehrerin scheint es daß sie eine große Ähnlichkeit mit ihrer eigenen Mutter habe — und sie stellt sich mit erstaunlicher Klarheit ihr Leben in Moskau vor dreizehn Jahren vor, als die Mutter noch lebte. „Und sie weinte, unbekannt weshalb [...]. Und es schien ihr, daß überall in den Fenstern, auf den

Bäumen ihr Glück, ihr Triumph leuchte. Ja, ihr Vater und ihre Mutter sind niemals gestorben, sie war niemals Lehrerin, das war ein lange, schwere, seltsame Traum, und jetzt ist sie erwacht [...]. Und plötzlich verschwand alles". Da finden wir in einigen Zeilen die typischen Züge des Čechovschen Stils: das „Vorbeihuschen" der Wirklichkeit, die unerwarteten, unbegründeten und einander widersprechenden Erlebnisse („sie weinte", „es schien ihr, daß überall [...] ihr Glück leuchte"), die im schnellen Fluß einander ablösen, das „plötzliche Verschwinden" der Erlebnisse auslösenden Wirklichkeit — und das ebenso plötzliche Verklingen der Erlebnisse.

Diese Hauptzüge des Čechovischen Stils sind nicht die einzigen Elemente seines Impressionismus. Das Beachten der Einzelheiten, die den Kritikern der Zeit so unnötig, ja widersinnig zu sein schien, gehört zur Darstellungsart des Dichters, wie auch zu der Art, in welcher die Helden die Wirklichkeit empfinden und auf sie reagieren: die Wirklichkeit, auch die Menschen, werden nach scheinbar zufälligen und unwesentlichen Zügen wahrgenommen und chrakterisiert, so etwa die Menschen nach ihrem Geruch („roch nach Kaffeesatz", „roch nach rohem Fleisch" usf.), nach ihrer Ausdruckweise mehr als nach dem Inhalt des Gesagten („Mensch im Futteral", der Arzt Čebutykin in den „Drei Schwestern" usf.), die Natur durch einzelne Farbflecken („Die Steppe"), was die Kritiker richtig als eine Neuerung hervorgehoben haben, oder durch völlig unklare Bilder („in unbegreiflicher Ferne [...] erhoben sich und kletterten auf einander nebelhafte, wunderliche Gestalten" (ebendort)) und endlich durch die unbestimmten Klänge, die vor allem eine wesentlich symbolische Funktion tragen: „es ertönt, die unbewegliche Luft beunruhigend, das sich wundernde „a-a!" von jemandem, und man hört den Schrei eines nicht einschlafenden oder träumenden Vogels" („Die Steppe", fast gleich ist ein Satz mehrere Seiten weiter in dieser Novelle), oder „plötzlich erklingt ein weiter Laut, wie vom Himmel herunter, der Klang einer zerrissenen Saite, abklingender, trauriger" („Kirschgarten" 2 Akt, fast gleich wird dieser Satz in der abschließenden Regiebemerkung des 4-ten Aktes wiederholt).

Daß Čechov unmittelbar vor dem Auftreten des Symbolismus wirkte, ist nicht nur eine chronologische Tatsache. Sein Impressionismus hat genau so wie der V. Garšins, Fets und einiger anderen Dichter in einem gewissen Sinne den Symbolismus vorbereitet. Das darf man nicht vergessen, wenn man die Frage nach der Stellung Čechovs in der Entwicklung der russischen Literatur aufwirft. Die Urteile Čechovs über den Symbolismus sind schlecht bezeugt und vielfach widerspruchsvoll. Von einem Dichter, der selbst immer seine Abneigung gegen jede „Parteilichkeit" betonte, kann man auch keine eindeutige Stellung-

nahme zu den neuen literarischen Richtungen erwarten. Diese „Partei-
losigkeit" Čechovs war übrigens auch einer der Gründe für die heftigen
Angriffe gegen diesen angeblich „gesichtslosen" und „ansichtslosen"
Dichter, den Verfasser von „inhaltslosen Bagatellen" (s. oben). Man
muß aber am Ende unserer Bemerkungen doch betonen, daß Čechov
schon in seinen „Humoresken", wie wir sahen, ein ernster und scharfer
Satiriker war. Und sein impressionistischer Spätstil beruht doch auf
einer bestimmten Welt- und Menschenauffassung, die besondere Aufmerksamkeit verdient (manches darüber hat bereits N. Šapir in seinem
oben zit. Aufsatz gesagt, s. besonders Band 80 der zit. Zeitschrift).
Aber noch bedeutungsvoller ist es, daß Čechov seine eigenen Antworten
auf die alten, von großen russischen Dichtern gestellten Fragen zu
geben versuchte. So ist sein „Duell" eine Antwort auf Tolstojs „Anna
Karenina", daneben steht die Auseinandersetzung mit den russischen
Darwinisten und dem russischen (falschverstandenen) Nietzsche. Die
Untersuchung solcher Anklänge und direkter Auseinandersetzungen
mit den ideologischen Problemen bei Čechov ist eine weitere For-
schungsaufgabe auf die ich hier nur hinweisen kann.

C. WILCZKOWSKI

UN AMOUR DE ČECHOV.

Pendant des années, Čechov aurait aimé une jeune femme, mariée et mère de trois enfants; il lui aurait avoué ses sentiments; un de ses plus beaux contes aurait été inspiré par cet amour caché et insatisfait — tels sont les faits affirmés dans le récit posthume de Lidija Alekseevna Avilova, née Strachova, paru en 1952 sous le titre „Čechov dans ma vie". [1]

Ces révélations surprenantes furent accueillies dans les milieux littéraires avec une méfiance compréhensible. On savait, en effet, que ni la correspondance de l'écrivain, ni les très nombreux souvenirs des témoins de sa vie ne contenaient la moindre allusion à ce roman mystérieux. Émanant d'une femme de lettres et rédigée sous une forme romancée, la confession paraissait doublement suspecte. Enfin, l'image de Čechov amoureux et souffrant du mal d'amour ne s'accordait guère avec certains clichés vieillis, mais tyranniques.

Boris Zajcev fut le premier à exprimer ce scepticisme quasi général dans sa „biographie littéraire" de Čechov, publiée en 1954. „Il est difficile de porter un jugement sur le „roman" avec Mme Avilova, écrivit-il. [2] „Je ne doute pas qu'il ait existé plus d'une dame estimant que Čechov „n'était pas indifférent" à son égard, qu'il était „blessé" par elle, ou „amoureux" d'elle — au choix, selon le tempérament."

Un an plus tard, Mme Sophie Laffitte se prononçait dans le même sens dans *Tchékhov par lui-même:* Estimant qu'Ol'ga Knipper avait été la „seule femme" qui aurait réussi à inspirer à l'auteur de la „Cerisaie" „un attachement profond, bien que très tchékhovien" [3] elle refusait, par là même, tout caractère sérieux à „l'amitié amoureuse" [4] qui liait l'écrivain à la „jeune Flore".

Bref, le procès semblait jugé quand les notes réunies par Bunin en vue d'une biographie de Čechov, et publiées par sa veuve [5] firent rebondir l'affaire. On apprit alors que l'auteur de „La Vie d'Arsen'ev", avait personnellement connu Mme Avilova et l'avait tenu en grande estime. À en croire cet observateur pénétrant et peu enclin à idéaliser son

---

[1] Dans le recueil „Čechov dans les souvenirs de ses contemporains", Moscou 1952 (en russe).

[2] Boris Zajcev, „Čechov. Une biographie littéraire," New York 1954 (en russe), p. 211.

[3] Sophie Laffitte, *Tchékhov par lui-même,* Paris 1955, p. 172.

[4] ibidem, p. 37.

[5] I. A. Bunin, „A propos de Čechov", New York 1955 (en russe).

prochain, la nouvelliste (dont le genre de beauté était précisément celui qui attirait Čechov) se distinguait par son amour de la vérité, par son intelligence et — soulignons-le — par *un sens de l'humour qui s'exerçait même sur son propre compte.* [6] Autant de traits excluant la mythomanie féminine... Rien d'étonnant donc que Bunin ait été convaincu par la lecture de „Čechov dans ma vie". „Dire que nombreux sont ceux qui pensent que Čechov n'a jamais éprouvé de sentiment fort!" écrivit-il. „Moi-même je le pensais jadis. Mais maintenant je dis fermement: *il l'avait éprouvé!* Il l'avait éprouvé envers Lidija Alekseevna Avilova". [7]

Cette prise de position contribua, certes, à faire pencher la balance en faveur de l'amie de Čechov, mais ne trancha pas le débat. En effet, un témoignage basé uniquement sur des impressions personnelles, demeure forcément contestable quelle que soit l'autorité du témoin. Il demande à être confirmé par des preuves objectives, qui, dans le cas qui nous intéresse, n'ont pas été produites jusqu'à présent.

La question reste donc ouverte, et pourtant elle est brûlante. Il est clair que s'il faut prêter foi à Mme Avilova, l'idée que nous nous faisons de Čechov est à revoir et toute l'histoire de sa vie à récrire. Aussi bien, du moment que des documents nouveaux tardent à se révéler et ne verront peut-être même jamais le jour, avons-nous cru utile de rouvrir ce dossier déjà connu, pour y rechercher tout au moins des arguments psychologiques pour ou contre l'héroïne présumée de „A propos de l'amour". Nous livrons ici les premiers résultats — encourageants — de cette enquête. Comme nous tenterons de le démontrer dans les pages qui suivent, l'étude comparée de l'oeuvre čechovienne et des faits biographiques solidement établis permet de faire ressortir, d'une façon indirecte, mais assez probante, la réalité d'une passion secrète de Čechov.

Pour que notre démonstration soit claire, il faut remonter d'abord à la crise morale que Čechov traverse aux approches de la trentaine, vers la fin des années 8o.

On sait qu'elle débute à l'époque où, ayant conquis une modeste place au soleil, l'écrivain, débarrassé des soucis les plus pressants, libre désormais de sortir du provisoire et décidé à organiser sa vie selon les meilleurs principes, procède, à cet effet, à un examen de conscience longtemps différé. A ce moment, il n'est pas heureux malgré les premiers sourires de la fortune. Sa vitalité est déjà atteinte par le surmenage et la maladie; il se sent solitaire, anxieux, hésitant entre diverses voies qui le tentent, et diverses doctrines dont aucune ne le satisfait.

---

[6] ibidem, p. 134.
[7] ibidem, p. 135.

L'effort d'introspection qu'il entreprend lui révèle progressivement des carences affectives qu'il ne semble pas avoir discernées jusqu'alors. Il constate que ce n'est pas seulement son esprit individualiste et critique qui lui rend difficile tout engagement sentimental ou idéologique, mais une certaine froideur qui lui est propre et, plus spécialement, l'indifférence égotiste — voire le mépris — qu'il ressent envers son prochain.

Pour cet homme foncièrement moral, pétri d'idées humanitaires, et rêvant d'un grand amour romantique, ce sont là des découvertes dures à supporter. De l'étonnement douloureux, l'écrivain glisse donc peu à peu à la détresse. Comme A. N. Derman fut le premier à le montrer, [8] elle atteint son paroxysme pendant l'été 1889 que Čechov passe au chevet de son frère phtisique. Durement, il se reproche alors son „insouciance" qui l'avait jadis éloigné du moribond, [9] et ce sentiment de culpabilité viendra aggraver l'effroi et la stupeur qu'il éprouvera auprès du premier cercueil dans la famille. [10] Pourtant, la violence du choc facilite la réaction. Très vite, l'écrivain se ressaisit, et, avec la ténacité qui le caractérise, s'applique à exorciser le démon de l'égotisme. L'étrange voyage au bout de la nuit — au bagne de Sachalin— qu'il entreprend en 1890 et les activités sociales auxquelles il s'adonne en 1891 et 1892 sont autant de thérapeutiques qu'il invente pour guérir son âme.

Au cours de cette période de crise et de redressement, où Čechov atteint sa maturité artistique, le caractère lyrique de son art s'affirme définitivement après une année de transition (1887). Étroitement liée à sa vie intérieure, son oeuvre — abstraction faite de quelques exceptions de plus en plus rares — reflète désormais ses états d'âme et illustre donc les problèmes intimes qui le tourmentent. Aussi bien, un dénominateur commun se retrouve-t-il dans presque tout ce qu'il écrit à l'époque dont nous parlons. Qu'il s'agisse de confessions à peine voilées, d'aveux savamment camouflés ou d'ouvrages à thèse nettement didactiques, c'est toujours le „silence du coeur" que l'auteur y dénonce.

Il s'y prend de deux façons, en développant deux thèmes apparentés mais distincts.

---

[8] A. N. Derman, „Portrait artistique de Čechov", Moscou 1929 (en russe).

[9] Après l'étude détaillée de A. N. Derman, il est difficile de ne pas voir dans „L'Histoire ennuyeuse" la confession au moyen de laquelle Čechov se délivre de son remords à l'égard du défunt. La clef de cette nouvelle est donnée dans la lettre à Pleščeev du 30 septembre 1889: „Mon héros — et c'est là un de ses traits principaux — se comporte avec trop d'insouciance à l'égard de la vie intérieure de ceux qui l'entourent, et, pendant que près de lui on pleure, on se trompe, on ment, il discute tranquillement de théatre et de littérature; s'il avait été différemment fait, Liza et Katja n'auraient pas, sans doute, péri" (XIV 406/407).

[10] Lettre à A. N. Pleščeev du 26 juin 1889 (XIV 379/380).

Le premier, d'ordre universel, est celui de l'indifférence coupable opposée à l'ouverture salvatrice, à la charité active. Après avoir inspiré deux chef-d'oeuvres („L'Histoire ennuyeuse" (1889) et „La Salle n° 6" (1892)), ainsi que tout ce que Čechov compose sous l'influence de Tolstoj ou en combattant la non-résistance tolstoienne, il se manifestera bien au delà du quinquennat critique (d'une manière directe ou indirecte) dans presque toute l'oeuvre mûre de l'artiste.

L'autre — plus étroit — est celui de l'égoïsme masculin, rendant l'homme incapable de répondre à l'amour d'une femme, ou de l'aimer d'une façon vraiment virile et généreuse. Il donne naissance entre 1887 et 1892 à six histoires d'amour („Veročka", „Ivanov", „Les Feux", „Le Récit d'un inconnu", „Le Duel" et „La Peur"), revient trois ans plus tard dans „La Mouette", pour ne plus réapparaître ensuite que d'une façon assourdie et accessoire dans la symphonie pathétique de „La Cerisaie".

C'est ce dernier thème qui nous intéresse ici d'une façon spéciale. En effet, en étudiant son historique, on se heurte à des anomalies que les biographes ne semblent pas avoir remarquées ou, en tout cas, qu'ils n'ont pas fait ressortir, bien qu'elles nous paraissent singulièrement révélatrices.

Les circonstances qui ont déterminé l'apparition du motif en question dans l'oeuvre de Čechov ne sont pas connues d'une façon directe, mais peuvent être reconstituées, en gros, avec assez de vraisemblance.

Il est certain que ce n'est pas simplement en méditant sur son passé que Čechov se rendit compte de sa froideur inquiétante. En effet, quoiqu'on en ait dit, ce passé ne présentait rien d'anormal. L'écrivain n'a jamais été frigide au sens physiologique du terme, et a même perdu sa virginité à l'âge de treize ans. [11] Lycéen, il s'intéresse aux lycéennes; [12] étudiant, il courtise des jeunes filles. [13] A l'âge de 25 ans [14] il eut une fiancée, qu'il avoua avoir beaucoup aimée [15] et dont le souvenir touchant lui inspira dix ans plus tard „La maison à mezzanine" — petit conte d'une tonalité toute turgenevienne.

Si la version qu'il y donne de sa brève idylle est proche de la vérité (et nous n'avons aucune raison de ne pas le croire) sa conduite en l'occurrence fut celle d'un homme d'honneur. D'ailleurs, le fait même qu'il ne l'évoqua que dix ans plus tard et la façon dont il en parla,

[11] Lettre à V. A. Tichonov du 22 février 1892 (XV 321).
[12] M. P. Čechov, „Autour de Čechov", Moscou 1959 (en russe), p. 66.
[13] ibidem, p. 79.
[14] Lettres de V. V. Bilibin, citées par N. I. Gitovič, „Chronique de la vie et de l'oeuvre de Čechov", Moscou 1955 (en russe), p. 123 et 126.
[15] Lettre à Mlle E. M. Šavrova du 26 novembre 1895 (XVI 288).

semblent prouver que cette affaire ne l'avait jamais bouleversé outre mesure et ne s'associait, dans son souvenir, à aucun remords. Ce n'est donc pas la rupture des fiançailles qui a pu déclancher la crise des années suivantes. Si Čechov se mit brusquement à douter de sa capacité d'aimer, ce fut, à coup sûr, à la suite d'autres expériences plus récentes, blessant à la fois son sens moral et son orgueil.

Sur ces expériences, les biographes ne nous apprennent rien, mais l'étude des ouvrages illustrant le thème qui nous intéresse permet quelques déductions indiscrètes. Notons d'abord que, de toute évidence, ,,Ivanov" ne peut nous fournir aucun des indices que nous recherchons. Le hobereau neurasthénique et indiscipliné ne ressemble aucunement à l'auteur, et l'intrigue mélodramatique n'a rien d'autobiographique. De même, ,,Le Récit d'un inconnu" entre à peine en ligne de compte. Orlov, le jouisseur correct et glacial n'est pas Čechov : il est plutôt l'incarnation parfaite d'une tendance dont l'auteur s'accuse, mais qui n'existe en lui qu'en germe. En revanche, Ognev, le héros maladroit de ,,Veročka" qui ne profite pas d'un amour qui s'offre — pour le regretter aussitôt — pourrait bien être le jeune Čechov. Et l'on peut en dire autant d'Anan'ev, le narrateur des ,,Feux", ce Don Juan mal assuré qui fuit piteusement sa maîtresse d'une nuit — par peur de complications gênantes — tout en se reprochant la vilenie de sa conduite. Le cadre de ces deux contes est, d'ailleurs, familier à Čechov et l'intrigue — très simple — n'y sent nullement l'artifice. On peut donc supposer que ce sont là deux récits, à peine stylisés, d'expériences vécues par l'auteur. Celle qui fournit le sujet des ,,Feux" aurait eu pour lui une importance particulière, car il reprend ce sujet, à peine modifié, deux fois encore, dans ,,Le Duel" et dans ,,La Peur".

Si l'on accepte ces hypothèses, largement admises, la façon dont le thème qui nous intéresse se développe chez Čechov devient parfaitement compréhensible. Le cynisme d'Anan'ev est une réaction un peu naïve, mais naturelle, contre la timidité d'Ognev. Les deux contes que nous considérons comme autobiographiques se suivent donc à bref intervalle, ,,Veročka" (1887) étant antérieure aux ,,Feux" (1888). Entre les deux se place ,,Ivanov" (septembre-octobre 1887) et c'est en 1887-1888 qu'est conçu ,,Le Récit d'un inconnu", rédigé définitivement en 1892. Bref, le thème dont nous parlons obsède Čechov dans les années 1887-1888, c'est-à-dire tant que les expériences humiliantes sont encore fraîches dans son souvenir et tant que son propre cas lui paraît incurable, ou presque. Puis quand, reprenant courage, il entreprend son grand effort de rééducation, quand l'espoir renaît et que les vieilles plaies se cicatrisent, le thème obsédant disparaît pour trois ans de ses écrits. Il se présente ensuite dans ,,Le Duel" (1891), où le héros (une sorte de sosie d'Anan'ev) arrive à vaincre son égoïsme et où tout finit le mieux du monde (novembre 1892). Quant à „La Peur" (bien que le sujet soit encore celui des „Feux"), l'accent s'y trouve posé non pas sur l'égoïsme du narrateur, mais sur la gêne qu'il éprouve à l'égard du mari trompé.

Jusqu'ici tout se tient et tout est clair. Mais les difficultés commencent avec „La Mouette", que Čechov rédige en octobre-décembre 1895, après avoir joué en 1892-1894 — et cette fois-ci dans des circonstances parfaitement connues des biographes — un rôle aussi peu reluisant que ceux d'Ognev et d'Anan'ev.

Rappelons brièvement cette lamentable histoire. Dès 1891, l'écrivain semble distinguer une demoiselle de 21 ans, la séduisante Lika Mizinova, amie de sa soeur. Il la taquine, il lui fait des déclarations bouffonnes et, en été 1892, sous les ombrages de Melichovo, pousse le flirt si loin que la jeune fille amoureuse lui propose une fugue à deux dans le Caucase. Čechov accepte, puis se récuse sous un prétexte futile. Pourtant, il poursuit le marivaudage encore plus d'un an, juseq'au jour où Lika, désespérée, cède par dépit aux sollicitations d'un Don Juan assez vulgaire, Potapenko, l'écrivain à la mode. En 1894, celui-ci l'abandonne à Paris, enceinte. De Suisse, elle fait appel à Čechov en termes émouvants. Mais derechef il se dérobe, bien qu'il se trouve à Nice et que rien ne l'empêche de la rejoindre.

Il semble qu'il y avait là de quoi troubler profondément l'artiste. On s'imagine facilement l'auteur des „Feux" accablé par cette preuve nouvelle et éclatante de son „insouciance" et de son égoïsme nullement vaincu. Mais, chose étrange, contrairement à tout ce qu'on pourrait normalement attendre, Čechov-écrivain ne réagit pas. Il n'est pas question de l'égoïsme masculin dans son oeuvre des années 1893-94 et, dans „La Mouette", inspirée de ce drame vécu, le rôle réel de l'auteur est escamoté. On ne trouve dans la pièce ni galant indécis, ni amoureuse poussée à bout par un velléitaire. Trigorin est bien Potapenko, mais Treplev n'est pas du tout Čechov.

Ainsi, des malheurs de Lika, dont il est en partie responsable, l'écrivain ne tire qu'un sujet littéraire. Le thème dont nous nous occupons ici n'a, dans „La Mouette", plus rien de personnel. Il ne semble plus émouvoir en Čechov que l'homme de lettres, et, dans les années qui suivent, il perdra pour lui tout intérêt. Tels sont les faits facilement constatables, mais inexplicables pour les biographes fidèles aux schémas canonisés.

Or, l'obscurité se dissipe si l'on prend au sérieux la confession de Mme Avilova.

Ouvrons une parenthèse pour résumer les étapes essentielles de ce roman, telles qu'elle les rapporte.

Čechov rencontre la „jeune Flore" pour la première fois le 24 janvier

1889 à St. Petersbourg où elle habite, au cours d'un dîner chez un éditeur. Il la revoit, pour la deuxième fois, trois ans plus tard, le Ier janvier 1892, de nouveau dans la capitale. Cette fois-ci, il semble la distinguer particulièrement et lui parle comme à une vieille amie. Puis il repart, et trois ans s'écoulent encore, sans que rien ne se passe entre eux, apparemment. Ils correspondent, certes, mais les lettres de Čechov (qui nous sont toutes parvenues) sont froides et ne traitent que de littérature. Pendant le carnaval de 1895, quand Čechov séjourne une fois de plus à St. Petersbourg, ont lieu la troisième et la quatrième rencontres, toujours dans le monde. Mais le Ier février, se retrouvant avec Mme Avilova en tête à tête, chez elle, après une soirée gâchée par la présence de visiteurs inopportuns qu'il croit conviés intentionnellement, l'écrivain lui avoue brusquement son amour en parlant — soulignons-le — au passé.

> „Savez-vous que j'ai été sérieusement épris de vous", lui dit-il. „C'était sérieux. Je vous aimais. Il me semblait qu'il n'y avait pas d'autre femme au monde que je pouvais aimer tellement (...). Je vous aimais, et je ne pensais qu'à vous (...). Je vous aimais, mais je savais que vous n'étiez pas comme le sont beaucoup de femmes, qu'on ne peut vous aimer que purement, saintement, pour la vie. Je craignais de vous toucher, pour ne pas vous blesser. Est-ce que vous le saviez?" [16]

Là-dessus il la quitte, d'un air courroucé. Avant de partir pour Moscou, il adresse à la novelliste son dernier livre avec une dédicace tout-à-fait officielle, accompagnée d'une lettre sèche.

À partir de ce moment, l'histoire entre dans une nouvelle phase. Mme Avilova envoie à son ami une breloque. On y lit: „Nouvelles et Contes. Par An. Čechov. Page 267, lignes 6 et 7." C'est une référence à la phrase des „Voisins": „Si jamais tu as besoin de ma vie, viens et prends-la." L'envoi anonyme reste sans réponse. La jeune femme ne revoit Čechov qu'un an plus tard, le 27 janvier 1896, au cours d'un bal masqué. Cette fois-ci, c'est elle qui lui parle de son amour, mais elle ne veut pas se nommer, et ne sait pas s'il la reconnaît sous le loup. L'écrivain lui promet de lui en donner la preuve, le 17 octobre suivant, lors de la première de „La Mouette". En effet, l'épisode de la breloque se trouve introduit dans la pièce, et les chiffres que lit Trigorin se rapportent à un conte de la novelliste. „Il ne sied pas aux jeunes filles de se rendre à des bals masqués", lit-elle, et cette réponse la rend heureuse et perplexe. Trois mois plus tard, Čechov lui fixe un rendez-vous à Moscou. Mais à la veille de l'entrevue projetée, une brusque poussée de tuberculose le terrasse. Son amie ne le retrouve qu'à la clini-

---

[16] „Čechov dans ma vie", op. cit. p. 172.

que, exsangue, et transformé du jour au lendemain en grand malade. Ainsi, une force majeure met fin au roman. Ses héros vont entretenir une correspondance amicale, mais ne se reverront qu'une fois, le Ier mai 1899, au départ d'un train.

Ce qui retient ici notre attention, c'est le fait qu'en février 1895 Čechov parle de son amour *au passé*. Quand donc l'avait-il ressenti pour la première fois? Sûrement pas après la première rencontre — celle de 1889 — qui, survenant au moment où l'écrivain s'enfonçait dans sa crise dépressive, pouvait difficilement avoir produit sur lui une impression profonde. C'est, de toute évidence, le réveillon de 1892 qui fut décisif. Ainsi, Čechov aurait connu les débuts d'un grand amour précisément à l'époque où se nouait le drame de Lika.

Si l'on admet cette chronologie, son comportement dans cette triste histoire apparaît sous un nouvel éclairage. Sa dureté à l'égard de la jeune fille demeure difficilement excusable, mais on en aperçoit les raisons. En effet, son flirt avec Lika commence *avant* la première année de Melichovo, [17] et, sans doute, l'attire-t-elle allors vraiment. Ce n'est qu'au cours du fameux été 1892 que leurs relations changent: elle, s'enflammant graduellement, lui, se refroidissant peu à peu, car l'image d'une autre femme le hante et remplit de plus en plus son coeur. S'il poursuit le jeu, c'est qu'il n'est pas fait pour des ruptures et que, peut-être, il hésite encore. Puisque, plus tard, il parlera d'avoir „raté" Lika, [18] ne serait-ce pas qu'il avait pensé, à un moment, pouvoir l'épouser quand même, faute de mieux pour ainsi dire, celle qu'il aimait vraiment n'étant pas libre? Quoiqu'il en soit, son indifférence envers la jeune fille est telle, qu'il ne s'oppose pas aux agissements de Potapenko et ne lui garde aucune rancune. Même après le dénouement, il reste avec lui en excellents termes; l'été suivant, lorsque Lika, déjà abandonnée, attend son accouchement en Suisse, il trouve naturel de passer avec le séducteur une partie de ses vacances, sur la Volga d'abord, puis en Ukraine.

C'est que toute son optique est devenue entre-temps différente. Son „insouciance" et sa sécheresse ne l'effraient plus, car il *sait désormais qu'il peut aimer profondément*. Ses dérobades ne lui paraissent plus lamentables, car c'est son *vrai amour* qu'il a le sentiment de défendre, en fuyant des aventures inopportunes. Bien sûr, il doit comprendre ce que sa conduite à l'égard de Lika a de répréhensible, mais la conscience de ce tort demeure chez lui purement intellectuelle. Absorbé par sa passion, il demeure inaccessible au repentir. Et, comme, sur le plan artistique, le mensonge lui est impossible, [19] le remords sera néces-

---

[17] M. P. Čechov, op. cit.

[18] Lettre à L. C. Mizinova du 18 septembre 1894 (XVI 166).

[19] Voir: C. Wilczkowski, *Le Témoignage de Tchékhov*, dans *Études*, septembre 1957.

sairement absent du chef-d'oeuvre qu'il tire des malheurs de Lika.
D'une façon générale, toutes les responsabilités y seront noyées ou
atténuées car elles n'intéressent plus Čechov et, sans doute, préfère-t-il
ne pas trop s'y appesantir. C'est le hasard ou la fatalité qui règnent dans
la pièce, et il faut que l'auteur appuie assez lourdement sur le symbole
de l'oiseau blessé à mort par un chasseur oisif, pour que son drame —
en réalité inclassable — prenne un faux-air didactique. [20]

Ainsi, entre „Les Feux" et „La Mouette" la parenté n'est qu'ex-
térieure, et l'on serait tenté de dire: accidentelle. Le passé et ses
angoisses paraissent maintenant si loin à l'homme qui aime enfin
vraiment, que le thème de la froideur masculine n'est plus pour lui
qu'un thème littéraire comme un autre, et non un thème existenciel.
Ainsi ce motif disparaîtra-t-il pour longtemps de l'oeuvre čechovienne,
axée désormais sur d'autres problèmes. Comme nous l'avons dit, il ne
réapparaîtra que timidement dans „La Cerisaie", tel un serviteur trop
vieux pour les grandes besognes, mais encore capable d'un travail
d'appoint

Soulignons, finalement, qu'indépendamment de tout ce que nous
raconte Mme Avilova, *un seul détail — parfaitement vérifiable celui-là*
— semble nous permettre de jauger l'amour de Čechov. Nous avons en
vue l'épisode de la breloque qu'il interpole dans la pièce — geste de
galanterie qui aurait été charmant dans un autre contexte, mais qui cho-
que dans les circonstances données. Profiter d'une espèce de requiem
à la mémoire de Lika pour aguicher sa rivale, quelle idée odieuse ! Si
Čechov, d'habitude si fin, ne remarque pas cette goujaterie, n'est-ce pas
la preuve qu'il est emporté par sa passion et se trouve dans un état
obsessionnel, propre à certains hommes très amoureux ?

Mais, nous dira-t-on sans doute, il y a un point faible dans cette
thèse. Comment, si l'amour de Čechov date du Ier janvier 1892, peut il
se plaindre tout au long de cette année de son état apathique et déclarer
même à Suvorin, le 18 octobre, qu'il s'ennuie „sans amour fort" ? [21]

A cela on serait tenté de répondre que les affirmations contenues
dans la correspondance de l'écrivain, toujours cachotier, ne doivent pas
nécessairement être prises à la lettre. Ses lettres, pleines de réticences,

---

[20] C'est évidemment Trigorin qui cause la perte de la Mouette, mais l'image
du chasseur lui convient peu. En effet, ce viveur influençable et mou ne fait
preuve d'aucune initiative et se laisse en quelque sorte séduire par la jeune fille
exaltée. L'auteur prend soin de souligner la faiblesse de son caractère, sa
distraction et sa franchise à l'égard de sa jeune victime, qu'il ne cherche nullement à éblouir. D'autre part, comment reprocher à Nina de dédaigner l'amour de
Treplev ? Ce jeune névrosé, plus prétentieux que doué, et vivant aux crochets
de sa mère, est un bien piètre soupirant.
[21] Lettre à Suvorin du 18 octobre 1892 (XV 431).

abondent en plaisanteries, en boutades, en pirouettes, destinées à le
protéger des indiscrétions. Cependant cet argument ne paraît pas
convainquant dans le cas qui nous intéresse. En effet, Čechov n'aime
pas du tout à être plaint et cherche généralement à mentionner le moins
possible ses misères. D'autre part, on imagine mal l'intérêt qu'il aurait
à mentir à Suvorin qui est précisément l'unique ami auquel il se
confie?

Une autre explication nous paraît plus probante. Cette phrase étrange
trahit simplement la lenteur des rythmes čechoviens. En octobre 1892,
il hésite encore à admettre la réalité de son amour et à désigner de son
vrai nom le sentiment qu'il éprouve à l'égard de l'Absente.

Rappelons, à ce propos, le comportement du héros de ,,La Dame au
petit chien'', de retour à Moscou, après l'idylle de Yalta, et persuadé
qu'il ne s'était agi que d'une passade:

> ,,Un mois encore s'écoulerait et Anna Sergeevna, lui semblait-il,
> se couvrirait de brume dans sa mémoire et ne lui apparaîtrait que de
> temps en temps en rêve, avec son sourire touchant, comme d'autres
> lui étaient apparues. Mais plus d'un mois s'était écoulé, on était en
> plein hiver, et tout restait net dans sa mémoire comme s'il n'avait
> quitté Anna Sergeevna que hier. Et les souvenirs devenaient de plus
> en plus intenses (...). Il arpentait la pièce, évoquait des souvenirs,
> souriait, et les souvenirs se transformaient en rêves d'avenir, et
> le passé se confondait avec ses imaginations (...). Anna Sergeevna
> ne lui apparaissait pas en rêve, mais le suivait partout comme une
> ombre et le guettait. En fermant les yeux, il la voyait pleine de vie,
> et elle lui semblait plus belle, plus jeune, plus tendre qu'elle n'avait
> été (...). De loin il percevait sa respiration, le doux bruissement de
> sa robe. Dans les rues, il suivait des yeux les femmes, cherchait si
> aucune ne lui ressemblait.'' [22]

Ce passage qui date de 1899 est sans doute inspiré par Ol'ga Knipper.
Mais ceci importe peu, car il semble traduire une démarche propre
à l'auteur: sa façon lente de prendre conscience de son sentiment, cette
longue période d'incubation qui lui paraît nécessaire après ce que
d'autres ressentent comme un ,,coup de foudre''.

Fait plus significatif encore, cette démarche est déjà évoquée en
quelques mots dans ,,A propos de l'amour'' (1898). Après sa première
rencontre avec celle qu'il aimera d'un si profond amour, le narrateur
part pour la campagne. ,,C'était le début du printemps. Ensuite j'ai
passé à Sof'ino tout l'été, sans m'absenter, et je n'avais pas le temps
de penser à la ville, mais le souvenir d'une femme svelte et blonde
restait en moi. Je ne pensais pas à elle, mais tout se passait comme
si son ombre légère reposait sur mon âme.'' [23]

[22] *Oeuvres en douze volumes*, Moscou 1956, T. VIII, p. 403.
[23] ibidem, T. VIII, p. 314.

Or, si l'on fait confiance à Mme Avilova, ce conte décrit, étape par étape, l'histoire à peine transposée de ses relations avec l'auteur des „Trois Soeurs". Vue dans cette perspective la lettre à Suvorin n'étonne plus. Et l'on comprend mieux, du coup, les contradictions de l'artiste, qui, en cet été 1892, préparent déjà la perte de Lika.

Il nous reste maintenant, pour compléter notre démonstration, à poursuivre l'examen des rapports entre les thèmes čechoviens et leur substrat biographique. C'est toujours dans le domaine de l'amour que nous nous cantonnerons, pour chercher à voir comment l'auteur l'aborde à diverses étapes de son oeuvre.

Voici quelques jalons essentiels :

En revenant aux histoires d'amour contées par Čechov de 1887 à 1892 nous pouvons noter deux faits caractéristiques. D'une part, elles sont axées sur le problème de l'égoïsme masculin, et ce vice y est traité *comme l'unique ennemi du bonheur*. En effet, si les choses y tournent mal, c'est uniquement par la faute du héros insensible, et si les choses s'arrangent („Le Duel"), c'est que le héros s'est amendé à temps. D'autre part, *il n'y est pas question d'obstacles extérieurs ou objectifs* empêchant l'homme de satisfaire sa passion, du moment qu'il s'y décide. Les femmes sont consentantes, elles sont libres, ou bien leur mari ne compte guère. La seule loi que l'auteur semble affirmer c'est la loi du coeur au sens romantique du terme, si bien que, contrairement à l'égoïsme tout court, l'égoïsme à deux n'y est pas condamné. [24] Au fond, il n'y a dans ces drames — petits ou grands — que deux protagonistes : *l'Égoïste et la femme qui l'aime*. Et c'est sur le premier que se concentrent tous les feux de la rampe, car, nous l'avons vu déjà, ce qui tourmente l'auteur à cette époque, c'est *l'état d'égotisme* dont il souffre, et la recherche des moyens par lesquels il pourrait s'en guérir.

À partir de la fin de 1892 [25] pourtant, les histoires d'amour prennent chez Čechov un autre caractère. Dans „La Peur", déjà, le drame se complique. Un troisième protagoniste intervient. On a l'impression que le narrateur, même s'il se décidait à sacrifier son confort à sa maîtresse (selon la loi de la passion romantique), n'aurait jamais la conscience tranquille à cause du mari.

Dans „Volodja-le-grand et Volodja-le-petit" (fin 1893) ce n'est plus un homme qui occupe l'avant-scène, mais une femme, et l'histoire

---

[24] Le couple amoureux n'a pas à se soucier des tierces personnes, ni des conventions sociales. Dans „Le Duel", par exemple, seule une pimbêche réprouve la situation irrégulière des amants, et dans „Les Voisins" (1892), l'auteur semble approuver l'union libre des amoureux.

[25] Nous ne parlons pas ici de „La Cigale" (fin novembre 1891), car ce conte, inspiré par les mésaventures du peintre Levitan, n'a rien d'autobiographique.

n'a rien de didactique. Il serait également difficile de tirer une morale quelconque du „Professeur de littérature" (achevé en 1894, mais commencé en 1889) et des „Trois Ans" (1894). Ces contes et cette longue nouvelle ne semblent, en somme, qu'exprimer la tristesse de Čechov et surtout, sans doute, sa misogynie. Cette dernière s'affirme en 1895, dans un groupe de trois contes („L'Épouse", „La Cravate de Ste Anne" et „Ariane") où les filles d'Ève sensuelles, avides, arrivistes, dominatrices, sont montrées dans un éclairage quasi naturaliste. Mais, déjà, la manière de l'auteur change à nouveau. Avec „La Maison à mezzanine" et, dans une certaine mesure, avec „La Mouette" nous accédons au dernier et au plus beau groupe d'histoires d'amour qu'il fut donné à Čechov d'écrire.

Ici, le poète semble refouler complètement le sociologue, le censeur et le moraliste, et le monde qu'il évoque est tragique. Si tous les romans ratent, aboutissent à des impasses ou se brisent, la faute n'en est à personne sinon à un destin aveugle, ironique, stupide et inflexible. Ou bien il s'agit d'idylle brutalement interrompue („La Maison à mezzanine"), ou bien d'amour non partagé (Treplev dans „La Mouette", Vojnickij dans „L'Oncle Vanja"), ou bien d'amours réciproques mais contrecarrées par d'insurmontables obstacles. Tels sont les cas des passions insatisfaites et débouchant sur la séparation des héros de „À propos de l'amour" (1898), ainsi que de Maša et de Veršinin („Trois Soeurs", 1900). Tel est, enfin, le cas des amants de „La Dame au petit chien" (1899), incapables de détruire leurs foyers, mais tout aussi incapables de rompre, et condamnés à une double vie déchirante.

Les biographies „classiques" nous fournissent fort peu d'éléments susceptibles d'expliquer cette évolution. D'où vient le nouveau motif apparaissant dans „La Peur"? À quoi correspondent, plus tard, les décevantes évocations de ménages bourgeois? Pourquoi, enfin, si Čechov n'a connu ni passion forte, ni amour interdit, ce passage au registre tragique, ces accents ardents et désespérés? Toutes ces questions restent sans réponse satisfaisante. Seule, l'inspiration des trois contes de 1895, peu flatteurs pour les femmes, paraît évidente. Il faut la chercher dans l'amitié assez trouble qui, au vu et au su de tout Moscou, liait Čechov, vers cette époque, à une ambitieuse actrice, la Javorskaja. [26]

En revanche, si nous admettons la réalité d'une liaison platonique et passionnée entre l'écrivain et la nouvelliste, les choses s'éclairent une fois de plus. En prenant „Čechov dans ma vie" pour cadre et en y insérant les faits biographiques dûment connus, on obtient une histoire

---

[26] Certains contemporains ont cru reconnaître Mme Javorskaja dans Ariane, l'héroïne du conte du même nom. Un ami de Čechov, A. S. Lazarev-Gruzinskij, prétend que c'est l'actrice elle-même qui aurait lancé ce bruit dans un but publicitaire („Čechov dans les souvenirs de ses contemporains", p. 106).

cohérente, où les attitudes successives de l'artiste paraissent parfaitement logiques.

Voici, en quelques mots, les diverses phases de cette histoire et leurs incidences littéraires.

La première phase, nous l'avons vu, est celle d'incubation. En automne 1892, Čechov n'est pas encore complètement sûr de son amour, bien qu'il commence à en prendre conscience. Le problème du mari d'ores et déjà le trouble. Il hésite entre la tentation et le scrupule. D'où „La Peur" — cet hybride où, sur le vieux thème du désir, se greffe le nouveau thème du tabou. Notons que Silin, le mari mal aimé, amoureux de sa femme, père de deux enfants charmants, n'est pas sans certaines ressemblances avec Michail Avilov, tel que pouvait le voir Čechov. Soulignons aussi que la façon dont débute le récit, ainsi que les relations initiales des personnages, rappellent, d'une façon assez frappante, les situations que nous retrouverons dans „À propos de l'amour", conte autobiographique dont nous possédons les clefs.

La deuxième phase est celle où, ayant reconnu la nature de son sentiment, Čechov décide de le garder „saint" et „pur", comme il le dira plus tard. Il ne cherche pas à revoir celle qu'il aime. Sa passion soigneusement cachée ne semble pas encore le torturer : c'est plutôt un mal doux qu'il arrive à circonscrire et que, sans doute, il pense pouvoir dépasser. Renoncera-t-il bourgeoisement à un bonheur impossible au profit d'un mariage raisonnable? Ou encore, Dame Vénus tentant Tannhauser, restera-t-il captif de l'actrice qui, flattée par ses hommages, cherche à le retenir dans son sillage? Mais les projets matrimoniaux le dégoûtent; quant aux sortilèges de la Javorskaja, ils ne durent guère. L'artiste, toujours véridique, ne peut le dissimuler. D'où les tristes tableaux conjugaux qu'il peint en 1894, et les portraits féminins de l'année suivante — prouvant sa lucidité et sa déception.

La troisième phase s'ouvre en 1895, quand Čechov revoit Mme Avilova. C'est alors que sa passion semble connaître une brusque flambée. Pris dans l'engrenage, il comprend que le temps ne pourra plus arranger les choses, et qu'il marche vers d'inévitables drames. Epargnera-t-il un foyer déjà ébranlé, en sacrifiant délibérément son amour? Entraînera-t-il celle dont il connaît maintenant les sentiments vers une aventure pleine de risques? C'est vers cette dernière solution qu'il semble pencher, quand le destin décide pour lui et met fin d'une façon brusque à ses espoirs, à ses craintes et à ses scrupules.

Tant que le dénouement n'est pas intervenu, l'oeuvre de l'écrivain ne trahit ni le débat intérieur qui le tourmente, ni ses joies incomplètes et fugitives. Si dans „La Mouette" apparaît le thème de la fatalité et, dans „La Maison à mezzanine" — celui de la séparation, les personnages qui y sont mis en scène et les situations où ils se trouvent, n'ont aucun rapport avec le roman que vit l'auteur. Mais quand il en aura tournée la dernière page, quand rien ne pourra plus être gâché et compromis, la douleur secrète sera plus forte que la réserve, et le sujet interdit s'imposera à l'artiste. „Horribles erreurs" [27] du destin, amours irréalisables, départs sans retour — c'est de sa propre expérience récente qu'il enrichira ses histoires d'amour tragiques. Il la racontera, presque ouvertement, dans „A propos de l'amour", étrange confession d'un romantique, où le pénitent ne regrette qu'une chose : le péché qu'il n'a pas osé commettre.

Il semble donc qu'en acceptant le témoignage apporté par „Čechov dans ma vie", nous ne tombons pas dans l'invraisemblance. Bien plus, ces révélations facilitent l'exégèse de l'oeuvre čechovienne. Elles expliquent si bien certaines attitudes de l'écrivain qu'on en arrive presque à regretter que l'amour secret de Čechov n'ait pas été découvert par voie déductive, comme un astre invisible au télescope. „Oui, les biographes devront compter sérieusement avec les souvenirs de Mme Avilova", écrivait Bunin. [28] Tout compte fait, nous nous rangeons à son avis.

---

[27] „A propos de l'amour". *Oeuvres en douze volumes,* T. VIII, p. 316.
[28] Bunin, op. cit., p. 147.

THOMAS G. WINNER *

ČECHOV AND SCIENTISM; OBSERVATIONS ON THE SEARCHING STORIES

After Čechov had ceased writing primarily for humor magazines and was beginning to contribute more ambitious works to serious literary journals, there can be observed in his art and private papers an avid search for a well-defined world view. Čechov was always unable to accept any of the existing predominant ideologies *in toto,* but we find during this period of searching a certain sympathy with some limited facets of Tolstoj's views, especially with Tolstoj's doctrine of non-resistance to evil. After Čechov's voyage to the Russian penal colony on the island of Sachalin, in 1890, he began increasingly to reject those of Tolstoj's views which had attracted him for a certain period. Many of his letters and stories written during the early 1890's clearly illustrate Čechov's growing aloofness to Tolstoj's doctrine, [1] and the stories of this decade reveal his ever increasing concern with the search for a more independent definition of his own world view. His inability to define clearly and systematically a satisfactory world view rings desperately in Čechov's letters. This intense quest finds its clearest expression in a series of stories written between 1889 and 1893 which are concerned more directly than any of Čechov's other works with specific philosophical questions and with a restless search for a world view. These stories, by virtue of the fact that they are united by the common theme of the search for a guiding idea, are here considered to form a specific cycle which is composed of the following stories: "A Dreary Story" (*Skučnaja istorija,* 1889), "The Duel" (*Duel',* 1891), "Ward No. 6" (*Palata No. 6,* 1892), *Gusev* (1891) and "The Black Monk" (*Černyj monach,* 1893). After "The Black Monk", which terminates what we might call the cycle of the psycho-philosophical searching stories, Čechov's stories no longer show so intense and restless a concern with intellectual and philosophical questions.

The cycle of "searching" stories is thus thematically united by the theme of the search for a guiding idea, and an ideological "center" of orientation. What is of particular concern to us here, however, is a

* The author wishes to acknowledge his indebtedness to his friends, Professors Sigmund Koch and Richard F. Kuhns for a number of stimulating discussions concerning some philosophical and psychological implications suggested by the stories here called the "searching" ones.

[1] See T. G. Winner, "Chekhov's *Ward No. 6* and Tolstoyan Ethics," *Slavic and East European Journal,* XVII 4, December 1959, pp. 321-34.

special problem which is treated in various ways in the stories, that is
the significant problem of man's dedication to science, to the scientific
point of view and thus the relationship of science to man. This was a
problem of focal significance in the age of scientific optimism of the
late nineteenth century, with its spirit of empiricism and positivism.

It has become almost a truism, in the critical literature about
Čechov, to speak of him as dedicated to the scientific view and the
scientific method. Clearly Čechov, who was himself a practicing
physician, was profoundly attached to the scientific viewpoint, and the
influence of science can be observed in many of his views and practices
in *belles-lettres*. In his clinical probing into his characters, in his lack of
moralism and his objective approach to his heroes and their problems,
Čechov frequently came very close to the theories of the French natu-
ralists, whom he greatly admired, though their influence on him must
not be overstated, as it sometimes has been. [2] Čechov was intimately
acquainted with Zola's *Roman expérimental,* as well as with Claude Bernard's fundamental *Introduction a la médicine générale* (1865), which
so strongly influenced Zola's literary theories. [3] Čechov's scientific
positivism, and his admiration for Darwin, were among the compelling
reasons for his lack of enthusiasm for Tolstoj's religious views. One
has merely to leaf through Čechov's stories and plays, to see that
scientists, and especially physicians belong to his most positive protagonists and that in one of the central conflicts of his works, that
between creativity and empty banality, it is frequently the humane
scientist who symbolizes the positive views. Nevertheless, it would be a
gross exaggeration to consider the scientist and the scientific way of
life in Čechov's works as unqualifiedly identified with the ideal. While
Čechov was clearly very much influenced by the spirit of the scientific
optimism of the *fin de siècle,* there is little doubt that he viewed with
scepticism a scientistic attitude, not uncommon in his days and very
much a part of our own age, which sought, he believed, to place science
above man and thus to reify it as a value in itself. In these stories,
which I have called the "searching" ones, Čechov treats some of the
problems related to the scientific view, which concerned also Dostoevskij and, after him, Nietzsche : the relationship of science to man, the
problem of the reification of science and thus the already emerging
conflict between the new science and traditional humanistic values.

---

[2] For a discussion of Čechov's views on the theories of the Naturalist movement, see Leonid Grossman, *Naturalizm Čechova, Vestnik Evropy* 7, 1914, pp.
218-247.

[3] The interesting question of the influence of Bernard's positivism on Čechov's
aesthetics is discussed by the late A. Roskin in *Zametki o realizme Čechova,* in
A. Roskin, *A. P. Čechov,* Moscow 1959, 193-219.

It is the thesis of this study that the theme of reification of science and intellectualism, in many variations, can be seen as one of the unifying themes of the "searching" stories and that this preoccupation with an attitude which would place the scientific man, or more broadly the intellectual, above mankind, is brought to a climax in the last of the "searching" stories, "The Black Monk". We shall find thus that Čechov has preempted many problems which have become most desperately important ones in our own days of cybernetics and of atomic science which threaten ever more to make man into a sorcerer's apprentice who has conjured up forces of which he has ceased to be fully a master. In "A Dreary Story" we shall see an over-dedication to science by a very capable scientist as one of the underlying causes for isolation and unhappiness; in "The Duel" views concerning the superiority of an intellectual and scientific Übermensch are voiced by a cold Nietzschean scientist. In "Ward No. 6" views about the superiority of the intellectual serve as justification for submission to evil. Finally, in "The Black Monk", this theme is most highly developed in the phantom monks enraptured vision of the intellectual extraordinary man who is made all-powerful by the strength of his scientific mind.

Various aspects of these problems are clearly evident in the first of Čechov's "searching" stories, "A Dreary Story". "A Dreary Story" (1889) is Čechov's most significant work of the 1880's. Its melancholy tone and intellectual questioning reflect most clearly the intellectual and emotional crisis through which Čechov passed at the end of the 1880's in his search for a world view. "A Dreary Story" portrays the tragedy of a noted professor of medicine, a distinguished and famous scientist, who, when he is old and incurably ill, realizes that his life has not been the glorious life he and his admirers had thought it to be, but that, for reasons which he is now attempting to define to himself, his life has been a total failure. The professor begins to feel himself increasingly isolated from everyone around him, even from those whom he has once loved and by whom he has been loved. Even his ward Katja, the person who has always been closest to him, walks away from him in despair, when he is incapable of heeding her cry for moral help. The theme of isolation, which endlessly preoccupied Čechov, is again of central importance in this story, but it is here presented in quite a new and different context.

There are few works of Čechov's which have been the object of as much discussion as has "A Dreary Story". The question so debated is that of the origin of the professor's isolation and unhappiness on the eve of his life. And here it must be recognized that there is a multitude of causes underlying the professor's psychological decline.

In the most common interpretation of the work the view is held that the professor's isolation is caused by his lack of a "general idea", of an overall world view, which has prevented his full participation in life. He is a scientist who, as he himself admits, has alway carefully avoided concerning himself with politics. While this interpretation can only be considered valid as far as it goes, we shall attempt, in this analysis, to come to a deeper understanding of the complexities of the professor's isolation. The professor says of himself:

> With such a lack [of a unifying idea, T.G.W.] one must only have a serious ailment, fear of death, or be influenced by circumstances and people, to have all that I considered formerly my world view, all that in which I saw a sense and the happiness of my life, turned upside down and disappear. So it is not at all surprising that the last months of my life have been clouded by thoughts and feelings worthy of a slave and a barbarian, that I am now so indifferent and do not even notice the dawn. When man lacks something which is higher and stronger than external influences, then all he has to have is a bad headcold in order to lose his equanimity and to make him see in every bird an owl, in every noise a dog's howling.

We meet the professor in a moment of spiritual and intellectual crisis, when he sees his life in a critical fashion for the first time, a criticism which is expressed in a bitter attitude towards himself. The professor now constantly feels irritated towards others, and complains about others. Yet, we learn that before his crisis, when he had observed such a negative attitude in Katja, he had felt that this was a certain sign of her personal decline. His growing crisis is further expressed in a more critical attitude towards social problems and in his lonesome realization of the ills of his country. His impotence in the face of his growing critical attitude toward reality makes his position the more helpless, if not grotesque. Thus he fails the only person he loves, Katja, and his isolation is then complete. The professor is tortured by his inability to form a new and more broadly positive philosophy. There is little doubt that the absence of a "general idea" is the outward expression of the professor's psychological decline, of his growing resentfulness, irritability and, finally, of his inability to help even those he loves. But one cannot agree with the critics who advance this as the sole cause for the professor's unhappiness and isolation.

The psychological collapse of the once successful and happy scientist is clearly related to many and various factors. It is related to the universal problems of the isolation of the famous and also to the despair of the aged, particularly those who are condemned to the restless questionings of a searching mind. I would hold that basic to the professor's isolation, and its most fundamental cause, is his committedness to the scientism of his age which, though realized at the highest level, proved in the end to be inadequate. A scientist such as the professor's assistant does not suffer from the limitations of his commitment to scientism. For the small soul of the assistant neither can, nor needs to, question the correctness and fruitfulness of his mechanistic world view. The professor vaguely feels the inadequacy of his science; he faintly yearns for beauty and art. But the integrated wholeness of life escapes him.

The failure of the old professor to find lasting satisfaction in a life devoted primarily to science is brought into relief by a contrapuntal theme, the fate of his ward Katja, which serves as an ironic commentary on the problem of the professor. Katja, like the professor, has committed her life to a specific center, which is in her case that of art, which, just as the professor's, appears in the end as elusive and unsatisfactory. But unlike the professor's, Katja's failure and resulting cynicism comes early in life and at an immature level. Her frustration is caused not so much by an awareness of the limitations of the center to which she had dedicated herself. Rather her unhappiness and her resulting paralysis of action is related most directly to her unhappy realization of her lack of talent. Thus, Katja's dilemma is, in a sense, more pathetic, because of the hopelessness of her inner inadequacy.

The professor's dilemma, however, which is caused partly by an awareness of the limitations of his over-committedness to science, is a realization of a fully mature and able mind, and is thus of a far more profound and philosophical nature. In this sense the theme of Katja, an ordinary person with pretensions, plays the role of an echo of pathos and irony to the tragic, or near-tragic, notes of the theme of the extraordinary scientist. Katja and the professor represent two extremes, both beloved by Čechov: science and aestheticism, although the first is tempered by artistic inclinations and the second enfeebled by lack of talent, maturity and profundity. The professor is constantly drawn to Katja, although he eternally fails her. In her he sees an escape from the rigidity of his own life, something free, unconventional, natural and beautiful. She symbolizes to him, however inadequately, the life of emotions and aesthetics which he cannot realize himself. Katja is, on the other hand, dependent on the professor, who is to her a father figure and a wise scientist who can, though he never does, help her. They each seek salvation from their own limitations in the temperament of the other. Yet, the professor cannot guide Katja, and the latter cannot provide the warmth and human contact which the professor seeks.

In "A Dreary Story", as in all of Čechov's "searching" stories, the philosophical level is united with the psychological, as Čechov examines particular aspects of a universal problem which never ceased to occupy him, man's search for, and inability to find, life's wholeness, and man's consequent isolation from himself and from society. The themes of this story, its subtexts and moods are suggested in this work by typical Čechovian use of detail and symbolism, as well as by the structure of the story. But these most significant problems of technique, which would necessitate a separate study, can only be mentioned here in passing.

The predominantly melancholy tone of "A Dreary Story" which marks Katja's and the professor's unresolved dilemma, and its lack of sympathetic humor, mark it forever as one of Čechov's saddest, if most searching, works.

In the story "Gusev", in which is related the conversation between two moribund patients in a hospital ward of a Russian troop ship, the problem of an overly narrow committment to intellectualism and science is not as crucial to the structure of the story as it was in "A Dreary Story". But the theme of reification of intellectualism does emerge in the passionate statement of Pavel Ivanyč, one of the two patients, as he attacks his naive ward neighbor, Gusev, who is willing to accept his evil fate, and even death, without protest:

> Yes, I always tell the truth straight out... I am not afraid of anyone or of anything. In this respect there is a tremendous difference between you and me. You are ignorant, blind, forgotten people, you see nothing and what you see you do not understand... *but I am different.* I live life consciously, *I see everything just as the eagle and the falcon when they fly over the earth,* and *I understand everything... And I am invincible,* no Spanish inquisition can force me to be silent. (Italics supplied.)

The line of the story provides ironic commentary on this assertion of individual omnipotence of the superior intellectual. For Pavel Ivanyč dies and is unceremoniously buried at sea. But in the technical treatment of this scene which is based on a new device of Čechov's, that of the indirect and hidden chorus consisting of seemingly unconnected statements, a further ironic commentary becomes manifest. Thus when Pavel Ivanyč has completed his peroration, it is noted that Gusev does not listen to him, but looks out of the porthole, where he sees a Chinese bird seller in his boat who lifts up a cage with canaries and calls out: "He sings! He sings!" The ironic identification between "He sings! He sings!" and the brave peroration which has just resounded is clearly evident. This suggestive chorus-like commentary is further strengthened by the implied contrast between Pavel's self image as a free bird omnipotence whom no walls can hold, and the encaged canary bird.

The theme of overdedication to science and intellectualism which we have observed in "A Dreary Story" and in "Gusev", is also one of the principal themes of the story "The Duel", published, as was "Gusev", in 1891. In "The Duel" this theme is part of the depiction of the young natural scientist von Koren. One of the lines of conflict of this story is that between the scientist von Koren and Laevskij, one of the superfluous men, so well known in Russian literature, as they meet in a Russian seaside resort. This conflict is outlined in the exaggerated form of carricature. The satirically treated von Koren, who espouses the extreme views of the intellectual *Übermensch,* speaks for the right of the intellectually superior extra-ordinary man to exterminate those who, because of weakness or inactivity, are detrimental to society. In von Koren's estimation Laevskij is one of these harmful creatures, uselessly idle, and morally corrupt. Von Koren's cold and arrogant worship of the abstract value of science is expressed in a statement by Laevskij :

> When ordinary mortals work for the common good, they keep their fellow man in mind : me, you, in one word, Man. For von Koren, however, people are but little dogs and nothings, too small and insignificant to constitute the aim of his life. He works ... not in the name of the love of fellow man, but in the name of such abstract concepts as mankind, future generations, an ideal race of men. He pleads for the improvement of the human race and in this relationship we are for him nothing but slaves, cannon fodder,... animals; some he would destroy, or send to forced labor, others he would force into discipline, would force them, like Arakčeev, to rise and go to sleep to the sound of drums...

In searching for the line of the theme under discussion, we see it also in "Ward No. 6", where an artificial intellectualism prevents contact with life and active combat of the corrupt and cruel conditions in a mental ward. However, the more dominant theme of "Ward No. 6" is concerned with problems of the philosophy of Tolstoyanism, although aspects of the theme of scientism, noted in the other "searching" stories, are reflected in the overly abstract intellectualism of the inactive Dr. Ragin, and in the disordered overpassionate intellectualism of the insane Gromov. "Ward No. 6" and "The Black Monk" are the two final stories of the "searching" cycle; both of them are satirical tragicomedies of great complexity. We shall limit ourselves to an analysis of the final story of the cycle, "The Black Monk", in which the theme comes to a final dramatic climax.

"The Black Monk" (1893) is the story of a scientist, Kovrin, who comes to his friend's estate to rest his wearied nerves and there begins to see visions of a black monk who preaches to him ideas of the intel-

lectual super-man. The belief in the scientific and intellectual super-man
is now posed in this ironic satire within the context of the insane
visions of an ordinary and pathetic man who cannot live without his
beguiling delusions. In "The Black Monk" there is suggested such a
complexity of philosophical and psychological problems, however, that
no single answer as to its predominant idea is completely satisfying.
In order to elucidate our problem, the theme of scientism in this cycle
of stories, we must limit ourselves to those very important aspects of
"The Black Monk" which are relevant to this theme. In considering
the philosophical theme of this story, it is only by a process of
abstraction, which is even more difficult to carry out here than in "A
Dreary Story", that the philosophical level can be considered inde-
pendently from the psychological one.

Kovrin and the phantom monk who comes to Kovrin, may be
considered to symbolize the problems of science, intellectualism and the
would-be extra-ordinary man. The depiction of Kovrin is silhouetted
against that of his friends, the family of the horticulturist Pesockij.
While there is something of the ridiculous about the old horticulturist,
his useful labor forms a contrast to the fruitless intellectual endeavors
of Kovrin. It is significant that throughout the entire work, which is
concerned with Kovrin's intellectual endeavors as a philosopher and
psychologist, we never really learn what his accomplishments are. It is
true that the monk talks persuasively of leading mankind to immor-
tality and to eternal truth. But, with a Čechovian ironic twist, the charm
which the monk exercises over us is broken, when he appears incapable
of answering Kovrin's question about the essence of problems concerning which the monk talks so eloquently and convincingly. Čechov
smilingly deflates the hope and optimism concerning the mission of intellectuals which the monk's enthusiastic words have created in Kovrin's
mind. "If only you knew how agreeable it is to hear you say these
things", Kovrin tells the monk. How strange, he tells the phantom, who
might be his alter ego, that "you repeat what so often comes also to my
own mind... it is as if you had looked into, and listened to, my innermost thoughts. But let us not talk about me. What do you mean by
eternal truth?" It is just at this critical point that the monk fails
Kovrin and the hallucination disappears.

> The monk did not answer. Kovrin looked at him and could not see
> his face; his features began to cloud over and to disintegrate. Then
> the monk had disappeared and his arms, his body began to merge
> with the bench and the dusk — and he had disappeared.

While the monk cannot directly satisfy Kovrin's search for final
answers, he can seduce him with flattery and thus still his doubts:

Yes, you are one of those few who can justly say of themselves that they are God's chosen. You serve eternal truth. Your thoughts, your intentions, your amazing knowledge and all your life have on themselves a divine heavenly stamp, since they are dedicated to the reasonable and to the beautiful, that means to that which is eternal.

And then, in Nietzschean fashion, the monk sharply contrasts Kovrin with the "herd" of ordinary people. Kovrin, he says, is all intellect, all nerves. That is why he sees phantoms. But this is as it should be, for people who are especially gifted, like Kovrin, have no need for *mens sana in corpore sano*. They are high above the ordinary men with their low and despicable bodily needs. They are disembodied intellectualism and aestheticism and by this distinction they stand above mankind. "My friend," the monk tells Kovrin,

> healthy and normal are only the ordinary people, the herd ... heightened mood, excitation, ecstasy — that is what distinguishes the prophets, the poets, the martyrs for an idea from the ordinary people, from the disgusting animal side of humanity, that is — from physical health. I repeat — if you want to be healthy and normal, go into the herd.

It should be noted that when the monk speaks of the extraordinary man, while he addresses his remarks to the scientist Kovrin, the extraordinary man means to the monk all specially gifted men, artists, poets, as well as scientists. Thus, significantly, in the last of the searching stories, the aesthetic and the scientific theme are brought to a kind of unity which had already been suggested in the sub-theme of Katja in "A Dreary Story", and which is expressed here symbolically by the recurrent *Leitmotif* of music which always precedes the appearance of the hallucination of the monk.

Kovrin believes passionately in his extraordinary character and talent and others also believe in the aura of greatness with which he has surrounded himself. Tanja and her father adore him and believe him to be a genius who honors them by his presence in their country estate.

The problem of the superiority of intellectualism is developed in this story in a fashion which is to become increasingly a part of the Čechovian method, a method which is characterized by the use of subtle symbolism and varied indirect comment. The monk presents his views concerning genius with enthusiastic persuasiveness. But his pronouncements are tempered by the irony of inappropriateness, of being addressed to Kovrin, who is not a genius. While Kovrin thinks of himself as striving, like Faust, for all-knowledge, this identification serves only as an ironic commentary. For Kovrin is far from being the extraordinary person of whom the phantom monk boasts, and is, in his way, as insignificant as the "herd' which the monk has taught him to despise.

The members of the Pesockij family, who may be seen as representatives of the herd of which the monk speaks so disparagingly, are also not freed from touches of Čechov's irony in the picture of their humdrum and boring lives. The character of the old Pesockij the horticulturist may be seen to serve in typical Čechovian fashion as a kind of contrapuntal echo to that of Kovrin. While Pesockij is clearly a simple man, in certain limited respects he also is part of the depiction of the extraordinary man. His excited and vituperative polemic articles on horticulture, his constant worry that his garden will perish with his death, a concern which overrides the problem of the future of his daughter, together compose a simple form of horticultural "scientism" which acts as a subtle comment on the more pretentious scientism of Kovrin.

Pesockij also pictures himself arrogantly above the herd, and thus he regrets that he can no longer flog the peasants, and he feels himself superior to his learned horticulturalist colleagues whom he accuses of lack of practical experience. The depiction of Pesockij is, in some sense, an inversion of the picture of Kovrin. While Kovrin's vaunted intellectual prowess leads him to feel special, it is Pesockij's practical abilities which cause him to value himself and his work above others. Yet, we are reminded that both men will perish without having left a trace of their extraordinary talent. Kovrin cannot give any lectures, and Pesockij's orchard is ruined.

Thus we see in "The Black Monk" a Čechovian treatment of the theme of the extraordinary man, a problem which also concerned Dostoevskij so deeply. In this story the problem reaches a climax which comes close to the tragic. But the scholar Kovrin is only a mediocre man, and is thus not capable of becoming a tragic hero. The character of the gifted scientist of "A Dreary Story", whose penetrating intellect would not leave him in peace, is only hauntingly mocked in the depiction of the untalented Kovrin, who is nevertheless too sensitive to accept his mediocrity, and who thus cannot live without his faith, no matter how unstably based, in his delusions of intellectual greatness. Thus he destroys his own life and that of those who love him. The last touch of irony is acchieved as Kovrin realizes his final ecstatic joy, when at death he rediscovers his delusion of greatness, as his hallucination reappears in the form of the black monk. But this last event, with which the story concludes, only leads us to another aspect of our theme, a more clearly psychological one; that is, the pathos of life without illusions, be they even delusions, a theme which would take us to an entirely new subject for discussion. We must conclude by observing that science as well as art were the aspects of life most precious to Čechov. But while Čechov in his "searching" stories experimented with a commitment to various philosophical ideas, and most specifically to that of science, he never found one completely satisfying general idea, not even as embodied in science or art. Thus it was that, after writing the tragic comedy of "The Black Monk", Čechov more or less abandoned the quest for final solutions, although these problems never ceased to concern him.

Perhaps the most telling observation which can be drawn from this study for its elucidation of the genius of Čechov, lies not simply in the conclusion that Čechov found wanting in the "searching" stories any over-dedication to one narrow aspect of life, even should that aspect be one so valuable to man as science, or so precious as art itself. I would like to conclude rather with a thought affirming again the peculiar genius of Čechov, which enabled him to experiment so subtly with so profound a theme. Man's commitment to science which was after all, in one way or another, a great part of Čechov's own commitment, is considered in this cycle of stories with the solemnity of tragedy in the almost tragic hero of "A Dreary Story", with the seriousness of moralism in the treatment of the problem of good and evil in "The Duel", and with the final subtlety of irony and pathos in the bitter tragicomedies "Ward No. 6" and "The Black Monk". But the individual personality, in its total complexity, is the ultimate reality for Čechov; and no intellectual system, no matter how enticing, can subjugate the intricacies of human action to its ordered reality.